HANDBOOKS

GLACIER
NATIONAL PARK

BECKY LOMAX

GLACIER NATIONAL PARK

Cardston

2

Mountain View

5

Buds River

Waterton River

6

6

5

Waterton Lakes

National Park

▲ Mt Blakiston
9,581ft

RED ROCK PKWY

CRANDELL ▲
MOUNTAIN

▲ Mt Dungarvan
8,419ft

AKAMINA PKWY

Waterton Townsite

▲ Mt Alderson

Lower Waterton Lake

Middle Waterton Lake

Upper Waterton Lake

Akamina-Kishinena

Provincial Park

BRITISH COLUMBIA

North Fork

KINTLA LAKE

Kintla Lake

Upper Kintla Lake

▲ Kintla Peak
10,101ft

Flathead River

OUTSIDE NORTH FORK RD

Bowman Lake

BOWMAN LAKE

Quartz Lake

QUARTZ CREEK

LOGGING CREEK

Logging Lake

Polebridge

Flathead

National

Forest

INSIDE NORTH

ALBERTA

MONTANA

PIEGAN-CARWAY CUSTOMS

St. Mary River

2

89

Duck Lake

464

Blackfeet Indian

Reservation

89

17

Babb

Lower St. Mary Lake

St. Mary

INTERNATIONAL HWY

CHIEF MOUNTAIN

BELLY RIVER

CHIEF MTN CUSTOMS

CANADA

USA

GOAT HAUNT

▲ Goat Haunt Mountain
8,641ft

▲ Mt Cleveland
10,466ft

▲ Kootenai Peak

▲ Chief Mountain
9,080ft

▲ Apikuni Mountain

MANY GLACIER

Lake Sherburne

ST. MARY

RISING SUN

St. Mary Lake

▲ Mt Siyeh
10,014ft

Logan Pass

Lewis

GRANITE PARK CHALET ●

Livingston

Range

▲ Heavens Peak
8,987ft

AVALANCHE CREEK

Mt Custer ▲
8,883ft

Contents

Discover Glacier National Park

Glacier National Park is the undisputed "Crown of the Continent." Its glaciers, tarns, and high meadowlands accent steep arêtes where mountain goats walk like acrobats across cliffs. Acres of lush green parklands plunge down jagged red pinnacles, exposing some of the world's oldest stones. Waterfalls roar, ice cracks, and rock falls echo in scenery still under the paintbrush of change.

In this rugged country, eyes taste a rare ecosystem of indigenous wildlife topped by grizzly bears and wolves. Wolverines romp in high glacial cirques. Bighorn sheep browse in alpine meadows. Pikas shriek warnings as golden eagles swoop low on the hunt. Only two animals present in Lewis and Clark's day are missing: woodland caribou and bison.

Here, one million wild acres crown the Continental Divide, where glaciers fuel North America's major rivers. Feet tread where waters shed to the Atlantic and Pacific. Glacier touches down at 3,150 feet at the confluence of two Wild and Scenic Rivers splashing along its boundary; yet its peaks scratch the sky with six mountains topping 10,000 feet. Stare at Mount Cleveland stretching the highest, its north face one of the tallest vertical walls in the U.S.

Bisecting the park, an engineering marvel — historic Going-to-the-Sun Road — twists and turns on its narrow cliff-climb, causing white-knuckled driving for some. Tunnels, arches, and bridges lead sightseers over precipices where no road seemingly could go. Breath intakes punctuate every curve with new sights: Broad glacially scooped valleys, thundering cascades, mammoth lakes, and serrated peaks. Ice abraded this world into a place where "wow" is never enough.

Known as a hiker's park, Glacier snakes more than 700 trail miles through remote wilderness. Hikers prance up verdant valleys, shimmy beneath frigid waterfalls, and crawl over high passes. Peak panoramas and blue-green lakes are strung like pearls along trails in places of solitude.

Earning its designation as a Biosphere Reserve and World Heritage Site, Glacier corrals a rich diversity of wildlife and a wealth of natural attributes. The park holds ancient geological secrets, and for centuries provided sacred lands for the Blackfeet. With Waterton Lakes National Park in Canada, Glacier celebrates being the world's first International Peace Park.

For 100 years, Glacier has preserved some of the nation's wildest country. Welcome to this rugged slice of nature's best.

Planning Your Trip

► WHERE TO GO

West Glacier and Apgar

Together, West Glacier and Apgar form the park's western portal. Divided by a nationally declared Wild and Scenic River, the pair whip into a summer frenzy with white-water rafting, trail riding, fishing, kayaking, boating, hiking, and backpacking. They house the largest campgrounds on the park's largest lake—Lake McDonald.

North Fork

For those looking to escape crowds, the remote North Fork has real rusticity—not just the look of it. By modern standards backwards without electricity, Polebridge Mercantile and Northern Lights Saloon attract travelers who relish bumpy dirt roads, solitude at Bowman and Kintla Lakes, and wolf serenades.

Going-to-the-Sun Road

As the park's biggest attraction, Going-to-the-Sun Road leads drivers on a skinny cliff-shimmy into craggy alpine country. The National Historic Landmark crosses the Continental Divide at Logan Pass, a wild-flower wonderland dancing with glaciers, waterfalls, mountain goats, and trails with top-of-the-world vistas.

St. Mary and Many Glacier

The small, seasonal St. Mary bustles as a hub of campgrounds, lodges, cabins, cafés, shops, and Going-to-the-Sun Road's eastern portal.

Historic Granite Park Chalet sits below the Continental Divide.

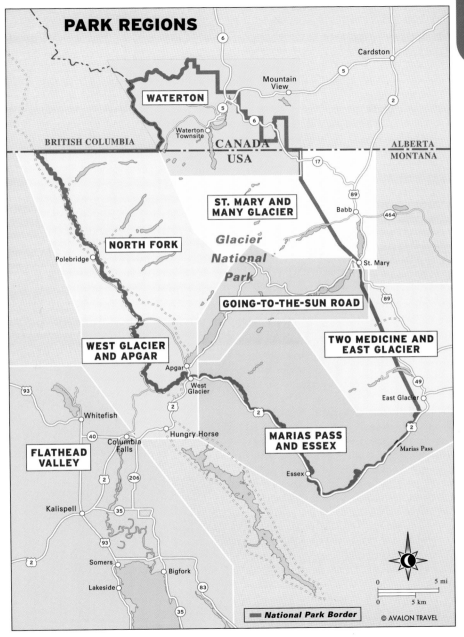

PARK REGIONS

WATERTON

BRITISH COLUMBIA

CANADA
USA

ST. MARY AND
MANY GLACIER

NORTH FORK

Glacier

National

Park

GOING-TO-THE-SUN ROAD

WEST GLACIER
AND APGAR

TWO MEDICINE AND
EAST GLACIER

MARIAS PASS
AND ESSEX

FLATHEAD
VALLEY

ALBERTA
MONTANA

Cardston

Mountain
View

Waterton
Townsite

Polebridge

St. Mary

Babb

Apgar

West
Glacier

Whitefish

Columbia
Falls

Hungry Horse

East Glacier

Marias Pass

Essex

Kalispell

Somers

Bigfork

Lakeside

0   5 mi

0   5 km

National Park Border

© AVALON TRAVEL

IF YOU HAVE...

- **ONE DAY:** Drive over Going-to-the-Sun Road.
- **THREE DAYS:** Add on Many Glacier.
- **ONE WEEK:** Explore West Glacier, Waterton, and Two Medicine.
- **TWO WEEKS:** Add the North Fork, Highway 2, and Flathead Valley.

hiking in Waterton

In prime bear country in Many Glacier, hikers find heaven with glimmering sapphire lakes, and the historic Many Glacier Hotel roosts idyllic below jagged peaks.

Two Medicine and East Glacier

The park's historic headliner hotel, Glacier Park Lodge greets travelers with its flowered walkway and huge lobby. It buzzes with golfers, swimmers, and trail riders. But Two Medicine Lake yields a quiet contrast for hikers, boaters, anglers, wildlife-watchers, and campers under Rising Wolf's red peak.

Marias Pass and Essex

Pale next to Going-to-the-Sun Road's drama, Highway 2 crosses mile-high Marias Pass in the fastest route over the Continental Divide. The scenic drive squeezes between Glacier and the Bob Marshall Wilderness, passing the Goat Lick and historic Izaak Walton Inn in Essex, and a Wild and Scenic River.

Waterton

In Canada, visitors tour Waterton Lake, travel by boat to cross the international boundary to Goat Haunt, U.S.A., and walk to the International Peace Park Pavilion. Presided over by the historic Prince of Wales Hotel, Waterton Townsite is a nucleus for boat tours, hiking, shopping, bicycling, dining, and camping.

Flathead Valley

More than Glacier's gateway, Flathead Valley is an attraction in itself with Kalispell, Whitefish, Bigfork, and Columbia Falls drawing visitors for their unique personalities. The valley lives up to its outdoor reputation with opportunities for boating, fishing, rafting, camping, biking, golf, swimming, hiking, and skiing.

Weeping Wall on Going-to-the-Sun Road

Goat Haunt, U.S.A.

Grinnell Glacier Valley

► WHEN TO GO

Summer attracts hordes when lodges, campgrounds, and trails are open. Baring deep snows, Going-to-the-Sun Road opens mid-June through mid-September, with peak visitation crammed into four weeks—mid-July–mid-August. Snow buries some trails into July, when moderate weather rides in. Mosquitoes descend with a vengeance in early summer, wildflowers peak in late July, and huckleberries ripen in August.

Although saddled with unpredictable weather, off-seasons offer less-hectic visits.

Low-elevation trails are usually snow-free, but few commercial services are open. While Going-to-the-Sun Road is closed to vehicles, bikers and hikers tour it sans cars. In spring, May and June rains intersperse with cobalt blue skies. In fall, warm, bug-free days and cool nights usher in peak-top snows by September's end. Often, early October sees a blue-sky spell, when larch and aspen turn gold. In winter, snow closes most park roads, which become snowshoeing and cross-country ski trails.

► BEFORE YOU GO

Non-driving travelers usually fly into Flathead Valley—the closest airport—or hop the Seattle-Chicago train that stops in East and West Glacier. Once at Glacier, shuttles aid travel, but only in summer and only to certain locations. Summer travelers should reserve rental cars in advance. Visitors heading to Waterton will need appropriate documentation to cross the international border.

Northwest Montanans have a saying: "Wait five minutes...the weather will change."

Because snows fall even in August, layers make sense—lightweight wicking synthetics, fleeces, and breathable waterproof or water-resistant fabrics. Bring gloves, a warm hat, and rain gear for cold snaps and a hat, sunscreen, and sunglasses for sun. Sturdy walking shoes or hiking boots work best on Glacier's rugged trails.

Dressing for dinner here means putting on a clean shirt. Casual attire is the restaurant norm, as are hiking boots and river sandals. Cool weather brings out fleece rather than cashmere. Despite the Wild West heritage, cowboy hats and boots garb only wranglers.

For hiking, bring a pack and a water bottle; you can get pepper spray for bears here. Bring binoculars and telephoto lenses for wildlife-watching. Don't forget the camera, for Glacier's scenery creates foolproof photo opportunities.

Explore Glacier National Park

▶ ON THE ROAD: THE BEST OF GLACIER

Glacier's roads cut through some of the most rugged country—along several-thousand-foot cliffs and sapphire lakes, high above forested valley floors, below parapets and icefields. This seven-day tour includes lots of roadside stops and short walks limited to less than two miles round-trip on fairly level terrain. You can arrange this tour to coordinate with staying in lodges or at campgrounds.

DAY 1

Begin on Glacier's west side, camping at Apgar, Sprague Creek, or staying at Lake McDonald Lodge for two nights. In the afternoon, get acquainted with Glacier in

heading past Haystack Creek on Going-to-the-Sun Road

GLACIER ON TWO WHEELS

BY BIKE

Bicycling Going-to-the-Sun Road stands in the annals of lifetime routes for many riders. While you can bike it from either east or west, most cyclists opt for starting in **West Glacier** for the dramatic 3,500-foot thigh-burning climb up the west side. Timing, however, is crucial with uphill road restrictions. Plan to leave West Glacier at 6 A.M. to reach **Logan Pass** by 11 A.M.

The best road tour loops 142 miles over the Sun Road and Highways 89, 49, and 2. Road racers ride the loop in one day; tourers do it in two days overnighting in **East Glacier** or three days staying one night in **St. Mary** and one in **East Glacier.** Enjoyable side trip rides from St. Mary can extend the length by including a day trip to **Many Glacier** or an overnight to **Waterton Lakes National Park.** Most park campgrounds have shared biker-hiker campsites available.

BY MOTORCYCLE

While motorcyclists can tour the park like any other vehicle, many bikers are attracted to riding Going-to-the-Sun Road with the wind blowing through their hair! Montana requires no helmets for motorcyclists over 18 years old, hence the feel of freedom amid an alpine wonderland. The park attracts scads of decked-out

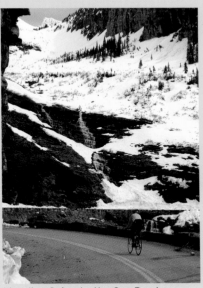

bicycling Going-to-the-Sun Road

Harleys and Goldwings as well as motorcycle clubs who come specifically to tour Going-to-the-Sun Road.

historic style on a red bus tour up Going-to-the-Sun Road to Logan Pass.

DAY 2

In the morning, take a scenic float on the Middle Fork of the Flathead River with one of the four raft companies in West Glacier. The float trip cuts through a dramatic steep-walled canyon with tame water. In the afternoon, explore Lake McDonald—touring Apgar, renting a canoe, taking the tour boat from the lodge, or just skipping rocks and catching the sunset at the lakeshore.

DAY 3

You already sampled a taste of Going-to-the-Sun Road, but now you'll get to savor it in different light on your own schedule. Pack a lunch to be free to take your time. Stop and walk Trail of the Cedars through the rainforest. Pull over on the National Historic Landmark highway to snap photos as you climb the west side, and stroll around Logan Pass. You'll see new country as you drop to St. Mary, stopping at Sunrift Gorge, Sun Point, and Wild Goose Island for a postcard picture of the park. When you reach St. Mary, do as the locals do and hit Park Café

Triple Arches is one of Going-to-the-Sun Road's engineering triumphs.

for fresh-baked pie before camping or lodging in Many Glacier or St. Mary for three nights.

DAY 4

In Many Glacier, hop on the tour boat across Swiftcurrent and Josephine Lakes; then walk to turquoise Grinnell Lake fed by a waterfall dropping from Grinnell Glacier. Sit on the shore for a picnic before returning to the upper Josephine dock to catch the return boat. While in Many Glacier, be sure to waltz through the historic Many Glacier Hotel if you're not staying there. Bask on the hotel's deck with binoculars in hand to spot grizzly and black bears foraging on Altyn Peak's hillside.

DAY 5

Drive Chief Mountain Highway to Waterton Lakes National Park for the day. Tour the Townsite and explore Cameron Falls. Book an early afternoon cruise on the historic MV *International* to Goat Haunt, U.S.A. and walk to the International Peace Park Pavilion. After returning, be sure to pop in the Prince of Wales Hotel for a look-see if you haven't already.

DAY 6

Drive to Two Medicine. Enjoy sitting on the benches near the boat dock beach. Take the boat tour across the lake to walk to Twin Falls. Camp in Two Medicine or stay in East Glacier at Glacier Park Lodge for one night.

DAY 7

For your last day in Glacier, drive U.S. Highway 2 over Marias Pass, stopping at the Goat Lick to catch sight of the white beasts and possibly elk high on the hillside above. Stop at Izaak Walton Inn for lunch before exploring river access spots on the Middle Fork of the Flathead River. Dine at the historic Belton Chalet in West Glacier to celebrate your trip.

► FROM DAWN TO DUSK: OUTDOOR OUTINGS

Leave Glacier's roads, and you're in a back-country paradise with hiker trails, rafting, and trail riding. This nine-day camping adventure explores the best of what the park's backcountry offers—sparkling glaciers, roiling rivers, blue lakes, goat-walk traverses, and peak galore.

DAY 1

Head toward Two Medicine to grab a campsite for two nights. In the afternoon, climb to Scenic Point to catch an eagle's eye view of the lakes and East Glacier. In the evening, walk along Two Medicine Lake's shore enjoying the sunset, or drop a line in for fish.

DAY 2

Leave from your campsite at 8 A.M. to hike Dawson-Pitamakin Loop. Turn right at the fork to heading toward Old Man Lake. The eight-hour hike traverses between Pitamakin,

PHOTOGRAPHER'S PILGRIMAGE

Both amateur and professional photographers find countless photo ops in Glacier. They hit **Going-to-the-Sun Road** at dawn to set up tripods for morning light. They haul out the giant telephoto lenses for wildlife photography at **Logan Pass** and macros for shooting delicate wildflowers. The Sun Road's top sunrise photo op spots include **Heaven's Peak** from the **West Side Tunnel** and **The Loop, Logan Pass, Sun Point,** and **Wild Goose Island Overlook.** The **Garden Wall** lights up best in the late afternoon or evening.

Cut Bank, and Dawson passes along a high goat walk before dropping to the tour boat at Pray Shelter at the lake's head to catch the boat back across Two Medicine Lake.

Hiking is one of the best ways to see Glacier.

WILDFLOWER WANDERS

When Glacier's spring hits Lake McDonald and St. Mary, Logan Pass still cowers under winter snows. Lower-elevation flowers bloom first, and as summer progresses, like a mist lifting, buds pop open in higher and higher habitats. Wildflowers do not bloom parkwide all at once, but peak at different times. But to hit the big displays aim for mid to late July. To help identify wildflowers, pick up a field guide from one of the Glacier Natural History Association bookstores.

FORESTS

Tiny and pale cream-colored forest wildflowers choose habitats under fir, hemlock, and cedars for their shade-producing canopies that protect fragile plants from the sun's drying rays. Queen's cup, fairybell, and pipsissewa scatter no more than boot-high. Most trails in the **North Fork** and **McDonald** valleys bloom with these gems, especially **Trail of the Cedars** at Avalanche. The rich duff also sprouts diminutive orchids. Look for pink calypso or fairy slipper orchids growing along the **Quartz Lakes** loop.

PRAIRIES

Wildflowers grow below timberline in prairie grasslands. Except for the **North Fork** prairies, most grasslands amass on the east side

fields of tall beargrass in July

at **Two Dog Flats,** along **Many Glacier Road,** and in **Waterton Lakes National Park** where 13 square miles of prairie is preserved. Without trees for shade, wildflowers adapt to dry conditions: high temperatures, wind, and less rain. Look for the sunflower-like arrowleaf balsamroot and dusty pink prairie smoke.

ASPEN PARKLANDS

Many flowers proliferate in a rich mix of meadows and aspen groves. Mountain death camas, paintbrush, pasque flower, lupine, stonecrop, and horse mint span the color rainbow. Along **Two Medicine Road,** blue camas blooms hardily. Beside **Many Glacier Road,** pink sticky geranium makes a show. Along **Chief Mountain International Highway,** wild roses and tiger lilies line the road to Waterton, which is home to 35 rare plants found only in its borders.

SUBALPINE

A drive on **Going-to-the-Sun Road** climbs into the subalpine zone—a rough place to be a wildflower. Long winters, high winds, little shade, and a short growing season mean that wildflowers must do their business fast. No time to smell pretty; just bloom. At **Logan Pass,** walk toward Hidden Lake Overlook or out along the Garden Wall to see colors a Monet would envy in pink shooting stars, yellow arnica, deep blue gentians, and fuchsia monkey flowers. Yellow glacier lilies—the harbingers of summer—force their blooms up, even through snow. Some years, three-foot-tall beargrass grows so thick that slopes appear to be snow-covered. For one of the best midsummer flower displays, hike three miles from Siyeh Bend to **Preston Park** with endless fields of color.

yellow columbine

ALPINE

Alpine wildflowers struggle against high winds, drying altitude, and rocky soils lacking organic matter. But these diminutive wildflowers that survive by hugging the ground bloom with a show during their short few-week season. In Two Medicine, hike the short steep **Scenic Point** trail, where you'll see several-hundred-year-old mats of pink moss campion, small bluebells, and the red tops of king's crown cowering between slabs. To see blue Jones columbine and creamy mountain avens, grunt up to 8,000-foot-high **Siyeh Pass.**

climbing around on argillite layers in Many Glacier

DAY 3

Pack up and drive to Many Glacier to get a campsite for three nights. Spend the afternoon exploring: walk to Many Glacier Hotel to enjoy the immense lobby, rent a canoe to paddle Swiftcurrent Lake, and watch bears through the park service telescope in Swiftcurrent parking lot. You can also grab showers here.

DAY 4

From your campsite, walk across the Swiftcurrent parking lot to the Iceberg Lake trail. Stop for a break at Ptarmigan Falls, and at the lake, swim with the icebergs if you can stand the cold. If you have gumption, add on Ptarmigan Tunnel.

DAY 5

Climb to Grinnell Glacier to hear ice breaking off the glacier. When you return to Josephine Lake, you can catch a return boat across the lake or hike all the way back. If you

want to shorten the hike to six miles round trip, catch the early hiker express boat across Swiftcurrent and Josephine Lakes from Many Glacier Hotel.

DAY 6

Pack up and get an early start. At St. Mary, turn up Going-to-the-Sun Road, driving to Logan Pass by 9:30 A.M. to get a parking spot. Hike the Highline Trail to Granite Park Chalet to spend the night. Your evening will fill with bear and sunset watching.

DAY 7

In the morning, hike out to The Loop to catch the shuttle back to Logan Pass and retrieve your car. Drive west on Going-to-the-Sun Road toward Lake McDonald, camping at Sprague Creek.

DAY 8

Join Swan Mountain Outfitters for their all

day horseback ride to Sperry Chalet, eating lunch in the dining hall and delighting in their home-baked pie. After the ride, head to your campsite and the beach for a swim in Lake McDonald.

DAY 9

Head to one of the four raft companies in West Glacier to celebrate your adventures with a half-day white-water rafting trip on the Middle Fork of the Flathead River.

► FAMILY ADVENTURES

Pack the kids in the car and head outdoors! While some tiny-mileage hikes may work with tots, this itinerary is aimed at getting 7- to 12-year-olds out to hike, raft, and ride horses. The seven-day tour can be geared toward staying in lodges and cabins or camping. Base the first three nights in West Glacier or Apgar; then move to Many Glacier or St. Mary to stay for the last three nights. To make hiking successful with kids, have each child carry his or her own water bottle and stuff a snack bar in a pocket. And yes, it's okay for them to make noise on the trails—that warns bears you're coming.

DAY 1

Begin in Apgar, heading to the visitors center to pick up copies of the Junior Ranger Newspaper. This will not only give them activities to do through the week, but they can earn a Glacier Park Junior Ranger badge by completing all the projects in the newspaper. While in Apgar, visit the Discovery Cabin, where kids can do free hands-on learning about wildlife, geology, and natural history. Head to Apgar Picnic Area to go swimming, go fishing along Lower McDonald Creek, or rent canoes to paddle Lake McDonald.

newborn goat kid

WILDLIFE-WATCHING HOTSPOTS

With 57 animals and over 210 varieties of birds, wildlife watchers have plenty to spot. Bring your binoculars and scopes, for your own safety as well as the animal's well being. Die-hard birders will want to hit June and July because migrations prompt some birds to head south as early as August.

Both Glacier and Waterton Parks have wildlife and bird checklists. Ask for them at visitors centers or check park websites.

Look for Watchable Wildlife programs in Glacier. Interpretive rangers set up spotting scopes for public viewing and answer all your animal questions.

GOAT LICK

Located on Highway 2, the Goat Lick is a natural mineral lick that attracts **mountain goats** in late spring and early summer. You'll see both billies and nannies with newborn kids.

INSIDE NORTH FORK ROAD

While **gray wolves** are elusive, you may have a chance of spotting one on the Inside North Fork Road near dawn or dusk.

MCGEE MEADOWS

For birders, the North Fork Valley holds over 196 species of **birds,** 57 percent of which are nesters. Fens, like McGee Meadows, bustle with red-winged blackbirds, snipes, and soras. Woodpeckers drum; songbirds chatter. Keep your eyes open for the western tanager's striking yellow and red.

LOGAN PASS

Mountain goats and **bighorn sheep** wander through the parking lot at Logan Pass and frequent the short trail to Hidden Lake Overlook. **Blue grouse** and **ptarmigan** strut in open meadows.

AVALANCHE CHUTES

In early spring, **grizzly bears** prowl avalanche slopes between Avalanche and The Loop on Going-to-the-Sun Road in hopes of finding carcasses. Look particularly at slopes on Mt. Cannon and the Glacier Wall on Going-to-the-Sun Road.

FALLS

St. Mary and Virginia Falls create perfect habitat for **American dippers.** Recognize these small dark birds by their bobbing.

HENKEL AND ALTYN

Both **grizzly and black bears** congregate on these two peaks in Many Glacier mid-July through September, looking for bulbs, ground squirrels, and huckleberries. You can even spot them from Many Glacier Hotel's deck. The park service often sets up a viewing scope in the Swiftcurrent parking lot.

DAY 2

In the morning, drive up Going-to-the-Sun Road to hike to Avalanche Lake. Start on Trail of the Cedars, where fallen cedars look like an imaginary gnome world. Warn the kids about slippery rocks at Avalanche Gorge before climbing to the lake to wade. Afterwards, enjoy a picnic at Avalanche before heading back to Lake McDonald, stopping to explore some of its beaches and skip rocks.

DAY 3

In the morning, saddle up a one-hour trail ride with Swan Mountain Outfitters at the Apgar corral. In the afternoon, go whitewater rafting on the Middle Fork of the Flathead with one of the four companies in West Glacier. (With younger kids, take a scenic float instead.)

DAY 4

Pack a sack or picnic lunch for touring Going-

SWIFTCURRENT VALLEY

A short, gentle hike tours through good **moose** country to Red Rocks and Bullhead Lakes. The valley is also good **bird** habitat for white-crowned sparrows, loons, finches, Townsend's solitaires, hummingbirds, kinglets, and Clark's nutcrackers. Look for **golden eagles** soaring high along cliffs.

TWO DOG FLATS

Early morning in spring and late fall, herds of **elk** drop out of the high country to feed at Two Dog Flats along Going-to-the-Sun Road near Rising Sun. This is also a good place to watch **woodpeckers, flickers, sapsuckers, mountain bluebirds,** and several species of **owls** in the aspen trees.

BISON PADDOCK

In Waterton, stop at the **bison** paddock to see the small herd of monster shaggy bovines maintained there.

WATERTON LAKES

In Waterton, the wetlands around Maskinonge and Linnet Lakes abound with **waterfowl, osprey, swans, and kingfishers.** Over 250 avian species pass through here on two major migratory flyways because of the rich wetlands and varied habitats.

KOOTENAI LAKES

Accessed via the Waterton tour boat, Glacier's Kootenai Lakes harbors **moose** and sometimes **trumpeter swans.**

grizzly sow and cub

to-the-Sun Road. Several assignments in the Junior Ranger Newspaper will be completed on this drive. Stop at Logan Pass to hike to Hidden Lake Overlook. In St. Mary, get ice cream cones at Curly Bear Café.

DAY 5

In Many Glacier, pack a lunch and take the boat tour across Swiftcurrent and Josephine Lakes. From Josephine, hike across a swinging bridge to turquoise Grinnell Lake for

a picnic and wading. Return via the boats and stop in the Swiftcurrent parking lot to look through the park service telescope at bears.

DAY 6

Pack trail snacks, water, and lunch for a long day hiking in Many Glacier. For older kids and in-shape youngsters, head to Iceberg Lake to swim with icebergs! For younger kids and those not used to hiking, aim for Red Rocks Falls.

TOP 10 DAY HIKES

Glacier is a hiker's park. With over 700 miles of trails, it's a place to explore on foot, June–September to sample the top trails. Shuttles running from July through Labor Day help accommodate point-to-point hiking over Going-to-the-Sun Road.

APGAR LOOKOUT

Located at Lake McDonald's foot, the lookout requires a less than three-mile climb to attain a far-reaching panoramic view of Glacier's peaks that stretches from Canada to the Bob Marshall Wilderness. It's a short hike with big view rewards.

AVALANCHE LAKE

A two-mile trail leaves the McDonald Creek Valley, heading up a red rock side canyon to the idyllic lake—hence the crowds. Fed by Sperry Glacier above, waterfalls spew thousands of feet down the cliffs surrounding the lake below the Little Matterhorn.

HIGHLINE TRAIL

Beginning at Logan Pass, the stunning 11.6-mile point-to-point goatwalk tiptoes through high wildflower meadows along the Garden Wall arête to historic Granite Park Chalet before dropping to The Loop. Acrophobes may clench their stomachs as the trail prances along cliffs looking down at Going-to-the-Sun Road.

SIYEH PASS

Just east of Logan Pass at Siyeh Bend, this point-to-point trail climbs 10.5 miles over a high elevation saddle with views of sparkling glaciers. The trail wanders through Preston Park ablaze with purple wildflowers and alongside bighorn sheep, as it circumnavigates Going-to-the-Sun Mountain.

SCENIC POINT

High above Two Medicine Lake, this short three-mile climb lets you look far out across the plains and then turn around to stare at rugged

DAY 7

Before you leave, swing by St. Mary Visitor Center or Many Glacier Ranger Station. Here, the kids will turn in their Junior Ranger Newspapers, be quizzed briefly by the rangers, and sworn in. Then, head off to Waterton Lakes National Park. Drive through the bison paddock before going through the park entrance. Then, explore the Townsite on surrey-bikes, pedaling to Cameron Falls.

▶ HISTORIC HOTEL HIGHLIGHTS

Great Northern Railway built the park's great lodges in the early 1900s to entice wealthy easterners to ride the train and visit Glacier. While some inns served as gateways, others were placed in striking scenery. Bear in mind that these are not luxury inns on this six-day tour, but lodges laden with historic ambiance. You'll enjoy this tour best enlightened by the history of each lodge as described in *Glacier's Historic Hotels and Chalets: View with a Room* available through Glacier Natural History Association.

DAY 1

Begin your tour in West Glacier at the first railway hotel to be built in the park chain in 1910—Belton Chalet. Sip wine on the deck overlooking the train depot or by the peaks as you stand atop a promontory of the Lewis Overthrust Fault.

DAWSON-PITAMAKIN LOOP

In a hike that includes a boat ride across Two Medicine Lake, the 16-mile loop actually crosses three passes: Dawson, Cutbank, and Pitamakin. You'll feel like you're walking on top of the world as the narrow path hangs dizzyingly thousands of feet above the valley floor.

ICEBERG LAKE

For the rarity of seeing icebergs in August, a 4.5-mile gentle ascent in Many Glacier leads to a glacial remnant lake where chunks of white ice float in its deep blue waters. Tradition dictates a quick dive in, but be ready for cold like you've never felt before.

GRINNELL GLACIER

In Many Glacier, the Grinnell trail provides the quickest path in the park to reach a glacier. In its scenic climb, its 5.5-mile path delights en route with wildflowers, bighorn sheep, grizzly bears, waterfalls, and stunning views of turquoise Grinnell Lake.

CARTHEW-ALDERSON

Beginning at Cameron Lake in Waterton, the nearly 12-mile **Carthew-Alderson** trail climbs high into windswept alpine tundra with panoramic views extending in to Glacier. Then it drops past gleaming tarns set against giant stone walls to the Waterton Townsite.

CRYPT LAKE

Requiring boat access across Waterton Lake, the trail throws a unique twist at you with a ladder, tunnel, and cliff walk in its five miles to reach the lake set in a hanging valley. But be prepared for hiking with hordes—everyone begins the hike together from the boat dock and races at the end of the day to catch the return boat.

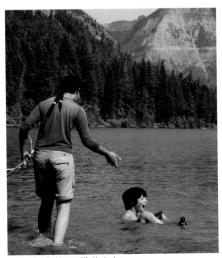

swimming in Upper Kintla Lake

fireplace in the tap room before dining in among historic photos in the Belton Grill. Don't forget your earplugs as the trains run all night!

DAY 2

Drive 12 miles stopping to enjoy Lake McDonald beaches en route to Lake McDonald Lodge. Stay in the main lodge built in 1914 or cabins rather than motor inn. For a historic ride, hop a morning red bus tour up Going-to-the-Sun Road. Dine early in Russell's Fireside Dining Room followed by the evening tour boat on the lake to feel how the lodge was originally approached from the water.

Lake McDonald Lodge, built in 1914

the circa-1927 Prince of Wales Hotel in Waterton

DAY 3

Tour Going-to-the-Sun Road at your own pace, stopping at Sun Point to see the sight of one of the original park chalets. Head to Many Glacier Hotel, where you can sit on the back deck to watch bears with binoculars. In the immense four-story lobby of the 1915 hotel, browse the historical photo display and curl up in front of the fire. Go for a Ptarmigan Dining Room table adjacent to the two-story windows. Stay in a lakeside room, for the balconies add another way to revel in the vista and view the night sky with, possibly, Northern Lights.

DAY 4

Drive Chief Mountain International Highway across the border to Waterton Lakes National Park. You'll spot the dramatic-spired, circa 1927 Prince of Wales Hotel long before you arrive. Splurge for a lakeside room staring down Waterton Lake. After exploring the Townsite, take a ride on the MV *International* to Goat Haunt, U.S.A. to walk to the International Peace Park Pavilion. Then, back at the hotel, delight in the downlake view through floor-to-ceiling windows in the Royal Stewart Dining Room.

DAY 5

Head back across the border to East Glacier to check in at the headliner Glacier Park Lodge, built in 1915. Walk its flowered pathway, sit in its huge Douglas fir lobby, peruse the historical photo display, swim in its pool, and golf on its course frequented by wildlife. Dine in the Great Northern Steak and Rib House. Finish the evening with a cocktail in the Sunset Lounge overlooking the orange sky above Dancing Lady and Mount Henry.

DAY 6

Drive Highway 2 over Marias Pass to Izaak Walton Inn at Glacier's southernmost tip. Originally built in 1939 to house railroad personnel, the building eventually became a four-season resort that caters to cross-country skiers in winter. Lunch in the Dining Car Restaurant and tour the historical photos in the basement Flagstop Bar. If you have an extra day, stay overnight in one of their cabooses (hope you kept your earplugs).

WEST GLACIER AND APGAR

Sitting just two miles apart, West Glacier and Apgar span Glacier Park's southwestern boundary—the Middle Fork of the Flathead River. While West Glacier sprouted up outside the park along Great Northern Railway's line, early trapper and logger homesteads dug in a foothold at Apgar on Lake McDonald—the port to the park's wild interior before Going-to-the-Sun Road was built. Connected by the "new bridge," the park entrance road, and a two-mile paved bicycling and walking pathway, the pair are doorways for exploring Glacier's western wilderness. As such, they throng with cars and visitors in summer; 60 percent of visitors access the park via this west entrance. The pair also launch sightseers in two disparate directions: to the untrammeled North Fork Valley and to Glacier's crowning highway, Going-to-the-Sun Road.

Today, many concessionaires headquarter themselves in West Glacier, just outside national park boundaries. The tiny town evolved into the seasonal mecca for rafting, guided hiking and backpacking, guided fishing trips, trail rides, and helicopter tours. Along with the train station, campgrounds, restaurants, motels, shops, and even an espresso stand, West Glacier is a place to gas up the car one last time before seeking Glacier's interior. On Lake McDonald's shores and inside the park, Apgar resounds with calm in comparison. Although its restaurant, lodging, camping, shopping, boat ramp, and petite west-side visitors center swarm in high season, miles of lake sprawl

HIGHLIGHTS

◖ Belton Chalet: Enjoy a tribute to a by-gone era of tourism in a chalet as old as the park. On chillier days, enjoy the ambience by its stone fireplace; on warmer days, lounge at sunset on its deck with a local brew (page 33).

◖ Robert Fire: See a forest renewing it-self after the 2003 fire on Apgar Mountain and Howe Ridge. The fire forced the evacuation of West Glacier, Apgar, and the McDonald Valley (page 35).

◖ Lake McDonald: Leap into the park's largest lake for a refreshing swim or paddle its shoreline in a kayak or canoe. Its clear waters lure boaters, anglers, scuba divers, photographers, and rock skippers (page 36).

◖ Apgar Lookout: Climb to where you can look down Lake McDonald, West Glacier, and the North Fork. You'll see a huge panorama of peaks from Canada to Glacier's southern tip (page 37).

◖ Huckleberry Lookout: Traipse along a top-of-the-world ridge walk where views stretch from Flathead Lake to Canada on this 12-mile round-trip hike (page 39).

◖ Middle Fork of the Flathead: Crash through white-water on a raft. The Wild and Scenic River drops through rapids such as Screaming Right Hand Turn, Bonecrusher, Jaws, and Could Be Trouble (page 42).

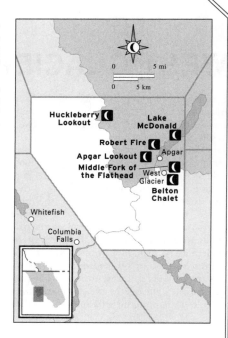

LOOK FOR ◖ TO FIND RECOMMENDED SIGHTS, ACTIVITIES, DINING, AND LODGING.

with blue waters and lakeshore enough to find a niche for solitude.

HISTORY
Native Americans

For the Ksanka or Standing Arrow people (known today as the Salish and Kootenai, whose tribal lands are at Flathead Lake's south end), Glacier's Lake McDonald area held special significance. Ten thousand generations ago, as legend says, the Ksanka were first given a ceremonial dance by the spirits at their winter camp near Apgar. Originally called the Blacktail Deer Dance, the ceremony became an annual event for the tribe, and the area became known as "the place where people dance." Today, the annual dance—now called the Jump Dance—takes place on the Flathead Reservation, but rapids on McDonald Creek still hold the original name, Sacred Dancing Cascade.

Early Tourism

When the Great Northern Railway completed its westbound track in 1891, early tourists jumped off the train in Belton (West Glacier) to see Glacier. With no bridge across the Middle Fork of the Flathead, visitors rowed across the

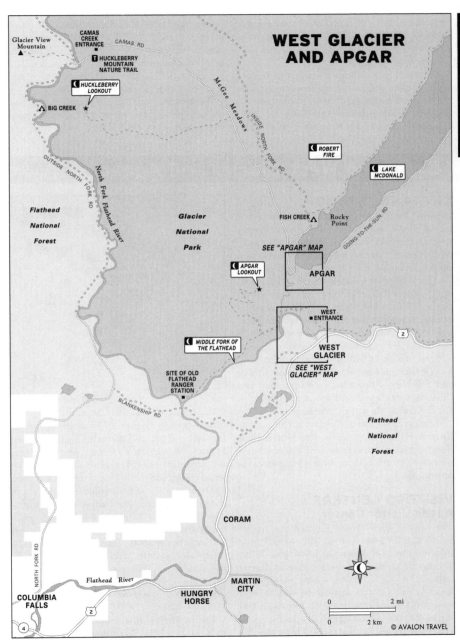

WEST GLACIER AND APGAR

Glacier View Mountain ▲

CAMAS CREEK ENTRANCE ■

CAMAS RD

HUCKLEBERRY MOUNTAIN NATURE TRAIL

☾ HUCKLEBERRY LOOKOUT ★

△ BIG CREEK

McGee Meadows

INSIDE NORTH FORK RD

☾ ROBERT FIRE

☾ LAKE MCDONALD

OUTSIDE NORTH FORK RD

North Fork Flathead River

Flathead

National

Forest

Glacier

National

Park

FISH CREEK △ Rocky Point

SEE "APGAR" MAP

GOING-TO-THE-SUN RD

☾ APGAR LOOKOUT ★

APGAR

■ WEST ENTRANCE

WEST GLACIER

2

☾ MIDDLE FORK OF THE FLATHEAD

SEE "WEST GLACIER" MAP

SITE OF OLD FLATHEAD RANGER STATION ■

BLANKENSHIP RD

Flathead

National

Forest

NORTH FORK RD

CORAM

Flathead River

COLUMBIA FALLS

2

4

HUNGRY HORSE

MARTIN CITY

0   2 mi

0   2 km

© AVALON TRAVEL

river and then saddled up for a horseback ride to Apgar. Finally, in 1895 a rough dirt road eased the two-mile journey, followed two years later by a bridge across the river.

As the railroad dumped visitors in Belton, Lake McDonald homesteaders leaped into the tourism business, offering cabins, meals, pack trips, boat rides, and guided tours. After Glacier became a national park in 1910, local landowners along the lake retained their property as inholdings. While private summer homes still exist here within the park boundaries (to the envy of everyone), when sellers are ready, the National Park Service purchases these properties at fair market value.

To coincide with Glacier's first summer as a national park, Great Northern Railway opened Belton Chalet in 1910 across from the depot.

Exploring West Glacier and Apgar

ENTRANCE STATION

Crossing the Middle Fork of the Flathead River on the West Glacier Bridge officially escorts you into Glacier National Park. There's even a pull-out before the park entrance sign for those who photo-document their travels by park signage. The park entrance is usually staffed during daylight hours all summer long and off-season on weekends. But don't sweat it if you miss someone in the station: you can use the self-pay cash-only kiosk on the right just beyond the booth. If you don't have an annual pass, 7-day passes cost $25 per vehicle or $12 for individuals on foot, bicycles, or motorcycles. (Rates drop to $15 and $10 Nov.–Apr.) Also, pick up a map and the summer or winter edition of the *Waterton-Glacier Guide,* the park's newspaper.

You can also enter Apgar via the Camas Entrance from the rough dirt North Fork Road. At its northwest end, an entrance station sits unstaffed along with a self-pay cash-only kiosk.

VISITORS CENTERS
Apgar Visitor Center

The tiny Apgar Visitor Center (on Apgar Rd. 0.2 mile from Camas Rd. or 0.9 mile from Going-to-the-Sun Rd., 406/888-7800, 9 A.M.–5 P.M. daily May–late June and after Labor Day–Sept., 8 A.M.–7 P.M. daily late June–Labor Day, 9 A.M.–4:30 P.M. winter weekends) seems crowded with 15 people, but it sees 190,000 visitors annually. In the small shell of what was once a two-room house, the

visitors center houses a few displays, an information desk, and a small Glacier Natural History Association bookstore. The backcountry permit office (May–Nov. 406/888-7859, winter 406/888-7800) sits a few doors west opposite the old red schoolhouse. In spite of the visitors center's diminutive size, park personnel are big on information. Pick up maps, naturalist activity guides, and Junior Ranger Program newspapers. You can also get the latest updates on trails, roads, campgrounds, fishing, and boating. Restrooms sit around the side of the building. The park service hopes to build a new visitors center eventually near the Apgar Transit Center.

For some free, fun, hands-on activities for kids, stop by the **Discovery Cabin** in the

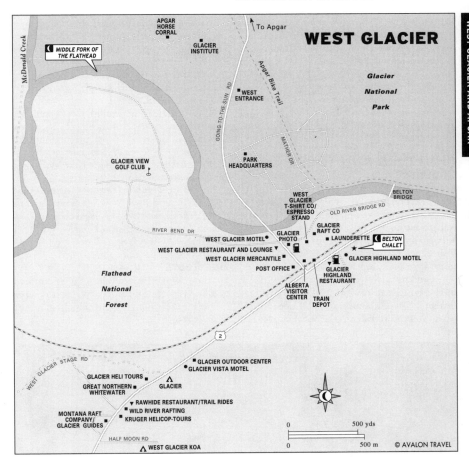

woods across the street from the Apgar Visitor Center. With the help of interpretive rangers, learning stations teach about wildlife, geology, and natural history. Limited hours change; consult the visitors center for the current schedule and walking directions to the cabin.

Apgar Transit Center

A new $4.3 million Transit Center constructed in 2007 houses the unstaffed **Discovery Center,** loaded with park information in visual displays and electronic kiosks. By car, find its parking lot off the Apgar T junction on Going-to-the-Sun Road, or walk by trail from the Apgar Visitor Center. The center reflects the highest green building standards: Restrooms with low-flow toilets, automatic lights, and indigenous flora landscaping. Outdoor signage highlights interpretive information for all major park regions. Catch the shuttle here to go up Going-to-the-Sun Road.

Alberta Visitor Information Center

Located in West Glacier, the Alberta Visitor Information Center (125 Going-to-the-Sun

Rd., 800/252-3782, www.travelalberta.com, 8 A.M.–7 P.M. daily late May–early Sept., expect closures around 5 P.M. during late Sept.) is a building-size advertisement for Canada, complete with dinosaur bones. For those heading over the border to Waterton, the center is worth a stop to help with travel planning. The staff has plenty of brochures and maps to give away. You'll also find big, clean public restrooms here!

SHUTTLES AND TOURS
Shuttles

Free shuttles circulate every 15–30 minutes July 1–Labor Day, 7:15 A.M.–7 P.M. Look for obvious interpretive signs marking the shuttle stops. Shuttles link Apgar Campground, Apgar Village, and the Apgar Transit Center. (From Fish Creek Campground, call 406/888-5961 to arrange pick up.) From the transit center, you can catch shuttles heading up Going-to-the-Sun Road toward McDonald Lodge, Avalanche, several trailheads, and Logan Pass, where you can transfer to the St. Mary shuttle.

The no-reservations, no-tickets-needed shuttles are popular, so you may have to wait for a seat during the peak season. Designed as hiker shuttles, they do not come with interpretive guides. If you are heading toward Logan Pass, be sure to take a daypack with water, snacks, and extra clothes.

Running late May through late September, **Glacier Park, Inc.** (406/892-2525, www .glacierparkinc.com, $6 per person) shuttles train passengers between West Glacier's Belton Depot and Apgar Village Inn or Lake McDonald Lodge. Reservations are mandatory.

Flathead-Glacier Transportation (406/892-3390 or 800/829-7039; www.fgtrans .com) runs shuttles by reservation only between Glacier International Airport and West Glacier ($36 one way) or Apgar ($40 one way).

Bus Tours

For those with oversized vehicles not permitted on Going-to-the-Sun Road, two tour companies offer the easiest way to tour Logan Pass when it is open.

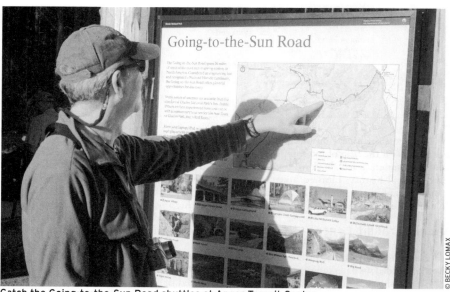

© BECKY LOMAX

Catch the Going-to-the-Sun Road shuttles at Apgar Transit Center.

Glacier Park's fleet of **Red Buses** (406/892-2525, www.glacierparkinc.com, late May–Sept., adults $35–90, kids half price) are the best way to tour in historic style, with roll-back tops allowing for uninhibited peak views and au natural air-conditioning. Make reservations a day in advance, especially in high season. Half- and full-day tours are based out of Lake McDonald Lodge but have pickups at West Glacier KOA, Glacier Campground, Belton Chalet in West Glacier, and the Village Inn in Apgar scheduled 30–60 minutes in advance of lodge departure times. When the pass is closed in shoulder seasons, the red buses tour around Huckleberry Mountain.

With a pickup at the Alberta Visitor Information Center, your campground, or Apgar, **Sun Tours** (406/226-9220 or 800/786-9220, www.glaciersuntours.com, June–Sept., adults $40, kids ages 12 and under $15, meals and park entrance fees not included) departs at 9:30 A.M. daily from West Glacier for four-hour tours to Logan Pass and back. The air-conditioned 25-passenger coaches are extremely comfortable, with extra-big windows enhancing views. Blackfeet guides who grew up on the reservation give insight into the park's rich Native American heritage—from buffalo days to modern spirituality.

Helicopter

Two helicopter tour companies—both within one mile of the train depot—fly half-hour and one-hour tours over Glacier Park. Per person rates vary $99–750, based on the number of passengers and flight duration. Even though tours are weather dependent, make reservations from home, especially if you want to be able to keep the cost down by sharing the ride with other passengers. You may have to adjust your schedule when you're here, but you'll still have your reservations. **Glacier Heli Tours** (11950 Hwy. 2 E., 406/387-4141 or 800/879-9310, www.glacierhelitours.com, 8 A.M.–8 P.M. daily May–Sept.) flies two helicopters, seating four or six guests. **Kruger Helicop-Tours** (11892 Hwy. 2 E., 406/387-4565 or 800/220-6565, www.krugerhelicopters.com, daily mid-

May–Sept., office hours vary with weather) carries four passengers per flight.

SERVICES

Gas services are *not* available inside the park, on Going-to-the-Sun Road, up the North Fork Valley, or on Highway 2 until East Glacier. The last chance for gasoline is West Glacier: **Glacier Highland** (gas available year-round with a credit card) across from the train depot or **West Glacier MRC Gasoline** (mid-May–Sept.) across from the Mercantile.

The **West Glacier Laundromat** (8 A.M.–10 P.M. daily mid-May–mid-Sept.) sits behind the Alberta Visitor Information Center. If it is packed, both the West Glacier KOA and West Glacier Campground have launderettes. You can also get a hot shower ($3–5) at both campgrounds.

The post office sits in West Glacier adjacent to **Going-to-the-Sun Gift Shop,** which has a wireless Internet hotspot (8 A.M.–7 P.M. daily May–Sept.). ATM machines are located in Apgar at Eddie's and in West Glacier near the MRC gas station.

Glacier Highland Resort (12555 Hwy. 2 E., 406/888-5427 or 800/766-0811, www.glacier highlandresort.com) across from the train depot rents cars.

Shopping

West Glacier and Apgar both have gift shops with souvenirs, T-shirts, and books. In Apgar, stop by **Montana House of Gifts** (406/888-5393, on Apgar Rd. next to the visitors center, 9 A.M.–8:30 P.M. daily in summer, until 5 P.M. in winter) for its locally made pottery, weaving, jewelry, crafts, and arts—some by Native Americans. Glacier Outdoor Center (11957 Hwy. 2 E., 406/888-5454 or 800/235-6781, open daily year round) carries outdoor gear for hiking, rafting, and fishing.

Located in the historic Belton Railway Station in West Glacier, the **Glacier Natural History Association** (GNHA, 406/888-5756, www.glacierassociation.com) headquarters sells books, posters, and maps of Glacier. This is the place to go for all park-reference,

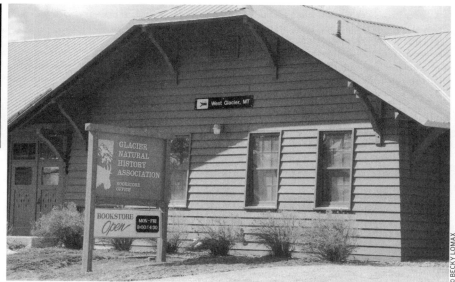

© BECKY LOMAX

The Belton depot in West Glacier houses the Glacier Natural History Association bookstore.

natural history, guide-, and picture books. GNHA also runs a small bookstore in the Apgar Visitor Center and six other park locations. You can also order products from the GNHA website.

Newspapers and Magazines

Look for three daily newspapers here: Kalispell's *Daily Interlake, The Missoulian* from Missoula, and the *Great Falls Tribune.* For the scoop on park news, the weekly *Hungry Horse News* gives a good inside look. You can also find the free weekly *Flathead Beacon* (www.flathead beacon.com), covering Flathead Valley news, and *Flathead Living,* a local free quarterly magazine featuring cultural and lifestyle tidbits.

Emergencies

For emergencies within park boundaries, contact a ranger or call 406/888-7800. Outside park boundaries, call 911. The nearest hospitals are in the Flathead Valley: Kalispell Regional Hospital (406/752-5111) and North Valley Hospital in Whitefish (406/863-3631).

The nearest ranger station inside the park is **Glacier National Park Headquarters** (406/888-7800), on Going-to-the-Sun Road just west of the park entrance station. The side road is well-signed; turn onto it and take the first right into the parking lot for the headquarters building. You can also get assistance at the Apgar Visitor Center.

Outside the park, the nearest U.S. Forest Service ranger station for Flathead National Forest is in Hungry Horse on Highway 2 at milepost 143.1. Call **Hungry Horse Ranger Station** (10 Hungry Horse Dr., 406/387-3800, www.fs.fed.us/r1/flathead) for any emergencies on the Flathead River system or in the Flathead National Forest.

DRIVING TOUR
Camas Road

Outside Apgar, the 11.3-mile Camas Road heads north across Lower McDonald Creek toward the North Fork of the Flathead River on one of the best paved roads in Glacier, open only in summer. The havoc of weather, time,

© BECKY LOMAX

West Glacier from Apgar Lookout

geology, and massive traffic has not taken its toll on the Camas Road as on other park roads. Climbing along the base of the Apgar Range, the road traverses through the **2003 Robert Fire** and the **2001 Moose Fire,** which offer a contrast in forest succession after burns. Several pullouts en route are worth a stop: If you can stand the mosquitoes, grab binoculars to peruse **McGee Meadows** (at 5.5 miles) for moose, deer, and bear. Just west of the Camas entrance station at 11.1 miles, a turnoff leads to **Huckleberry Mountain Nature Trail,** a 0.9-mile self-guided loop and views of the remote Livingston Range. After crossing the park boundary—the North Fork River—the Camas Road terminates at North Fork Road. When bears frequent the Camas Road, you may see rangers hazing them away from the roadway. They are trying to condition the bears to steer clear of trafficked areas for their own safety.

SIGHTS

While most visitors head straight to Lake McDonald, the biggest attraction in the area, there's plenty more to see in West Glacier and Apgar.

West Glacier

The town of West Glacier (originally known as Belton) centered historically around the Belton Train Depot and Belton Chalet. Today, Highway 2 divides the pair, and West Glacier now harbors recreational concessions such as rafting, backpacking, hiking, helitours, and fishing. To leave the highway bustle, drive through the railroad tunnel and enter a historic world preserved by the Lundgren family, operators for over 50 years of the West Glacier Mercantile Company. The vintage brown 1938 buildings house a bar, restaurant, gift shops, grocery, and motel. Fall finds lazy birch leaves covering the ground as shops board their windows, leaving the town's 224 year-round residents to themselves.

◖ Belton Chalet

In 1910, Glacier became a park, and the Belton Chalet opened its doors to guests arriving via Great Northern Railway. The first in a series of railroad company Swiss-themed chalets built throughout the park, the Belton served as the park gateway. Milkmaid-attired hostesses and flowered walkways greeted guests. (In the Taproom, you can see its original look in the photo that includes the trellised walkway from the train depot to the chalet.) Over the years, the chalet changed hands, serving as housing for Civilian Conservation Corps crews building Going-to-the-Sun Road as well as a pizza parlor and bakery. After heavy snows destroyed roofs and floors in the late 1990s, owners from Bigfork restored the lodge and cabins to the tune of $1 million. In 2000, Belton Chalet was recognized on the National Register of Historic Places—commemorated here on a walkway bench.

Historic Belton Bridge

The Belton Bridge opened in 1920; park visitors could drive across the Middle Fork of the

WILDFIRES

In an average summer, 13 wildfires burn in Glacier, altering the forest landscape on 5,000 acres. Most are lightning-caused, with over 80 percent of strikes touching down in the park's heavily timbered west side. Some are small and unseen while others send huge smoke plumes thousands of feet in the air.

Two large fire seasons ripped through Glacier in the past decade. In 2001, the Moose Fire burned almost 30,000 acres in the North Fork Valley and Apgar Mountain Range. In 2003, an onslaught of lightning strikes and possibly an illegal campfire burned 150,000 acres in several locations around Glacier in one of the largest fire seasons in the park's history. (You can see the evidence from Going-to-the-Sun Road across Lake McDonald and at The Loop.) In 2006, the Red Eagle fire ate up 32,000 acres outside St. Mary. But even in these recent fire zones, plants and forests are already regenerating.

As flames eat up wood, ash falls to the ground, releasing nutrients. Similar to putting a good fertilizer on a garden, the ash fosters energetic plant growth, especially with the open tree canopy permitting more sunlight. As a natural succession of greenery takes over, wildlife dependent on plant foraging finds improved habitat. In short, fires help maintain a natural balance. They also remove deadfall and infested insects, reduce the power of future fires, and create forests more resistant to drought and nonnative plant invasions. Fire isn't the end of a forest, but an ongoing process of succession in an ever-changing landscape.

Some species even rely on fires for reproduction: The lodgepole's serotinous cones require high heat to release its fast-growing seeds from the sticky resin. Ceanothus, hollyhock, and morel mushrooms flourish after fires. Others, like the larch or ponderosa, will survive a fire through thick resin-less bark and minimal low branches.

From 1916 to 1968, federal policy suppressed all fires — resulting in excessive fuel buildup,

Apgar Lookout Trail takes you through terrain that's regenerating from a 2003 fire.

bug infestations, and elimination of some floral species. Today, the Park Service manages each fire individually. If fires threaten human life or structures, they will be suppressed along with most human-caused fires, but lightning fires ranging in the wilds will often be monitored, allowing the ecosystem's natural cycle to take place. Sometimes, park crews set intentional fires to reduce fuel buildup or protect a resource, such as a prairie, from invasion by other species.

Glacier's wildfires used to be monitored from 17 different lookouts. Today, satellite and airplane surveys have reduced the need for staffed lookouts to four: Huckleberry, Scalplock, Numa, and Swiftcurrent.

© BECKY LOMAX

Flathead River without rowing. Ironically, this wood and cement bridge remained standing during the 1964 flood while torrents of water destroyed the new bridge downstream. For a time, this bridge served again as the new bridge was repaired. The park service recently fixed up the "Old Bridge," as locals call it, open now for foot traffic only. It accesses the Boundary Trail, Middle Fork fishing spots, and calm but deep chilly pools for swimming. To find it, turn right in West Glacier on Old Bridge Road, driving to the end.

Middle Fork of the Flathead

The Middle Fork of the Flathead collects its waters from deep within the Bob Marshall Wilderness Complex and Glacier National Park. Its north shore high-water mark denotes the national park boundary. Designated a Wild and Scenic River, the Middle Fork—the shortened moniker most people use for the river—vacillates between raging rapids and mesmerizing meanders. Anglers and swimmers gravitate to its blue-green pools. Rafters and kayakers splash through rapids known as Bonecrusher and Jaws. Hikers toodle along its Boundary Trail.

Apgar

Two miles from West Glacier, Apgar sits on the shore of the park's largest body of water—Lake McDonald. With Apgar Campground within walking distance and Fish Creek Campground a couple of miles away, Apgar is crowded in high season but still quiet compared to the West Glacier highway hubbub. It's the quintessential national park community. The tiny west-side visitors center, a restaurant, a camp store, two inns, Lake McDonald's only boat ramp, swimming beaches, and picnic areas all cluster here at Lake McDonald's foot. One local gift shop is in Apgar's historic red schoolhouse. Like West Glacier, most of Apgar shuts down by October and opens again in May.

◖ Robert Fire

Summer 2003 unleashed some of the biggest flames in Glacier Park's history. Raging winds shoved the Robert Fire over Apgar Mountain,

Historic Belton Bridge was recently renovated.

© BECKY LOMAX

© BECKY LOMAX

Lake McDonald, Glacier's largest lake, looks toward the Continental Divide.

gobbling 7,000 acres in four hours. Campers, motel guests, and park headquarters personnel evacuated from West Glacier and Apgar while helicopters doused the fire with water scooped from Lake McDonald. The fire's 39,000 acres comprised 29 percent of the park's aflame forests that summer. See post-fire forest regeneration on the Camas Road, the Lake McDonald Trail starting at Fish Creek Campground, or for an overview climb to Apgar Lookout. While some lament the charred timbers, fast-growing new vegetation isn't singing a funeral dirge. From the fire's ash, nutrient-rich soils prompt prolific flower blooms, like pink fireweed. Three-toed woodpeckers converge to dig bugs from dead timber, and some tree species require fire to sprout again.

Lake McDonald

Catching waters from Glacier's longest river, Lake McDonald is 10 miles long by 1.5 miles wide—the largest lake in Glacier National Park. Squeezed between Mount Brown and Stanton Peak at its head, the lake plummets to depths of 472 feet—the deepest waters in the park. Resting in an ice-scoured trough, the 6,823-acre lake is buffered by larch forests that turn gold in fall. Here, visitors fish, boat, and swim in its quiet no-jet-skis-allowed blue. While waterskiing attracts a few wet-suited diehards, the lake's cold temperatures and hefty breezes deter many. Access the lake's shores via Fish Creek or Apgar Picnic Area, the Apgar boat ramp, or the many pullouts along Going-to-the-Sun Road.

Recreation

If Glacier has a recreation center, it's West Glacier and Apgar. For between them you can hike, bike, raft, ride horses, kayak, boat, fish, swim, and golf. It's the unofficial park headquarters for whitewater rafting with two Wild and Scenic Rivers (nationally-designated rivers protected for their wilderness and beauty) a short step from the back door.

HIKING

Hiking in Apgar improved substantially with the 2003 Robert Fire. Views opened up amid thick dark forests, and the nutrient-enriched soil from the fire sprouted lush growth. Wildflowers now run amok on slopes that once had meager color. This also is the only park area where a trail permits dogs: The two-mile paved Apgar Bike Trail connecting West Glacier and Apgar is open to walkers, leashed dogs, and bicyclists.

Rocky Point

- Distance: 2 miles round-trip

- Duration: 1 hour

- Elevation gain: none

- Effort: easy

- Trailhead: Fish Creek Campground by Apgar

Rocky Point is a short romp along Lake McDonald Trail through the 2003 Robert Fire to a promontory on Lake McDonald's north shore. You'll notice places of heavy burn and slow regrowth versus lighter burn clogged now with lush greenery. Don't forget your camera: The view from Rocky Point looks up lake toward the Continental Divide and grabs grand shots of Mounts Jackson and Edwards to the south. If the lake is calm, you'll nab some stunning reflection photos. Snow leaves early and comes late to this trail, making it good for spring and fall hiking.

◖ Apgar Lookout

- Distance: 5.6 miles round-trip

- Duration: 3.5 hours

- Elevation gain: 1,835 feet

- Effort: moderate

- Trailhead: end of Glacier Institute Road 1.9 miles from Going-to-the-Sun Road

- Directions: Take the first left after the West Entrance Station at the Glacier Institute sign. At the first fork, follow the sign to the horse barn; at the second, go left, crossing over Quarter Circle Bridge. Drive approximately one mile up the hill to a small clearing at the trailhead.

Beginning with a gentle walk along an old dirt road, Apgar Lookout Trail soon climbs steeply uphill toward one of three long switchbacks. As the trail ascends, large burned sentinels stand as relics from the 2003 Robert Fire. Because of the fire, hikers now have views during the climb of the Middle Fork drainage, Rubideau Basin, the railway line, and West Glacier. Following the third switchback, the trail traverses the ridge—which holds snow in June—to the recently rebuilt lookout. A panoramic view unfolds from Canada to the park's southern sector: The North Fork Valley sprawls below, and you can see all six park peaks over 10,000 feet.

From this 5,236-foot aerie, you can see the path of the Robert Fire, where it burned 7,000 acres in four hours. Prior to the fire, heavy timber and brush occluded views, but Apgar Lookout now ranks as one of the park's most scenic hikes. While fire improved the views, trees no longer shade the southwest-facing slope, scorching the trail on hot days. Increased park communication radio antennas clutter the summit, but at least they are clustered in one location at the lookout instead of spread out.

HIKING ESSENTIALS

Hiking in Glacier National Park demands preparedness. Unpredictable, fast-changing weather can mutate a warm summer day into wintry conditions in hours. Different elevations vary in temperatures, winds, and visibility: Sun on the shore of Two Medicine Lake may hide knock-over winds barreling over Dawson Pass six miles away. Hot valley temperatures may give way at Grinnell Lake to chilly breezes blowing down from the Continental Divide and across the ice. To be prepared in Glacier's backcountry, take the following:

Extra clothing: Rain pants and jackets can double as wind protection, while gloves and a lightweight warm hat will save fingers and ears. Carry at least one extra water-wicking layer for warmth. Avoid cotton fabrics that stay soggy and fail to retain body heat.

Extra food and water: Depending on the hike's length, take a lunch and snacks, like compact high-energy food bars. Low-odor foods will not attract animals. Heat, wind, and elevation lead quickly to dehydration, so always carry extra water. Don't plan to drink directly from streams or lakes. Due to possible giardia and other bacteria, always filter (with a one-micron filter) or treat water sources before drinking.

Map and compass or GPS device: Although Glacier's trails are extremely well-signed, a map can be handy for ascertaining distance traveled and location. A compass or GPS device will also help, but only if you know how to use it. In deep heavily-forested valleys, a GPS may not pick up satellites.

Flashlight: Carry a small flashlight or headlamp. In an after-dark emergency, the light becomes invaluable. Take extra batteries, too.

First-aid kit: Two Band-Aids may not be enough! Carry a fully equipped standard first-aid kit with blister remedies. Many outdoor stores sell suitably prepared kits for hiking.

Don't forget to add personal items like beesting kits and allergy medications.

Sun protection: Altitude, snow, ice, and lakes all increase ultraviolet radiation. Protect yourself with 30 SPF sunscreen, sunglasses, and a sun hat or baseball cap.

Emergency bathroom supplies: Not every hike conveniently places a pit toilet at its destination. To accommodate an alfresco bathroom, carry a small trowel, plastic baggies, and toilet paper and move at least 200 feet away from water sources. For urinating, aim for a durable surface, such as rocks, logs, gravel, or snow. "Watering" fragile plants, campsites, or trail sides attracts mineral-starved animals that dig up the area. Bury feces 6–8 inches deep in soil. Do not bury toilet paper; use a baggie to pack it out.

Feminine hygiene: Carry heavy-duty Ziploc baggies and pack tampons, pads, and everything out. Do not dispose of any feminine hygiene products in backcountry pit toilets.

Insect repellent: Summer can be abuzz at any elevation with mosquitoes and blackflies. Insect repellents containing 50 percent DEET tend to work best. Purchase applications that rub or spray in a close range rather than aerosols that become airborne onto other people, plants, and animals.

Pepper spray: If you want to carry pepper spray, purchase an 8-ounce can as nothing smaller will be effective, but do not bother unless you know how to use it and what influences its effectiveness. It is not to be used like bug repellent.

Miscellaneous: A knife may come in handy, as can a few feet of nylon cord and a bit of duct tape (wrap a few feet around something small like a flashlight handle or water bottle). Many hikers have repaired boots and packs with duct tape and a little ingenuity.

◖ Huckleberry Lookout

- Distance: 12 miles round-trip

- Duration: 5–6 hours

- Elevation gain: 3,403 feet

- Effort: strenuous

- Trailhead: six miles up Camas Road from Apgar just past McGee Meadows

Huckleberry Lookout trail is aptly named, for huckleberries do abound in this area. During certain times of the season, usually late summer to early fall, the trail closes due to bear activity. The heavy concentration of huckleberries attracts a significant bruin population looking to bulk up for the winter. Check with the park service for current status. When the trail is closed, the trailhead posts obvious closure signage.

The trail begins with a gentle walk through lodgepole forest. Shortly, the path climbs, steadily gaining elevation among larch until it emerges on steep-sloped meadows and reaches a saddle at 4.5 miles. In a short reprieve from the climb, the trail traverses a wide bowl until it crests the Apgar Range for the final ascent to the lookout at 6,593 feet. A spectacular view of the North Fork Valley and the park's Livingston Range unfolds. During fire season, the lookout is staffed. Evidence of the 2001 Moose Fire clings to Huckleberry Mountain as well as Demers Ridge below and the North Fork Valley. Snow often packs the upper trail until mid-July.

Huckleberry Lookout and trail

© BECKY LOMAX

Lake McDonald Trail

- Distance: 6.6 miles one-way

- Duration: 3 hours

- Elevation gain: none

- Effort: easy

- Trailhead: Fish Creek Campground or North McDonald Road

This year-round trail (use skis or snowshoes in winter) follows the north shore of Lake McDonald, wandering back in the trees, then close to shoreline. While views of peak-flanked Lake McDonald are dramatic, more remarkable is the study of post-fire forest succession along the trail. Burned by the 2003 Robert Fire, the trail passes through lush new growth spurred by nitrogen-rich ash returned to the soil. With a car shuttle, hikers can walk this point-to-point, but most opt to saunter out for a few miles from either direction, perhaps drop a fishing line into the lake, and turn around again.

South Boundary Trail

- Distance: 10.6 miles round-trip to Lincoln Creek

- Duration: 5 hours

- Elevation gain: minimal

- Effort: easy

- Trailhead: behind park headquarters on Mather Drive's south end or the old bridge in West Glacier

After parking at headquarters, walk through the headquarters housing area to the trailhead. Follow the old Glacier Park Entrance Road to the historic Belton Bridge, where a trail continues upstream. You can also access this trail via the Belton Bridge, but the trailhead here does not have as much parking. With gentle ascents and descents, the path hugs the north-shore hillside above the Wild and Scenic Middle Fork of the Flathead River.

This year-round trail won't feel like wilderness: Noise from the railroad and highway competes with the river's roaring white water. But it's a great place to watch rafters shoot rapids, swim in deep pools, or fish. The trail descends to a fine rocky beach at Lincoln Creek, a stopping point for rafters before they hit the white water. From here, backpackers can opt to continue another 15 miles upriver to Coal Creek or turn 9.4 miles up Lincoln Creek to Lincoln Lake.

Guided Hikes

National Park Service **naturalist rangers** guide hikes and walks around Apgar from mid-June through mid-September. Days and times vary, as do the hikes—easy to strenuous. In winter, they offer guided snowshoe trips to look for animal tracks. Grab a copy of *The Glacier Explorer* at visitors centers to check for the current schedule. And they're the best price of all: free!

Glacier Guides (11970 Hwy. 2 E., 406/387-5555 or 800/521-7238, www.glacierguides.com) leads day hikes; however, most destinations are outside the West Glacier-Apgar area. Solo travelers hook up with their Tuesday Hikes ($75 per person, July–Aug.) and Group Day Hikes ($375, 1–5 people, June–Sept.), which depart from their office. Custom Day Hikes ($450, up to 5 people) depart from your lodge or campground. All hikes require reservations and include guide service, deli lunch, and transportation to the trailhead. The guide service also leads extended day hiking trips in their

Camping Safari (6 days, $910), Inn Walking Tour (6 days, $1,949), and backcountry chalets hikes (3 or 6 days, $658 or $1,700). Also, three-, four-, and six-day backpacking trips depart weekly ($135 per day, June–mid-Sept.).

Rentals

Glacier Outdoor Center (11957 Hwy. 2 E., 406/888-5454 or 800/235-6781, www.glacierraftco.com) carries the most extensive line of rental gear for hikers: Day packs ($10), backpacks ($20), trekking poles ($5), and child carrier packs ($20). They also rent a full car camping setup for four people for $125 per day and individual gear from ice axes to sleeping bags, tents, cook stoves, and water purifiers.

BIKING

Bicycling Glacier National Park is not for everyone. Narrow, shoulderless roads are packed with curves, and trails prohibit bikes. However, West Glacier–Apgar is one area in the park that does provide two off-road biking options.

Bike Trails

A level, newly repaved bicycle trail connects West Glacier with Apgar. Approximately 2.6 miles long, the **Apgar Bike Trail** begins on the north side of the West Glacier Bridge. After dropping through the woods, it crosses through the park service employee housing area before entering the forest again, where it continues on to Apgar, connecting finally with the campground. Be cautious at two road crossings en route. This is one park trail where dogs are permitted on a leash, and it's good flat riding for kids.

The **Old Flathead Ranger Station** is a fun 10-mile round-trip ride on a combination dirt road and trail that was once a road. It terminates at the confluence of Flathead River's North and Middle Forks. Access the route from midway between West Glacier and Apgar on the Apgar Bike Trail, turning west on the dirt Glacier Institute Road. At the first junction, follow the sign to the horse barn; at the second, hang a left toward Quarter Circle Bridge. About 0.5 mile past the bridge, the

© BECKY LOMAX

bicycling over Quarter Circle Bridge to Old Flathead Ranger Station

Old Flathead Ranger Station Trail begins. Turn left here, biking 3.7 miles to the Old Flathead Ranger Station site and the confluence. Although the trail continues north, bikes are not permitted beyond here.

Bicycle Road Tours

Many bicyclists enjoy short road rides from Apgar up Camas Road, the dirt Inside Road (see *North Fork* chapter for details), or just to Fish Creek Picnic Area.

For a longer mountain-bike tour (approximately 37 miles, four hours) on a mix of dirt and paved roads, the **Apgar Mountain Loop** takes off from West Glacier heading west over Belton Stage and Blankenship Roads to connect with North Fork Road. From here, ride north, parallel with the North Fork River to the Camas Road entrance and back into the park. Follow paved rolling Camas Road back to the Apgar Bike Trail. The scenic loop is well

worth a ride, especially in late spring before Going-to-the-Sun Road is open, but be prepared to suck serious dust on the dirt sections during dry spells and battle bears and mosquitoes along Camas Road.

West Glacier is also the launch point for those bicycling Going-to-the-Sun Road. For details, see the *Going-to-the-Sun Road* chapter.

Rentals

No bicycle rentals are available here. You can rent bikes in Flathead Valley (see *Flathead Valley* chapter).

TRAIL RIDING

Catch the horseback experience in both Apgar and West Glacier. For trail riding, be sure to wear long pants; you'll be a lot less sore afterward. For safety, wear sturdy shoes or hiking boots—not sandals.

For guided trail rides in Apgar, make reservations with **Swan Mountain Outfitters** (mid-Sept.–mid-May 800/919-4416, summer 877/888-5557, www.swanmountainoutfitters .com). Their **Apgar Corral** (406/888-5010, late May–mid-Sept.), located on the Glacier Institute Road just inside the park's west entrance, leads three daily trail rides ($32–68): a one-hour easy saunter to McDonald Meadows, a popular two-hour ride along the C.M. Russell Trail, and a three-hour ride around the Oxbow on McDonald Creek. Rides depart several times daily. You can also arrange rides via their Apgar phone kiosk across from the red schoolhouse in Apgar Village. Look for the horseshoes! The company does not take children under seven nor riders weighing over 250 pounds.

In West Glacier, **Rawhide Trail Rides** (12000 Hwy. 2 E., 406/387-5555 or 800/388-5727, www.glacierrawhide.com, mid-May–mid-Oct.) leads horseback tours through the lodgepole foothills of Flathead National Forest. One-, two-, three-hour, or half-day rides begin daily at 8 A.M. ($25–60 per person); tours depart multiple times throughout the day with the last ride leaving at 4 P.M. You can just show up for these, but if you want to guarantee a time, make reservations. Rawhide can accommodate kids 4–7 years old with small saddles. You can also do a full-day ride with a minimum of four people ($105 per person, including lunch, reservations req.). The company also works in tandem with a raft company to offer half- and full-day ride and raft trips. Departing on Sundays (early June–late Aug., adults $625, kids $550), a four-day headliner trip includes overnight horse-packing into Flathead National Forest followed by rafting the Wild and Scenic Middle Fork.

RAFTING
C Middle Fork of the Flathead
Bordering Glacier's southern boundary, the Middle Fork of the Flathead interrupts scenic float sections with raging white water. Designated a Wild and Scenic River, the Middle Fork draws its headwaters from deep within the Bob Marshall Wilderness Complex and drains Glacier's immense southern valleys. Together with the North Fork of the Flathead, the rivers provide 219 miles of wilderness, scenery, and recreation; the rafting season runs May–September, with high water usually peaking in June.

If there's one thing you should do while you're in the area, it should be a raft trip on Middle Fork. While the white water cannot compete with the Grand Canyon's monster waves, the Middle Fork is a fun, splashy place to raft. It's easy enough for kids and good introductory fun for a first-time river trip.

Managed by the Forest Service, the Middle Fork River offers several put-ins and take-outs easily accessed along U.S. Highway 2. Different sections are appropriate for overnights, day trips, fishing, and short floats. While a few rapids at certain water levels are rated Class IV, the river along Glacier's boundary is primarily Class II and III. No permits are required; however, all camping must be done on the south shore; no camping is permitted on Glacier's shoreline. Since private property abuts some of the south shore, you'll need to be knowledgeable about where you can camp. Consult the Flathead National Forest Ranger

Station (milepost 143.1 on Hwy. 2, 406/387-5243) in Hungry Horse, nine miles west of West Glacier, for assistance in planning a self-guided overnight trip.

North Fork of the Flathead
From Canada, the North Fork of the Flathead flows through the remote North Fork Valley. As the river enters the United States, it forms the western boundary of Glacier. Accessed via the bumpy, dirt Outside North Fork Road, the Class II river is great for multi-day float trips, day rafting, and fishing. Put-ins and take-outs range up and down North Fork Road. No permits are required, but campsites must all be set up on the western shore; no camping is permitted on Glacier's bank except for Round Prairie. Just past its confluence with the Middle Fork, the take-out at Blankenship is 10 minutes from West Glacier.

Guides
The commercial rafting season runs May–September with high water usually peaking in June. All four West Glacier rafting companies lead half-day and full-day float trips on the Middle Fork River. Each company also launches four to five half-day raft trips daily through the white-water section. All also guide overnight and multi-day trips as well as scenic floats, dinner, barbecue, or evening floats. If you're comparing rates between companies (they're all very similar in cost), be sure to ask if the 7 percent service fee is included in the rate or added on. Also, ask about the size of the raft and the number of people it carries. Smaller rafts will have a more exciting ride. Expect to pay (not including service fees) around $46 per person for an adult half-day raft trip or $78 for full day; kids run about $10 cheaper. For more fun rafting, tackle the white water in an inflatable kayak, otherwise known as a rubber ducky (around $10 more per person)! Guides instruct inflatable kayakers on routes as they tag along with their raft trips. Paddles and lifejackets are included in all rates, but some companies charge additional fees for wet suits and/or booties. Clarify fees

when you make your reservation. Plan on tipping guides $3–5 per person.

Overnight rafting trips range two to five days; longer ones are usually paired up with hiking, horseback riding, or backpacking. Expect to pay around $160 per person per day for an overnight rafting trip and $30–40 less per day for children. Tip about 10 percent for overnights. When making reservations, clarify what you'll need to bring for your overnight. The companies can provide tents, sleeping bags, pads, and dry bags for your gear.

Glacier Raft Company (6 Going-to-the-Sun Rd., 406/888-5454 or 800/235-6781, www.glacierraftco.com) sits right in West Glacier village adjacent to the river—close enough to the take-out that white-water rafters debark at the Middle Fork Bridge to walk two blocks back to the office. They are also the only local company permitted to guide trips on the Class III–IV Upper Middle Fork of the Flathead River. Their four-day Great Bear Wilderness excursion ($1,395) requires flight access to a remote put-in near the headwaters; their five-day trip ($2,000) reaches the put-in via 2.5 days of horse-packing. Located one mile west from downtown West Glacier, **Great Northern Whitewater** (12127 Hwy. 2 E., 406/387-5340 or 800/735-7897, www.gnwhitewater.com) specializes in saddle-paddles and two- to three-day floats on the Middle Fork River.

Just off the highway 1.5 miles west of West Glacier, **Montana Raft Company** (11970 Hwy. 2 E., 406/387-5555 or 800/521-7238, www.glacierguides.com) adds splashy Thrill-seekers—small rafts that hold four paddlers and one guide ($73 per person)—to their arsenal of day trips. They overnight on both the Middle Fork and the North Fork of the Flathead River and run an extensive menu of hike-raft or backpack-raft combinations—full day trips to week-long adventures. One signature family-friendly trip puts together a three-day North Fork float with staying in rustic cabins (adults $669, kids $562).

Located adjacent to Rawhide Trail Rides, **Wild River Adventures** (11900 Hwy. 2 E., 406/387-9453 or 800/700-7056, www.riverwild.com) specializes in horse-raft combo trips from one full day to four days. They also guide overnights on the North Fork River and trips where you'll get soaked in their sporty 12-foot rafts that hold only four paddlers and a guide ($68).

Rentals

Got the river savvy to guide yourself? If so, you can rent a raft ($160–185) or inflatable kayak ($99) from **Glacier Outdoor Center** (11957 Hwy. 2 E., 406/888-5454 or 800/235-6781, www.glacierraftco.com). Rates include paddles, helmets, life jackets, pump, and repair kit. You can also rent dry bags, wet suits, booties, and camping gear for overnights. The company will also shuttle your vehicle from the put-in to take-out for $25–140, depending on distance up the Middle Fork or the North Fork, or shuttle you in their rigs for $40–240.

BOATING

With its vast acreage of water, Lake McDonald attracts boaters, but it's never crowded—usually just a few quiet anglers in the early morning followed by a couple die-hard water-skiers, sightseers, and kayakers touring the shoreline. Because the frigid waters inhibit most water-skiers and jet skis are not permitted, the lake never has a frenzied hubbub of noise. In fact, national park regulations enforce a maximum noise level of 82 decibels. Similar to many of the park's lakes, you'll rarely see a sailboat or windsurfer: unpredictable, swirly winds on Lake McDonald make other lakes outside the park more appealing. Located adjacent to Village Inn, Apgar's boat ramp provides the lake's only public ramp access.

Rentals

For boating and fishing on Lake McDonald, **Glacier Park Boat Company** (406/257-2426, www.glacierparkboats.com) rents rowboats and eight-horsepower motorboats for $14–24 per hour from the Apgar boat dock next to Village Inn. Paddles, life jackets, and fishing regulations are included in the rates. Come prepared with cash, for the company does not take credit cards out of its tiny boat dock office.

Regulations

Two shoreline closures affect boaters: from the Apgar boat ramp north to the lake's outlet, and between the Apgar Amphitheater and Going-to-the-Sun Road. To protect swimmers here, boaters must stay 300 feet off the shoreline and are not permitted to beach. Watch also for additional temporary wildlife closures marked with buoys, especially at the lake's east end, where bald eagles nest.

While any craft over 12 feet must be registered in Montana, temporary use of out-of-state boats is permitted without registration. On Glacier's waters, federal boating regulations and water travel etiquette apply. For a complete list of boating regulations, check with visitors centers or Glacier's website: www.nps.gov/glac.

WHITE-WATER KAYAKING

White-water kayakers drop into the **Middle Fork of the Flathead** that churns up Class II–III rapids. You'll find kayakers playing in the froth between Moccasin Creek put-in and the West Glacier take-out, surfing the waves on Tunnel Rapid. Some eliminate the flat water before and after the rapids by using railroad accesses.

Great Northern Whitewater (12127 Hwy. 2 E., West Glacier, 406/387-5340 or 800/735-7897, www.gnwhitewater.com, $150–250, all equipment incl.) leads half-, full-day, and playboat kayak trips on the Middle Fork rapids and teaches a **kayak school.** Instructors, who are all ACA White-water Certified walk beginners through the basics or teach playboating skills to those with some experience. While none of the companies rent white-water kayaks (you have to go to Flathead Valley), **Glacier Outdoor Center** (11957 Hwy. 2 E., West Glacier, 406/888-5454 or 800/235-6781, www.glacierraftco.com) rents one- and two-person inflatable kayaks for $45–75, including paddles, helmets, life jackets, pump, and repair kit. The center will also shuttle your vehicle

from put-in to take-out starting at $25; shuttle rates depend on distance.

SEA-KAYAKING AND CANOEING

The scenic section of the **Middle Fork of the Flathead** is gentle enough for canoeing and sea-kayaking from West Glacier downriver to Blankenship. But it includes one challenging rapid that has been known to flip lazy paddlers. The very scenic **Lower McDonald Creek** route starts at Lake McDonald's boat launch and goes to Quarter Circle Bridge. With its monstrous shoreline, **Lake McDonald** is a treat for both canoeing and sea-kayaking, but watch for winds whipping up large whitecaps. When glassy, calm waters prevail, you'd be hard-pressed to beat it at sunrise or sunset. Touring the shoreline, you may encounter wildlife closures, especially for nesting bald eagles at the lake's head.

At the Apgar boat dock next to Village Inn, **Glacier Park Boat Company** (406/257-2426, www.glacierparkboats.com) rents canoes and kayaks for $14 per hour. Boats come with

kayaking Lake McDonald

© BECKY LOMAX

paddles and life jackets. Bring cash; the company does not take credit cards. For sea-kayak rentals, you'll have to go to Flathead Valley.

FISHING

While **Lake McDonald** may be the biggest body of water in Glacier, expert anglers head to other lakes. Those who want to troll for lake trout here should use a boat. For catch-and-release fly-fishing, **Lower McDonald Creek** from the lake to Quarter Circle Bridge works, but it's also heavily fished because of its easy access. For several miles in both directions from West Glacier, the **Middle Fork of the Flathead** presents good fishing, but be ready to contend with rafters and fishing outfitters. Because of the concentration of visitors in the West Glacier–Apgar area during high season, you may not feel like you're off in the wilderness when you toss a line in here, but you just might pull in some native trout.

Park Regulations

Fishing inside Glacier Park does not require a license, but waters here have some restrictions. Lake McDonald has no limit on lake trout or whitefish. Lower McDonald Creek from the lake outlet to Quarter Circle Bridge is catch-and-release only. Despite its name, Fish Creek is closed to fishing.

Licenses and Gear Rental

Fishing outside Glacier on Flathead River drainages requires a Montana fishing license. You can pick one up at **Glacier Outdoor Center** (11957 Hwy. 2 E., West Glacier, 406/888-5454 or 800/235-6781, www.glacierraftco.com). A two-day license costs $25; a seasonal license is $70. The center, which is also a fly shop, rents fishing gear ($5–50). You can get rods, waders, and float tubes.

Guides

Four fly-fishing companies guide half-, full-, and multi-day trips in drift boats on Glacier's boundary waters in the Middle Fork or North Fork of the Flathead River, but none guide fishing adventures inside Glacier Park. For beginners, all four offer fly-fishing schools to teach the basics of casting, mending, and catch-and-release. Reservations are mandatory.

For a half-day guided fishing trip for one or two people, expect to pay around $320 and add on about $100 more for full days. Overnights run around $350 per person per day. Plan on tipping the guides about 10 percent, or more if you catch lots of fish. It's pricey, but the guides usually get you to the good fishing holes. Rates include all equipment, such as life jackets, rods, and flies. As with rafting trips, a 7 percent service fee is added to all fishing trips, but some companies include it in the price. You'll also need to have your own fishing license.

Glacier Anglers (Glacier Outdoor Center, 11957 Hwy. 2 E., 406/888-5454 or 800/235-6781, www.glacierraftco.com) leads fishing trips on the Middle Fork and North Fork of the Flathead mid-April–mid-October. Their specialty four- to seven-day Great Bear Wilderness fishing trips cost around $595 per person per day. **Glacier Guides** (11970 Hwy. 2 E., 406/387-5555 or 800/521-7238, www.glacierguides.com) has fly-fishing trips on the North Fork and Middle Fork of the Flathead River July–mid-September. **Montana Fly-fishing Guides** (Great Northern Whitewater, 12127 Hwy. 2 E., 406/387-5340 or 800/735-7897, www.gnwhitewater.com) leads trips on the Middle Fork River late June–October. **Wild River Adventures** (11900 Hwy. 2 E., 406/387-9453 or 800/700-7056, www.riverwild.com) provides anglers with day trips on the Middle Fork of the Flathead and overnight trips on the North Fork late June–early September.

GOLF

Glacier View Golf Club (640 River Bend Dr., 406/888-5471 or 800/843-5777) may tax your concentration as you tee off. Moose, elk, bears, and deer wander across the fairways, and the mountain views are hard to ignore. The 18-hole course has a pro shop, restaurant, practice green, driving range, lessons, and cart rentals ($25). Open daily to the public April–October (snow permitting), the course charges only $25–30 for 18 holes. To locate the golf course

FISHING IN GLACIER

With 27,023 acres of lakes, 563 streams, and 22 species of fish, no angler should sit with a slack line. Although only a scant 10 percent of park visitors fish, those who do typically enjoy calm vistas and a few native trout. While variables from weather to skill influence success, a few tips for Glacier's waters can help.

FISHING TIPS

- Avoid making a long hike to a remote lake to fish...unless you want to go there for the sake of the journey. While many anglers find more success angling in waters away from roads, remoteness doesn't mean good fishing. Waterfalls prevent fish from reaching some streams and lakes.

- Since arrival at a high mountain lake will most likely be at midday when fishing is not the best, stay overnight in the backcountry or at a lodge nearby. This way, you can fish in the morning or evening for best results; that's when fish feed. Overcast days also tend to be better than sunny days.

- During early summer runoff when river waters cloud with sediments, fish hang out on the bottom to feed. Try lures that mimic insect larvae. Or fish lakes instead.

- When streams run clear, fly-fishing is the most productive. Try to match a prominent hatch, but traditional high-floating attractor patterns will also move fish.

- At lakes, look for inlets and outlets to fish, but be considerate of heavily trafficked areas.

- Trolling from a motorboat (where allowed) or canoe is the most effective way to fish for lake trout.

FISHING AND BEARS

- Fishing in bear country poses special considerations. Since smells attract bears that travel along waterways, minimize your chances of a bear encounter by keeping fishy smells away from your clothing. In general, catch-and-release fishing minimizes the chances of attracting a bear.

- For cleaning fish in the front country, dispose of fish entrails in bear-resistant garbage cans. In the backcountry, do not bury

---

in West Glacier, turn west onto River Bend Drive and follow signs to the clubhouse. The club also has onsite RV hookups!

CROSS-COUNTRY SKIING AND SNOWSHOEING

Between late November and April, winter converts the roads and trails around Apgar into easy cross-country ski and snowshoe paths. Quiet and scenic, road skiing makes for easy route finding with little avalanche danger in lower elevations. Roads are plowed into Apgar and up Lake McDonald's south shore. Beyond plowing, popular ski tours follow roads and trails to **Fish Creek Campground, Rocky Point, McGee Meadows,** and the **Old Flathead Ranger Station** near the Middle

Fork and North Fork confluence. Those with stamina and skiing expertise climb to **Apgar Lookout.** For route descriptions, pick up *Skiing and Snowshoeing* in visitors centers or online: www.nps.gov/glac. Skiers and snowshoers should be well-equipped and versed in winter travel safety before venturing out even on snow-covered roads.

Glacier Outdoor Center (11957 Hwy. 2 E., 406/888-5454 or 800/235-6781, www.glacier raftco.com) daily grooms a delightful 10 kilometers of trails for both skate and classic skiing. Trail fees are $5 per day and $20 per week. Until noon, the trails are for skiers only, but after noon, dogs are permitted. You can even rent skijoring gear ($10 for half-day) to be pulled around the course by Fido. The or burn the innards as that may attract bears. Instead, be at least 200 feet away from a campsite or trail, puncture the air bladder, and throw the entrails into deep water. If you plan to eat your fish, keep only what you can eat, and eat as soon as you can.

NATIVE SPECIES

Glacier Park's fishing regulations enforce protection of native species through selected area closures and limits on the taking of native species. The park service no longer stocks fish, as many of the introduced species took a toll on native fish through competition for food and predation. Until 1972, an estimated 45-55 million fish and eggs were planted in Glacier's waters, introducing **arctic grayling, rainbow trout, kokanee salmon, brook trout,** and **Yellowstone cutthroat trout. Lake trout** and **lake whitefish** also invaded the park's west-side water systems through stocking in Flathead Lake, although lake trout are native to park waters east of the Continental Divide and **mountain whitefish** are native throughout the park.

Of Glacier's 10 sport and 12 non-sport fish,

the **bull trout** is the one listed as a threatened species under the Endangered Species Act. In Montana, this predatory fish, which can grow to two feet long, now inhabits less than half of its original streams, due to a number of factors, including habitat degradation. No fishing for bull trout is allowed; any incidentally caught must be immediately released. Look on the dorsal fin: No black, put it back.

Glacier is also one of the few remaining strongholds for **westslope cutthroat trout,** which now inhabit only 2.5 percent of their original range. Mostly threatened by interbreeding with rainbow trout, genetically pure populations of cutthroat remain in 15-19 park lakes.

While bull trout are protected by law, other native fish need conscientious anglers to help preserve the native fishery. Learn to identify native and nonnative species and follow park guidelines for which fish to harvest and which native fish to release. But in general, release native fish; keep only your limit of nonnative species.

For the best fishing recommendations, grab a copy of Russ Schneider's *Fishing Glacier National Park.*

© BECKY LOMAX

Glacier Outdoor Center grooms cross-country ski trails in winter.

center also rents skate skis, waxless touring skis, and snowshoes for $12–22 daily; weekly rates run $70 for snowshoes and $90 for cross-country ski gear. You can also rent a pulka to pull a tot.

Guides

The park service guides free weekend snowshoe tours from Apgar Visitor Center (406/888-7939), January through mid-March. The two-hour walks depart at 10:30 A.M. and 1:30 P.M. Interpretive rangers point out how flora and fauna adapt to harsh winters and look for tracks. Hikers should wear winter footwear, dress in layers, and bring water. Snowshoes rent for $2.

November–April as snows permit, **Glacier Adventure Guides** (406/892-2173, www.glacier adventureguides.com, $200–310 for 1–4 people per day, $30 for each additional person) guides full-day ski tours for a variety of skill levels into Glacier—road schussing to backcountry tele-mark and randonee skiing. If you're a solo trav-eler, it's the best way to get accompanied into the backcountry with avalanche-certified guides to find pristine powder stashes. Lunch and snacks

are included. For deep backcountry, ski in to an igloo to spend the night (add $35 per person per day to above rates). On full-moon nights, you can also take a ski tour, skiing by ethereal moonglow ($35 per person).

ENTERTAINMENT

This isn't a place for nightlife. Instead, most park visitors take advantage of long daylight hours (dark doesn't descend until almost 11 P.M. in June) to explore everything they can. If you're looking to party, you can hang at the West Glacier bar shooting pool with the river-rats or head into Flathead Valley.

Park Naturalist Evening Programs

Fish Creek Campground Amphitheater and **Apgar Campground Amphitheater** host free park naturalist evening programs on wildlife, fires, and natural phenomena. Check a cur-rent copy of *The Glacier Explorer* for subjects, times, and dates for these programs (usually mid-June–mid-Sept.). The 45-minute talks are usually posted in campgrounds, hotels, and visitors centers, too.

Accommodations

On Lake McDonald's shore, the limited lodg-ing at Apgar is extremely popular, so West Glacier options often serve as backup. But given that the communities are only two miles apart and connected by a bike path, they are equally convenient to each other and their unique activities. Keep in mind that Montana tacks on a 7 percent bed tax to each lodging night, so your bill will be higher than quoted room rate.

APGAR

Reservations are a must at the two adjacent lodges in Apgar at Lake McDonald's foot. Both share a block with Eddie's Restaurant and Grocery, the visitors center, the boat dock, several gift shops, and free park shuttles. The

Apgar Bike Trail begins here, and there's ac-cess to McDonald Creek for fishing or canoe-ing. The Apgar Campground Amphitheater for naturalist talks is a seven-minute walk away or quick shuttle ride. Although the area is a busy hive during the day, at night it's quiet.

Set back in huge old-growth cedars on McDonald Creek, **Apgar Village Lodge** (on Apgar Rd. 0.3 mile from Camas Rd. or 0.8 mile from Going-to-the-Sun Rd., 406/888-5484, www.westglacier.com, early May–Sept., $95–270 per night) clusters 20 motel rooms and 28 rustic cabins—most with kitchens—within a few steps the lake. The creek cabins (6, 7, 8) are particularly serene—mixed with a wonderful ambience of wildlife and the sound of the stream. Although older, the nonsmoking cabins have all been upgraded since the mid-1990s, but none have televisions, phones, or air-conditioning. (Pay phones are outside the lobby.) Look for shoulder season discounts.

On Lake McDonald's beach, every one of the 36 nonsmoking rooms in the **Village Inn** (on Apgar Rd. 0.3 mile from Camas Rd. or 0.8 mile from Going-to-the-Sun Rd., 406/892-2525, www.glacierparkinc.com, late May–mid-Sept., $120–185 per night) wakes up to a striking view uplake toward the Continental Divide. Some rooms include kitchenettes, but to preserve the get-away-from-it-all ambience, none of the rooms have air-conditioning, phones (a pay phone is outside the lobby) or televisions, nor is there an elevator to the second floor. Although it's been redecorated, not much else has changed since the inn was built in 1956. Despite nondescript rooms, the stunning view makes the stay worthwhile.

WEST GLACIER

Lodging in West Glacier is convenient for hopping the train, going river-rafting or fishing, and heading off on guided backpacking trips. It's also such a quick jaunt to Lake McDonald that if park lodging is full, West Glacier options work as an easy backup. Be prepared, however, for nightly noise—not from people (they're crashed from packing in so much activity during the long days), but from almost 30 trains that ride the Burlington Northern Santa Fe rail daily. Bring earplugs if you're a light sleeper. During high season, most West Glacier lodging options fill nightly with bookings, so reservations are wise.

Lodges and Cabins

Located across from Belton Train Depot, the National Historic Landmark **Belton Chalet** (12575 Hwy. 2 E., 406/888-5000 or 888/235-8665, www.beltonchalet.com) improved its buildings a decade ago with a $1 million restoration. Centered around a large stone fireplace, the cozy lobby contains a piano, stuffed rockers, and a fun table displaying the owners' soap collection. Stay in the main lodge rooms (late May–early Oct., $145–170)

Belton Chalet, a National Historic Landmark

© BECKY LOMAX

or private year-round cottages ($299 summer, $99–225 winter), both of which are discounted in spring and fall. Rooms are a slice of history: original wainscoting and wood floors, push-button lights, twig tables, and historic photos. The original closets have been converted into in-room bathrooms with showers only. To enjoy your evening at the Belton, stay in one of the nine balcony rooms, sitting in wicker rockers with a glass of wine as the sun sets over the Apgar Range. Remedies Day Spa also provides massages on-site. The chalet's restaurant serves outstanding dinners; other restaurants are within a five-minute walk, as are gift shops and rafting.

Glacier Outdoor Center (11957 Hwy. 2 E., 406/888-5454 or 800/235-6781, www.glacierraftco.com, open year-round, $280–425 per night) has nonsmoking one- and two-bedroom log cabins that sleep 6–14 people. Set way back from the road amid birch trees around a trout pond with views of Glacier, the cabins come with fully equipped kitchens, televisions, log furniture, decks, grills, and gas fireplaces, and the deluxe cabin has a washer and dryer. Horseshoe pits, an outdoor pavilion, and a volleyball court sit adjacent, and amenities include rentals for hiking, biking, skiing, snowshoeing, and fishing. Multi-night stays chop off $5–20 per night depending on the duration, and off-season rates drop by 30 percent, more in winter.

Part of the Great Northern Whitewater complex with the rafting, fishing, and kayaking company located on-site, **Great Northern Chalets** (12127 Hwy. 2 E., 406/387-5340 or 800/735-7897, www.gnwhitewater.com, Apr.–Oct., $260–295) rents two small (six-person) and three large (eight-person) nonsmoking log chalets with fully equipped kitchens. Set around a landscaped garden pond, the cozy chalets are decorated in Glacier outdoor themes, and several have sweeping views of the park. A three-night minimum stay is required during high season. West Glacier's restaurants and shops are one mile away: You can walk down the highway, but it's not the most pleasant walk with big trucks zipping by. Outside of late June–late August, you can get off-season discounts…some quite good.

Motels

For basic, nothing fancy rooms, motels in West Glacier give sheer convenience to shopping, rafting, restaurants, and the park entrance. All are nonsmoking. **West Glacier Motel** (200 Going-to-the-Sun Rd., 406/888-5662, www.westglacier.com, open mid-May–mid-Sept.) has 32 motel units ($85–105) and three cabins ($145–175, two-night min.). None have televisions, air-conditioning, or phones (pay phones are outside the lobby), but the motel does have a wireless Internet hotspot. Sitting directly across from the Belton Train Depot, the **Glacier Highland** (12555 Hwy. 2 E., 406/888-5427 or 800/766-0811, www.glacierhighlandresort .com, open mid-Apr.–Oct., $82–93, off-season discounts available) has 33 modern rooms that include satellite television and access to a hot

tub, adjacent to their restaurant. **Glacier Vista Motel** (milepost 152.5 on Hwy. 2 E., 406/888-5311, www.glaciervistamotel.com, open mid-May–mid-Sept., $67–140) sits perched on a hill above the highway a half-mile west of the Belton Train Depot. It's a family-run, older motel—the only one with an outdoor heated swimming pool. Rooms facing the highway have an amazing view into Glacier.

OUTSIDE WEST GLACIER

Typically, lodging facilities in West Glacier and Apgar both book up before summer for high season. However, plenty of motels and cabins line the nine miles of Highway 2 from West Glacier to Hungry Horse—good alternatives, just a short drive to reach the park entrance.

Cabins

A new cabin complex built in 2003, **Glaciers Mountain Resort** (1385 Old Hwy. 2 E., 406/387-5712 or 877/213-8001, www.glaciers mountainresort.com, open year-round, $200 per night, off-season rates drop 25–40 percent) has five one-bedroom knotty pine cabins—with fully equipped kitchens with dishwashers, satellite television, VCRs, log furniture, private bathrooms, and barbecue grills—lined up on landscaped property. There's a two-night minimum stay mid-June–mid-September. Touted for its "designer chalets," **(Silverwolf Log Chalet Resort** (Gladys Glenn Rd. and Hwy. 2 E., 406/387-4448, www.silverwolfchalets .com, open mid-May–mid-Oct., $158, off-season discounts available) rents 10 modern, two-person log chalets decorated with log furniture and set on a landscaped lawn under lodgepoles. Separated from the road by a privacy fence, the resort is a neat, well-maintained, sharp-looking adults-only place; kids, smoking, and pets are taboo. Multi-night stays reduce rates by $11 per night. Spring and fall have discounts.

Bed-and-Breakfasts

For those who want the intimacy of a B&B setting, three operate year round near West Glacier, all serving full, hearty breakfasts. **A Wild Rose Bed and Breakfast** (10280

Hwy. 2 E., 406/387-4900, www.awildrose .com, $120–150) has four nonsmoking luxury Victorian rooms with all-natural linens and cushy robes. Amenities include an outdoor hot tub and breakfast served in the dining room, which is furnished with 1920s antiques. The **Glacier Park Inn** (9128 Hwy. 2 E., 406/387-5099, www.glacierparkinn.com, $80–140) tucks five rooms in its remodeled, octagonal, nonsmoking home with a giant wraparound deck overlooking the Apgar Mountains and Flathead River—the perfect place to unwind with a view. Built in 1907, the **Tamarack Lodge** (9549 Hwy. 2 E., 406/387-4420 or 877/387-4420, www.historictamaracklodge .com, $105–135) renovated its six main log-beam lodge rooms in 1994—running them now as a bed-and-breakfast.

CAMPING
Apgar

In Apgar, two campgrounds sit amid thick forests with easy access to Lake McDonald. Rustic—with no hookups—both Fish Creek and Apgar Campgrounds have flush toilets, disposal stations, hiker-biker sites, amphitheaters for evening naturalist talks, and sites that accommodate large RVs. Because of their location inside the park, they are popular campgrounds away from highway and railroad noise. Both have shuttle stops connecting with Apgar Transit Center. Bring your own firewood, as wood-collecting is prohibited.

Fish Creek (end of Fish Creek Rd., 406/888-7800, June–early Sept., $23 per night), one of two campgrounds in the park that can be reserved through the National Park Reservation System (877/444-6777, www.reservations.gov), is one of the larger campgrounds in the park, with 180 sites tucked under cedars, lodgepoles, and larch. Loops C and D have the best sites adjacent to the lake. Eighteen campsites accommodate RVs up to 35 feet long; 62 sites fit RVs up to 27 feet. To find Fish Creek, a six-minute drive from Apgar, drive 1.25 miles north on Camas Road and turn right, dropping one mile down to the campground. Lake McDonald Trail departs from the campground.

Apgar Campground (on Apgar Rd. 0.4 mile from Going-to-the-Sun Rd., 406/888-7800, May–mid-Oct., $20 per night) is within short walking distance to Apgar Village and Lake McDonald. The 192-site campground is the park's largest with group campsites and 25 sites accommodating RVs up to 40 feet. The Apgar Bike Trail begins nearby, and a restaurant, gift shops, visitors center, and boat dock are in adjacent Apgar Village. Primitive camping ($10, Apr. and mid-Oct.–Nov.) has pit toilets available, but no running water. In winter, you can camp free at the Apgar Picnic Area, but it's just a plowed lot with a pit toilet. Check the winter camping instructions on the bulletin board here for details.

West Glacier

Commercial campgrounds in the West Glacier vicinity are convenient for rafting, fishing, biking, and trail rides, but are located outside the park. If you require hookups, this is where you'll need to be. Standard amenities in these campgrounds include flush toilets, laundries, hot showers, camp stores, picnic tables, fire grates, firewood, propane, disposal stations, playgrounds, and WiFi Internet or modem dataports. Also, these campgrounds can handle the big RV rigs. If you're a light sleeper, bring your earplugs, for many of the campgrounds hear the rumble and screech from trains.

Although most commercial campgrounds lean toward servicing RVers and car campers, bikers and hikers should ask about special rates in shared area sites, for they can often pay much less, around $6 per person. Many of the campgrounds also offer rustic camping cabins or yurts, which have no kitchens or bathrooms, and you'll need to bring sleeping bags or pay extra for clean linens, blankets, and towels (around $9–15 per person). Commercial campgrounds tack on a 7 percent Montana bed tax to their rates. When you make your reservations, check for deals; many give 10 percent discounts over the Internet or to Good Sam, AAA, or Woodall's members. Reservations are highly recommended for July and August, especially for big rigs requiring sites with a certain amount of room. Most offer discounts in early and late season, too.

On 40 timbered acres only a half-mile from West Glacier, **Glacier Campground** (12070 Hwy. 2 E., 406/387-5689 or 888/387-5689, www.glaciercampground.com, May–Sept., $19–27) sits one mile west of the park entrance. Sites are very private, separated by birch and fir trees as well as lush undergrowth, so you don't feel you are camping in a parking lot. Several cabins ($35–45) share a covered outdoor cooking area with gas burners and BBQ. Leashed pets are totally welcome. With the campground set back from the road, trees reduce highway and railroad sounds. For evening entertainment, the campground sponsors Forest Service presentations.

Set back in the woods one mile off Highway 2 and 2.5 miles west of the park entrance, the **West Glacier KOA** (355 Half Moon Flats Rd., 406/387-5341 or 800/562-3313, www.west glacierkoa.com, May–Sept., $27–47) is the only campground with a heated swimming pool (June–mid-Sept.) and a couple of hot tubs that are open all season. It also has evening programs, cabins ($45–70), horseshoes, and a pancake breakfast. Due to its location away from the highway and railroad, this is one of the quieter campgrounds.

Outside West Glacier

Five more commercial campgrounds sprawl in the nine miles between West Glacier and Hungry Horse. These three each offer something different. At 2.5 miles from the park entrance, **San-Suz-Ed RV Park** (11505 Hwy. 2 E., 406/387-5280 or 800/630-2623, www.san suzedrvpark.com, open year round, $21–30) centers its campground around a nightly community campfire pit: BYOM (bring your own marshmallows) or BYOHD (bring your own hot dogs) to roast. For those needing open space for clear satellite reception, the **North American RV Park and Campground** (10784 Hwy. 2 E., 406/387-5800 or 800/704-4266, www.north americanrvpark.com, mid-Apr.–mid-Oct., $20–35) sits in a big grassy setting with fewer trees. One of the quietest campgrounds, **Mountain Meadows RV Park** (9125 Hwy. 2 E., 406/387-9125, www.mmrvpark.com, May–Sept., $33–36) spans 77 acres of forested hillside with sites separated for privacy and a stocked catch-and-release rainbow trout pond.

Food

Glacier is a place for good down-home cooking where tasty, fresh-baked fruit pies are still the rage, rather than upscale or ethnic delicacies. Seasonal restaurants cater to summer visitors, but don't expect much open between October and May. Many of the restaurants pack lunches to go for travelers.

RESTAURANTS
Apgar

Eddie's Restaurant (on Apgar Rd. 0.3 mile from Camas Rd. or 0.8 mile from Going-to-the-Sun Rd., 406/888-5361, open daily early June–mid-Sept., 7 A.M.–9:30 P.M. in high season, 8 A.M.–8 P.M. in shoulder seasons) is the only game in town, but it has good family-friendly breakfasts and lunches ($7–11), including hiker lunches to go. You'll often find long waiting lines in high season for dinner ($7–20), but will find the menu broad with sandwiches, dinner salads, and full entrees—fresh pan-fried trout to roasted chicken. With large waiting lines, takeout can be quicker; walk a few steps away to Lake McDonald's shore to picnic. Leave room for their sweet chocolate Bear Paw pie ($6).

West Glacier

At the historic **◖ Belton Chalet** (12575 Hwy. 2 E., 406/888-5000 or 888/235-8665, www .beltonchalet.com, Taproom 3 P.M.–midnight daily, dining room 5–10 P.M. daily, breakfast

7–11 A.M. Thurs.–Mon., late May–early Oct.) you can dine in the intimate Belton Grill, by the fireplace in the Taproom, or on the deck watching trains and the sunset over Apgar Mountain. The Belton is a treat—not just for its ambience, restored to its 1910 grandeur, but for its fine-dining flavors made with fresh local ingredients. The lodge's old boiler was converted into the kitchen's outdoor grill. Entrees ($20–33) like the flavorful Montana meatloaf—buffalo wrapped in hickory-smoked bacon with chipotle gravy—pair well with Taproom wines and Montana microbrews. The dessert tray changes nightly, but if available, try the huckleberry crisp or cheesecake with sauce made of cherries from the owners' Bigfork orchard. Lighter Taproom meals ($8–19) feature hors d'oeuvres, sandwiches, and salads. You can also get the Montana meatloaf in a sandwich with chipotle mayo. Order box lunches to go, too. Breakfasts are served Thursdays–Mondays only. Breakfast specials are big on local organic foods. In winter (Dec.–Mar.), the Belton opens on Friday and Saturday (3–9 P.M.), serving chili and elk moussaka ($5–22) to hungry skiers and Sunday brunch (11 A.M.–3 P.M.).

◖ West Glacier Restaurant and Lounge (200 Going-to-the-Sun Rd., 406/888-5359, 7 A.M.–10 P.M. daily mid-May–late Sept.) serves up good tasting café fare. Located between the park entrance bridge and the railroad tunnel, the restaurant packs out with a line in high season. Breakfast and lunches run $7–10. Try their blueberry pancakes for breakfast. Dinners ($9–17) span fish, pasta, steaks, sandwiches, or salads. Ironically, you'll find the best thing to sate a hungry hiker stomach—the Glacier Monster Cheeseburger—listed under "Lighter Appetites," but it's no such thing with bacon and cheese atop a half-pound hamburger, with fries. The burger-and-beer crowd heads to the adjacent bar to order off the restaurant menu.

Across from the Belton Train Depot, the **Glacier Highland** (12555 Hwy. 2 E., 406/888-5427, www.glacierhighland.com, 7 A.M.–10 P.M. daily mid-Apr.–Oct.) bakes large huckleberry muffins and cinnamon rolls to start the day. Their breakfasts, lunches, and

© BECKY LOMAX

Belton Chalet dining room, looking out at Apgar Mountain

dinners cover typical café fare—sandwiches and burgers ($6–8) or steaks and trout (up to $18). Beer and wine are served, too. The restaurant closes at 8 or 9 P.M. in shoulder seasons.

Convenient following trail rides, the **Rawhide Trading Post Restaurant and Steakhouse** (12000 Hwy. 2 E., 406/387-5999 or 800/388-5727, www.glacierrawhide.com, 11 A.M.–10 P.M. daily mid-May–mid-Oct.) serves a fast lunchtime pulled BBQ brisket on a hoagie ($10). For dinner, you can dive into the house specialty of mesquite-grilled steak ($19–23)—a 10-ounce cowgirl, 12-ounce cowboy, or the 14-ounce Wayne's cut. The restaurant also does take-out meals for easy campfire dinners. Until mid-June and after Labor Day, the Rawhide opens only from 4–8 P.M.).

Outside West Glacier

In Coram, five and a half miles west of West Glacier, **Glacier Grill and Pizza** (10026 Hwy. 2 E., 406/387-4223, 11 A.M.–11 P.M. daily) serves café fare ($6–12) year-round, but the main reason to go here is the pizza ($11–18). The loaded all-meat pizza is packed wall-to-wall with sausage, Canadian bacon, and pepperoni; the Mediterranean special with feta cheese is baked with a delightful twist on spices.

CAFFEINE

The **Glacier Espresso** stand (8 A.M.–3 P.M.-ish daily June–mid-Sept.) near the Alberta Visitor Information Center in West Glacier carries a few baked goodies to go with your latte. If temps climb, get an Italian soda or granita instead. In high season, it stays open sometimes as late as 7:30 P.M.

GROCERIES

Groceries (food, beer, wine) and camping items (ice, firewood, stove gas) may be purchased in both West Glacier and Apgar. In Apgar, get supplies at **Eddie's Campstore** (on Apgar Rd. 0.8 mile from Going-to-the-Sun Rd. or 0.3 mile from Camas Rd., 8 A.M.–10 P.M. daily in high season, closes at 6 P.M. in shoulder seasons, open June–mid-Sept.). In West Glacier, the **West Glacier Mercantile** (0.1 mile west of Hwy. 2 junction on Going-to-the-Sun Rd., 8 A.M.–10 P.M. daily in high season, early and late season closure at 5 P.M., open May–Sept.) has the bigger selection of meats, fresh veggies, and fruits. Convenience store items are also available at **Glacier Highland** (across from the Belton Train Depot on Hwy. 2, 7 A.M.–9 P.M. daily mid-Apr.–Oct., may close earlier in shoulder seasons); you'll find cheaper beer and wine prices here.

The nearest year-round grocery store is in Hungry Horse, on Highway 2 nine miles west of the park entrance. Look for the "supermarket" sign, but you'll have to drive 30 minutes into Flathead Valley to hit the megastores that carry huge brand selections.

PICNIC AREAS

Two picnic areas, both with beach access, rim Lake McDonald's western shores. **Apgar Picnic Area** is just off Going-to-the-Sun Road on the lake's southwest corner, with a beautiful uplake view to the Continental Divide. **Fish Creek Picnic Area** sits next to Fish Creek Campground, where a one-mile hike leads out to Rocky Point for more views. Both have picnic tables, flush toilets, and fire grates, but firewood is not provided and gathering is prohibited, so plan to purchase firewood in Apgar or West Glacier before heading here for your picnic.

NORTH FORK

It's remote. It's wild. It's not for everyone. The North Fork Valley defines rustic. Not rustic as in cute, comfortable rustic, but real rustic as in you nearly have to fend for yourself. No gas stations, no electricity. Pit toilets are de rigueur. But for those who want to get away from the mayhem, it's the place to go. A visit to the North Fork transports you back in time. The pace of life slows with the ambience of the Polebridge Mercantile and Northern Lights Saloon.

For the average traveler, the North Fork's nasty dirt roads alone deter interest. Brutal potholes, jarring washboards, and clouds of dust launch periodic vehement debates about paving the North Fork Road, but pavement into this remote enclave would alter its nature forever.

The North Fork Valley spans diverse habitats from grassland prairies to alpine glaciers. It's home to an immense range of wildlife—huge grizzly bears to tiny pygmy shrews. Spruce trees 300 years old root the valley in deep history. Surrounded by thick subalpine fir forests, Bowman and Kintla Lakes have miles of empty shoreline dotted with only a boat of anglers or a few kayaks. Trails from the North Fork see only a few people, even in high season. For those who have patience to sit with binoculars, wildlife-watching and birding are the best. Nothing chills the soul quite like the wild call of wolves in the dead of night.

HISTORY

In the late 1800s, handfuls of homesteaders, loggers, hunters, and trappers eked out a living

© BECKY LOMAX

HIGHLIGHTS

◖ Inside Road: Survive this rough road! This scenic byway presents a real challenge for both vehicles and mountain bikes. Drive or ride its 28 miles for a close encounter with its wildlife and potholes (page 62).

◖ Polebridge Mercantile: Smell fresh-baked cookies and breads when you walk in this historic hub of the North Fork Valley. With no electricity, an old-fashioned cash register clangs up your groceries (page 62).

◖ Northern Lights Saloon: Order a microbrew and sit outside to enjoy the view or just soak up the chatter from locals inside. In spite of its remote location, the saloon serves incomparable food in its tiny log cabin (page 63).

◖ North Fork of the Flathead River: Throw your watch away to let river time take over as you float this scenic river. Forming the park's western boundary, the river courses through prairie and forests where grizzly bears and wolves hunt prey (page 63).

◖ Bowman Lake: Look down the lake; you're looking straight into wild country. Rainbow Peak juts straight up 4,500 feet from the lakeshore, while Thunderbird Mountain scrapes the sky behind nesting bald eagles (page 64).

◖ Kintla Lake: Get far away from civilization at this remote lake. Although it may have been the site for oil drilling a century ago, today it's a mean 42 miles from pavement and launches into some of the park's most isolated backpacking terrain (page 64).

◖ Quartz Lakes: Hike to three lakes lined up like pearls on a necklace. The lakes lure anglers for native westslope cutthroat trout — but pack the bug spray, for they're mosquito havens as well (page 64).

◖ Glacier View: Climb a short grunt up with scenery galore. The route may tax the lungs, but you'll smell wild roses, and your eyes will relish Glacier's panorama at the top (page 68).

LOOK FOR **◖** TO FIND RECOMMENDED SIGHTS, ACTIVITIES, DINING, AND LODGING.

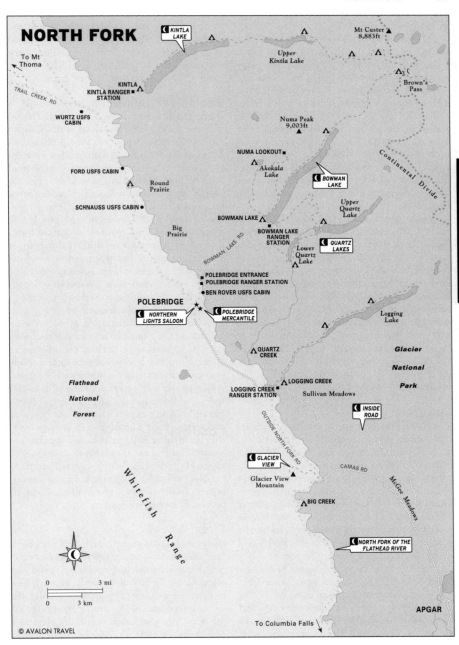

NORTH FORK

To Mt Thoma

TRAIL CREEK RD

KINTLA LAKE

Upper Kintla Lake

Mt Custer 8,883ft

Brown's Pass

KINTLA
KINTLA RANGER STATION

WURTZ USFS CABIN

Numa Peak 9,003ft

NUMA LOOKOUT

FORD USFS CABIN

Round Prairie

Akokala Lake

BOWMAN LAKE

Continental Divide

Upper Quartz Lake

SCHNAUSS USFS CABIN

Big Prairie

BOWMAN LAKE

BOWMAN LAKE RANGER STATION

Lower Quartz Lake

QUARTZ LAKES

BOWMAN LAKE RD

POLEBRIDGE ENTRANCE
POLEBRIDGE RANGER STATION
BEN ROVER USFS CABIN

POLEBRIDGE

NORTHERN LIGHTS SALOON

POLEBRIDGE MERCANTILE

Logging Lake

Glacier

QUARTZ CREEK

National

Flathead

LOGGING CREEK

LOGGING CREEK RANGER STATION

Sullivan Meadows

Park

National

INSIDE ROAD

Forest

OUTSIDE NORTH FORK RD

GLACIER VIEW

Glacier View Mountain

CAMAS RD

McGee Meadows

BIG CREEK

Whitefish Range

NORTH FORK OF THE FLATHEAD RIVER

0   3 mi
0   3 km

APGAR

To Columbia Falls

© AVALON TRAVEL

in the North Fork Valley, connected to each other only by a network of trails. In 1900, a Butte business, on a quest for oil at Kintla Lake, built the Inside North Fork Road—a 65-mile wagon track riddled with ruts, bogs, and stumps. It was sufficient, however, for hauling drilling equipment from Belton (West Glacier) to Kintla Lake, where sleds skidded supplies across the frozen lake to drill Montana's first oil well in 1901. The road attracted more homesteaders, but talk of Glacier becoming a national park was already afoot—a change the homesteaders disliked because parkhood meant an end to their hunting and timber livelihoods.

When Glacier achieved national park status in 1910, construction of the rough Outside North Fork Road two years later prompted many of the 35 homesteading families within the park boundaries to move across the North Fork of the Flathead River, outside the park boundary. One resident, Bill Adair, built a new mercantile in 1914 near Hay Creek—a two-story plank building. The "Merc," as locals call it, is now listed on the National Register of Historic Places. The area today is known as Polebridge—named for the funky North Fork River bridge, a one-lane lodgepole affair that burnt in the 1988 Red Bench Fire.

Culture

The North Fork is unique. It's a small, intimate community that prides itself on its rustic nature. Not L.L.Bean squeaky-clean look-alike rustic, but real bucolic earthiness with no electricity and few phone lines. The population of the four-mile-wide floodplain comprises year-round residents living off-the-grid and summer cabins. Most residents could care less if visitors complain about dust and potholes on the roads, and talk of paving the North Fork Road raises the hackles of many. The hub of valley life, the Merc and Northern Lights Saloon are where residents catch up on news, sometimes not much differentiated from gossip.

In Polebridge, the town's dogs run amok and lounge on the Merc's front porch. However, as a visitor, you have a different responsibility with

your canine. Visitors' dogs must be leashed. Hand-painted signs will tell you so: "Local dogs at large—please leash pets." One of the warning signs on the Northern Lights Saloon claims, "Unleashed dogs will be eaten."

Ecological Significance

The North Fork area contains all five of Glacier's ecosystems: grassland prairies, aspen parklands, montane forests, subalpine, and alpine tundra. Rich floodplains teem with wildflowers, berries, shrubs, and trees. Fens abound with orchids, bladderworts, sundews, mosses, sedges, ferns, and bulrushes. McGee Meadows, which is actually a fen, houses at least 50 species of flora. The valley is rife with grizzly and black bears, moose, coyotes, mountain lions, and elk—all manner of wildlife down to its tiniest occupant, the pygmy shrew, which preys on 25 species of bugs, insects, and snails. Birders have documented 196 species of woodpeckers, owls, raptors, waterfowl, and songbirds, over half of which nest here.

With the natural migration of wolves from Canada in the 1980s, Glacier saw its first wolf pack in 50 years with its first litter of pups in 1986. Numbers have since rebounded. Now wolf packs live throughout northwest Montana, which prompted federal delisting of the wolf from the Endangered Species Act in 2008. However, don't expect to see a wolf around every tree; their numbers vary year to year, they roam up to 300 square miles, and they are elusive. But you may hear them—especially at night. High deer and elk concentrations make the North Fork Valley prime habitat; to maintain its health, every day a wolf must eat 10 percent of its body weight in meat.

Fires

Rich timberlands of the North Fork are prime fire lands due to years of fire suppression policies that led to thick lodgepole stands and bug infestations. The 38,000-acre Red Bench Fire in 1988 saw a change in policy, for the fire ran its natural course, nearly wiping Polebridge off the map. Silver sentinels stand as a reminder near town. In 2001, the Moose Fire shot over

NORTH FORK WONDERS

TINY FAUNA

The North Fork Valley is home to the rare **northern bog lemming,** a small, brown-backed, gray-underbellied rodent that seeks mats of thick, wet sphagnum moss for habitat. Weighing only one ounce (the same as one heaping tablespoon of sugar) but growing up to six inches long, the tiny cousin of the Arctic lemming is a relic of the Pleistocene ice age, which began two million years ago. Although it's rarely seen, look for small, neat piles of clipped grass along the mossy thoroughfares en route to underground nests. One study found that bog lemmings make up two 2 percent of the pine marten's diet.

Glacier's smallest predator, the **pygmy shrew,** inhabits floodplains in the North Fork Valley. This tiny carnivore is one of North America's rarest mammals. Less than 2.5 inches in size and weighing less than a quarter ounce, this shrew's voracious appetite for insects, slugs, snails, and carrion can put larger shrews to shame. One study watched a female eat three times her own body weight daily for 10 days. Their high metabolism echoes their respiration rate – 25 times more than humans – and their hearts beat up to 1,320 times per minute when excited. To feed their high metabolic rates, pygmy shrews eat every couple hours 24/7 year-round.

PLANTS

Carnivorous plants inhabit North Fork fens. The **sundew** attracts insects to its sparkling droplets like morning dew on leaves. Sitting atop hairs lining its leaves, the sticky droplets like wet cement entrap unsuspecting visitors. Slowly, the leaves curl around the victim as digestive juices work their magic. The **bladderwort** also refined trapping. Buoyant bladders trap anything that swims by – mosquito larvae to fish fry. When the prey passes, it brushes hairs, opening a trapdoor that sucks water in along with the naive prey. Digestive enzymes make short work of the meal, with the trap reset in 15 minutes to two hours.

BIRDS

Birders find a feast for their eyes and ears in the North Fork. With 196 species of birds documented here – at least 112 nesters – the valley teems with avian activity. Migratory birds stop on their flight highways to wintering ranges or summer nesting.

Raptors: Birds of prey find abundant food in the North Fork Valley. Numerous rodents, ground squirrels, songbirds, and carrion feed their appetites here. The valley's forests attract sharp-shinned and Cooper's hawks. Bald eagles nest on Kintla and Bowman Lakes. Northern harriers, red-tailed hawks, goshawks, and American kestrels all prowl above the prairies. At night, the hoots of large great-horned and pygmy owls haunt the air.

Waterfowl: With the Flathead River, many large lakes, swamps, and wetlands, waterfowl have no shortage of suitable habitat. Herons, ducks, grebes, geese, loons, and swans migrate through or nest in the plentiful waters here.

Songbirds: The North Fork could be considered downright noisy at times – not from traffic, but from the scads of songbirds flitting among its trees and cattails. American redstarts, warbling vireos, kinglets, nuthatches, crossbills, sparrows, and warblers are just a few of the neotropical songbirds that migrate annually into the valley. In winter, you'll spot tree sparrows and redpolls.

Woodpeckers: After the recent Moose (2001) and Wedge Canyon Fires (2003), dead standing timber attracted the three-toed woodpecker, picking away for bugs. Watch also for the large, red-headed pileated woodpecker looking for a favorite food – carpenter ants. To help with identification of Glacier's birds, pick up a bird list from visitors centers or on the park's website.

Demers Ridge, burning 71,000 acres, over one-third inside Glacier. In 2003, the Wedge Canyon Fire burned 53,315 acres, jumping the North Fork River into the park and traveling up the side of Parke Peak, while the Robert Fire burned the valley's south end. Evidence of each of these fires is obvious, but swift new growth is building a new forest with rampant blooms of fireweed, arrowleaf balsamroot, and pussytoes.

Exploring North Fork

ENTRANCE STATION

The North Fork River is the boundary between national forest and national park. From the North Fork Valley, two roads cross the river into the park. The paved **Camas Road** enters from the dirt North Fork Road, with an unstaffed entrance station and a self-pay cash-only kiosk. A mile northeast of Polebridge, the **Polebridge entrance station** is staffed during summer only, but a self-pay cash-only kiosk is available, too. If you don't have an annual pass, seven-day passes cost $25 per vehicle or $12 for individuals on foot, bicycles, or motorcycles. (Rates drop to $15 and $10 Nov.–Apr.)

TOURS AND SHUTTLES

The closest thing to guided tours in the North Fork is guided outdoor recreation: river-rafting or backpacking. However, the companies that guide these trips are based in West Glacier (see the *West Glacier and Apgar* chapter for contact info and pricing). You can also hook up with a **Glacier Institute** course that might be wildlife-watching in the area (see *Background* chapter).

The North Fork does not see any routine bus service; however, **Flathead-Glacier Transportation** (406/892-3390 or 800/829-7039, www.fgtrans.com) provides a shuttle between Polebridge and Glacier International Airport ($80 one way). Because of Glacier's North Fork wilderness policies precluding commercial operations, visitors can get shuttled to Bowman or Kintla Lake only by renting a vehicle from FGT to drive themselves to the lake; then FGT picks up the vehicle the following day ($150). This accommodates backpackers hiking between the North Fork and Waterton or Chief Mountain Customs.

SERVICES

You won't find strip malls nor services up the North Fork. The nearest gas stations are in Columbia Falls and West Glacier. Forget the ATMs, newspapers (unless they are a couple days old), a post office, television, visitors centers, and shopping. You won't find public flush restrooms; only outhouses and vault toilets. Phone lines only run as far as Polebridge. The **Polebridge Mercantile** (265 Polebridge Loop, 406/888-5105, 8 A.M.–6 P.M. daily, until 9 P.M. in summer) has a pay phone on its front deck.

With the re-opening of the **Home Ranch Store** (8855 North Fork Road, 406/888-5572, www.homeranchbottoms.com, 9 A.M.–9 P.M. late May–early Sept.), you can now get hot showers ($7) and do laundry ($3.50 wash, $3.50 dry). Both are pricey due to the power source—a generator. A phone is available for calling-card calls and so is a dial-up modem computer with Internet (30 minutes for $5). If you're buying food and beer in the tavern, you can jump on for free.

Emergencies

For emergencies within park boundaries, contact a ranger or call 406/888-7800. Outside park boundaries, call 911. The nearest hospitals are in the Flathead Valley: Kalispell Regional Medical Center (310 Sunny View Ln., 406/752-5111) and North Valley Hospital in Whitefish (1600 Hospital Way, 406/863-3631).

The **Polebridge Ranger Station** (staffed year-round, 406/888-7800) sits one mile from Polebridge across the North Fork River next to

TIPS FOR WILDLIFE-WATCHING

- Safety is important when watching wildlife – safety for you and safety for the wildlife. The easiest tool for watching wildlife is a good pair of binoculars for spying up close.

- Do not approach wildlife. Although our inclinations tell us to scoot in for a closer look, crowding wildlife puts you at risk and endangers the animal, often scaring it off in fright. Sometimes simply the presence of people can habituate an animal to hanging around people; with bears, this can lead to more aggressive behavior.

- Let the animal's or bird's behavior guide your behavior. If the animal appears twitchy, nervous, or points eyes and ears directly at you, back off: You're too close. The goal is to watch wildlife go about their normal business, rather than seeing how they react to disruption. If you behave like a predator stalking an animal, the creature will assume you are one. Use binoculars and telephoto lenses for moving in close rather than approaching an animal.

- Most animals tend to be more active in morning and evening. These are also optimum times for photographing animals in better lighting.

- Blend in with your surroundings. Rather than wearing loud colors, wear muted clothing that matches the environment.

- Relax. Animals sense excitement. Move slowly around them because abrupt, jerky movements can startle them. Look down, rather than staring animals directly in the eye.

- Don't get carried away watching big, showy megafauna like bears and moose only to miss a small carnivore like a short-tailed weasel.

- Use field guides to help with identification and understanding the animal's behavior.

- If you see wildlife along a road, use pullouts or broad shoulders to drive completely off the road. Do not jam the middle of the road. Use the car as a blind to watch wildlife, but keep pets inside. If you see a bear, you're better off just driving by slowly. Bear jams tend to condition the bruin to become accustomed to vehicles, one step toward getting into more trouble.

the park entrance; backcountry camping permits are available here when someone is available to write one. During summer, Logging Creek Ranger Station on the Inside North Fork Road is staffed, as are stations at Bowman and Kintla Lakes; however, these seasonal rangers may be out patrolling miles of backcountry trails.

DRIVING TOURS
Outside North Fork Road

Open year-round, the Outside North Fork Road is the easier drive of the two dirt and gravel access roads. Although the road running from Columbia Falls to Canada is wide enough for two cars to pass, be prepared for washboards, potholes, ruts, dust in summer, slush in fall or spring, and ice in winter. Locals

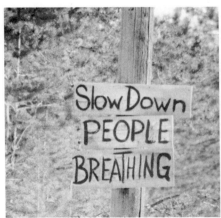

sign entering Polebridge

© BECKY LOMAX

refer to this road as simply the North Fork, dropping the "Outside," for it is the valley's main gateway. Every few years, clamor arises about paving the North Fork, which many locals oppose because pavement would promptly change the valley's nature. The North Fork Road is intermittently plowed in winter to the Canadian border, but do not attempt it without good snow tires and four-wheel drive. Carry chains and emergency supplies in the car.

From Columbia Falls, the North Fork Road leaves pavement just past Blankenship Road and follows the North Fork River for 13 miles. After a junction with the paved Camas Road (an alternate access from Apgar), the road passes a few small bucolic ranches whose pastures provide browse for cows and wild elk herds. You'll hit six miles of rough pavement again at Home Ranch, where cattle walk the road; drive with caution, especially when coming around corners. At 32 miles and a little over one hour's drive, the road meets Polebridge Loop—the cutoff to the Merc, the Inside North Fork Road, and **Bowman** and **Kintla Lakes.** You'll see hand-painted signs when you enter town: "Slow Down, People Breathing" and "10 mph: Bear, dog, kid, wolf, rabbit, squirrel crossing." Respect residents here; speed kicks up a tremendous amount of dust in summer!

From the Polebridge junction, the road continues 22 more miles north toward Canada—another hour's drive. It accesses the upper Whitefish Range, the North Fork River, and Forest Service cabins. Although drivers used to cross into Canada, the Trail Creek port of entry is closed due to a road washout on the Canadian side.

C Inside Road

Not for everyone, the summer-only (May–Oct.), dirt Inside North Fork Road throws precipitous drops, curves, and climbs at drivers. Monster potholes and washboards are commonplace; spaces wide enough for two vehicles to pass are rare. You're definitely off the beaten path on this bumpy trek where speeds top out at 20 mph. Marked as Glacier Route 7 on some maps and known as simply the "Inside Road"

to locals, the Inside North Fork Road is the rougher of the two choices and requires high-clearance vehicles. Big RV rigs will definitely have trouble, and it's a rough ride for a trailer. Although it's only 29 miles to Polebridge, it will take two hours to drive. Many link it up with Outside North Fork and Camas Roads for a 53-mile scenic loop drive.

From the south, the Inside Road begins at Fish Creek Campground and climbs through the 2003 Robert Fire. Atop the ridge, look for peek-a-boo views of **McGee Meadows,** good wildlife-watching spots if you can squeeze your vehicle off the road and tolerate swarms of mosquitoes. Then compare fire reqrowth as you drive through the 2001 Moose Fire. After dropping down steep Anaconda Hill (12.5 miles from Fish Creek) and crossing the creek, the road bisects Sullivan Meadows, famous for Glacier's wolves, before passing two small campgrounds—Logging Creek (17.5 miles) and Quartz Creek (20 miles). At 28 miles, the road intersects with the Polebridge park entrance. From here, cross the North Fork River, drive one mile to **Polebridge,** and connect with Outside North Fork Road.

You can also continue up the Inside Road to **Bowman** and **Kintla Lakes.** A few minutes north of the Polebridge Ranger Station, the curvy Bowman Lake road turns off, a six-mile (25-minute) snake-like drive eastward up the valley. Continuing northward toward Kintla, the Inside Road crosses **Big Prairie,** the largest of the North Fork's unique grasslands. **Round Prairie** follows at one-third the size. The road re-enters the forest and passes through the 2003 Wedge Canyon Fire zone before dead-ending at Kintla Lake, 14 miles north of the North Fork entrance station.

SIGHTS
C Polebridge Mercantile

Located 25 miles north of Apgar, the hub of the North Fork community is the red-planked "Merc." The Polebridge Mercantile, listed on the National Register of Historic Places, was built in 1914. It is more than a place to buy that forgotten can of pork and beans for camping. It

NORTH FORK

sells everything from local handmade jewelry to not-to-be-missed bakery goods fresh from the oven. While the smell of cookies and pastries fills the small room, an old-fashioned cash register clangs up sales.

◖ Northern Lights Saloon

Next door to the Merc, the tiny Northern Lights Saloon looks like a ramshackle log cabin but packs out with diners, extras spilling outside onto picnic tables. Open nightly in summer and weekends in winter for dinner, it may be the only restaurant in the North Fork, but the food clearly beats many eateries elsewhere. Hikers, celebrating their adventures here with whatever Montana microbrew is currently on tap, lounge outside staring at Rainbow Peak.

◖ North Fork of the Flathead River

Forming the western boundary of Glacier National Park, the North Fork of the Flathead River draws its headwaters from Canada and

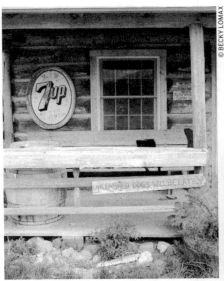

Northern Lights Saloon: food, beer, and scenery

Polebridge Mercantile: much more than a market

ends near West Glacier at its confluence with the Middle Fork. Fifty-nine miles of waters flow through private, state, and federal lands while descending the North Fork Valley's diverse habitats. Designated as a Wild and Scenic River in 1976, the Class II river with six accesses is great for multiday float trips, day rafting, fishing, and scenic floating.

McGee Meadows

McGee Meadows is a wildlife-watching spot, but during much of the spring and early summer, the fen is too wet to walk due to its soggy nature. It is also a mosquito haven. As a fen, its low oxygen waters build up dead plant matter, but nutrients feed it via precipitation and ground water, making it fertile ground for diverse vegetation. The meadow is home to rare plants and over 50 species of flora—bulrushes, bladderworts, sphagnum moss, sundews, and orchids. It is also a place to see bears, moose, deer, and a host of birds. Access McGee Meadows from the Camas Road (six miles from Apgar) or from the Inside Road (four miles from Fish Creek). Bring bug spray if you plan on wildlife-watching.

◖ Bowman Lake

The closest of Glacier's northwestern lakes to reach, Bowman Lake sits in a narrow trough seven miles northeast of Polebridge on a dirt road with a bouncing ride. The lake's six miles sprawls toward nesting bald eagles and Thunderbird Peak; its half-mile width squeezes in between the hulks of Numa Peak and Rainbow Peak, the latter rising 4,500 feet straight up from the south lakeshore. In summer, lake waters offer solitude: Drop in a canoe to tour its shoreline. In winter, the icy expanse and snow-laden crags call to cross-country skiers, who ski in on the road pockmarked with wolf and elk tracks.

Big Prairie

Located 30 miles up the Inside North Fork Road, just two miles past the Bowman Lake turnoff and three miles from Polebridge, Big Prairie is the largest of four Palouse prairies in the North Fork. At one mile wide and four miles long, the prairie is a grassland with wheatgrass, fescues, oatgrass, and sagebrush. Because the Whitefish Range causes a rain shadow effect, the North Fork receives only 20 inches of precipitation per year, which fosters this drier flora.

◖ Kintla Lake

Kintla Lake is a place to go only on purpose. Fifteen miles of washboarded, rutted road links Polebridge with the remote lake. Its tiny campground tucked deep in the trees offers quiet, a place to decompress. Cowering between Starvation and Parke Ridges, the half-mile-wide lake curves a little over five miles up valley, a prelude to Upper Kintla Lake. Only one trail takes off along the north shore toward the isolated Kintla-Kinnerly peak complex and Boulder Pass. Haul a canoe or kayak to Kintla Lake for unbeatable secluded paddling.

Recreation

HIKING

Hiking in the North Fork leads to stunning vistas, but be prepared for tromping through long, mosquito-ridden, thick-forested valleys to earn your views. While day hikers trek to lakes and lookouts, backpackers gain altitude into rugged glaciated alpine bowls above the tree line. In this undeveloped area, you're on your own to get to trailheads; no regular shuttle service runs up the North Fork. From both sides of the valley, hikes depart in Glacier and in the national forest of the Whitefish Range. For those looking for hikes for the pooch, Flathead National Forest is the answer.

While trails in Glacier Park are well-signed, Flathead National Forest trails are less so. Trail signs may consist of just a number with no distances, destinations, or directions. For that reason alone, always hike with a topographical map in Flathead National Forest, and know how to read it. Trails also in the national forest are maintained less frequently: Expect to encounter deadfall and downed trees as well as brushy routes. For hiking maps of Flathead National Forest, contact the Glacier View Ranger District in Hungry Horse (406/387-3800). Topographical quads of the Whitefish Range can be purchased at outdoor sporting-goods stores in Flathead Valley. For hiking Glacier's trails, take along a topographical map, available through Glacier Natural History Association (406/888-5756, www.glacierassociation.org).

◖ Quartz Lakes

- Distance: 12.4-mile loop

- Duration: 6 hours

- Elevation gain: 1,470 feet to Upper Quartz, 1,000 feet on return over ridge

- Effort: moderate
- Trailhead: backcountry parking area at Bowman Lake

In June, early parts of the trail burst with calypso orchids while the path crossing Cerulean Ridge is still buried under snow. Within a half-mile up the trail, the path splits. You'll return to this junction at the end of the loop. Take the left fork, heading to Quartz Lake. With peek-a-boo views of Numa Peak, the trail climbs through thick spruce and fir forests until it crests Cerulean ridge. As the trail drops 1,000 feet to Quartz Lake, it enters the 1988 Red Bench burn, where open meadows afford views of Vulture Peak's steep north face and the lake.

At Quartz Lake, the trail cuts through the backcountry campsite and rounds the lake through boardwalk bogs, passing Middle Quartz Lake. Even as the trail moves away from water, mosquitoes pester hikers. The trail drops to a backcountry campsite at Lower Quartz Lake's outlet. From here, it climbs 1.5 miles with good views to the top of Cerulean Ridge before dropping back to the junction. For families with kids, an out-and-back excursion just to Lower Quartz Lake may be easier at seven miles round-trip.

Numa Lookout

- Distance: 11.2 miles round-trip
- Duration: 5.5 hours
- Elevation gain: 2,930 feet
- Effort: moderately strenuous
- Trailhead: from Bowman Lake Campground near lakeshore

Although the bulk of the trail crawls through deep forest, the view from Numa Lookout is well worth the climb. Following the northwest shore of Bowman Lake, the trail winds 0.7 mile through damp cedars to a junction. Take the left fork. The trail climbs

Boulder Pass in Glacier's remote northwest corner is accessed via trails from Bowman or Kintla Lakes.

steadily uphill to a saddle with a small boggy pond. During mosquito season, hike fast to get by the swarms.

After the trail switchbacks up the final climb within eyesight of the lookout, the treed slope breaks into dry open meadows. At 6,960 feet high, the lookout, which is staffed during fire season, stares across Bowman Lake at the steep massif of Square, Rainbow, and Carter Peaks.

Bowman Lake

- Distance: 14.2 miles round-trip to head of lake

- Duration: 6 hours

- Elevation gain: none

- Effort: easy, but lengthy

- Trailhead: from Bowman Lake Campground near lakeshore

This easy-walking trail wanders the forested northeast shoreline of Bowman Lake. For a stroll, walk it as far as you want and then turn around. The trail nears the shore close enough for beach access only a couple times where June water levels flood beaches. Intermittent views of the Square, Rainbow, and Carter massif poke out from the trees.

At the head of the lake, a backcountry campground with a marvelous pebble beach is a great place to lunch, but do so by the community cooking site rather than in or near backcountry sleeping sites. Bring binoculars, because bald eagles nest at the lake's head. For backpackers, the trail continues on, climbing to Brown's Pass atop the Continental Divide, where it splits, either dropping east to Goat Haunt on Waterton Lake (23 miles total) or climbing around Hole-in-the-Wall and over Boulder Pass to Kintla Lake (37 miles total).

Kintla Lake

- Distance: 12.4 miles round-trip

- Duration: 6 hours

- Elevation gain: none

© BECKY LOMAX

hiking above Hole-in-the-Wall en route to Boulder Pass

in-the-Wall cirque to Brown's Pass on the Continental Divide and then splits, either dropping east to Goat Haunt on Waterton Lake (32 miles total) or down to Bowman Lake (37 miles total).

Logging Lake

- Distance: 8.8 miles round-trip
- Duration: 4 hours
- Elevation gain: 477 feet
- Effort: easy
- Trailhead: Logging Creek Campground on the Inside North Fork Road

With large views en route, the trail attracts mostly anglers fishing for cutthroat, some with gumption enough to haul in float tubes to get away from the brushy shoreline. Above Logging Creek, the trail climbs quickly at the start but then levels out across a timbered ridgeline that offers a glimpse or two of the creek canyon. At the lake, far beyond its opposite shoreline eight miles away, you can spot Mount Geduhn and Anaconda Mountain.

Mount Thoma

- Distance: 10 miles round-trip
- Duration: 5 hours
- Elevation gain: 2,917 feet
- Effort: strenuous
- Trailhead: on north side 3 miles up Trail Creek Road in Flathead National Forest
- Directions: Drive north of Polebridge on the Outside North Fork Road approximately 13 miles to Trail Creek, 6 miles from the Canadian border. Turn left and drive 3 miles to the trailhead.

The forested trail starts off gently but soon pitches into an uphill grunt. Brushy and rarely maintained, the trail frequently has downed trees barring the path, requiring climbing and worming through branches. But soon it breaks out into a high ridgeline meadow with

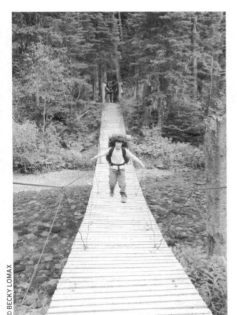
© BECKY LOMAX
swinging bridge above Upper Kintla Lake

- Effort: easy, but lengthy
- Trailhead: from Kintla Lake Campground near lakeshore

The gentle trail cruises along Kintla Lake's north shore with an expanding view up the lake before its midsection tours deep back in the trees. Look for woodland flowers: trilliums, twisted stalk, queen's cup, fairybells, bunchberry, and bog orchids. Toward the head of the lake, the trail returns to a shoreline tour.

At 6.3 miles, the trail reaches the Kintla Lake backcountry campground. Pull out the binoculars, for you might see moose, bear, or bald eagles from its shoreline. When eating lunch, do so by the community cooking site rather than in or near backcountry sleeping sites. For backpackers, the trail continues on through the 2003 Wedge Fire growing with prolific pink fireweed to Upper Kintla Lake. Here, it begins a substantial climb to Boulder Pass, where it drops through Hole-bluebells. At the end of the ridge, it climbs a series of switchbacks to the summit.

The summit is well worth the hike. Glacier's peaks sprawl southeasterly. The border swath between Canada and the United States slices an unnaturally straight line across the valley. In Canada, a mosaic of clearcuts leads up to Akamina-Kishinena Provincial Park bordering Waterton National Park. To the south, the Whitefish Range layers off peak after peak as far as the eye can see.

Hornet Lookout

- Distance: 2 miles round-trip

- Duration: 1 hour

- Elevation gain: 498 feet

- Effort: easy

- Trailhead: at Hornet Road's terminus in Flathead National Forest

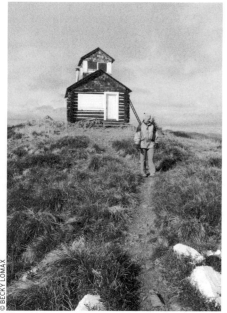

© BECKY LOMAX

Hornet Lookout

- Directions: 10 miles north of Polebridge, turn west on Whale Creek Road #318 for 4 miles, then turn north climbing on narrow Hornet Road #9805 for 5.2 miles.

A short climb uphill through huckleberry, fireweed, and beargrass slopes leads to a small lookout with great views of Glacier's skyline and the North Fork Valley. Silvered trees remain from the 2003 Wedge Fire; you'll get a good look at the full scope of the burn. While the drive may take longer than the hike, the lookout makes a great kid destination with an eyeful of view rewards for adults. Two people can rent the USFS lookout to spend the night.

◖ Glacier View

- Distance: 4.5 miles round-trip

- Duration: 4 hours

- Elevation gain: 2,687 feet

- Effort: strenuous

- Trailhead: at the junction of Camas and North Fork Roads in Flathead National Forest

A steep climb up the side of Demers Ridge leads to Glacier View. Its name says it all: views from the top span the park's peaks. You'll even see Flathead Lake in the distance. The trail passes right through the 2001 Moose Fire zone with charred stumps and silver toothpick trees. In the valley below, you can see the fire's mosaic as it burned with different intensities and leaped tree glades. In June, wild roses scent the air amid a botanical dream of wildflower species.

Right from the start, the trail makes no bones about going uphill: No flats to catch your breath, no warm-up for the legs. But with a decent pair of lungs, the ascent is not bad. Just adopt a slow, steady plod, and you'll reach the top where meadows afford a scenic top-of-the-world place to lunch. The fire removed shade from the slopes, so the trail is a baker in hot August heat. In winter, snowshoers trek up.

© BECKY LOMAX

The Inside North Fork Road crosses through several old burns.

Guides

Glacier Guides (406/387-5555 or 800/521-7238, www.glacierguides.com), in West Glacier, has the sole guiding concession for Glacier Park. Most of their day-hiking trips head elsewhere; however, many of their multiday backpacking trips begin or finish at Bowman and Kintla trailheads. See the *West Glacier and Apgar* chapter for details. No companies have guiding services for hiking in the Whitefish Range of Flathead National Forest.

BIKING

With the North Fork's rough gravel roads, mountain biking is the only way to go; road bikes won't cut it here. Bike rentals are not available in the North Fork—only in Flathead Valley.

Many mountain bikers choose to make a 54-mile loop from Apgar up the Inside North Fork Road, overnighting in Polebridge, and down the Outside North Fork and Camas Roads. Because the Inside Road packs in serious elevation gain as it climbs and drops through five creek drainages, the loop is a good two-day ride, but it requires carrying only minimal supplies. (Some do the trip in one long day, but then you don't have much time for exploring en route.) By staying at the North Fork Hostel and renting linens, you can leave the tent and sleeping bag home. Plan for dinner at the Northern Lights Saloon and breakfast on baked goodies at the Merc. Just carry your lunch, the day's water, emergency supplies, and, of course, bug juice. In June, while moisture still clings in the gravel, the ride is less dusty, but you'll eat your share of mosquitoes on the Inside Road. By late July, you might need a dust mask to survive the ride back south on the Outside North Fork Road.

RAFTING

Floating the Wild and Scenic **North Fork of the Flathead** decompresses you to river pace on its Class II waters. Six river put-ins stagger down the river's length from the Canadian border to its confluence with the Middle Fork: the border, Ford, Polebridge, Big Creek, Glacier Rim, and Blankenship. High water hits in June and low water in August. In July, the average float time from the border to Blankenship is 16 hours. Most rafters tend to break that into three days. If you're in the park, it's convenient to rent rafts, frames, oars, paddles, and PFDs from **Glacier Outdoor Center** (406/888-5454 or 800/235-6781) based in West Glacier. They also offer vehicle shuttle services. If you're accessing the North Fork via Columbia Falls, it's more convenient to rent a raft from a Flathead Valley location.

Overnight Permits

No permits are required for overnights, but all camps must be set up on the western shore rather than Glacier's eastern shoreline. Camps in Flathead National Forest and on state lands are first-come, first-serve. Round Prairie is the one exception on Glacier's bank, and it requires a permit ($5 per person per night). Permits are available by advance reservation ($30 per trip) and must use the official Backcountry Camping application: download it at www.nps .gov/glac. You can stop in the Polebridge Ranger Station near the Polebridge entrance station the day before your departure and hope it is available. Call ahead to be sure someone is available to write the permit (406/888-7742). The Apgar Backcountry Permit Center (406/888-7859) may be more convenient as you launch your trip up the North Fork. Hours are generally 8 A.M.–4:30 P.M. for both permit centers.

Respect the rights of private property owners along the river. Signage at river accesses identifies land ownership en route. For questions regarding rafting on the North Fork, call Glacier View Ranger District (406/387-3800).

Guides

Several raft-guiding companies lead overnight trips down the North Fork; however, none base their operations in the North Fork Valley. All commercial outfitters begin their trips in West Glacier. Due to the Class II nature of the river, most trips are camping and float trips, appropriate for families and kids. **Glacier Guides** (406/387-5555 or 800/521-7238, www.glacier guides.com) runs unique three-day North Fork

float trips that combine rafting with overnight cabin stays rather than camping ($669 adults, $562 kids).

BOATING

All types of rowed boats and sail craft are allowed on both Bowman and Kintla Lakes; however, the narrow canyons create swirly winds that make sailing and sailboarding almost impossible. While Kintla does not permit any motorboats, Bowman allows motors of 10 horsepower or less. Both lakes, however, are closed to jet skis and waterskiing. No boat rentals are available in the North Fork Valley; plan ahead for rentals in Flathead Valley.

Be aware of wildlife closures on the lakes. Both lakes harbor nesting bald eagles at their heads; seasonal closures marked with orange buoys protect the nests.

KAYAKING AND CANOEING

River kayakers and canoers head to the Wild and Scenic **North Fork of the Flathead.** But canoers must be able to handle Class II ripples. For access, six river put-ins dot the North Fork from the Canadian border to its confluence with the Middle Fork. Sea kayakers and most canoers aim for the larger waters of **Bowman and Kintla Lakes.** While the lakes on calm days make for stellar paddling, both waters kick up with lusty winds in minutes. Be aware, too, of wildlife closures marked with orange buoys at the heads of both Bowman and Kintla Lakes, where bald eagles nest. The nearest rental shops for kayaks, canoes, and camping gear are in West Glacier and Flathead Valley.

No permits are required for those overnighting along the North Fork River, but all camping must be done on the western shore rather than Glacier's eastern shoreline. Round Prairie and the backcountry sites at the heads of Bowman and Kintla Lakes require a permit. See *Rafting* permit information for details.

FISHING

Anglers are attracted to the North Fork for its indigenous fish: westslope cutthroat and bull trout. However, you should be able to identify bull trout; they are a protected species and must be returned to the wild immediately. No black, put it back!

Kintla and **Bowman Lakes** are the main lakes accessible by car for fishing. Bowman allows motorized boats, but not Kintla. For those willing to hike to a worthy fishing lake, the three **Quartz Lakes** hop with native trout and whitefish. Along the Inside North Fork Road, most of the western creek drainages provide some fishing, with various degrees of accessibility. Fishing closures in the area include Upper Kintla Lake and Kintla Creek between the two Kintla Lakes, Bowman Creek above the lake, and Logging Creek between Logging and Grace Lakes.

The most popular North Fork Valley fishing is on the **North Fork River** itself, where six river accesses (Canadian border, Ford, Polebridge, Big Creek, Glacier Rim, and Blankenship) allow for raft or boat launching and fishing. The Camas Bridge also provides fishing access.

Several commercial outfitters guide overnight fishing trips on the North Fork River; however, all fishing outfitters base their operations out of West Glacier.

Licenses and Regulations

The North Fork River's high water line on the eastern shore provides Glacier's western boundary. Inside the park, fishing licenses or permits are not required, but outside the park, anglers must possess a Montana State Fishing License. This includes anglers on the North Fork River. Purchase one before you come up the North Fork; none are sold in Polebridge. Check details on licenses in the *Background* chapter.

HUNTING

Hunting is illegal in Glacier National Park. But in the North Fork, Flathead National Forest holds popular deer, elk, and bird hunting grounds. Get hunting regulations, seasons, and license info from Montana Fish, Wildlife, and Parks (406/444-2535, www.fwp .montana.gov).

CROSS-COUNTRY SKIING

Roads in the North Fork convert to cross-country ski and snowshoe trails in winter. But don't expect pristine smooth snows: The North Fork thrives as a winter habitat for moose, wolves, deer, elk, snowshoe hares, coyotes, and bobcats. Their tracks pockmark roads. The roads, which make easy skiing, also make for easy animal travel. Grab a track identification book to help in deciphering the footprints splattered across your trail. If you need rental gear, pick it up in West Glacier or the Flathead Valley before coming up the North Fork; no skis are available in Polebridge.

Bowman Lake makes a perfect day ski; park at the Polebridge entrance station and ski less than a half-mile north on the Inside Road before climbing six miles up to Bowman Lake's frozen shores. Be cautious about continuing out onto the ice in shoulder seasons. You're better off sticking close to shore if you want to ski the lake. **Big Prairie, the Inside Road, and Hidden Meadows** all provide other routes starting from the same point. Pick up a copy of *Skiing and Snowshoeing* online or from visitors centers or ranger stations for route descriptions.

For an overnight, skiers traverse 12 miles up Whale Creek Road to stay in one of the Forest Service cabins—Ninko—on the flanks of Thompson-Seton Mountain. For information on this trip, call Glacier View Ranger Station (406/387-3800).

SNOWMOBILING

While snowmobiles are not permitted in Glacier, they are allowed in Flathead National Forest in the Whitefish Range, where snowfall piles up 6–12 feet. December–April, unplowed roads heading west off the North Fork Road are used by snowmobilers, and a few are groomed by Flathead Snowmobile Association. Contact Montana Snowmobile Association (406/788-2399, www.snowtana .com) for current information on the local association and maps. Glacier View Ranger Station (406/387-3800) regulates the snowmobile use, season, and closures; check for current cross-country skiing along the North Fork of the Flathead River

© BECKY LOMAX

conditions and restrictions. The nearest rentals are in Flathead Valley.

ENTERTAINMENT

Instead of red, white, and blue marching bands, witness cross-dressers, beer-can draggers, bicycles, the 1956 Polebridge fire truck, and rafts in Polebridge's annual **Fourth of July Parade**—the more slightly off-kilter, the better. Hundreds of people line the dirt main street for the noon parade-that's-really-not-a-parade. (Warning: Parking is an absolute nightmare!) It's a two-for-one show as the parade goes up the street and then back down the same street. Enter for free; watch for free. Who's in charge? No one knows.

Accommodations and Food

North Fork lodging is seriously off-the-grid. With no electricity, power comes from generators, lights are most often propane, and woodstoves provide heat. Telephone lines reach only as far north as Polebridge. However, despite conditions in this outpost, the state of Montana still charges its 7 percent bed tax.

IN POLEBRIDGE

Located a quarter mile south of the Merc and Northern Lights Saloon, the **North Fork**

Hostel (80 Beaver Dr., 406/888-5241, www .northforkhostel.org) may be off the electric grid, but you don't "rough it" here. A huge storage battery powers phone, fax, and computer with Internet access. You can even recharge your digital camera batteries from it. Propane powers lights, a cooking stove, and a refrigerator, with a few kerosene lights added in. Amenities include a shared living room, fully equipped kitchen, outhouses, washrooms with hot showers, dorm bunks ($15 per person), rooms for couples ($40), and a wood-fired cedar hot tub. Bring linens (or rent them for $5) or sleeping bags and food. In addition, the hostel rents tipis ($35), tent camping spaces ($10), and cabins ($35–45). They also rent mountain bikes, canoes, cross-country skis, and snowshoes for guests. Some facilities are open year round, but make reservations to be sure.

Nearby at **Square Peg Ranch,** the hostel also rents two log homes (sleeping 4 each, $80 per night)—one a 1918 homestead. Propane lights, refrigerator, and cooking ranges stock the equipped kitchens, and wood heats the buildings. Cold running water, solar showers, and outhouses complete the rustic stay. Bring sleeping bags or sheets, food, towels, and containers to haul fresh drinking water from the hostel.

Cabins

Open year-round, the units at **Polebridge Cabins** (265 Polebridge Loop, 406/888-5105, $30–35 per night double occupancy) are stark. Some visitors complain of smoky woodstoves and lack of amenities. Adjacent to the Merc and Northern Lights Saloon, the tiny cabins come equipped with beds, tables, chairs, and propane refrigerators. Bring your sleeping bag, pillow, cooking utensils, a water jug, and a flashlight for middle-of-the-night trips to the outhouse. Call ahead to see if you need to bring firewood.

OUTSIDE POLEBRIDGE

For those looking to get away from it all, **◖ The Way Less Traveled Bed and Breakfast** (16485 North Fork Rd., 406/261-5880, www.thewaylesstraveled.com, open year-round) is about as far away as you can get and still have the comforts of civilization. Here, proprietors Paul and Nancy Winkler encourage guests to forget about the outside world. Located 17 miles north of Polebridge near the Canadian border, the smoke-free, alcohol-free B&B has three themed rooms. Two of the rooms ($85) share a bathroom, but the Lewis and Clark room ($105) has a private bath and deck. The

dining room, where the full breakfast features goodies like cinnamon-raisin-vanilla French toast, is surrounded by wildlife-watching windows; in summer, breakfast on the deck is accompanied by loons singing on a nearby lake. A generator provides power for lights, hot water, a satellite television for those who just cannot live without it, and wireless Internet. While phone lines don't reach this far, you can make Internet calls.

Cabins

The Flathead National Forest (Glacier View Ranger District in Hungry Horse, 406/387-3800, www.fs.fed.us/r1/flathead) maintains six cabins for rent scattered throughout the North Fork. All with a three-night maximum stay, the cabins ($20–65 per night) come with beds, vault toilets outside, equipped kitchens, and outdoor fire pits. Water is carried from streams or pumped, and firewood is supplied. Bring your own bedding and food. They are all nonsmoking and do not permit pets, tents, or RVs. Reservations are mandatory for all the cabins (877/444-6777, www.recreation.gov). After confirmation, the reservation service gives you the cabin combination. You must clean up at the end of your stay and pack any garbage out with you.

In a rather drafty building, **Hornet Lookout** (open year-round, sleeps two) has a 1-mile hike in summer or 11-mile ski or snowmobile trek in winter. The deck at **Schnauss** (open year-round, sleeps 12) yields sweeping views of the Livingston Range, making it a local favorite for its sunrises and sunset alpenglow over Glacier. It has vehicle access right up to the front door and a less than one-mile walk to the North Fork River. Located right on the North Fork River, **Ben Rover** (open year-round, sleeps eight) is convenient for skiing to Bowman in winter, walking to Polebridge in summer, and fishing right out the front door. In a remote forested setting, **Ninko** (Dec.–Mar., sleeps seven) is reached via a 12-mile ski or snowmobile trek. Adjacent to the North Fork Road with drive-up access, **Ford** (May 20–Mar. 10, sleeps eight) was built in 1922 as part of the ranger station. Located north of Ford cabin, **Wurtz** (open year-round, sleeps 12) is an old 1913 homestead on the west side of the North Fork Road.

CAMPING

Don't expect commercial campgrounds here—only more rustic national park or national forest campgrounds. If you require hookups, your nearest options are West Glacier and Columbia Falls. The national forest and national park campgrounds are all first-come, first-serve.

Glacier National Park Campgrounds

Glacier's seasonal North Fork campgrounds (406/888-7800) are only accessible via rough dirt roads. Between rugged roads and smaller sites, these campgrounds don't accommodate huge RVs nor trailer combinations well. Neither do they have hookups nor disposals. But that's precisely their attraction: Fewer people equals solitude and quiet. They all have pit toilets, fire pits, and picnic tables. While the park prohibits firewood collecting in most places, including the campgrounds, you are allowed to collect dry, downed firewood on the Bowman Lake Road and the Inside Road from one mile north of Fish Creek Campground to Kintla Lake. Cutting live timber is not permitted. After fall closures, Bowman and Kintla campgrounds permit primitive camping ($10). You can haul cooking water from lakes and streams to boil or purify. The four campgrounds are buggy in June, serene in August, and closed in winter when the roads bury in snow.

At the foot of Kintla Lake, **❰ Kintla Lake Campground** (late May–mid-Sept., $15 per night) sits 15 miles north of Polebridge. Even by park standards, the tiny 13-site campground in large trees is rough, with hand-pumped water and small sites. One hiking trail leads up lake and beyond to Upper Kintla Lake and Boulder Pass. With no reservations, plan to arrive early enough that if all campsites are full, you can still drive back toward Bowman Lake.

At the foot of Bowman Lake, **❰ Bowman Lake Campground** (late May–mid-Sept., $15

per night) sits seven miles from Polebridge. Its 48 sites, comprising the largest of the region's campgrounds, are sprinkled under a mixed conifer forest. It has running water, and a short five-minute walk leads to the lakeshore and the boat ramp. Trails lead to Quartz Lakes, Numa Lookout, Akokala Lake, and up Bowman Lake to Brown's Pass.

Two tiny campgrounds (July–Nov., $10 per night) sit on the Inside Road—both set in the woods midway between Apgar and Polebridge and best for tent campers who can drive the rugged road. No running water is available, so bring your own or plan to purify stream water. Arrive by mid afternoon, which should allow plenty of time to go elsewhere if the campground is full. **Quartz Creek Campground,** a tiny seven-site campground six miles southeast from Polebridge, is adjacent to Quartz Creek. From the campground, a 6.8-mile rough trail with infrequent maintenance follows the creek up to Lower Quartz Lake. Located 8.3 miles southeast from Polebridge, **Logging Creek Campground** adjacent to Logging Creek Ranger Station has only eight sites. This is a popular site for anglers heading to Logging Lake.

Glacier Backcountry Camping

North Fork trails lead to some of the park's most coveted backcountry campsites in the high country between Bowman and Kintla Lakes. Spectacular **Boulder Pass, Brown's Pass,** and **Hole-in-the-Wall** campsites are snow free late July–early September. Low elevation campsites—great canoe and sea-kayak destinations—are snow free on **Bowman and Kintla Lakes** May–October. Anglers head to **Quartz Lakes** and **Logging Lake.** Pick up permits ($5 per person per night; kids 8–18 $2.50; kids 7 and under free) in person at ranger stations or the Apgar Permit Office (406/888-7900) 24 hours in advance or by reservation ($30). Check additional requirements online: www.nps.gov/glac.

National Forest Campgrounds

Located 20 miles north of Columbia Falls and 13 miles from Apgar on North Fork

Road, **Big Creek Campground** (Glacier View Ranger District, 406/387-3800, mid-May–mid-Oct., $12 per night) sits in Flathead National Forest rather than Glacier Park. It can be accessed via a five-minute gravel road drive from the Camas Road park entrance. Several of the campground's 22 sites can accommodate 40-foot RVs and trailers among its large cottonwoods. Drinking water is available, along with vault toilets. Since the campground sits on the North Fork of the Flathead River, fishing access is easy. You can collect firewood here, but by late season the surrounding woods are scoured. Plan on bringing your own.

FOOD

Some folks drive up the North Fork just to dine at the (**Northern Lights Saloon** (255 Polebridge Loop, 406/888-5669, nightly at 5 P.M. and Sunday 8:30 A.M.–3 P.M. Memorial Day–Oct., only Friday and Saturday nights in winter, entrees $9–18). A chalkboard proudly proclaims the ever-changing menu with seasonal specialties ranging from stuffed morel mushrooms to buffalo, fish, and elk entrees sided with colorful fruit chutneys. Served in bottles or fishbowls, Montana beers or your favorite cocktails accompany healthy portions of food. Friday nights pack the dinky old log building with pizza night, and Sundays for breakfast and lunch. It may be the only game in town, but waiting lines attest to its ambience and flavors.

Open year-round, the (**Polebridge**

Mercantile (265 Polebridge Loop, 406/888-5105, 8 A.M.–6 P.M. daily, until 9 P.M. in summer), or The Merc, as it is called, stocks limited groceries, white gas, propane, fishing tackle, and beer. You can pick up forgotten camping items, but don't expect a broad selection of choices, and there might just be some road dust on the canned foods. However, it's the place to go for yummy baked goodies yanked fresh from the oven—pastries, lunch breads, snacks, and sandwiches to go. You can get three cookies for $1.

Closed for several years after a grizzly ripped apart the building, **Home Ranch Store** (8855 North Fork Rd., 406/888-5572, www.homeranchbottoms.com, 9 A.M.–9 P.M. late May–early Sept.) opened again in 2005 after Beth and Greg Puckett rebuilt the cabin. It's worth a stop just to see the preserved grizzly-clawed floor and photos of the ripped-up wall. Well-signed with hand-painted advertising, the small store sells convenience-type groceries, beer, coffee, pop, T-shirts, firewood, ice, and frozen foods such as ice cream, pizza, and hamburgers. In 2006, the Pucketts added **The Bottoms Tavern** featuring a large log bar where you can get pizza, buffalo wings, potato skins, and daily lunch specials like chili. It's also known for the coldest beer in the North Fork. They fire up the wood stove on chilly days, and folks lounge on the deck when it's warm. Music jams happen here, with a guitar and banjo kept on hand for those with skills. If there's a crowd, they'll stay open later than 9 P.M.

NORTH FORK

GOING-TO-THE-SUN ROAD

Historic Going-to-the-Sun Road is a testament to human ingenuity and nature's wonders. Tunnels, switchbacks, arches, and a narrow two-lane highway cutting across precipitous slopes nod to engineering feats—marvels in themselves. Yet in the road's 52 miles, an incomparable diversity unfolds with surprises around each corner. Cedar rainforests give way to windblown subalpine firs, broad lake valleys lead into glacial corridors, thousand-foot cliff walls abut wildflower gardens, and waterfalls spew from every pore. Defying gravity, ragged peaks rake the sky, crowning all.

This National Historic Landmark is a highway to savor every nook and cranny. "Ooohs" and "aaahs" punctuate every sweep in the road as stunning scenery unfolds. Stopping at myriad pullouts along the road, many sightseers burn through their digital pixels only halfway up the alpine section. The sheer immensity of the glacier-chewed landscape leaves visitors gasping, "I can't fit it all in my camera!"

To stretch the legs, well-signed short paths guide hikers through a dripping rainforest, along a glacial moraine, amid mountain goats, and beside a roaring waterfall. Those ready to put miles on their boots should tackle at least one of the longer high alpine trails, where you'll feel you've reached the apex of the world to send the human spirit soaring.

The Sun Road, as locals call it, is one place you won't want to miss. Its rugged beauty leaves a lasting impression.

HIGHLIGHTS

(Red Bus Tour: Ride over Logan Pass in historic style. The 1937 vintage touring sedans, designed especially for national parks, roll their canvas tops back for superb views and perhaps dousing from the Weeping Wall (page 82).

(Boat Tours: Hop aboard *Little Chief* for the best way to see St. Mary, or aboard the *DeSmet* to see Lake McDonald–the park's two largest lakes (page 83).

(Lake McDonald: Stop to see Glacier's largest lake, which fills a monstrous valley gouged by an ancient ice age glacier. Rent a boat to fish, or swim from any of the pullouts on Going-to-the-Sun Road (page 87).

(Lake McDonald Lodge: Sit on the back porch of the historic lodge gracing Lake McDonald. The lodge's rustic hunting motif harkens back to a pre-national park era when the area served as a hunting preserve (page 87).

(Logan Pass: Touch the Continental Divide, where waters stream toward both the Pacific and the Atlantic. The apex of Going-to-the-Sun Road sprawls with broad alpine meadows teeming with wildflowers and mountain goats (page 91).

(Wild Goose Island Overlook: Bring the camera! Hands down the most photographed spot in the park, tiny Wild Goose Island stares up St. Mary Lake to the rugged skyline of the Continental Divide (page 93).

(Trail of the Cedars: Walk through the easternmost rainforest in the U.S. The trail follows a boardwalk and paved pathway under a tree canopy that keeps temperatures cool even in midsummer (page 95).

(Highline Trail and Granite Park Chalet: Hike a wildflower-packed trail clinging high on cliffs along the Garden Wall to a historic backcountry chalet. Here, bear-watching is a worthy pastime (page 95).

(Siyeh Pass: Climb over one of the most scenic and diverse trails in Glacier. The path wanders wildflower parks and descends colorful sedimentary strata – perhaps touching every color in the spectrum (page 97).

(Swan Mountain Outfitters: Saddle up for the best trail ride in the park. Join the Swan Mountain Outfitters for a ride to Sperry Chalet, where you can lunch in the historic dining room and smack your lips on fresh-baked pie (page 100).

LOOK FOR **(** TO FIND RECOMMENDED SIGHTS, ACTIVITIES, DINING, AND LODGING.

GOING-TO-THE-SUN ROAD

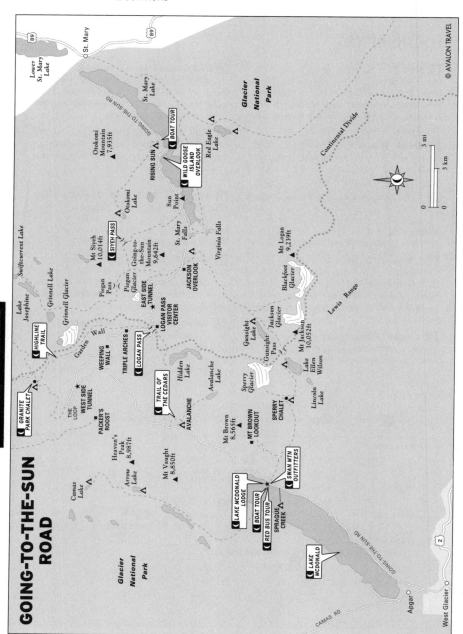

GOING-TO-THE-SUN ROAD

© AVALON TRAVEL

West Glacier

Apgar

CAMAS RD

GOING-TO-THE-SUN RD

LAKE MCDONALD

RED BUS TOUR

BOAT TOUR

LAKE MCDONALD LODGE

SPRAGUE CREEK

SWAN MTN OUTFITTERS

Glacier National Park

Camas Lake

Arrow Lake

Mt Vaught 8,850ft

Heaven's Peak 8,987ft

THE LOOP

PACKER'S ROOST

WEST SIDE TUNNEL

GRANITE PARK CHALET

HIGHLINE TRAIL

Garden Wall

WEEPING WALL

TRIPLE ARCHES

LOGAN PASS

TRAIL OF THE CEDARS

AVALANCHE

Mt Brown 8,565ft

MT BROWN LOOKOUT

Hidden Lake

Avalanche Lake

Sperry Glacier

SPERRY CHALET

Lincoln Lake

Lake Ellen Wilson

Gunsight Lake

Gunsight Pass

Jackson Glacier

Mt Jackson 10,052ft

Lake Josephine

Lake

Swiftcurrent Lake

Grinnell Lake

Grinnell Glacier

Piegan Pass

Piegan Glacier

EAST SIDE TUNNEL

LOGAN PASS VISITOR CENTER

Mt Siyeh 10,014ft

SIYEH PASS

Going-to-the-Sun Mountain 9,642ft

St. Mary Falls

JACKSON OVERLOOK

Virginia Falls

Mt Logan 9,239ft

Blackfoot Glacier

Lewis Range

Otokomi Mountain 7,935ft

Otokomi Lake

Sun Point

RISING SUN

BOAT TOUR

WILD GOOSE ISLAND OVERLOOK

Red Eagle Lake

St. Mary Lake

Lower St. Mary Lake

St. Mary

Glacier National Park

Continental Divide

89

89

2

GOING-TO-THE-SUN RD

3 mi

3 km

0

0

HISTORY
Early Development
By 1895, Lake McDonald boomed with tourism brought on by the railroad's arrival in West Glacier. Hauling a 40-foot steamboat up from Flathead Lake, George Snyder shuttled guests from Apgar to his 12-room hotel where Lake McDonald Lodge currently sits. With Sperry Glacier's discovery in 1896, Snyder's guests had a popular horse trip destination above his lodge. Funded by Great Northern Railway, Dr. Lyman Sperry and 15 of his students built the Gunsight Pass and Sperry spur trail to accommodate travel between St. Mary and Lake McDonald. While the west side surged with turn-of-the-century tourism, on the east side, Roes Creek (Rose Creek at Rising Sun) boomed as a short-lived mining town—vacated with the Alaska gold rush.

Lodges and Chalets
Under dubious circumstances—perhaps a poker game—ownership of Snyder's hotel went to John and Olive Lewis in 1906, who moved the old hotel and built a cedar and stone lodge facing Lake McDonald. Opening in 1914, Lewis's Glacier Hotel imitated the Swiss theme of Great Northern Railway's hotels and chalets springing up parkwide. Lewis promoted Going-to-the-Sun Road, spending his own money to cut part of the route along the lake, grade the road, and build bridges. From West Glacier, the road reached his hotel in 1922, increasing the hotel's visitors with automobile popularity.

Because of Lewis's foothold in McDonald Valley, Great Northern Railway ignored the area around the park's largest lake—instead frenetically erecting chalets between 1912 and 1914 at Sun Point, Gunsight Lake, and Sperry and using Sperry's trail over Gunsight Pass to link the three. A year later and quite behind schedule, Granite Park Chalet was finally completed—a destination from Many Glacier Hotel and Sun Point. With packed bunk-bed dorms and canvas tents outside, Granite and Sperry could house 144 and 152 guests, nearly four times the number each sleep today. Their

popularity increased in the 1920s as wealthy easterners spent an average of 21 days in the park touring on horseback with Park Saddle Company. However, Gunsight Chalet lasted only five years, wiped out by an avalanche.

In 1930, Great Northern Railway purchased Lewis's hotel, adding it to its lodge arsenal. When ownership changed, so did the name—to Lake McDonald Lodge. Two years later, the lodge was sold to the National Park Service.

Ironically, along with the Depression and increased auto travel, Going-to-the-Sun Road, which was completed in 1932, hastened the demise of the chalets. Horse-trip visitation dropped from 26 to 3 percent. Natty automobile drivers sought more affordable places to stay. In 1940, the railroad company built East Glacier Auto Cabins (now Rising Sun Motor Inn), where two people could rent a cabin without a shower for $1.75. Finally, World War II park closures, deteriorating buildings, and increased costs of supplying the chalets taxed the railway company to the point where it razed Going-to-the-Sun Chalets and sold Sperry and Granite Park to the National Park Service for a dollar.

Building the Road
Nearly 20 years of planning and construction went into building Going-to-the-Sun Road, fueled by burgeoning excitement over the automobile. While proponents proposed various passes for the "Transmountain Highway," its original name, in 1918 Logan Pass won the park service selection. However, the plan called for 15 switchbacks up the west side, replaced later with one long switchback. Over several years, Congress appropriated $2 million for its construction.

Surveying the route required tenacity to hang by ropes over cliffs and tiptoe along skinny ledges—perhaps causing the 300 percent crew turnover in three months. Over six seasons, three companies excavated rock using only small blast explosives and minimal power tools to create tunnels, bridges, Triple Arches, and guard walls. With power equipment unable to reach the East Side Tunnel, crews cleared its 405-foot length by hand-boring 5.33 feet per day.

In 1932, during late fall, the first automobile chugged over Logan Pass. The following July, over 4,000 people attended dedication ceremonies at the pass, celebrating the road's completion and ending with a peace ceremony for the Blackfeet, Kootenai, and Flathead tribes.

Although guardrails, surfacing, and grading were not completed until 1935, nearly 40,000 visitors in its first year flocked to the road despite its rough tread and the Depression. Until the late 1930s, crushed rock covered its surface. Finally, in 1938, the park service embarked on a 14-year project to pave the scenic highway—at last completed in 1952.

Exploring Going-to-the-Sun Road

Going-to-the-Sun Road connects West Glacier and St. Mary by 52 miles of one of the most scenic highways in America. The road joins two immense glacier-carved valleys—McDonald and St. Mary—via Logan Pass, which crosses the Continental Divide at 6,646 feet. From Lake McDonald, the road ascends up 3,400 feet to the pass; from St. Mary, it rises about 2,200 feet. Given the road's extremes in elevation, it takes rash punishment from brutal weather.

ENTRANCE STATIONS

Both ends of Going-to-the-Sun Road have entrance stations: one at West Glacier, the other at St. Mary. Staffed during daylight hours all summer long and off-season on weekends, the stations have national park maps and the *Waterton-Glacier Guide,* the park's newspaper which is updated twice annually. If you miss working hours, you can use the self-pay cash-only kiosks on the right just beyond the booths. If you don't have an annual pass, seven-day passes cost $25 per vehicle or $12 for individuals on foot, bicycles, or motorcycles. (Rates drop to $15 and $10 Nov.–Apr.)

VISITORS CENTER

The one place everyone wants to go is Logan Pass, but its visitors center is small and the parking lot cramped on sunny days. We all put up with the hassle, for no one wants more pavement and a larger building impinging the meadows. Unprepared visitors arrive expecting a resort atmosphere at **Logan Pass**

Visitor Center (406/888-7800, 9 A.M.–7 P.M. mid-June–Labor Day, 9:30 A.M.–4:30 P.M. daily Labor Day–Sept.). It's a seasonal outpost with a tiny Glacier Natural History Bookstore (406/888-5756, www.glacierassociation.org), an information desk, and a few displays. Set your hand in the grizzly paw cast to marvel at the size difference!

While a fireplace crackles upstairs on cold days, one bench allows only a few to snuggle up to its heat. Restrooms downstairs have the coldest running water you'll ever dip your fingers into. In shoulder seasons when the water is turned off, port-a-potties line the parking lot. No food or beverages are sold here, not even coffee and candy bars. Due to the elevation, expect harsher weather—wind, rain, and snow even in August. Don't be surprised if you left the lowlands in sunny summer only to arrive at Logan Pass in winter.

SHUTTLES AND TOURS
Shuttles

To avoid Logan Pass parking lot hassles, shuttles are the way to go. Better yet, shuttles enable point-to-point hiking on some of Glacier's most spectacular trails. In 2007, Glacier added a free shuttle service (406/888-7800, www.nps.gov/glac) to eliminate congestion on Going-to-the-Sun Road during construction. These shuttles are extremely popular: Mid-summer, you may find yourself waiting in lines to get on, or see full shuttles bypass a stop. But going car-free to trailheads is still worth it, compared to not finding a parking spot.

RED BUSES

In the 1930s, red buses led sightseeing tours in Glacier. Built by Ohio's White Motor Company specifically for national park touring, the red buses became a symbol of the country's western parks. Yosemite, Yellowstone, Zion, Mount Rainier, Grand Canyon, and Bryce all had their own fleets, and so did Glacier. Nearly 500 red buses toured visitors in Glacier, Yosemite, and Yellowstone alone.

Although red bus fleets disappeared from the other parks in the 1950s, Glacier steadfastly held on to its 33 scarlet prizes, upgrading parts as necessary. The canvas tops rolled back to create an open-air touring car, so guests rode in historic style over Going-to-the-Sun Road, covering up with blankets if temperatures chilled down. Nicknamed "jammers" or "gear jammers" for the tremendous noise their gears made while shifting, the vintage 25-foot-long 17-passenger vehicles first drove Glacier's curvy roads in 1937 as the park's second generation of touring sedans. Sixty years later, as automatic transmissions replaced the manual transmissions and power steering eased driving Going-to-the-Sun Road's curves, jammers continued to tour folks through Glacier until 1999, when safety concerns sidelined the red rigs.

Glacier Park, Inc., operator of the historic park lodges, owned the jammers, but after the fleet was donated to the National Park Foundation, Ford Motor Company jumped aboard to rehabilitate the vehicles in keeping with their historic appearance. In the process, Ford also converted them to bi-fuel, able to run on gasoline or propane. New wiring, interiors, and paint

© BECKY LOMAX

grillwork on red jammer bus (Ford revamped original White line)

jobs completed the project. (Check a jammer up close: You'll see both White and Ford logos.) Thirty-two of the red buses are back in service; one was kept intact for historical value.

You may also see uniformed park employees pedaling red retro bikes to match the historic buses. The bikes are part of a National Park Service program to employ alternative transportation in the park, save fuel costs, and reduce emissions. The bikes were purchased with help from The Glacier Fund, a nonprofit organization.

GOING-TO-THE-SUN ROAD

The park service runs **free shuttles** over Going-to-the-Sun Road, July 1–Labor Day, stopping at 16 locations. Get on or off at any of the stops denoted by interpretive signs—each one featuring a different animal print. No tickets are needed; no reservations are taken. Both east- and west-side shuttles begin running up the road at 7:00 A.M.; the last shuttles depart Logan Pass at 7 P.M.

On the west side, shuttles depart every 15–30 minutes with stops at the Apgar Transit Center, Sprague Creek Campground, Lake McDonald Lodge, Avalanche Creek, The Loop, and Logan Pass. The 32-mile ride from the Apgar Transit Center to Logan Pass takes 90 minutes or more. Several different routes service the west side: confirm your destination when boarding to be sure you catch the right bus.

On the east side, shuttles depart every 30 minutes, starting at St. Mary Visitor Center.

The one-hour shuttle reaches Logan Pass in 18 miles after stopping at Rising Sun, Sun Point, Sunrift Gorge, St. Mary Falls, Gunsight Pass Trailhead, and Siyeh Bend. At St. Mary for a fee, you can connect with the **Glacier Park, Inc.** (406/892-2525, www .glacierparkinc.com, no reservations, cash only) daily van service running early June–late September linking St. Mary with East Glacier, Two Medicine, Many Glacier, and Waterton ($8–40 one-way; kids 11 and under half price). For hikers on The Highline or Piegan Pass trails dropping to Many Glacier, two afternoon shuttles run July–Labor Day (4:45 and 5:30 P.M., $8 one way) between Many Glacier and St. Mary.

For those arriving by Amtrak with reservations at Lake McDonald Lodge, GPI also runs a shuttle late May through late September ($6 per person) to and from the Belton Depot in West Glacier. Reservations are mandatory.

Flathead-Glacier Transportation (406/ 892-3390 or 800/829-7039; www.fgtrans .com) also runs shuttles by reservation only between Glacier International Airport and Lake McDonald Lodge ($50 one way).

◖ Red Bus Tour

In historic style, red jammer buses tour visitors over Going-to-the-Sun Road in vintage 1930s White Motor Company sedans operated by **Glacier Park, Inc.** (406/892-2525, www.glacierparkinc.com, mid-June–mid-Sept., $35–78; kids 11 and under half-price, meals and park entrance fees not included). On good weather days, the jammers (tour bus drivers known for their storytelling) roll the canvas tops back for spectacular views of the Continental Divide. Without a roof, it's one of the most scenic ways to feel the expanse of the glacier-carved terrain. From Lake McDonald Lodge, tours depart daily to explore Going-to-the-Sun Road: the 7.5-hour Crown of the Continent tour departs at 10 A.M. and three-hour Logan Pass tours depart four times daily. You can make reservations by phone or at hotel activity desks.

For those staying at Rising Sun Motor Inn,

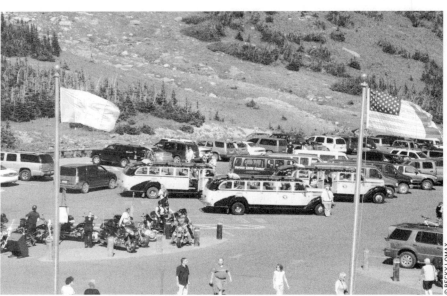

Jammer buses line up at Logan Pass at the top of the Continental Divide.

© BECKY LOMAX

daily tours originating at Many Glacier Hotel or Glacier Park Lodge will stop to pick up riders. Inquire at the motel's front desk.

Native American Tour

A Blackfeet-led tour provides a different perspective with emphasis on Native American cultural and natural history. **Sun Tours** (406/226-9220 or 800/786-9220, www.glacier suntours.com, June–Sept., meals and park entrance fees not included) drives air-conditioned 25-passenger comfortable coaches with extra-big windows for taking in the massive mountains on Going-to-the-Sun Road. You can catch four-hour Logan Pass tours (adults $40, kids $15) daily from St. Mary (9 A.M.) with a Rising Sun pickup shortly following or from Apgar and West Glacier (9:30 A.M.). Seven-hour daily tours (adults $70, kids $20) leave East Glacier (8 A.M.) and Browning (8:30 A.M.) to drive up the east side of Going-to-the-Sun Road, exploring Logan Pass, and driving down the west side to Big Bend to see the Weeping Wall before returning. Make reservations at least one day in advance.

◖ Boat Tours

Lake McDonald and St. Mary, the park's largest lakes, dominate the lowlands here, and **Glacier Park Boat Company** (406/257-2426, www.glacierparkboats.com) runs boat tours on both. You buy tickets (cash only) at the boat docks. In high season, purchase your spot a few hours in advance; midday, cocktail, and sunset cruises fill up. Some launches have ranger naturalists aboard (check *The Glacier Explorer* for scheduled times).

At the boat dock behind Lake McDonald Lodge, hop on the historic *DeSmet* (late May–late Sept., adults $14; kids half-price) for a one-hour tour down the lake at 11 A.M. (through early Sept. only) and 1:30, 3:00, 5:30 (July–late Aug. only), and 7 P.M. With a 90-passenger capacity, the 1930 vintage 57-foot wooden boat tours to the lake's core, where surrounding snow-clad peaks pop into sight. Go for a prime seat on the top deck, even in marginal weather—just bring along a jacket.

At the Rising Sun boat dock on St. Mary Lake, catch a ride on *Little Chief* (mid-June–early Sept., adults $20; kids half-price) as it braves the lake's choppy waters. Views of Sexton Glacier and Wild Goose Island can't be beat, but be ready for some healthy wind. Four daily departures offer different options for the 90-minute cruise: at 10 A.M., noon, and 2 and 4 P.M. Some add guided 15-minute hikes to Baring Falls or two-hour hikes to St. Mary Falls. The one-hour sunset cruise costs only $14 for adults.

SERVICES

Prepare for driving Going-to-the-Sun Road because no services exist on Logan Pass. The closest gas stations are outside the park at St. Mary and West Glacier. With no food services available at the pass, you'll enjoy your time better in less of a rush if you pack a lunch.

Restrooms are few and far between on this historic highway. Flush toilets and running water (at least cold) are available at Lake McDonald Lodge, Logan Pass Visitor Center, and Rising Sun. New vault toilets (no running water) are available at Avalanche Picnic Area, Logan Creek, The Loop, Jackson Glacier Overlook, and Sun Point.

Hot showers (one token $1.25 for eight minutes) are available at Rising Sun. For laundry, you'll have to hit West Glacier or St. Mary.

While some cell phones pick up service at Logan Pass, most do not work throughout the road's length due to the high surrounding peaks and narrow valleys. No Internet service is available at the lodges or chalets; if you have a laptop, you can plug in at Lake McDonald Lodge to dial up your own service long distance. Public pay phones are at Lake McDonald Lodge and Rising Sun as well as Avalanche Campground.

Find ATM machines at Lake McDonald Lodge and Rising Sun Motor Inn. Lake McDonald Lodge area also has a small seasonal post office across from the camp store; see current hours posted on the door.

Find local newspapers in gift shops and camp stores at Lake McDonald Lodge and

Rising Sun. They carry the *Great Falls Tribune* and Flathead Valley's *Daily Interlake.*

Shopping

The gift shops in Lake McDonald Lodge and Two Medicine Grill at Rising Sun and both camp stores carry a good selection of guidebooks, coffee-table photo books, maps, and natural-history books along with gifts, T-shirts, postcards, and jewelry.

Emergencies

If you have an emergency on Going-to-the-Sun Road, contact the park service (406/888-7800). If you cannot leave the scene to make a phone call, flag down a vehicle heading up or down the pass to notify the nearest ranger (usually at Logan Pass, St. Mary Visitor Center, or by phone from Lake McDonald Lodge). The nearest hospitals are North Valley Hospital (1600 Hospital Way, Whitefish, 406/863-3631), Kalispell Regional Medical Center (310 Sunny View Ln., Kalispell, 406/752-5111), or Northern Rockies Medical Center (802 2nd St. E., Cut Bank, 406/873-2251).

DRIVING TOUR

Of all the driving tours in Glacier National Park, **Going-to-the-Sun Road,** the 52-mile historic transmountain highway bisecting Glacier's heart, stands in a class by itself. For some, scary tight curves that hug cliff walls produce white-knuckled driving. But for most, its beauty, diversity, color, flora, fauna, and raw wildness will leave an impression like no other. For that reason, many park visitors drive it more than once during their stay.

In July and August, expect crowds, especially around Logan Pass. To avoid the hordes, drive in early morning or early evening, when lighting is often better for photography and wildlife is more active. In high season, Logan Pass parking lot crams full by 11 A.M. Signs at the entrance will indicate so and include an estimated wait of 30–60 minutes for a parking space. If the parking lot is full, forego Logan Pass for the time being and return later in the day. While pullouts sit a half-mile east and west

of the pass, the shoulderless road does not afford safe walking to the pass, and tromping across the fragile alpine Oberlin meadows is taboo. Avalanche, The Loop, and St. Mary Falls parking lots also pack full.

Although you can drive its 52 miles in less than two hours with no stops, most visitors take all day. Construction, sightseeing, and traffic slow travel. Don't be anxious with it; just sit back and enjoy the view. Pack drinking water, snacks, and a lunch to avoid frustration over lack of food services. Most restaurants around Glacier sell box or sack lunches; order them the day before you want them. The road passes through a wonderland whose development has been kept in check; no one wants to see that changed to accommodate hunger.

Season

Going-to-the-Sun Road is undergoing a decade of federally funded construction to

Alder Creek plunges under the Sun Road.

DRIVING TIPS: GOING-TO-THE-SUN ROAD

FIVE SIGNS OF A ROOKIE GOING-TO-THE-SUN ROAD DRIVER

A burning brake smell.

Hint: Use second gear for slowing speeds on descents rather than riding the brakes all the way down the mountain.

A dangling extension mirror.

Hint: Retract or remove those extension mirrors for fifth wheels or trailers before driving the narrow west side below Logan Pass.

A center-line hugger.

Hint: Stay in your own lane. You're more apt to scrape another vehicle on the skinny road than drive off the cliff. If you're acrophobic, let someone else drive.

A traffic slug.

Hint: Rather than holding up traffic by slowing to a stop in the road to take pictures, pull off into one of the many pullouts.

A car videographer.

Hint: While a handheld video camera hanging out a vehicle window seems like a grand idea, the Sun Road is bumpy. Videos come out very amateurish, and locals laugh at folks who do it.

OTHER TIPS

Follow posted speed limits and turn on your headlights.

During high season (mid-July–mid-Aug.), Logan Pass parking lot fills up by late morning with long waits for parking spaces. Consider getting an early start for touring Going-to-the-Sun Road.

Take lunch, snacks, and drinks. Between Lake McDonald Lodge and Rising Sun, no food or drinks are sold.

Watch for bicyclists. Although bicycle restrictions are in effect during July and August on Going-to-the-Sun Road's west side, the narrow roadway, lack of shoulder, and curves squeeze cyclists. Show them courtesy by slowing down and easing around them.

Expect construction delays. Reconstruction work usually reduces traffic to a single lane controlled by construction personnel. When workers are not present, timed traffic lights control flow. Obey both, for the single lanes allow for no pullover room for passing.

Check for summer closures. Heavy rains, snowstorms, fires, and accidents may close portions of the road – even in July and August. Entrance and ranger stations as well as lodges have current updates of the road status available.

Be prepared for all types of weather. Sunny skies may prevail in the valleys while visitors at Logan Pass creep along slowly in a dense fog on icy pavement.

Passengers with a fear of heights should sit on the driver's side of the car for ascending the west side and descending the east. This will put you farthest away from the cliff edges.

For updates on Going-to-the-Sun Road status, call 406/888-7800 or check www.nps.gov/glac.

GOING-TO-THE-SUN ROAD

rehabilitate the aging and ailing roadway. Shoulder seasons are used to accelerate construction, while keeping the entire length open mid-June to mid-September for sightseers. That's provided snow allows for a mid-June opening. On heavy snow years with stormy springs, Logan Pass has opened later—July 3, at the latest. During the season, snowstorms, washouts, and accidents may cause temporary closures. The park updates road status reports regularly: 406/888-7800 or www.nps.gov/glac.

During spring and fall, when parts of Going-to-the-Sun Road are closed to vehicles, sometimes bicyclists and hikers can tour the snow-free road, especially on weekends when construction crews may not be working. Call the park first, as construction changes daily. The traditional late fall and early spring closure runs from Avalanche to Rising Sun. During winter, the road is closed from St. Mary to Lake McDonald Lodge, but cross-country skiers and snowshoers trek lowland corridors.

Road Restrictions for Vehicles

Large vehicles are restricted on Going-to-the-Sun Road between Avalanche Campground and Sun Point. Because the road is narrow and over-hung, vehicles must be smaller than 21 feet in length, 10 feet high, and 8 feet wide. These dimensions include side mirrors, bumpers, towed units, and bike racks. Remember to pull in side extension mirrors; you'll see ones claimed by the cliff wall reflecting from the road. Even though smaller truck-camper units may be legal, drivers will still feel pinched on the skinny road.

Road Maintenance

Maintenance work seems interminable on Going-to-the-Sun Road. Avalanches, torrential downpours, and snows all wreak havoc. Constantly. Summer snowstorms and heavy rains cause washouts requiring annual repairs. Here, road construction is a fact of life, but it's also a unique chance to watch how workers cling to the side of thousand-foot cliffs.

The alpine section of Going-to-the-Sun Road is in a critical state—from drainage damage to wear-and-tear from the 475,000 vehicles that travel the road annually. Because heavy snows constrict road work to four to six months, construction must happen during summer. Starting in 2007, the park embarked on an 8- to 10-year $240–270 million rehabilitation project to improve road safety, parking, guardwalls, drainage, cracks, and deteriorating road beds—all while maintaining the historic character, fabric, and width of the road and done without closing the road during the peak visitor season.

Prior to mid-June and after mid-September, some road portions may be closed to speed up construction. But during high season and peak hours, drivers should see a maximum traffic delay of 30 minutes total while crossing the road. Usually this is true. Longer delays are scheduled for early mornings and evenings.

While road construction elicits complaints and moans, repairing this road is not like re-paving a local highway! You can watch state-of-the-art road technology at work in a cliff-ridden

Plows dig snow out of Logan Pass parking lot.

GOING-TO-THE-SUN ROAD

© BECKY LOMAX

environment: Cranes and bobcats jockey for position along one narrow lane, somewhat akin to working on a tightrope. Anyone with a mild engineering interest will be blown away, and you get a feel for the immensity of the original road's building.

Plowing Going-to-the-Sun Road

Every April, snowplows take to Going-to-the-Sun Road to heave over 100,000 cubic yards of snow off the pavement. It's a big deal here. Drifts range 30–50 feet thick from The Loop to Logan Pass. Just east of the pass, a 50- to 80-foot-deep snowdrift, the Big Drift, clings to a 40-degree slope. No wonder the job takes several months! For the duration, 25–30 equipment operators, mechanics, and snow specialists dig in with over 20 different machines—excavators, bulldozers, sweepers, loaders, and rotary blowers.

With over 60 avalanche swaths between The Loop and Siyeh Bend, slides smash into the road, forcing crews to replow the same pavement over and over, or plow themselves out at night. Compounding the snow removal difficulties, heavy rains, fog, and whiteouts hamper progress.

When spring snows prohibit the road opening until late June, everyone gets nervous: from local businesses to the governor of Montana. The opening of the road is bound to the local economy. Glacier Park's website tracks plow progress with daily reports (www.nps.gov/glac), and the park's communications center phones (406/888-7800) post updates. In May, the National Park Service leads a "Show Me Day" to show visitors the plowing operations. Call the park for details. If avalanches threaten, the event will be canceled in favor of safety.

SIGHTS

Going-to-the-Sun Road is a sight to behold! The following sights are listed as visitors see them driving from Lake McDonald to St. Mary. Approximate mileposts are listed parenthetically with eastbound first, beginning at the road's junction with Highway 2, followed by westbound mileposts beginning with the junction

with Highway 89. The total mileage is actually 50.8 miles, yet maps claim 52 miles. Where the missing 1.2 miles has gone, no one knows, nor is anyone too concerned about the math.

◖ Lake McDonald

The largest lake in the park, Lake McDonald (2.8–11, 39.9–47.9) hogs a valley hollowed out by a monstrous several-thousand-foot-deep glacier. Lining both sides, Howe and Snyder Ridges are lateral moraines left from that ice age bulldozer. At 10 miles long and 1.5 miles wide, the lake is big enough to plummet to a frigid depth at 472 feet. Its deep waters collect from melting glaciers and snowfields high atop the Continental Divide. Kayakers and boaters tour the shoreline, anglers pull trout from its pool, and a few water-skiers brave the cold. The road hugs its southeastern shore with frequent pullouts for access. If rare glassy waters reflect Stanton Peak, shoot off photos!

◖ Lake McDonald Lodge

At Lake McDonald's east end, the historic Lake McDonald Lodge (11.2, 39.2) was designed to resemble a hunting lodge. A taxidermist's delight or an animal-rights activist's nightmare, the tall, stately cedar-log lobby is cluttered with stuffed goats and mounted heads of bighorn sheep, deer, elk, and moose. Look for the woodland caribou—still represented among the furry creatures here, even though it no longer exists in the park. Because the lodge was built prior to the road, the front door actually opens on lakeside, facing the original boat approach. In 1976, the lodge was listed on the National Register of Historic Places. Explore the lobby, take a boat tour, or sit a spell in a log rocker on the back porch.

McDonald Creek

Originating near the Continental Divide, McDonald Creek (12.8–22, 29.6–38) is the longest river in the park at 25.8 miles and definitely more than a creek, but we won't quibble about nomenclature here. The Sun Road follows the river path until it begins its ascent to Logan Pass. In the seven miles where the road borders the river, several tumbling rapids and waterfalls are worth a stop. But be extremely cautious of hazardous slippery rocks. Unseen algae, mosses, and swift cold waters have been lethal for the unwary. At **Upper McDonald Creek Falls** (14.7, 36.2), waters roil through scoured rock; wooden stairs drop you onto a convenient observation platform right over the falls.

? Trail of the Cedars   ½ mile hike

Trail of the Cedars (16.6, 34.1) travels through a rainforest, the easternmost in the country. On a 0.7-mile wheelchair-accessible boardwalk and pavement, the shaded trail passes water-carved Avalanche Gorge. Several-hundred-year-old western red cedars, hemlocks, and towering black cottonwoods form a dense canopy that cools the forest floor where mosses, lichens, Pacific yew, and devils club grow in the rich duff. Fire has bypassed this small ecosystem, leaving gigantic old grandfather trees—some toppling from heavy rains, snows, and winds. You'll need many arms to hug one large cedar growing through the boardwalk.

Avalanche Paths

As the road sneaks through a slim corridor between the Glacier Wall and Mount Cannon (19.5, 31.3), look for avalanche paths. Snow, set in motion sometimes thousands of feet above, roars down gullies uprooting trees and snapping them like toothpicks. In early summer, scour the slope for remnants of avalanches— ice, snow, and rock rubble piled up. Grizzly and black bears forage along these avalanche paths in hopes of stumbling across some unfortunate mountain goat. Bring binoculars or spotting scopes to aid in bear-watching from a safe distance.

West Side Tunnel

An engineering marvel, the West Side Tunnel (24, 26.8) is 192 feet long with two stunning alcoves framing Heavens Peak. In early season, the alcoves drip with thin-sheeted waterfalls, but hop through the spray to reach the dry rock-hewn guardwalls. Photographers,

especially, will enjoy working the alcoves into framing pictures of Heavens Peak. To walk into the tunnel, park below in large pullouts on both sides; above the tunnel, the road narrows, making walking hazardous. In early season, a waterfall on the tunnel's uphill side splatters car windshields. If you're driving a convertible, too bad.

The Loop

Going-to-the-Sun Road has one massive hairpin turn known as The Loop (24.7, 26.1). With parking lots both below and above the switchback, it's a popular stop for views and the trailhead to Granite Park Chalet. Across the valley, the 8,987-foot **Heavens Peak** makes a stunning backdrop for a family photo. In early season, it will be snow covered; by late August, only a few ice fields remain. In 2003, the **Trapper Fire** blew through The Loop; evidence of the burn lingers here in skeletal trees.

Heavens Peak through West Side Tunnel alcove

Haystack Falls on Going-to-the-Sun Road

Bird Woman and Haystack Falls

About two miles past The Loop, look for the sign marking Bird Woman Falls (mile 27, 24.7). Many tourists assume the sign denotes the cascade crossing under the road. That stair-step waterfall is **Haystack Creek,** whose ledges evolved from eroding layers of Belt Sea sedimentary rock created between 800 million and 1.6 billion years ago. To see Bird Woman Falls, look across the valley for waters tumbling nearly 500 feet from a hanging valley, carved by a glacier in the last 6,000 years and lounging like a hammock in between Mount Oberlin, Mount Cannon, and Clements Peak. Early summer runoff pumps both falls full of water that dwindles to late-August trickles.

Glaciation Exhibit

Look for a signed interpretive pullout (28.3, 22.5) with terrific views of McDonald Valley.

THE CONTINENTAL DIVIDE

At Logan Pass, you can take your photo next to a sign that says you're atop the Continental Divide. But what is it?

The Continental Divide runs the length of North America from Alaska and the Yukon to Mexico. Along the Rocky Mountains, it is the highest point in the land dividing stream runoff in two directions: the Pacific and the Atlantic. In Glacier Park, the Continental Divide runs along the tops of the Livingston Range from Canada south to Trapper Ridge and West Flattop, where it leaps to the Lewis Range.

To cross the Continental Divide, drive over Logan or Marias Pass. You can hike across the divide on several passes: Brown's, Swiftcurrent, Hidden Lake, Gunsight, Cut Bank, Dawson, Two Medicine, and Firebrand. Beginning in New Mexico, the 3,100-mile Continental Divide Trail finishes its length with its last 110 miles in Glacier National Park.

Glacier's Continental Divide also stands in a class by itself, for it houses a tri-oceanic divide – the only one in the United States. (Canada's Mount Columbia is the continent's other significant three-way oceanic divide.) Not particularly high by Glacier Park standards, Triple Divide Peak stands at only 7,397 feet above sea level. But its placement on the Continental Divide with connecting ridge spurs splits waters in three streams: Hudson Bay Creek, Atlantic Creek, and Pacific Creek. Their names cite their eventual destinations in the continent's major watersheds of the Saskatchewan, Missouri, and Columbia.

On the southeast corner of St. Mary Lake, Divide Mountain with St. Mary Ridge forms the division between waters flowing to Hudson Bay and the Gulf of Mexico. To drive over this unmarked divide, head from St. Mary south on Highway 89.

GOING-TO-THE-SUN ROAD

Triple Arches is one of the Sun Road's striking engineering feats.

Once filled with several-thousand-foot thick ice, the valley's U shape shows the gouging, scouring, and carving of the behemoth glacier as it chugged around the Glacier Wall approximately two million years ago. Through the trough, McDonald Creek courses 26 miles and ends at Lake McDonald. Test your vertigo by gazing 2,500 feet below; you'll see Going-to-the-Sun Road with cars looking tiny like ants as they drive the narrow corridor.

Weeping Wall and Big Bend

As its name implies, the Weeping Wall (29.5, 21.3) does weep, but it's a moody thing. In early summer, the wall wails profusely, enough to douse cars driving the inside lane. Roll up your windows unless you want a shower! In August, drips slow to a simper. At the Weeping Wall, the road affords no room to pull over; instead, drive ahead into the bowl named Big Bend (29.7, 21) to find ample parking on both sides of the road. Here, where avalanches careen from Mount Gould into the bowl, snow often remains until mid-July.

Triple Arches

One of the most striking engineering marvels on Going-to-the-Sun Road, Triple Arches (30.4, 20.2) requires a slow drive to see, for no pullouts offer a good view. You can see this feature only driving uphill, for it sits at the back of downhill traffic. Approximately one and a half miles past Big Bend, you'll come upon the arches abruptly. Start watching for them as you enter a very narrow, curvy part of the road. At several sharp S turns, you'll see them. As you drive over the arches, don't think about the stonework repairs that overhang hundreds of feet of air!

Garden Wall

From Big Bend to Logan Pass (29.7–32, 18.8–21), the peaks above the road actually form an arête, a wall carved by glaciers on two sides. Below its top cliffs, wildflower meadows bloom with every color of the rainbow: white cow parsnip, pink spirea, yellow columbine, purple nodding onion, and blue gentian. In a short half-mile, you may pass over 30 varieties of plants. For this reason, this wild botanical wonderland has been dubbed the Garden Wall. For the best look at the Garden Wall, hike the Highline Trail from Logan Pass.

Oberlin Bend Overlook

As Going-to-the-Sun climbs its final mile to Logan Pass, it sweeps around a large curve below Mount Oberlin. Park on the uphill lane side for the wheelchair-accessible walk to Oberlin Bend Overlook (31.4, 18.4). Mountain goats wander in the subalpine fir thickets here; look for newborns with only nubbins for horns. The overlook provides the best spot for photographing the road's west-side climb, as well as viewing the Continental Divide and peaks marching toward Canada. Look for Mount Cleveland, the park's highest peak.

Logan Pass

Logan Pass (32.6, 18.2) sits atop the Continental Divide at 6,646 feet. With its altitude and location between mountainous hulks,

weather can be chilly here even in midsummer. For evidence, look at the trees—gnarled, growing low in krummholz or thick mats for protection against the elements. Explore the visitors center and scan surrounding slopes for goats, bighorn sheep, and bears. In late July, the wildflowers reach their prime—pink alpine laurel, paintbrush, and monkeyflower. Two must-do unsurpassed trails depart from Logan Pass: Hidden Lake and the Highline Trail to Granite Park Chalet. Meadows at this elevation are fragile with short-lived flora, so stick to the paths.

Big Drift

Those driving over Logan Pass when it first opens get a treat: Big Drift (32.8, 18.1) towers on both sides of the road, making a thin corridor bounded by immense snow walls. Winds deposit heavy snows in this zone just east of Logan Pass. Often 80 feet thick, Big Drift remains the last obstacle for spring road clearing. By August, snow piles melt to small patches and

GOING-TO-THE-SUN ROAD

© BECKY LOMAX

Cross the Continental Divide at Logan Pass.

disappear. In the next few miles, the guardwall is sporadic—just for some added thrill.

Lunch Creek

Spilling from a cirque between Piegan and Pollock peaks, Lunch Creek (33.4, 17.4) makes for a scenic stop at the first bend east of Logan Pass. Sans picnic tables, the pullout's rock guardwall serves as a good impromptu lunch counter. Drag out your binoculars; often bighorn sheep cruise the slopes here, but they're hard to see with their camouflage tan matching the rocks. Fed by a glacier melting into an underground stream, waterfalls spew from the side of Piegan Mountain.

East Side Tunnel

The largest tunnel, the East Side Tunnel (33.8, 17), was excavated entirely by hand—all 408 feet. For safety, flip your headlights on as you drive through this tunnel. To stop for photos, drive through to its downhill side to find pullouts, also good stops for spotting bighorn sheep. Photograph the large peak looming ahead—**Going-to-the-Sun Mountain**—from which the road acquired its name.

Siyeh Bend

Three miles below Logan Pass, the road swoops through Siyeh Bend (35.5, 15.5), with ample parking above and below the curve. The trailhead leads to Piegan and Siyeh Passes via Preston Park, a meadowland of fuchsia paintbrush and purple fleabane. For a short stroll, walk up the creek crossing under the road to the junction of two creeks. The city-block-long walk passes gorgeous wildflower blooms in late July. From Siyeh Bend ("Siyeh" means "Mad Wolf"), named for the 10,014-foot barren peak towering above, you can see Blackfoot Glacier toward the south.

Jackson Glacier Overlook

This is the best view of a glacier on Going-to-the-Sun Road, but binoculars are handy to aid vision. Although trees are beginning to occlude the view from Jackson Glacier Overlook (mile 37.3, 13.4), you can still spot Jackson

Siyeh Bend on Going-to-the-Sun Road

© BECKY LOMAX

Glacier six miles away. One of the six highest peaks in the park, Jackson Peak rises to its west. Jackson Glacier joined its neighboring Blackfoot Glacier in the early 1900s, but the two glaciers melted into separate ice fields by 1939. A trail departs here for Gunsight Lake and Pass.

Sunrift Gorge

A narrow canyon, Sunrift Gorge (40, 10.5) requires a short 75-foot uphill stroll to see it. Baring Creek cascades through the dark gorge like a knife slicing cake. The dank rock walls create a perfect grotto for ferns and mosses. Parking on both sides of the road is somewhat crowded here, and it is a trailhead for Siyeh Pass, although most hikers opt to start at Siyeh Bend and finish here.

Sun Point

The often windy Sun Point (40.6, 10) on St. Mary Lake marks the site of the park's most popular early chalet colony: Going-to-the-Sun Chalets. Accessed via boat from St. Mary, the chalet launched visitors into Glacier's interior. For the best views, walk five minutes on the nature trail from the parking lot to the top of the red-rock promontory, where you'll see Going-to-the-Sun Peak, Fusillade, and the Continental Divide. A trail leads 0.6 mile to Baring Falls and connects to the St. Mary Falls Trail.

St. Mary Lake

The second-largest lake in the park, St. Mary Lake (42.2–49.8, 1–8.6) fills a much narrower valley than its larger counterpart—Lake McDonald. At nine miles long and 292 feet deep, it forms a blue platform out of which several stunning red argillite peaks rise. Its width shrinks in The Narrows (44.1, 6.6) to less than half a mile, where buff-colored Altyn limestone resisted erosion—the most ancient exposed rock sediments on the park's east side. While its waters attract boaters, anglers, water-skiers, and windsurfers launching from Rising Sun, frequent high winds whip up wicked whitecaps in minutes.

◖ Wild Goose Island Overlook

One of the most photographed spots in Glacier Park, tiny Wild Goose Island (43.8, 7) is dwarfed in St. Mary Lake's blue waters. Locate parking on both sides of the road from the signed viewpoint and walk the few steps to the overlook. The Continental Divide serves as the backdrop for the tiny island, with

Fusillade Mountain as the prominent central pyramid. For the best lighting, visit this spot in early morning or at sunset. Shoot a photo, then check the nearest gift shop for the same photo—you'll find it on postcards, on calendars, and in books.

Rising Sun

Rising Sun (44.5, 6.3) on St. Mary Lake is not really a scenic stop so much as one for necessity and services. A picnic area, campground, boat dock and ramp, camp store, restaurant, and cabins make up the area's amenities. It's also a jumping-off spot for hiking to Otokomi Lake and touring St. Mary Lake on the *Little Chief.* To access a beach, head to the picnic area (44.7, 6), but hold on to your hat, for winds often rage here.

Two Dog Flats

A series of grassland meadows interspersed by aspen groves lines the road from Rising Sun to St. Mary. Known as Two Dog Flats (46.5–49, 1.8–4.3), the meadows can be good elk-, coyote-, bear-, and bird-watching areas in early morning or late evening. From here, you can see two hydrological wonders to the south—Triple Divide Peak and Divide Mountain. Triple Divide Peak sits atop the Continental Divide, where its waters head to three seas—the Pacific Ocean, Hudson Bay, and the Caribbean. Divide Peak, along with the sweeping moraine heading east, marks the division between the huge Saskatchewan and Missouri watersheds.

Recreation

HIKING

Hikes off Going-to-the-Sun Road are top-notch, no matter what time of the summer. Around Lake McDonald, trails all begin in the forest, but several climb to undaunted heights. At Logan Pass and eastward, most trails access high alpine meadows and spectacular glacially carved scenery fairly quickly. Shorter trails are crowded in midsummer:

you may feel like you're walking in a parade to St. Mary Falls or Hidden Lake Overlook. If you want to get away from the masses, head for longer hikes that will take you farther into the backcountry: Granite Park Chalet, Siyeh Pass, Piegan Pass, or Gunsight Lake. The hikes described here are in order of their trailheads from west to east, and all are shuttle stops.

Mount Brown Lookout

- Distance: 10.8 miles round-trip
- Duration: 6 hours
- Elevation gain: 4,325 feet
- Effort: strenuous
- Trailhead: Sperry Trailhead across from Lake McDonald Lodge parking lot

One word describes this hike: steep. While the trail starts out climbing through moderate switchbacks, once you turn off the Sperry Trail at 1.8 miles, the next five switchbacks are lung-busters. After these, the remaining 20-some switchbacks level out into a more reasonable ascent.

While trees preclude views for most of this trail, snippets of Mount Edwards poke through now and then. Toward the top, alpine meadows bloom with beargrass and huckleberry patches as the trail works its way along the ridge to the renovated lookout. From this false summit (Mount Brown is higher to the east), you'll get dizzy peering down to Lake McDonald and the lodge. While you zoom binoculars in on Granite Park Chalet, Swiftcurrent Lookout, and the Continental Divide, protect your lunch from the overly curious mountain goats.

Sperry Chalet

- Distance: 12.8 miles round-trip
- Duration: 6.5 hours
- Elevation gain: 3,432 feet
- Effort: strenuous
- Trailhead: Sperry Trailhead across from Lake McDonald Lodge parking lot

The historic chalet is an attraction in itself, serving lunch and homemade desserts to hikers, but many overnight at the chalet, especially to access Sperry Glacier. The climb begins with moderate switchbacks through a hemlock forest. After crossing Snyder Creek at two miles, the trail takes a long traverse around Mount

Edwards, slowly easing up in elevation before switchbacking again up alder-strewn avalanche slopes. Because of the mule and horse trips using this same route, the trail sometimes smells like a barnyard and can be miserable, as you dodge equine droppings buzzing with black flies.

With more than a mile still to climb, you'll spot the chalet clinging to a clifftop high above. The trail crosses Sperry Creek before ascending its final switchbacks, passing the turnoff to Sperry Glacier en route. If mountain goats don't stand in your way, you'll arrive at the dining hall's door, ready for lunch and home-baked pie served inside 11:30 A.M.–5 P.M. To spend the night, you'll need reservations.

Sperry Glacier

- Distance: 8 miles round-trip
- Duration: 4 hours
- Elevation gain: 1,600 feet
- Effort: strenuous
- Trailhead: Sperry Chalet

From the chalet, drop down several switchbacks to the Sperry Glacier trail sign. From here, the trail wraps upward around a glacial cirque below waterfalls and immense cliffs. It switchbacks up past alpine tarns, flower gardens, snowfields lingering in to August, and glacially carved rock ledges before it seemingly disappears into a cliff. But, voilà: A steep stairway leads through the cliff into the basin above.

In the Sperry Glacier basin, a different world awaits. Snowfields, moraines, and ice mark this environment, with trees and flowers very sparse. From here, follow vertical markers across the snow-covered trail to the glacier overlook. Do not walk out on the glacier, which has hidden crevasses and waterways. Seasoned hikers pull a 21-mile round-trip Sperry Glacier hike off in one day from Lake McDonald Lodge: It's a 10-hour-plus day with a 5,000–foot climb followed by a knee-pounding descent.

◖ Trail of the Cedars

- Distance: 0.7-mile loop
- Duration: 30 minutes
- Elevation gain: none
- Effort: easy
- Trailhead: adjacent to Avalanche Campground and Picnic Area

A boardwalk guides hikers through the lush rainforest with interpretive signs. Here, fallen cedars become nurse logs, fertile habitat for hemlocks and tiny foamflowers. Immense black cottonwoods furrow with deep-cut bark. A huge cedar requires more than three people to reach around its girth. At the boardwalk's end, the trail crosses Avalanche Creek, spitting from its narrow gorge. To make a loop, continue on the paved walkway past large burled cedars to return to the trailhead.

Avalanche Lake

- Distance: 4 miles round-trip
- Duration: 2–3 hours
- Elevation gain: 500 feet
- Effort: moderately easy
- Trailhead: use Trail of the Cedars adjacent to Avalanche Campground

One of the most popular hikes, Avalanche Lake is the easiest-to-reach subalpine lake on the west side. Sitting in a steep-cliffed cirque tumbling with waterfalls, the lake attracts anglers and hikers alike. High season sees an endless stream of people, some incredibly ill-prepared with no drinking water and inappropriate footwear like flip-flops or heels. Avoid midday crowds by hiking this trail earlier or later in the day, but not at dawn or dusk.

When Trail of the Cedars crosses Avalanche Creek, turn uphill onto the lake's trail. A short grunt leads above the carved gorge. Be extremely careful: Far too many people have had fatal accidents here. From the gorge, the trail climbs steadily through woods littered with glacial erratics—large boulders strewn when the ice receded. Some still retain scratch marks left from the ice abrading the surface. At the lakeshore, enjoy watching waterfalls, mountain goats, and bears.

Granite Park Chalet via The Loop Trail

- Distance: 8 miles round-trip
- Duration: 4 hours
- Elevation gain: 2,400 feet
- Effort: moderately strenuous
- Trailhead: The Loop

The Loop trail is mostly used by hikers exiting the Highline Trail; however, when the road is only open to The Loop, this trail makes a worthy hike with Granite Park Chalet as a scenic destination. Since the 2003 Trapper Fire, views improved, but lack of shade offers little relief from the sun's blazing heat.

At its beginning, the trail crosses a tumbling creek before joining up with the Packer's Roost trail at 0.6 mile. Note this junction: You do not want to miss it hiking back down. From here, the trail climbs two long switchbacks before it crests into the upper basin to the chalet. In June, you'll have snow in the last mile. Open July–mid-September, the chalet has no running water but does sell candy bars. Bring cash to purchase bottled water, carry your own, or filter water from the campground stream just below the chalet.

◖ Highline Trail and Granite Park Chalet

- Distance: 7.6 miles to Granite Park Chalet, 11.6 miles to The Loop
- Duration: 5–6 hours
- Elevation gain: 830 feet
- Effort: moderate
- Trailhead: across Going-to-the-Sun Road from Logan Pass parking lot

© BECKY LOMAX

Highline Trail heads north from Logan Pass.

Many first-time hikers stop every ten feet to take photos on this hike that scares severe acrophobes with its exposed thousand-foot dropoffs. The trail drops from Logan Pass through a cliff walk above the highway before crossing a flowerland that gave the Garden Wall arête its name. At three miles, nearly all of the elevation gain packs into one climb: Haystack Saddle appears to be the top, but it is only halfway. After the high point, the trail drops and swings through several large bowls before passing Bear Valley to reach Granite Park Chalet atop a knoll at 6,680 feet.

En route, side trails lead to Grinnell Glacier Overlook (1.6 steep miles round-trip) and Swiftcurrent Lookout (4.6 miles round-trip). To exit the area, some hikers opt to hike out over Swiftcurrent Pass to Many Glacier (7.6 miles) and catch the Glacier Park, Inc. shuttle; backpackers continue on to Fifty Mountain

(11.9 miles farther) and Goat Haunt (22.5 miles farther). Most day hikers head down The Loop trail (4 miles) to catch the hiker shuttle.

The chalet (open July–mid-Sept.) does not have running water. Plan on purchasing bottled water here, carrying your own, or filtering water from the campground stream below the chalet. Day hikers may also use the outdoor picnic tables or chalet dining room but do not have access to the kitchen. On a rainy day, a warm fire offers respite from the bluster and a chance to dry out. Pop and candy bars are sold, too.

Hidden Lake Overlook

- Distance: 3 miles round-trip

- Duration: 2 hours

- Elevation gain: 550 feet

- Effort: moderate

- Trailhead: behind Logan Pass Visitor Center

Regardless of crowds, Hidden Lake Overlook is a spectacular hike. The trail is often buried under feet of snow until mid-July or later, but tall lodgepoles mark the route. Once the trail melts out, a boardwalk climbs the first half through alpine meadows where fragile shooting stars and alpine laurel dot the landscape with pink. The trail ascends through argillite: Look for evidence of mud-cracked and ripple-marked rocks from the ancient Belt Sea.

The upper trail climbs past moraines, waterfalls, mountain goats, and bighorn sheep. At Hidden Pass, the trail reaches the overlook with views down to Hidden Lake's blue waters. For ambitious hikers or anglers, the trail continues 1.5 miles down to the lake. Just remember: What drops 675 feet, must come back up!

Piegan Pass

- Distance: 9 miles round-trip, 12.8 to Many Glacier

- Duration: 4–5 hours

- Elevation gain: 1,670 feet

- Effort: moderate

- Trailhead: Siyeh Bend

Piegan Pass, named for the Pikuni or Piegan tribe of Blackfeet, is a reasonably unpopulated trail. After climbing two miles through subalpine forest and turning north at the first trail junction, the trail breaks out into Preston Park, bursting with purple fleabane, blue gentians, white valerian, and fuchsia paintbrush. As the trail gains altitude, Piegan Glacier is visible above. A signed trail junction splits the Piegan Pass trail from the Siyeh Pass trail.

Shortly after the junction, the Piegan Pass trail heads into the seemingly barren alpine zone as it crosses the base of Siyeh Peak. But look carefully, for all kinds of miniature flowers bloom here. In a long traverse, the trail sweeps around a large bowl to Piegan Pass, tucked under the Continental Divide. Rather than returning to Siyeh Bend, some hikers opt for continuing another 8.3 miles to Many Glacier Hotel, where they can link in with Glacier Park, Inc.'s east-side shuttle.

⒞ Siyeh Pass

- Distance: 10.3 miles

- Duration: 5 hours

- Elevation gain: 2,240 feet

- Effort: strenuous

- Trailhead: Siyeh Bend

Siyeh Pass trail crosses through such different ecosystems that the entire trail nearly captures the park's diversity in one 10-mile segment. The trail begins with a two-mile climb through subalpine forest broken by meadows, where it passes two well-signed junctions. (Go left at the first, right at the second.) The trail waltzes through Preston Park, one of the best flower meadows with purple fleabane and

fuchsia paintbrush, before switchbacking above tree line.

The switchbacks appear to lead to a saddle—a false summit. Eight more turns climb above the saddle before swinging through a cliff to the pass. Be wary of your lunch with aggressive golden-mantled ground squirrels here. Due to the elevation, snow can bury switchbacks south of the pass until mid-July. The trail descends past goats, bighorn sheep, and a multicolored cliff band before traversing the flanks of Goat Mountain and dropping to Going-to-the-Sun Road.

Gunsight Lake and Pass

- Distance: 12.4 miles round-trip

- Duration: 6 hours

- Elevation gain: 550 feet

- Effort: moderate

- Trailhead: Jackson Glacier Overlook

Gunsight Lake is a tantalizer. For those who hike in for the day, more high country lures beyond. The trail begins with a one-mile drop down to Reynolds Creek before gently climbing through a forest of boggy moose ponds that kick up mosquitoes. After passing a spur trail leading to Florence Falls, the trail breaks out into flower meadows, climbing along the flanks of Fusillade Mountain. Incomparable views of the wild Blackfoot and Jackson Glaciers sprawl across the scoured basin.

Surrounded by avalanche corridors, the lake sits at the base of Jackson Peak (10,064 feet), one of the six highest peaks in the park. From here, a two-mile spur trail wanders back into Jackson Glacier basin before disappearing in meadow seeps. Another trail climbs to Gunsight Pass (3 miles farther) and on to Sperry Chalet (7.8 miles farther) before descending to Lake McDonald Lodge (20 miles total). Seasoned hikers do the entire trail over Gunsight Pass to Lake McDonald Lodge in one day.

Jackson Overlook to Sun Point via St. Mary and Virginia Falls

- Distance: 7.5 miles one way
- Duration: 2 hours
- Elevation gain: 280 feet
- Effort: easy
- Trailhead: Jackson Glacier Overlook

With shuttles, you can do a point-to-point hike from Jackson Overlook to Sun Point, with side trips to St. Mary and Virginia Falls. From Jackson Overlook, drop to Reynolds Creek, where the trail forks eastward along the river. At the falls junction, turn right to explore mesmerizing blue-green St. Mary Falls and climb several switchbacks to misty Virginia Falls less than one mile farther. Return to the junction to continue east over stonecropped bluffs overlooking St. Mary Lake. (Ignore two signs for Going-to-the-Sun Road parking lot spurs.) Tally up your third waterfall—Baring Falls—just before the trail climbs to Sun Point.

St. Mary and Virginia Falls

- Distance: 3.6 miles round-trip
- Duration: 2 hours
- Elevation gain: 280 feet
- Effort: easy
- Trailhead: St Mary Falls Trailhead

In midsummer, the trail sees a constant stream of people, but the two falls are still gorgeous. The trail drops through two well-signed junctions en route to St. Mary Falls, where a wooden bridge crosses blue-green pools. From here, the trail switchbacks up to Virginia Falls, a broad falls whose waters spew mist. Be wary of slippery rocks and strong, cold currents at both falls. Also, look for water ouzels, or American dippers. The dark gray birds that nest near streams and waterfalls are easily recognized by their dipping action, up to 40 bends per minute.

Baring Falls

- Distance: 1.2 miles round-trip
- Duration: 1 hour
- Elevation gain: 50 feet on return
- Effort: easy
- Trailhead: southeast corner of Sun Point parking lot

Start by popping up to Sun Point, a large promontory in St. Mary Lake, the site of the original Sun Point Chalets. From here, a sign identifies peak names circling the often windy lake. After returning to the trail, follow it around the knoll as it gradually descends to lake level. The trail crosses the creek below Baring Falls, originally named "Weasel Eyes" in Blackfeet, meaning "huckleberries."

Otokomi Lake

- Distance: 10 miles round-trip
- Duration: 5 hours
- Elevation gain: 1,882 feet
- Effort: moderate
- Trailhead: behind Rising Sun Motor Inn

While Otokomi Lake makes a good early season hike, its sights pale in comparison to other trails in midsummer. Climbing immediately uphill, the trail soon levels out into a gentle timbered traverse above Rose Creek. Pause for breaks at the two scenic creek sections where fragile shooting stars grow next to rock slabs sliced by the creek. As the trail motors uphill, it has minimal views until the last mile of open beargrass meadows and red argillite talus slopes. At the lake, scan the cliffs above for mountain goats, and wade the outlet to get to open lunch spots on its west shore.

Guides

Mid-June through mid-September, park naturalists (406/888-7800, www.nps.gov/glac) guide free hikes at Avalanche, Sun Point, and Logan Pass. Both the Avalanche Lake and

Hidden Lake Overlook hikes are extremely popular, so expect to walk in a rather long train. They also guide longer hikes, like Siyeh Pass, and hikes with boat tours on St. Mary Lake. Pick up a copy of *The Glacier Explorer* from visitors centers for current destinations and schedules, also online.

Glacier Guides (11970 Hwy. 2 E., 406/387-5555 or 800/521-7238, www.glacierguides.com) lead several types of day-hiking trips. Solo travelers can hook up with their Tuesday Hikes ($75 per person, July–Aug.) and Group Day Hikes ($375, 1–5 people, June–Sept.), which depart from their West Glacier office. Their Custom Day Hikes ($450, up to 5 people) will depart from your lodge or campground. Many of their favorite haunts use Sun Road trailheads. All hikes require reservations and include guide service, deli lunch, and transportation to the trailhead. The guide service also leads three-day trips to Granite Park Chalet ($658, all meals, transportation from West Glacier to trailhead, guide services, linens, and lodging included), and a very popular six-day Ultimate Chalet trip ($1,700) spends two nights at Sperry Chalet, a night at Belton Chalet for a shower, and two nights at Granite Park Chalet. All meals (except one dinner), transportation, and lodging are included. The company also has three-, four-, and six-day backpacking trips that depart weekly ($135 per day, June–mid-Sept.), some via Sun Road trailheads. Tip your guides at least 10 percent.

BIKING

Going-to-the-Sun Road is a bicycle trip you won't forget. While the 3,500-foot climb in elevation seems intimidating, it's not steep…just a constant thigh-burning grind. During construction in the 1920s, the road grade stayed at 6 percent because cars shifted at a 7 percent.

Locals relish spring and fall riding when the Sun Road is closed to cars. Biking begins as soon as snowplows free pavement—beginning annually in early April—while the road remains closed to vehicles on the west side from Lake McDonald Lodge or Avalanche, and closed on the east side from Rising Sun. Riders

Bicycles start climbing the Sun Road as soon as it is plowed.

© BECKY LOMAX

climb up as far as plowing operations and construction permits. Even tricycles and training wheels hit the west-side flats after Avalanche! After mid-September, the road closes again to vehicles, but permits bicycling. Call the park (406/888-7800) first to check on the miles open for riding as some shoulder season construction precludes bicycling.

When Logan Pass opens, riders head for the top, some returning the way they came, others continuing on to the other side. Local racers make a 142-mile one-day loop (Going-to-the-Sun Road, Hwy. 89, Hwy. 49, and Hwy. 2); tourers ride the loop in two days. Locals also celebrate the full moon with a bone-chilling night ride. It's dangerous (injuries and at least one fatality have occurred), but it's an otherworldly experience.

Restrictions and Safety

Bicycles are restricted on the shoulderless Going-to-the-Sun Road during summer due

GOING-TO-THE-SUN ROAD

to heavy midday traffic. From June 15 to Labor Day, bicycles are not permitted between the Apgar Road junction and Sprague Creek or climbing uphill between Avalanche Campground and Logan Pass 11 A.M.–4 P.M. If starting from the west side, head out from Lake McDonald by 6:30 A.M. for adequate time to pedal to Logan Pass. In late June and early July, long daylight hours allow for riding after 4 P.M. when traffic lessens.

While helmets are not mandatory by law, it's stupid not to wear one here—considering most drivers are gaping at views rather than paying attention to the road. Wear bright colors for visibility and consider tacking a flag on your bike. At dusk or night, tail reflectors and a front light are required. Be sure to carry plenty of water: exertion, wind, and altitude can lead to a fast case of dehydration. Before heading out, check your brake pads, for the screaming downhill off the Continental Divide can wear them down to nubbins. Both mountain bikes and road bikes are appropriate here, but with skinny tires, be wary of obstacles: debris, grates, rockfall, and ice. Because shoulderless Going-to-the-Sun Road is so narrow, it is not the place for a family ride—except when the road is closed to cars. For bike rentals, head to Flathead Valley.

TRAIL RIDING
◖ Swan Mountain Outfitters

Only one trail-riding concession operates along Going-to-the-Sun Road. Swan Mountain Outfitters (mile 11.2 or 39.2, 406/888-5121 or 877/888-5557 summers, 800/919-4416 winters, www.swanmountainoutfitters.com) depart from the horse barn across from McDonald Lodge parking lot. July–mid-September, their specialty all-day ride ($135)—the best trail ride in the park—departs at 8:45 A.M. and climbs to Sperry Chalet, where you can lunch in the historic dining hall. The last two miles of the ride break out of thick trees into avalanche chutes, where you'll have better views of the steep-walled valley. Lunch is not included in the rate, so be sure to bring cash to eat at Sperry Chalet, and plan on ordering fresh homemade pie for

dessert! One-hour rides ($32, late May–early Sept.) depart five times daily on a trail through cedars and firs dripping with lichen. You'll get peek-a-boo views of peaks, but mostly a good close look at McDonald Creek. Wear long pants and hiking boots or tennis shoes. Kids need to be at least seven years old, and they cost the same as adults, so rates for families add up fast.

BOATING

Lake McDonald and St. Mary permit motorized boats, kayaks, sailboards, and canoes on both lakes, but Lake McDonald imposes a 10-horsepower limit on motorboats. As with all lakes in the park, jet skis are banned. Due to vehicle length restrictions (21 feet), towed boats may not cross Going-to-the-Sun Road between Avalanche and Sun Point.

Lake McDonald

Because Lake McDonald has only one boat ramp, you must drive to Apgar to launch anything larger than what you can carry. For hand-carried crafts, you can launch from Sprague Creek Picnic Area or several pullouts along the lake. For boating and fishing on Lake McDonald, **Glacier Park Boat Company** (406/888-5727 summers only, 406/257-2426, www.glacierparkboats.com) rents rowboats for $14 per hour and 8-horsepower motorboats for $22 per hour. Paddles, lifejackets, and fishing regulations are included. Find the rentals at the boat dock behind Lake McDonald Lodge. Bring cash; the company doesn't accept credit cards.

St. Mary

St. Mary Lake permits motorboats with unlimited horsepower. No boats are available to rent, but launch your own from the boat ramp at Rising Sun. Hand-carried crafts can also launch easily from Rising Sun Picnic Area. Be aware: Wild winds whip up quickly here, so keep your eye on conditions.

KAYAKING AND CANOEING

Both sea-kayaking and canoeing are popular on Lake McDonald and St. Mary Lake.

On calm days, shoreline tours are exceptionally scenic, and evening paddles are relaxing. On Lake McDonald, launch from any of the Going-to-the-Sun Road pullouts for shoreline tours or from the Apgar Boat Launch. On St. Mary Lake, launch from Rising Sun boat ramp to paddle to Silver Dollar Beach below Red Eagle Mountain; however, watch the weather as high winds churn up monstrous waves quickly in the narrow valley. Although river kayakers drool at the rapids on McDonald Creek, the creek is closed to all boating due to nesting harlequin ducks.

FISHING
McDonald Valley

Heavily fished, Lake McDonald is a haven for kokanee, lake trout, whitefish, and cutthroat. Lake McDonald has no limit on lake trout or lake whitefish. Since boat fishing tends to produce better results than shore fishing here, you'll have more luck if you rent a boat at the Lake McDonald Lodge dock. If you have your own boat to launch (heavier than what you can carry), head to Apgar for the lake's only public ramp.

Other than Lake McDonald, fishing in McDonald Valley is sporadic at best. Although scads of anglers rim McDonald Creek, the river actually has a reputation for leaving hooks bare. As for Fish Lake, a steep three-mile hike from Lake McDonald Lodge accesses the tiny lily-padded shallow lake; a few westslope cutthroats reside here. Snyder Lake, a 4.4-mile climb from Lake McDonald Lodge, also has small cutthroat and is a little more open than Fish Lake's brushy shore. Ignore Avalanche Creek and head instead for the lake, where indigenous westslope cutthroat have been kept genetically pure by the gorge's falls. This lake is fished extensively, so drop your line far away from the trampled outlet or wade to one of the inlet streams to fish its chilly south end.

Logan Pass

With a quick three-mile access from Logan Pass, Hidden Lake holds good-sized westslope cutthroat trout in spite of its elevation and its reputation as the highest lake in the park with fish. However, the lake is catch-and-release only; during spawning, both the lake and outlet are closed.

St. Mary Valley

St. Mary Lake's reputation is similar to Lake McDonald's: beautiful scenery, but not spectacular fishing. It's best fished from boats rather than the shoreline. Upper St. Mary River doesn't fare much better: You often see anglers up and down its reaches especially around St. Mary Falls, but few catching fish. Gunsight Lake, the best fishing lake, rests 6.2 miles from Jackson Glacier Overlook; prepare for wind and late snowpack along the shoreline.

Rentals and Guides

For those in need of fishing gear, the camp stores at Lake McDonald Lodge and Rising Sun sell a few items like line and flies. The nearest rental-gear location is **Glacier Outdoor Center** (11957 Hwy. 2 E., 406/888-5454 or 800/235-6781, www.glacierraftco.com) in West Glacier. The park has no fishing guides, but West Glacier has four companies that guide on rivers bordering the park. Glacier requires no fishing license, but be aware of regulations (as detailed in the *Background* chapter) and learn to recognize protected bull trout, which must be thrown back.

WATERSKIING

While both Lake McDonald and St. Mary permit waterskiing (although Lake McDonald has a 10-horsepower limit), you won't find the lakes packed shore to shore with skiers. Frankly, these glacier-fed lakes are frigid. Those who do water-ski wear wet suits. Precocious winds also whisk up sizable whitecaps—especially on St. Mary Lake. Serious water-skiers head to Flathead Valley's warmer, less whimsical lakes. Flathead Valley also has the nearest ski boat and water-ski rentals.

WINDSURFING

Of all the park's lakes, St. Mary Lake is the one windsurfers occasionally use. Lake

McDonald attracts a few, but inconsistent winds leave sails slack. On St. Mary Lake, winds rage down the valley; however, high mountains and erratic valley confluences create swirly winds on its west end. For that reason, the lake is really not a beginner windsurfing area; experience in self-rescue is paramount. Those who sail its frigid waters usually launch from Rising Sun Picnic Area and wear a wet suit. No windsurfing equipment is available for rent in the region.

CROSS-COUNTRY SKIING AND SNOWSHOEING

Since winter snowplowing ends at Lake McDonald Lodge, most skiers simply continue up the gated road on their skis through a relatively avalanche-free zone. The gentle grade makes for good gliding suitable for beginners as the road leads past McDonald Creek and Upper McDonald Creek Falls to Avalanche Campground (at six miles). Some skiers cross the bridge at Sacred Dancing Cascade to loop back on the river's north side, but snow coverage is more variable in the trees. For snowshoers on Going-to-the-Sun Road, etiquette requires blazing a separate snowshoe trail rather than squishing the parallel ski tracks flat.

In McDonald Valley, a gentle forest ski leads to John's Lake, but as a destination, it's not much. Some skiers head up to Snyder Lakes, but the narrow trail descending through tight trees on the way back down makes for a hair-raising adventure. Blue-sky days attract snowshoers to Mt. Brown Lookout.

On the east side, Going-to-the-Sun Road is closed in winter at St. Mary. A good, relatively avalanche-free six-mile flat ski heads to Rising Sun along Two Dog Flats; however, high winds often strip sections of the roadway bare.

Between Rising Sun and Avalanche Creek, Going-to-the-Sun Road sees significant avalanche activity. Do not attempt to ski any of this section without experience and know-how. Avalanche transceivers, shovels, and probes must be carried. Check current conditions at www.glacieravalanche.org.

Rentals and Guides

For guided winter ski or snowshoe excursions, call **Glacier Adventure Guides** (406/892-2173, www.glacieradventureguides.com, $200–310 for 1–4 people per day, $30 for each additional person, Nov.–Apr. as snows permit) for full-day ski tours. If you're a solo traveler, it's the best way to get accompanied into the backcountry with avalanche-certified guides. Lunch and snacks are included. For deep backcountry, ski in to an igloo to spend the night (add $35 per person per day to the above rates). On full-moon nights, you can also take a ski tour, skiing by ethereal moonglow ($35 per person).

ENTERTAINMENT
Park Naturalists

Lake McDonald Lodge, Avalanche Campground Amphitheater, and Rising Sun Amphitheater offer 45-minute evening park naturalist programs usually starting around 8 p.m. Check for schedules at campground information boards and hotel activity desks or pick up a copy of *The Glacier Explorer* at visitors centers. Topics range from fires to birds. Best of all, they're free. Once a week at Rising Sun, the program features a Native American speaker, a great way to gain an understanding of the park's rich Native American culture and history.

Jack Gladstone

Grammy-nominated Jack Gladstone, a Blackfeet, presents his multimedia **Legends of Glacier** (adults $5, kids 12 and under free) usually once a week at the Lake McDonald Lodge auditorium. The show blends slides, storytelling, and original music. His highly entertaining show provides insight into Blackfeet history, culture, and animal legends that have sprung from parklands. For show times and days, pick up the current newspaper copy of *The Glacier Explorer* at visitors centers or check online: www.nps/gov/glac.

Accommodations

Accommodations on Going-to-the-Sun Road are scarce. The west side has Lake McDonald Lodge, 16 miles west of Logan Pass. Twelve miles east of the pass, Rising Sun offers plain cottages and motel units. For those with the feet to carry them, there are two more outstanding options—Granite Park and Sperry Chalets—but both require hiking and, for Granite Park, the ability to carry your own food. All chalets and inns charge a 7 percent state bed tax.

LAKE MCDONALD

Historic 🄲 **Lake McDonald Lodge** (milepost 11.2 or 39.2 on Going-to-the-Sun Road, 406/892-2525, www.glacierparkinc.com, late May–late Sept., $114–160) sits on the lakeshore with boating, trail riding, red bus, and boat tours. Centered around a massive stone fireplace and its hunting lodge-themed lobby full of trophy specimens hung by John Lewis, the complex offers three types of accommodations: main lodge rooms, adjacent cottage rooms, and motel rooms a five-minute walk away. The lodge and cottage exteriors have a quaint cabin look with lakeside rooms having views, but the 1950s-style motel sits in deep cedars with no views. While all rooms are small, cottage rooms tend to be the tiniest, many with space for only two twin beds; main lodge rooms are the largest. Be prepared for all three room types to have petite bathrooms—dinky sinks and skinny elbow-knocking shower stalls—in many cases closets converted into bathrooms. Rooms have phones but no televisions, air-conditioning, nor elevator access, and the entire facility is nonsmoking. While the rooms are small, this is a place to get out and explore—not sit in a room. Dial back your expectations to the 1940s or 1950s,

© BECKY LOMAX

Lake McDonald Lodge is a National Historic Landmark.

GOING-TO-THE-SUN ROAD

TWO CHALETS: GETTING AWAY FROM IT ALL

To sample a few of Glacier Park's top trails and historic charm, head to the backcountry chalets. Here, you get away from the hubbub of modern life – no phones, no televisions, no electricity, no hot running water, and no flush toilets. Load up daypacks with a few extras like toothbrushes; you'll relish backpacker advantages without lugging huge heavy packs. Backcountry solitude, sunrises, and sunsets are prime amenities at the two rustic chalets, reached only by trail. Plan a five-night lodging itinerary that includes two nights each at Granite Park and Sperry Chalets. In between the two chalet stays, treat yourself to a night at Lake McDonald Lodge for a shower. Make chalet reservations early, for high season often books up by March.

Trails to the chalets usually open in early July, although heavy snow years may delay some high elevation access routes until mid-July. Open until mid-September, the chalets often have rooms available at the last minute midweek in early fall. With the park's hiker shuttles, you can hike in one trail and out another.

The two historic chalets still stand as enclaves of comfort in the backcountry and as tributes to a bygone era of horse tours. Their stone and log edifices are set in spectacular surroundings, and each offers different amenities. Don't forget earplugs, for noise from heavy snorers travels between rooms.

SPERRY CHALET

Leave your vehicle at Lake McDonald Lodge and catch the earliest hiker shuttles over Logan Pass to Jackson Glacier Overlook. Hike the long 14-mile route over **Gunsight Pass.** As it traverses the Continental Divide, it climbs roughly 3,500 feet and crosses two passes, so you need a very early start and plenty of stamina. (For a shorter access, hike up the 6.5-mile route from Lake McDonald Lodge.)

Set in a cirque, the full-service Sperry Chalet provides everything, including mountain goats clomping on walkways. With the package including meals – dinner, breakfast, and sack or dining room lunch – and rooms complete with fresh linens and bedding, you need to carry only your water, clothes, and a few snacks. If you can handle the weight in your pack, throw in a bottle of your favorite beverage for evening sipping.

On your second day at Sperry, grab your lunch and head for **Sperry Glacier.** The eight-mile round-trip trail climbs past bedrock tarns before it squeezes up a narrow stairway through a cliff into the ice-scoured basin housing the glacier, moraines, and crevasses. To exit Sperry on your final day, prep your toes, knees, and nose for a 3,500-foot descent down the 6.5-mile horse-manure-laden trail to **Lake McDonald Lodge,** where a hot shower awaits.

GRANITE PARK CHALET

Hop an early hiker shuttle to Logan Pass. Walking with the goats, hike the **Highline Trail** heading north along the Garden Wall. With only an 800-foot climb, the 7.6-mile trail heads out to a knoll with a 360-degree view of surrounding peaks and glaciers.

Granite Park Chalet functions as a hiker hostel: You bring and cook your own food in and you'll be delighted with its location and historic ambience. Restaurants, a lounge, gift shop, and camp store are in the lodge or within a five-minute walk. Best of all, trails to Mount Brown Lookout, Snyder Lake, Sperry Chalet, and Sperry Glacier depart right across the street. Reservations are highly recommended in June and September and an absolute must in July and August.

RISING SUN

Rising Sun Motor Inn (milepost 44.7 or 6 on Going-to-the-Sun Road, 406/892-2525, www.glacierparkinc.com, mid-June–mid-Sept., $107–124) became the answer for motorists traveling to Glacier during World War II as it was the only facility that stayed open. Built in 1940, the inn still retains its old-time feel with no television, air-conditioning, in-

© BECKY LOMAX

Granite Park Chalet sits atop a knoll surrounded by peaks.

a fully equipped kitchen or purchase packaged meals on-site to cook yourself. Either tote your sleeping bag or order linen service. In the evening, bring your binoculars outside to watch bears foraging in the valley below; at sunset, walk to the chalet's northwestern side as orange and pink hues spread across the sky.

On your second day, pack in two half-day hikes: one to **Swiftcurrent Lookout** for views of the park from end to end, and the other to **Grinnell Glacier Overlook** to see the melting glacier from the crest of the Continental Divide. Together, the hikes total eight miles.

To depart on your last day at Granite, either drop four miles downhill to The Loop to catch the shuttle, or cross over Swiftcurrent Pass. The 7.6-mile Swiftcurrent Trail descends through a spectacular cliff wall dripping with waterfalls before leveling out for an easy walk past moose browsing in lakes along the valley floor. From Swiftcurrent, grab a GPI shuttle to St. Mary to link in with the Sun Road shuttle back to your car.

room phones, or elevators. (A pay phone is in front of the camp store.) The compound comprises nonsmoking cottages and motel units, all with very diminutive private bathrooms; expect to bump your elbows in the shower stalls. The motel also has a restaurant, camp store, and hiker shuttle stop. The trail to Otokomi Lake begins right behind the motor inn, and access to St. Mary Lake is right across the street, along with the boat tour dock.

While not much has changed at this funky old-time motor inn with its board-and-batten construction, it's hard to beat its location 12 miles from Logan Pass. Although the rooms don't have much in the way of amenities, you won't want to spend your time there anyway with so much outside to explore. In the evening, go on a gorgeous sunset cruise on St. Mary Lake or drive to look for wildlife on Two Dog Flats between Rising Sun and St. Mary.

BACKCOUNTRY CHALETS

Glacier has two historic gems remaining in its backcountry—part of a series of backcountry chalets built by Great Northern Railway. Both Sperry and Granite Park Chalets are rustic stone and log buildings owned by the National Park Service and operated by Belton Chalets, Inc. (406/387-5654 or 888/345-2649, www.sperry chalet.com, www.graniteparkchalet.com, early July–early Sept.). They are set in the scenery-packed territory of mountain goats and grizzly bears. Pack along earplugs because snores resound through the historically thin walls. With no electricity, no phones, and no televisions, evening entertainment entails watching wildlife and sunsets and, in the dead of night, grabbing a flashlight to find the composting vault toilets. No alcohol is sold on the premises or allowed in the dining hall; you can pack along your favorite beverage for elsewhere, though, and you will need to pack the containers out with you. To reach the chalets requires hiking 6–14 miles, depending on routes. Reservations are required, often filling by March.

 Sperry Chalet offers hikers and horseback riders three meals and a warm bed, which means hauling only a day pack with some extra clothing. Set in a timbered cirque, the chalet has a dining hall, a dorm, and several park service buildings. Seventeen dorm rooms sleep 2–6 people each in bunks or beds ($170 for first person per night, $115 for each additional person per night in same room). Country meals with roasted turkey sate ravenous hiker appetites, but the menu has maintained culinary sensibilities from the late 1950s with canned fruits and vegetables. Trail lunches packed for you are plain, with a meat and cheese sandwich (no lettuce nor tomato), candy bars, and raisins. However, bakery goods—cookies, freshly baked breads, and pies—are outstanding, using traditional decades-old recipes. To reach Sperry, hike 6.5 miles up from Lake McDonald or 14 miles over two passes from

Jackson Glacier Overlook. For easy logistics, hiker shuttles stop at both trailheads.

Set at the same elevation as Logan Pass, **Granite Park Chalet** sits atop a knoll, where the 360-degree view alone makes the stay worth it. Granite comprises the main chalet (kitchen, dining room, and guest rooms), a dorm, a park service building, and the composting outhouse. Twelve guest rooms sleep 2–6 people each ($80 for the first person, $68 for each additional person in the same room). This chalet functions somewhat like a hostel: Bring your own sleeping bag, or if you don't want to carry one, purchase linen service ($15 for sheets, pillow, blankets). Meals are not supplied; hikers haul their own food to cook in the kitchen—lasagna to stir fry. If you don't want to carry food, you can purchase freeze-dried meals on-site, along with candy bars, juices, pop, and bottled water. You can also pre-order freeze-dried food to be there for you. Pots and pans are available for cooking on the huge 12-burner propane stove (oven, too), but you'll need to bring your own mugs, plates, bowls, eating utensils, and water filter. (You can purchase environmentally friendly disposable plates and utensils.) You'll also need to carry out your own garbage. Running water is not available. Most hikers reach the chalet from Logan Pass (7.6 miles), The Loop (4 miles), or Swiftcurrent (7.6 miles). Hiker shuttles stop at all three trailheads.

CAMPING

In the 52 miles of Going-to-the-Sun Road, five campgrounds stretch along the corridor, but none sit in the 28-mile central Logan Pass section. On the west side, Apgar, Sprague Creek, and Avalanche offer more sites than Rising Sun and St. Mary on the east side. (Details on Apgar and St. Mary are listed in their respective chapters.) In high season, the coveted Avalanche, Sprague Creek, and Rising Sun campgrounds fill by noon with all sites first-come, first-serve. For all campgrounds on Going-to-the-Sun Road, amenities include shuttle stops, flush toilets, cold running water, picnic tables, and fire grates; bring your own firewood, as collecting is prohibited. For hook-ups, hit commercial campgrounds outside the park in St. Mary or West Glacier. For bicyclists, hikers, and motorcyclists, shared hiker-biker sites ($5 per person) with bear-resistant food storage are held until 9 P.M. at all five campgrounds.

If campgrounds are full, oversized RVs must backtrack because vehicles over 21 feet cannot travel the Sun Road between Avalanche Campground and Sun Point. On the west side, head to Fish Creek and commercial campgrounds in West Glacier. On the east side, aim for commercial campgrounds in St. Mary.

West Side

Sprague Creek Campground (milepost 10.2 or 40.5 on Going-to-the-Sun Road, 406/888-7800, mid-May–mid-Sept., $20 per site) sits right on Lake McDonald's shore one mile west of the lodge in a timbered setting with shaded sites. Unfortunately, several sites also abut Going-to-the-Sun Road, with a nice view of cars driving by. After dark, the road noise calms down substantially, so it's not like tenting next to a major highway. As the small-est campground—only 25 sites accessed via a paved road, Sprague Creek does not allow towed units; however, a few sites can accommodate small RVs up to 21 feet. No trailheads depart from here, but beach sunsets rank as spectacular. Kayakers and canoers can't beat the lakefront access. At 23 miles from Logan Pass, it still has quick access to the high country and is five-minutes from Lake McDonald Lodge and campstore.

Set in a cedar-hemlock rainforest, **(Avalanche Campground** (milepost 16.6 or 34.1 on Going-to-the-Sun Road, 406/888-7800, early June–early Sept., $20 per site) opens for a shorter season than Sprague Creek. Six miles east of Lake McDonald Lodge, Avalanche makes the closest west-side base for exploring Logan Pass 16 miles away and is convenient for hiking to Avalanche Lake, since the trailhead departs from campground's rear.

You'll know you're in a rainforest with its dark overgrown forest canopy allowing little sun-light to hit your picnic table. The moist area sprouts thick patches of thimbleberries and sometimes a good collection of mosquitoes. Although the campground can fit RVs up to 26 feet in over half of its sites, no disposal station is available.

East Side

Located only 12 miles east of Logan Pass and six miles west of St. Mary, **(Rising Sun Campground** (milepost 44.5 or 6.3 on Going-to-the-Sun Road, 406/888-7800, late May–mid-Sept., $20 per site) tucks at the base of Otokomi Mountain by St. Mary Lake. Adjacent to Rising Sun Motor Inn, the 83-site campground is a few-minutes' walk to a res-taurant, camp store, hot showers, and a shuttle stop. Beach access is across Going-to-the-Sun Road at the boat ramp or picnic area; boat tours also depart from here. Otokomi Lake trailhead sits behind the inn. The campground has a dump station, but only 10 sites that can accommodate RVs up to 25 feet. Here, the sun drops down early behind Goat Mountain, cast-ing a long twilight on the campground.

Backcountry Campsites

Some of the park's most popular trails depart from the Sun Road for backcountry camp-sites high along the Continental Divide. The Highline Trail connects with **Granite Park** and **Fifty Mountain,** both set near wildflower meadows with stunning views. It also makes a loop to Packer's Roost via **Flattop.** The Gunsight Trail has three popular campsites at **Gunsight Lake, Lake Ellen Wilson,** and **Sperry.** From Rising Sun, **Otokomi Lake** also makes a scenic overnight. Pick up permits ($5 per person per night; kids 8–18 $2.50; kids 7 and under free) in person at ranger stations, visitors centers, or the Apgar Permit Office (406/888-7900) 24 hours in advance or by res-ervation ($30). Check additional requirements online: www.nps.gov/glac.

GOING-TO-THE-SUN ROAD

Food

No food services are available at Logan Pass. The nearest restaurants on the west side are at Lake McDonald Lodge, 21 miles below the pass. On the east side, Rising Sun has the only restaurant, 12 miles from Logan Pass and 6 miles from St. Mary. Most restaurants in and adjacent to the park sell box or sack lunches ($7–10) to accommodate hikers and sightseers spending the day driving the Sun Road.

RESTAURANTS
Lake McDonald
You'll find three distinctly different nonsmoking restaurants located at Lake McDonald Lodge (milepost 11.2 or 39.2 on Going-to-the-Sun Road, 406/892-2525, daily late May–late Sept.), but all operated by the same concessionaire. The headliner dining room inside the lodge is **(Russell's Fireside Dining Room.** It's worth a meal, just for its ambience with woven seats and painted Native American chandeliers. The north windows have a peek-a-boo lake view, but during dinner the blinds usually need to be pulled down as the sun blazes in hot. Breakfasts (6:30–10:00 A.M., $11–14) are the same in all the lodges run by Glacier Park, Inc.—a massive buffet spread with fruit, pastries, waffles, eggs, pancakes, French toast, sausage, and bacon. It offers a huge selection and enough to fill big eaters, but entrees will not be steaming hot off the grill. Those looking for something smaller can order à la carte. The dining hall is also open for lunch (11:30 A.M.–2 P.M., $8–14) and dinner (5–9:30 P.M., $16–33). While wild game, pasta, and fish take on a decidedly Montana taste at the lodge, your waitstaff is from around the globe. When you dine here, don't pass up a northern Rocky Mountain dessert—huckleberry ice cream. No reservations are taken, so you may have to wait for a seat.

If you want a lighter dinner without leaving the lodge, drop in the cozy **Stockade Lounge** open 11:30 A.M.–midnight. It serves a respectable $8–14 appetizer and sandwich menu

2–10 P.M., which includes the requisite burger and fries. The bar also stocks plenty of local microbrews along with wine and cocktails.

Across the parking lot from Lake McDonald Lodge, **Jammer Joe's Grill and Pizzeria** (11:30 A.M.–9:30 P.M., $8–16, closes in early Sept.) serves lunch and dinner in a cafeteria-type atmosphere. Pizzas, pasta, and sandwiches, including buffalo burgers, dominate the menu, making it the best place to take the kids. They also have an Italian buffet, which includes pizza, pasta, a large salad bar, and desserts.

Rising Sun
Located at Rising Sun Motor Inn, **Two Dog Flats Grill** (milepost 44.7 or 6 on Going-to-the-Sun Road, 406/892-2525, 6:30–10:00 A.M. and 11 A.M.–9:30 P.M. daily mid-June–mid-Sept.) serves breakfast ($6–10), lunch ($8–14), and dinner ($13–16) in its building reminiscent of an old coffee shop. Ask for a south window table for views of Red Eagle Peak. Fare is standard American: soups, salads, sandwiches, steaks, and fish. Montana microbrews and wine, too. No reservations are taken for the nonsmoking restaurant, which sometimes crowds with bus tours. You may have to wait for a table in high season. If the line is really long, you can bop six miles down the road to St. Mary for more dining options; the evening return drive offers good wildlife-watching along Two Dog Flats.

GROCERIES
Camp stores are located at Lake McDonald Lodge 21 miles west of Logan Pass (a five-minute walk from Lake McDonald Lodge) and Rising Sun 12 miles east of the pass. Open 7 A.M.–9 P.M. daily mid-June–mid-September, both camp stores carry limited brand selections, but you can pick up ice, firewood, stove gas, and other camping supplies as well as convenience store groceries, beer, wine, gifts, and newspapers. For hikers, both stores are a

suitable place to buy trail lunch supplies—crackers, cheese, chips, fruit, and cookies.

PICNICKING

Only four areas accommodate the picnic basket on Going-to-the-Sun Road: Sprague Creek, Avalanche Creek, Sun Point, and Rising Sun. All but Sun Point permit fires in the fire pits with grates, but you'll need to bring your own firewood as gathering is prohibited. All four sites have picnic tables. At no time should you leave your picnic gear unattended, due to bears. (Read the fines stapled to the tables.) To the right as you drive in the campground, **Sprague Creek Picnic Area** (milepost 10.2 or 40.5) is tucked tightly in the trees between Going-to-the-Sun Road and Lake McDonald, with more road view than scenery; however, short paths access the shoreline. It has access to flush toilets. ◖ **Avalanche Creek Picnic Area** (milepost 16.6 or 34.1) sits across the street from the campground and has newly rebuilt larger vault toilet restrooms. Picnic sites sit under cedar shade adjacent to McDonald Creek. Trailheads for Trail of the Cedars and Avalanche Lake are across the street. **Sun Point Picnic Area** (milepost 40.6 or 10) is more or less a parking lot with tables scattered around its perimeter;

however, it has great views up St. Mary Valley to the Continental Divide. Its trails access spectacular Sun Point and Baring Falls. Watch the paper plates, for the wind can blow here. It also has new vault toilets. ◖ **Rising Sun Picnic Area** (milepost 44.7 or 6) sits adjacent to St. Mary Lake with open sites slightly buffered from wind by aspen trees. If winds rage, however, hold down everything. Short paths through the trees access the shoreline. It has flush toilets.

Logan Pass has no picnic area, and the park service does not allow coolers outside of vehicles except for picnic areas...although you can eat a sandwich anywhere. If you want to "picnic" up with the views, the best method is to pack a sack lunch to eat on a trail or at one of the many pullouts along the road. Most restaurants in and around the park sell take-out lunches ($7–10) that you can order a day in advance of your trip. Especially scenic and aptly named, Lunch Creek pullout (1.4 miles east of Logan Pass) has a good historic rock wall that makes a great place for a tailgate party, but keep the cooler inside the car. On the west side, many picnic on the rock retaining walls at The Loop or big boulders at Big Bend (2.3 miles west of Logan Pass).

ST. MARY AND MANY GLACIER

Mountains don't pinch the sky here, but instead drop abruptly to wide open grasslands—eastern Montana prairie. Below sheer cliffs, elk browse. Aspen leaves chatter quietly with a hint of breeze. From valley floors, a wild panorama of Glacier's peaks draws across the western skyline, dominated by red sediments and milky-blue sapphire lakes. Icefields cling for dear life to cliffs as the summer sun strips them smaller each year. It's a place of extravagant color, where pink, purple, white, and yellow wildflowers intoxicate the eyes as much as the tumbling waterfalls.

Here, on the Continental Divide's east side, wind is a constant companion. It shapes trees into gnarled, bent wonders and whips up whitecaps on lakes in seconds. But every minute yields another view to burn up pixels. No wonder the Blackfeet called Glacier the "Backbone of the World."

While St. Mary is the eastern portal to Glacier's famed Going-to-the-Sun Road, Many Glacier is a setting of dreams: rugged peaks, idyllic lakes, pastoral meadows. Here, morning sunrise gleams gold across a rampart of peaks speckled with glaciers. Loons call across glassy lakes. Grizzly bears forage on hillsides, clawing at the ground for glacier lily bulbs. By evening, when trails vacate, the sunset paints royal hues above the Continental Divide. Dark descends, with a multitude of stars. And if you're lucky, the northern lights dance across the sky.

© BECKY LOMAX

HIGHLIGHTS

《 Boat Tours: Jump aboard the Many Glacier boat tour that combines two scenic rides with a short stroll. Launch on Swiftcurrent Lake and walk to Lake Josephine for the second boat – both with unbeatable views (page 117)!

《 Many Glacier Road: Enjoy a scenic evening drive into Many Glacier. Sunsets turn the peaks rosy with alpenglow, and wildlife is frequently afoot. At its terminus, the NPS often sets up a spotting scope for its Watchable Wildlife program (page 119).

《 Divide Mountain: Look for a pyramid southwest of St. Mary. This aptly named peak separates waters flowing north to the Saskatchewan drainage and those heading south into the Missouri (page 120).

《 Many Glacier Hotel: Visit the grandest of the park's lodges. This historic hotel lives up to its reputation for beauty with its enormous four-story log lobby and two-story floor-to-ceiling dining room windows matching the majesty of its idyllic setting (page 123).

《 Grinnell Glacier: Hear ice calve off Grinnell Glacier while waterfalls tumble from Salamander Glacier above. Hikers on this trail to the glacier often spot grizzly bears (page 125).

《 Swiftcurrent Valley and Lookout: Haul out gumption to hike and stand atop the Continental Divide. You'll survey glaciers and peaks for as far as the eye can see (page 126).

《 Iceberg Lake: Swim with icebergs! Tucked below goat-studded cliffs, the lake gleams with icebergs floating its blue waters... even in August. But you have to hike to get here (page 126)!

《 Ptarmigan Tunnel: Climb to a hiker's tunnel built in the 1930s. A walk through its dark corridor spits you out with a burst of color: Red argillite smears across hillsides with Elizabeth Lake's indigo waters below (page 127).

《 Duck Lake: Fish the world-famous lake known for its large rainbow trout. The views aren't bad either with Chief Mountain looming above the blue waters (page 132).

《 Native America Speaks: Gain an understanding of Blackfeet culture and heritage by catching one of these programs, which feature storytellers, singers, and dancers. Popular shows have standing-room only (page 132).

LOOK FOR **《** TO FIND RECOMMENDED SIGHTS, ACTIVITIES, DINING, AND LODGING.

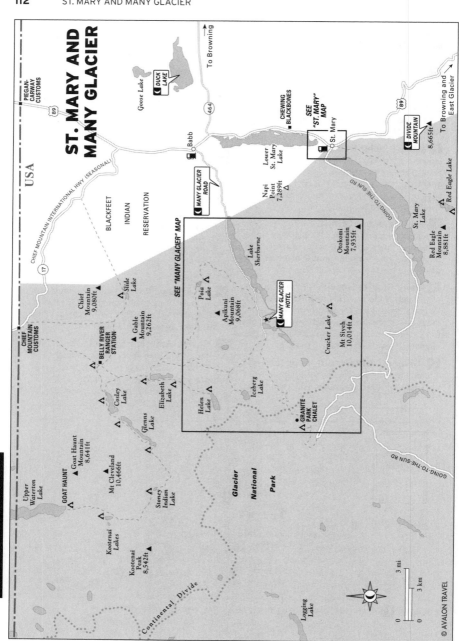

ST. MARY AND MANY GLACIER

HISTORY
Parkhood

George Bird Grinnell first set eyes on his namesake glacier in 1887. The editor of *Forest and Stream,* the precursor to *Field and Stream,* speckled two decades with several excursions to Glacier, during which he lobbied Congress for support for the area's preservation. Congress agreed to purchase lands to open to the public from the Blackfeet, and Grinnell helped negotiate the sale.

After the federal government purchased the land from the Blackfeet, Glacier became a forest reserve, thrown open to prospecting and hunting. The Many Glacier Valley attracted hordes of would-be miners, digging for copper, silver, and gold. In 1898, the mining boom gave rise to Altyn, a townsite located where Sherburne Reservoir is today. At its peak, the burg housed 800 residents, but by December of 1902 it was a ghost town, its yields meager and its inhabitants lured north into Klondike's gold rush.

Grinnell pressed on in his efforts to preserve Glacier. Finally, in 1910, President Taft signed the act creating Glacier National Park, America's 12th national park. In recognition of Grinnell's efforts, a glacier, a peak, a point, and two lakes have been named after him, all in Swiftcurrent Valley.

Lodges and Chalets

On old wagon roads, the Great Northern Railway built a dirt road between 1911–1912 from Midvale (East Glacier) to St. Mary and Swiftcurrent Valley—soon to be the home of the "Showplace of the Rockies," Many Glacier Hotel. When dry, the road was drivable; when rains fell, it mutated into treacherous muck. In the hustle to create guest lodging for train riders, the train company threw up Many Glacier and St. Mary Chalets in 1912–1913. Guests rode the 36 miles from Midvale to St. Mary by

car in 2.5 hours or stagecoach in four hours. Others arrived via the Inside Trail on an overnight saddle horse trip, stopping at Cut Bank Chalets. After avalanches demolished two of the Many Glacier chalets and the dining hall, poor site selection prompted choosing another location for the grand Many Glacier Hotel. Finally, the luxury hotel on Swiftcurrent Lake opened its doors in 1915 with running water— both hot and cold—steam heat, telephones, and electric lights in every room.

Blackfeet Highway

In the late 1920s, the State of Montana rerouted and paved the Midvale to St. Mary road—the Blackfeet Highway, found on most maps today as Highways 49 and 89. The new route bypassed St. Mary Chalets, which fell into disuse as growing automobile traffic diverted toward Going-to-the-Sun Road and sprouted the town of St. Mary. Saddled with the Depression and fewer people who could afford pricey hotels, the park service pressured the railroad company into building Swiftcurrent Cabins in 1933—immediately a popular place to stay at $2.25.

1936 Fire

When high winds forced the 1936 Heavens Peak fire over the Continental Divide, it beelined down Swiftcurrent Valley, eating up 33 of the auto cabins en route to Many Glacier Hotel. Employees doused the hotel roof with water to protect their lodge. After the fire spared the hotel, employees telegrammed the railway vice president, apprising him of the success. His reply: "Why?" The hotels and chalets had become a financial noose around the railway's neck. The St. Mary chalets were torn down in 1948; Many Glacier chalets succumbed to fire and avalanches. Only the historic showplace Many Glacier Hotel remains.

Exploring St. Mary and Many Glacier

Glacier's eastern ecosystem sprawls across national park lands and the Blackfeet Reservation—divided by an artificially straight border. Bears and elk know no boundaries, and sometimes neither do cattle, ranging astray inside Glacier.

Blackfeet Reservation

Bordering the park's eastern boundary are 1.5 million acres of Blackfeet Nation tribal lands. The boundary slices across the summits of Chief Mountain, Napi Point, and Divide Peak, crossing the lower end of Sherburne Reservoir and sliding between the two St. Mary Lakes. Tribal permits are required for recreating on the reservation: camping, fishing, hiking, and boating.

St. Mary

St. Mary is the eastern portal to Going-to-the-Sun Road. Sitting at the junction of the Sun Road and the Blackfeet Highway (Hwy. 89,) the town clusters at the park boundary. Only the visitors center and St. Mary Campground are within the park; the town, restaurants, grocery stores, lodging, and commercial campgrounds are all on the Blackfeet Reservation.

Many Glacier

You'll have to become used to the lingo here: Although the popular Many Glacier Hotel sits in the Swiftcurrent Valley, locals refer to the whole valley area simply as Many Glacier, even though that technically is not its name. (Only two features actually use that name—the hotel and the campground.) Many Glacier derived its name from the string of small glaciers that populated its peaks: Grinnell, Salamander, Gem, North Swiftcurrent, and South Swiftcurrent.

Babb

Between St. Mary and Many Glacier sits Babb, a blink-and-you'll-miss-it village about one block long. A few houses cluster behind a petite year-round grocery store, along with two bars, two restaurants, and a tiny motel.

It seemingly has no purpose in the middle of nowhere, but its year-round post office and elementary school service families ranching between St. Mary and the Canadian border.

Belly River

A confluence of two valleys lined with good fishing lakes, the Belly River is home to tales of one of the park's most notorious rangers—Joe Cosley. Guides and rangers tell stories of his exploits—from poaching to womanizing. The Belly, as locals call it, is undeveloped backcountry; there are no hotels and or restaurants. While hikers can reach a couple of the Belly River's lakes in one long day, it's an area best explored by backpacking.

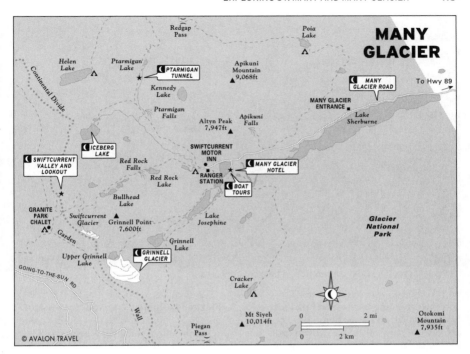

PARK ENTRANCE

The park staffs entrance stations at St. Mary at the gateway of Going-to-the-Sun Road and in Many Glacier just inside the park boundary. Both have self-pay cash-only kiosks for when the stations are unstaffed. If you don't have an annual pass, seven-day passes cost $25 per vehicle or $12 for individuals on foot, bicycles, or motorcycles.

VISITORS CENTER

In St. Mary, **St. Mary Visitor Center** (0.4 mile west on Going-to-the-Sun Rd., 406/732-7751, 8 A.M.–8 P.M. mid-May–late June and Labor Day–Sept., open until 9 P.M. late June–Labor Day) is the largest visitors center in the park. Indoor facilities comprise displays, a small Glacier Natural History Association bookstore, and a theater. In 2005, the center added a tipi, the first step in developing a tipi encampment with outdoor dancing and a performance stage for the popular Native America Speaks program. Plans also include renovation of the center's indoor exhibits to emphasize more Native American cultural park history.

Inside the center, you'll find backcountry permits, fishing regulations, Going-to-the-Sun Road updates, Junior Ranger newspapers, and information on free guided park naturalist hikes and presentations in *The Glacier Explorer.* The small indoor theater also shows slide presentations and schedules evening naturalist programs.

The visitors center is also a shuttle stop: To avoid parking hassles at Logan Pass, you can park your car here all day for free and catch the free shuttle up Going-to-the-Sun Road.

TOURS AND SHUTTLES
Shuttles

St. Mary Visitor Center serves as the east-side transit hub. You can catch the **free shuttle** backpackers in The Belly, undeveloped backcountry

heading up Going-to-the-Sun Road here. No tickets needed; no reservations taken. Starting at 7:00 A.M., the shuttle leaves every half-hour for Logan Pass with six stops en route at trailheads. It's a one-hour ride. At Logan Pass, you can catch the west-side shuttles into the Lake McDonald Valley. The last buses leave Logan Pass at 7 P.M. to return to St. Mary.

For hikers heading to the Highline-Swiftcurrent Pass or Piegan Pass trails that end in Many Glacier, **Glacier Park, Inc.** (406/892-2525, www.glacierparkinc.com, $8 one-way) runs a hiker van from Swiftcurrent Motor Inn and Many Glacier Hotel to St. Mary Visitor Center (7:00 and 8:30 A.M., 4:45 and 5:30 P.M., July–Labor Day). For details of point-to-point hikes ending in Many Glacier, see *Going-to-the-Sun Road* chapter. Between late May and late September, GPI's east-side hiker vans run north–south connecting Waterton, Many Glacier, St. Mary, Cut Bank, Two Medicine, and East Glacier ($8–40 one way; kids 11 and under half-price). Schedules are available online, at hotel activity desks, visitors centers, and ranger stations. No reservations are accepted for either shuttle; pay cash when you board.

Flathead-Glacier Transportation (406/892-3390 or 800/829-7039; www.fgtrans.com) runs shuttles by reservation only between Glacier International Airport and points on Glacier's east side. You can get to St. Mary, Many Glacier, or Chief Mountain Customs ($230–260 one-way). If you are booking as a group with one person paying, you can split the rate.

Tours
Glacier Park, Inc. (406/892-2525, www.glacierparkinc.com, mid-June–mid-Sept., adults $35–80, kids 11 and under half-price, prices do not include meals or park entrance fees) runs daily tours leaving Many Glacier Hotel on the historic red buses. These scenic buses are charmers; on good weather days, the jammers (tour bus drivers) roll the canvas tops back for unlimited skyward views—no air-conditioning needed then! Mid-June–mid-September, the 7.5-hour Crown of the Continent tour departs at 9 A.M. for Lake McDonald Lodge, hitting almost every scenic stop on Going-to-the-Sun Road. Running July–mid-September only, a four-hour tour departs at 9:30 A.M. and 2:30 P.M., goes to Logan Pass, sees the Garden

Wall, and then returns. Both of these tours stop in St. Mary to pick up riders at St. Mary KOA, Johnson's of St. Mary, and St. Mary Lodge. The five-hour International Peace Park Tour departs daily at 11:30 A.M. (mid-June–mid-Sept.) for an excursion to Waterton and arrives at Prince of Wales Hotel in time for afternoon tea. This tour, which originates in East Glacier, also picks up riders in St. Mary. Reservations can be made by phone or at Many Glacier Hotel's activity desk.

Departing St. Mary daily, **Sun Tours** (406/226-9220 or 800/786-9220, www.glaciersuntours.com, June–Sept., $40 adults, $15 kids, meals and park entrance fees not included) drives 25-passenger air-conditioned buses with extra-large windows for big scenery, an asset on the historic Going-to-the-Sun Road. Led by local Native American guides who grew up on the reservation, the tours highlight Glacier's rich connection with the Blackfeet—tribal history in the park, plants used for traditional medicines, stories behind peak names, and life in buffalo days. A four-hour tour departs at 9 A.M. with pickups at various St. Mary locations. Call for reservations 24 hours in advance.

◖ Boat Tours

In Many Glacier, jump on a pair of historic wooden boats for a tour of two lakes with **Glacier Park Boat Company** (406/257-2426, www.glacierparkboats.com, early June–mid-Sept., adult round-trip $18; kids half-price). Catch the 1961-vintage *Chief Two Guns* at Swiftcurrent Lake's boat dock behind Many Glacier Hotel. In an hour and fifteen minutes, you'll cruise across the lake, hike 0.2 mile over a hill, hop aboard the 1945 *Morning Eagle,* and return. On this tour, you're right in the thick of moose, bear, and wolverine country. Don't forget your camera, but you may have difficulty cramming the view into the lens. Tours depart six times daily: 9 and 11 A.M., 1 (July–Aug. only), 2, 3 (July–Aug. only), and 4:30 P.M. Two of the daily launches (9 A.M. and 2 P.M.) offer a guided walk to Grinnell Lake. In high season, the guided hike tours fill up fast, so buy your

tickets (cash only) at the dock a few hours early. Once the Grinnell Glacier trail melts out, the boat company adds an 8:30 A.M. launch to the schedule, allowing hikers quicker access across the valley. Hikers may also catch a return boat at the upper Lake Josephine dock (pay as you board); you may have to wait for a few launches to get on, but the captain runs the boat until all hikers are shuttled.

On St. Mary Lake, boat tours on the *Little Chief* depart from Rising Sun. Check the *Going-to-the-Sun Road* chapter for details.

SERVICES

Two gas stations are in St. Mary on Highway 89, one on either side of the Going-to-the-Sun Road junction. One more gas station sits in Babb across from Thronson's General Store. Many Glacier has no gas services.

In Many Glacier, public showers ($1.25 for eight minutes)—which are often cold-to-lukewarm—and laundry facilities are available

© BECKY LOMAX

The *Morning Eagle* tours Lake Josephine.

behind Swiftcurrent Campstore; purchase tokens for both in the store. In St. Mary, you'll find $5 showers and a coin-op laundry at St. Mary KOA, and $3 showers and coin-op laundry at Johnson's Campground. Find ATMs and pay phones at Many Glacier Hotel, Swiftcurrent Motor Inn, Country Market, and St. Mary Lodge and Resort. At the junction of Many Glacier Road and Highway 89, Babb has the nearest post office to Many Glacier; St. Mary has a seasonal post office in the Country Market. The local newspaper is the *Great Falls Tribune.* In St. Mary, you can find public restrooms at the visitors center and behind Curly Bear Café.

Cell Phones

Planning to use your cell phone in Many Glacier? Keep dreaming. There's no coverage here. If you require cell service, stay in St. Mary.

Shopping

Several gift shops in St. Mary offer a break from the same selections found in all the park hotel gift shops, but expect to see merchandise heavily branded with popular moose and bear themes. **Trail Creek Outfitters** (junction of Hwy. 89 and Going-to-the-Sun Rd., 406/732-4431, June–Sept.) carries minimal hiking, fishing, and camping gear at specialty-store prices.

Emergencies

If you are inside the park, contact a ranger or call 406/888-7800 for emergencies. The nearest hospital is in Cut Bank—the Northern Rockies Medical Center (802 2nd St. E., 406/873-2251).

Rangers like to keep apprised of all bear sightings and encounters—especially bears close to the trail—so report your sightings at the **Many Glacier Ranger Station** (milepost 12.4 on Many Glacier Rd., 406/732-7740, 8 A.M.–5 P.M. daily late May–mid-Sept.), between the picnic area and Swiftcurrent parking lot on Many Glacier Road.

VISITORS CENTERS

St. Mary Visitor Center (406/888-7800, Going-to-the-Sun Road at the entrance station, mid-May–Sept., 7 A.M.–9 P.M.) houses a small Glacier Natural History Association bookstore (406/888-5756, www.glacierassociation.org) and interpretive displays. It also functions as the east-side transit center for those catching the free shuttles up Going-to-the-Sun Road. Hours shorten in May, June, and September.

DRIVING TOURS

St. Mary is the eastern portal for Going-to-the-Sun Road. Winding along St. Mary Lake and Two Dog Flats, the road reaches Logan Pass in 18 miles before dropping 32 miles to West Glacier. The seasonally open Chief Mountain Highway connects the St. Mary Valley with Waterton and crosses the Canadian-U.S. border.

Blackfeet Highway

The Blackfeet Highway, otherwise known as Highway 89, runs entirely on the Blackfeet Reservation along the east side of Glacier Park from the Canadian border at Piegan-Carway to East Glacier—the last portion on Highway 49. Its only gas services are at Babb, St. Mary, and East Glacier. From the town of St. Mary, the highway rolls northward undulating on a fairly wide road past **Lower St. Mary Lake,** where you'll see Thunderbird Island. This section of the highway is one of the few roads around with shoulders, making the driving significantly easier. As you round the lake's outlet, watch for waterfowl and spectacular views to the north of Chief Mountain and Old Sun Glacier on Mount Merritt. En route north from St. Mary, the road travels through ranchland, passing Duck Lake Road (7.3 miles), Many Glacier Road and Babb (9 miles), and Chief Mountain Highway (14 miles) before reaching the Canadian border (24 miles). At the boundary, the highway turns into Alberta Highway 2 as it continues north in Canada.

On the Blackfeet Highway, be prepared for impediments! Much of the road crosses open range where you may encounter cattle on the road. Drive slowly if you run into a small herd. Ole Bessy may just stand there staring at you and refuse to budge. If so, a toot on the horn can sometimes help, but avoid being obnoxious about it. If necessary, carefully pass in the other lane. In the seven miles north of St. Mary, horses frequently run alongside or across the road. Slow down and give them room. Due to livestock, slow down night driving, even though the speed limit sign says 70 mph. You'll frequently hear the screech of brakes as drivers come too quickly upon a cow in the middle of the road.

From St. Mary, the Blackfeet Highway heads south toward **Two Medicine, Browning,** and **East Glacier.** Even if you have only a couple of minutes, bop southward two miles up the hill from town to grab a panoramic view of the St. Mary Valley and see the results of the 2006 Red Eagle Fire. Several unmarked wide pullouts afford good places to stop for a photo. As the road climbs St. Mary Ridge at 6,015 feet, it crosses the Hudson Bay Divide—sending waters to the Missouri or Saskatchewan. Several lanes allow for passing, but within a few miles the road shrinks to a curvy, rolling, narrow shoulderless trek through willow bogs and beaver ponds divided by aspen groves. Turns are blind; take them slowly in case bicyclists or cows are on the road. (Remember: It's open range here.) At 20 miles, you can turn off onto Highway 49—a road with more curves than a snake and part of the original Blackfeet Highway—toward Two Medicine (38 miles) or East Glacier (33 miles). If you continue on Highway 89, you'll reach Browning (32 miles).

◖ Many Glacier Road

The 12-mile-long Many Glacier Road—also called Glacier Route Three on some maps—is a stunning drive into **Swiftcurrent Valley.** On this road, there are two reasons to drive slowly: Motorists here have a good chance of spotting wildlife, and the road is chock full of potholes and torn-up pavement. From Babb, the road follows Swiftcurrent Creek upstream across Blackfeet Nation lands, where open

© BECKY LOMAX

Sherburne Reservoir leads into Many Glacier.

ST. MARY AND MANY GLACIER

range may put you nose-to-nose with cows on the road. Give them room, and drive at a snail's pace around them. Watch for bears, particularly around dusk. If you spot a bear, drive by slowly to watch rather than stopping and creating a bear jam, which conditions bears to be around cars. Above all, stay in the car for safety. Several sections of road are denoted by signs as wildlife corridors. No stopping is permitted in these.

After the road rises to reach Sherburne Dam (mile 4.8), it follows the reservoir's north shore, crossing into the park over the cattle grate, but you won't reach the park entrance station for another three miles. Check the shoreline for deer, bears, and sometimes errant cows straying into the park. Aspen groves and wildflower meadows with July's pink sticky geraniums line the road. Scenic stops lend views of Sherburne Reservoir and up the valley to **Grinnell, Salamander,** and **Gem Glaciers.**

At **Many Glacier Hotel** (turn south at 11.6 miles), stop to tour the historic building if you are not staying here. After the hotel turnoff, the road passes Swiftcurrent Lake, the picnic area (mile 12.2), the ranger station, campground, and Swiftcurrent Motor Inn, where it terminates in Swiftcurrent parking lot.

Duck Lake Road

Montana Highway 464, known as the Duck Lake Road, leaves the Blackfeet Highway at the east end of Lower St. Mary Lake (7.3 miles north of St. Mary, 1.7 miles south of Babb). Locals tend to use this road via Browning for a faster access between the park's northeast sections and East Glacier. Although the mileage is longer (53 miles from St. Mary to East Glacier rather than 33 miles via Hwy. 89), the straighter road affords easier driving. It's also faster: speed limits reach 70 mph on stretches, and fences keep cattle off the road. RV drivers and those pulling trailers in particular find it easier to handle than the curvy Blackfeet Highway. The road climbs over St. Mary Ridge, passing Duck Lake at three miles. From the top of the ridge above Duck Lake—the divide between the Missouri

and Saskatchewan river drainages—the highway heads southward across the Blackfeet Reservation to Browning (34 miles from Highway 89) through bison and cattle ranchland with Glacier's peaks dominating the western skyline across the prairie.

SIGHTS
St. Mary River

Between St. Mary Visitor Center and St. Mary Campground, Going-to-the-Sun Road crosses St. Mary River, a waterway connecting the two St. Mary Lakes. You can park near the bridge to take a look, but a better option is to park at the visitors center and walk 0.3 miles through prairie smoke flowers to a scenic wooden bridge—the same one Forrest Gump jogged across in his run across America. Watch for killdeer among other birds. For anglers, this river offers some of the best local fishing. You can drop a line in from the wooden bridge, but not the Going-to-the-Sun Road Bridge.

St. Mary Lakes

In pockets left from 1,200-foot-deep Pleistocene ice age glaciers that gouged out St. Mary Valley, **St. Mary Lake** and **Lower St. Mary Lake** fill most of the valley floor. The lakes collect water from snowmelt and some of the largest glaciers left in the park—Blackfoot and Jackson Glaciers. Their waters then meander toward the Canadian border and into the Saskatchewan River to Hudson Bay. With the valley sucking air down from the Continental Divide, frequent winds swirl up large whitecap waves. You'll see both lakes easily from roads: Going-to-the-Sun Road and Highway 89.

◖ Divide Mountain

Divide Mountain rises 8,665 feet in elevation, the last in a string of peaks guarding St. Mary Valley's south. Charred remnants of the 2006 Red Eagle Fire flank its slopes. From its summit, it drops to St. Mary Ridge, running for miles onto the prairie. The ridge is a lateral moraine, deposited by the Pleistocene glacier that formed the valley. This ridge, along with Divide Mountain, separates the waters flowing

THE EXTINCTION OF GLACIERS

"Where's the best place to go to watch the glaciers go by?" Every so often, someone asks this crazy question. But in reality, the question carries certain poignancy. For Glacier National Park's ice fields are moving rapidly. Melting, that is.

Climatologists from the United States Geological Survey (USGS) estimate northwestern Montana will be devoid of glaciers by 2030. These once glamorous diamonds strung along the Continental Divide – relics from a mini ice age that peaked around 1850 – now look barely different from snowfields hanging late into August. But 25 of them do remain, tiny in comparison to Alaska's rivers of ice.

When Glacier National Park was formed in 1910, more than 150 glaciers were documented within its borders. Today, only 25 percent of those remain. And not for long.

A glacier's upper end – the accumulation zone – piles up snow, adding to the ice's mass. Downslope, summer's heat brings on melt. When more ice turns to water at the bottom end than is created at the upper end, a glacier shrinks.

While tree-ring studies show that a warming trend began about 1850 causing glaciers to retreat, melting rates tended to be relatively slow. But in the latter 1920s, warmer summers and less snow triggered rapid melting. Some larger glaciers split in two, like Grinnell and Salamander Glaciers. In 1850, Sperry Glacier stretched across 960 acres, but today it covers less than one-fourth that area. Likewise, 27 glaciers clustered over 5,300 acres in the Mount Jackson area; now 15 of those glaciers have disappeared and those remaining broke into several pieces. Today, no glaciers remain in Waterton or in Two Medicine Valley.

As glaciers retreat, they fracture into patches. Some form lakes at their snouts. In 1927, Grinnell Glacier's recession formed a lake, growing in size as the glacier receded. Within 20 years, the lake had grown to 20 acres and was named Upper Grinnell Lake.

Because small glaciers are susceptible to worldwide climate change, the USGS monitors the park's glaciers as climate barometers. For information on melting glaciers, see www.nrmsc.usgs.gov.

© BECKY LOMAX

Grinnell Glacier is fast melting into an ever-growing lake.

into the Saskatchewan drainage and those heading toward the Missouri.

1913 Ranger Station

Follow the signs on a five-minute drive off Going-to-the-Sun Road (0.2 mile from the Hwy. 89 junction and just south of St. Mary Visitor Center) to the 1913 Ranger Station. A small parking area leads uphill on a three-minute walk to the historic building. Adjacent to it stands the Lubec Ranger Station Barn, which was moved here in 1977 for its preservation. However, with its restored weather-split logs and chinking, the barn is more photo-worthy than the original ranger station.

Grinnell Glacier

Like all glaciers in northwest Montana, Grinnell Glacier is sadly melting. Located in Many Glacier, the ice field reached its peak size around 1850, when it filled the entire upper lake pocket under Mount Gould and connected with Salamander Glacier. Lateral moraines mark its original size. By 1930, the glacier receded—forming a lake formed at its snout and separating from Salamander. Today, the ice has shrunk to less than one-third its 1850 size. By 2030, the glacier's moving ice will be gone, the lake looking akin to Iceberg Lake. In the meantime, you can see the glacier with binoculars from the Many Glacier Road. For a closer inspection, hike to the glacier while you can; it's the most easily accessed glacier in the park.

Swiftcurrent Lake

Originally called McDermott Lake, Swiftcurrent Lake took its name from the Blackfeet term for swift-flowing water—a name that George Bird Grinnell promoted for the area and also used on a peak, glaciers, creek, falls, and ridge. The lake, however, does not have fast-flowing waters. Located in Many Glacier, its bays attract waterfowl like loons and mergansers. Moose browse in the willows along the shoreline. A beaver lodge sits at the inlet of Swiftcurrent Creek. Enjoy

Ptarmigan Tunnel connects Many Glacier with The Belly.

the lake from Many Glacier Hotel's deck, launch a canoe from its boat ramp, ride across it on the tour boat, or walk an easy two miles around it.

◖ Many Glacier Hotel

Built in 1915 and placed on the National Register of Historic Landmarks in 1987, the five-story 211-room Many Glacier Hotel sits on Swiftcurrent Lake's shores. Listed as one of the 11 most endangered places in the country, the hotel, owned by the National Park Service and operated by Glacier Park, Inc., began a $30 million restoration in 2001. Beginning with structural damage, the rehabilitation has repaired exterior walls, windows, doors, decks, the roof, and siding. Further interior improvements are planned to continue as Congress appropriates more money for its preservation. Warm up on a cold day around the huge fireplace in the massive lobby or lounge on its large deck, checking out dramatic views of the Continental Divide. Join park naturalists for a one-hour tour of the historic hotel: Check *The Glacier Explorer* for the current schedule.

Iceberg Lake

Tucked in a cirque below Mount Wilbur and Iceberg Peak in Many Glacier, Iceberg Lake is a treat for the eyes. The lake itself sits in a glacial pocket, once carved by the moving ice that left a small moraine along the beach. With winter snows depositing heavy loads in the bowl protected by Wilbur's shadow, summer icebergs float in the lake—even on the hottest of August days. It's worth a quick dive in, just to say you swam with the icebergs. But be ready: Icy waters will suck the air out of your lungs!

Ptarmigan Tunnel

Built in 1931 to access the Belly River Valley from Many Glacier, Ptarmigan Tunnel is a phenomenon found on few trails. Large steel doors prevent winter snows from piling up inside; good thing, too, as those snows would never melt out. The doors open usually in July and close in early October. The 183-foot-long tunnel is high enough to permit riders on horseback without scraping heads. A walk through its dark corridor doesn't require a flashlight, but more than one hiker has encountered a bear racing through its bowels.

Recreation

HIKING

Hiking in the **St. Mary** vicinity doesn't offer the wealth of options that Many Glacier does. Easy trails access mosquito-ridden beaver ponds, while rough trails or scrambles lead to high peaks and bluffs. For trails, most visitors at St. Mary choose to travel back up Going-to-the-Sun Road or bop 21 miles to Many Glacier, where well-marked paths access high alpine meadows, lakes, glaciers, and passes. St. Mary Visitor Center has a free non-topographical map of hiking trails in St. Mary Valley, and it's also online (www.nps.gov/glac). For hiking outside the park on Blackfeet tribal lands, pick up a $10 annual Tribal conservation permit at the St. Mary Visitor Center.

Using the hiker shuttle that runs between Many Glacier and St. Mary and the park shuttle on Going-to-the-Sun Road, visitors easily avail themselves of point-to-point hikes: the Highline over Swiftcurrent Pass and Piegan Pass to Many Glacier Hotel. (For trail descriptions, see the *Going-to-the-Sun Road* chapter for details).

Hiking **Many Glacier** is a treat. Trails trot up fast into the high country, and not much old-growth forest obliterates views. Most trailheads are accessed from Many Glacier Hotel, Swiftcurrent parking lot, or the picnic area. Although trail junctions are extremely well signed, you'll find a map helpful to navigate the maze of trails—especially those crisscrossing the Grinnell Valley. Free area non-topographical hiker maps are available at

St. Mary Visitor Center, Many Glacier Ranger Station, park lodge front desks, and online (www.nps.gov/glac). In Many Glacier, seasonal footbridges are usually installed in late May and removed in October. Check with the ranger station or the trail status report online for installation or removal dates.

Because of dense bear populations and high hiker traffic in Many Glacier, trails see closures from time to time to let an aggressive bear cool off. Check for current trail status with the ranger station, Many Glacier Hotel's activity desk, or online.

Backcountry camping permits are available at St. Mary Visitor Center or Many Glacier Ranger Station for Red Eagle, Otokomi, Gunsight, Cracker and Poia Lakes and the Belly River drainage. No backcountry camping is permitted at Iceberg, Ptarmigan, Red Rocks, Bullhead, and Grinnell Lakes, or at Grinnell Glacier and Piegan Pass.

Hikes listed below begin in the south at St. Mary and move north to the Canadian border.

Divide Peak

- Distance: 5 miles round-trip

- Duration: 3.5 hours

- Elevation gain: 1,800 feet

- Effort: strenuous

- Trailhead: unmarked end of dirt road

- Directions: Depart off Highway 89 south of St. Mary at the dirt road at milepost 25.5 on top of St. Mary Ridge south of town.

On Blackfeet land, this hike requires a Tribal recreation label ($10) available at St. Mary Ranger Station. You'll have to poke around a bit to find the trail (of which there are several) that wanders through the 2006 Red Eagle Fire. Not only is the trail unmarked, but it's very steep—only those confident in their backcountry scrambling skills should attempt this. Several steep trails lead up to an old hexagonal fire lookout on Divide's northeast ridge. Pick one, scouting constantly ahead for where

it goes. If you don't like the steepness of what's ahead, back down and try another trail.

At the lookout, incredible views span the St. Mary Valley up to the Continental Divide and sprawl to prairies. From the lookout, a 45-minute scramble leads to the top of the peak, where you can stand atop the division of the Saskatchewan and Missouri drainages.

Red Eagle Lake

- Distance: 15 miles round-trip

- Duration: 7.5 hours

- Elevation gain: 300 feet

- Effort: easy, but long

- Trailhead: at 1913 Ranger Station parking lot at St. Mary

After following an old road for one mile, the trail climbs gently through the 2006 Red Eagle Fire where wildflowers are madly growing back. The burn continues to the lake, where it started. Watch for bear diggings—places where grizzlies rototill for glacier lily bulbs or chase after ground squirrels. Red Eagle Mountain looms ahead, and grand views upvalley to Going-to-the-Sun Mountain unfold. About halfway, the trail crosses Red Eagle Creek twice on swinging bridges. In between the two bridges, the St. Mary Lake trail splits off.

In the 1920s, Red Eagle Lake held a large tent camp, famous for its fishing. Today, diehard anglers hike in with float tubes hitched to their packs.

Apikuni Falls

- Distance: 2 miles round-trip

- Duration: 1 hour

- Elevation gain: 550 feet

- Effort: moderate

- Trailhead: Grinnell Glacier Interpretive site 10.4 miles on Many Glacier Road

Apikuni Falls springs forth from a hanging valley, which you can see from the trailhead.

The short walk starts out across a flat meadow but soon climbs uphill. In July, wildflowers bloom thickly here: geraniums, arrowleaf balsamroot, paintbrush, lupine, and stonecrop. The trail climbs to the cliffs between Altyn Peak and Apikuni Mountain where the falls drops out of the basin above. Those with scrambling skills can climb a rough trail into the scenic basin.

Cracker Lake

- Distance: 12.2 miles round-trip
- Duration: 6 hours
- Elevation gain: 1,400 feet
- Effort: moderate
- Trailhead: south end of Many Glacier Hotel parking lot

If you can stand the muddy, horse-rutted, manure-filled first 1.3 miles where trail rides travel four times a day, the rest of the hike is extremely scenic and not nearly as crowded as other Many Glacier hikes. If you meet horses, step below, not above the trail to let them pass. At the Cracker Flats junction, leave the messy trail behind and stomp the mud and manure from your boots. Climb up switchbacks into the Cracker Valley, where the forested trail breaks out into bluebell and lupine meadows about halfway up.

Once you reach Cracker Lake, bypass the backcountry campground and drop to the inlet for the best lunch spot on the shore. Glacial flour clouds the lake water, turning it a rich milky turquoise. Some historic mining debris still litters the cirque above the lake; it's protected by law, so leave items be. Siyeh Peak at 10,014 feet rises abruptly up a gigantic cliff face, a skyscraping 4,000 feet above the lake.

Josephine and Grinnell Lakes

- Distance: 1.8–7.8 miles round-trip
- Duration: 1–4 hours
- Elevation gain: minimal

- Effort: easy
- Trailheads: on the south side of Many Glacier Hotel, at the picnic area, or via the tour boat

With the maze of trails through the Grinnell Valley, a map is helpful to navigate even though trails are well signed. Pick up a free non-topographical map from the hotel desk or the ranger station. For a two-mile round-trip walk, catch the tour boat across Swiftcurrent and Josephine Lakes to hike to Grinnell Lake. For a longer hike, begin from Many Glacier Hotel, following the trail winding around Swiftcurrent Lake to the boat dock opposite the hotel. A third starting point begins at the picnic area, where it follows Swiftcurrent Lake to that same boat dock.

From here, bop over the hill to Josephine Lake, where the trail hugs the north shore until it splits off to Grinnell Glacier. Stay on the lower trail to wrap around Josephine's west end until you reach the Grinnell Lake junction. Turn toward the lake and follow the trail over a swinging bridge. At the lakeshore, enjoy Grinnell's milky turquoise waters and the falls tumbling into the lake from the glacier basin above. Although you can return to the trailheads via the south lakeshore trail, it is not as scenic, buried mostly in deep forest. You can also shorten the hike by catching the tour boat back.

Grinnell Glacier

- Distance: 11 miles round-trip
- Duration: 6 hours
- Elevation gain: 1,600 feet
- Effort: moderately strenuous
- Trailheads: on the south side of Many Glacier Hotel, at the picnic area, or via the tour boat

In early summer, a large steep snowdrift frequently bars the path into the upper basin; check with the ranger station for status before hiking. The most accessible glacier in the park, Grinnell Glacier still requires stamina to access,

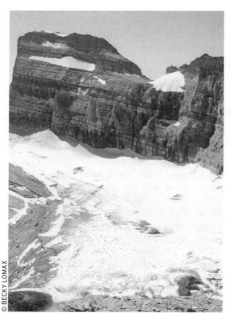

© BECKY LOMAX

Grinnell and Gem Glaciers

for most of its elevation gain packs within two miles. For that reason, many hikers take the boat shuttle, cutting the length to 7.8 miles round-trip or just trimming 2.5 miles off the return. To hike the entire route from the picnic area, follow Swiftcurrent Lake's west shore to the boat dock. From Many Glacier Hotel, round the southern shore to meet up with the same dock. Bop over the short hill and traverse around Lake Josephine's north shore.

Toward Josephine's west end, the Grinnell Glacier trail diverts uphill. As the trail climbs through multicolored rock strata, Grinnell Lake's milky turquoise waters come into view below. The trail ascends on a cliff stairway where a waterfall douses hikers before passing a rest stop with outhouses. A final grunt up the moraine yields a stunning viewpoint. Trot through the maze of paths crossing the bedrock to Upper Grinnell Lake's shore, but do not

walk out on the glacier's ice harboring deadly hidden crevasses.

◖ Swiftcurrent Valley and Lookout

- Distance: 3.6–16 miles round-trip
- Duration: 2–8 hours
- Elevation gain: 100–3,500 feet
- Effort: easy to strenuous
- Trailhead: Swiftcurrent parking lot in Many Glacier

This popular trail provides various destinations along a scenic trail dotted with lakes, waterfalls, moose, glaciers, and wildflowers. The trail winds through pine trees and aspen groves as it rolls gently up to Red Rocks Lake and Falls at 1.8 miles. At the top of the falls, a knoll provides a viewpoint to scan hillsides with binoculars for bears. The trail continues level through meadows rampant with sitka valerian in July to Bullhead Lake at 3.9 miles, a good destination with bighorn sheep wandering above on scree slopes.

From the lake, the trail knows nothing but uphill switchbacks. It cuts through a cliff face before reaching the pass at 6.6 miles. From here, Granite Park Chalet is a 0.9 mile downhill. To reach the lookout, take the spur trail up 1.4 miles of more switchbacks—you'll lose count of them. From the lookout, you'll survey almost the entire park: glaciers, peaks, wild panoramas, and the plains. Many Glacier Hotel looks minuscule. (Enjoy the one-of-a-kind view from the outhouse!) For a different descent, drop to The Loop to catch the shuttles.

◖ Iceberg Lake

- Distance: 9.8 miles round-trip
- Duration: 4–5 hours
- Elevation gain: 1,200 feet
- Effort: moderate

- Trailhead: behind Swiftcurrent Motor Inn cabins in Many Glacier

One of the top hikes in Glacier, the trail to Iceberg Lake begins with a short-lived steep jaunt straight uphill with no time to gradually warm up the muscles. However, within 0.4 miles, you reach a junction. Take note of the sign here and watch for it when you come down. Some hikers in zombie-walk mode blaze right on past it on the return heading on this high bear traffic spur.

From the junction, the trail maintains an easy railroad grade to the lake. Make noise on this trail known for frequent bear sightings. Wildflowers line the trail in July: beargrass, bog orchids, penstemon, and thimbleberry. A mile past the junction, the trail rounds a red argillite outcropping with views of the valley. As the trail swings north, it enters a pine and fir forest and crosses Ptarmigan Falls at 2.6 miles, a good break spot where aggressive ground squirrels will steal your snack. Do not feed them; feeding only trains them to be more forceful. From here, the trail traverses avalanche paths until it climbs the final bluff, where a view of icebergs stark against blue waters unfolds.

◖ Ptarmigan Tunnel

- Distance: 10.4 miles round-trip

- Duration: 5 hours

- Elevation gain: 2,300 feet

- Effort: moderately strenuous

- Trailhead: behind Swiftcurrent Motor Inn cabins in Many Glacier

Depending on snowpack, the tunnel doors usually open in July and close in early October; check with the ranger station to confirm status. Traversing the same trail as Iceberg Lake, the route begins with a steep uphill climb before leveling out into a gentle ascent around Mount Henkel. Just past Ptarmigan Falls at 2.8 miles, the Ptarmigan Tunnel route leaves

© BECKY LOMAX

Iceberg Lake retains icebergs well into August.

BELLY RIVER COUNTRY

North of Many Glacier, the Belly River is wild backcountry. It isn't easy to get here! No roads access the valley, making the entrance via foot or horseback. From Many Glacier, two routes cross into the Belly – Ptarmigan Tunnel and Red Gap Pass via Poia Lake. Three other trails reach the Belly via other routes: the shortest from Chief Mountain Customs, one from Goat Haunt over Stoney Indian Pass, and one from Lee Ridge. To locals, the area is simply known as The Belly.

The Belly houses two headwaters of the Saskatchewan River, which flows to Hudson Bay. The **Belly River** may have been named for the Gros Ventre (French for "Big Belly") tribe, and the **Mokowanis River** for a Blackfeet term that refers to a buffalo's stomach. Thirty-three backcountry campsites string up and down their two valleys. Lakes, too...Elizabeth, Helen, Cosley, Glenns, and Mokowanis. At the confluence of the two valleys, the historic Belly River Ranger Station is staffed in summer. It sits idyllic amid aspen groves and fields of wild sticky geraniums staring up at the three fingers of the Stoney Indian Peaks and Mount Cleveland, the park's highest peak.

THE LEGEND OF JOE COSLEY

The Belly is rife with legends of the park's favorite renegade ranger – **Joe Cosley.** A fur trapper long before Glacier became a national park, Cosley scoured The Belly for hides. He trapped in both Glacier and Waterton, carving his name on thousands of trees.

When Glacier achieved parkhood in 1910, Cosley was hired as The Belly's first ranger. What man knew the remote park corner better? For Cosley, ranger duties became a vehicle for poaching. Near West Glacier right under the superintendent's nose, rangers caught Joe poaching. Maybe communication of new hunting prohibitions posed confusion or officials needed Cosley's mountain skills, but he wore The Belly's ranger badge for two more years.

Sprouting from truth and fiction, Cosley's mountain man reputation grew, his self-generated legend watered with changeable facts. He told more than one woman he named Elizabeth Lake for her, said he buried a diamond ring in a Belly poplar, and claimed to have hiked 35 miles between Polebridge and Waterton in 3.5 hours for a dance.

Cosley supplied big game to paying customers and sold hides in Canada. Heeding local gossip, park officials dispatched rangers to snag him poaching, and despite lack of evidence, in 1914 the superintendent ousted Joe from the payroll.

After serving with Canadian forces in World War I, Joe snuck back into The Belly to trap and hunt in 1919. Meanwhile, 24-year-old **Joe Heimes,** who inherited The Belly's ranger badge, stumbled over a footprint leading to one of Cosley's caches. Heimes arrested the legend twice his age. Cosley repeatedly bolted; Heimes tackled him, finally sitting on him and tying his feet.

The only route to jail demanded a snow slog over Gable Pass to Slide Lake, a car to East Glacier, and a train to Belton (West Glacier). Heimes loaded Joe's own pack for the march with evidence – traps and beaver pieces.

In 1929, Glacier Park witnessed its most infamous trial. Heimes testified; Cosley pled guilty, but claimed the evidence was not his. The commissioner fined Cosley $125 and sentenced him to 90 days in jail. In an Oscar performance, Cosley begged for clemency due to a fatal disease. Fearful of a death in his jail, the commissioner axed the sentence to 30 days, then suspended it due to Joe's fast-failing health. Local friends paid his fine; Cosley strolled free.

Two hours post-sentencing, gifted with snowshoes and trail grub, the cured Cosley hiked over the Continental Divide, bee-lining for his cache in The Belly. When Heimes reached the camp, one log pole remained like a lonely bone left after a wolf kill. Two days after his trial, Cosley sold 55 beaver, 21 marten, and 22 mink hides for $4,129 in Canada.

For more of Cosley's adventures, read *Belly River's Famous Joe Cosley*, by Brian McClung.

the Iceberg Trail. From here, it climbs aggressively uphill for nearly a mile before assuming an easier uphill grade through meadows to Ptarmigan Lake.

From the lake, the route to the tunnel switchbacks another 800 feet up a scree slope. Tiny fragile alpine plants struggle to survive on this barren slope: Protect them by staying on the trail rather than cutting switchbacks. The 183-foot tunnel (6 ft. wide by 9 ft.) cuts through Ptarmigan Wall. Walk through for the burst of red rock greeting you on the other side. Admire the trail engineering along the north side's cliff wall and drop down a quarter mile to see Old Sun Glacier on Mount Merritt.

Belly River Ranger Station

- Distance: 12.6 miles round-trip

- Duration: 6 hours

- Elevation gain: 750 feet on return

- Effort: moderate

- Trailhead: Chief Mountain Customs parking lot on Chief Mountain Highway

A trail used by backpackers to access Elizabeth, Helen, Cosley, Glenns, and Mokowanis Lakes and Stoney Indian Pass, the Belly River Trail attracts day hikers more for the views en route of Chief Mountain and Pyramid Peak in the distance. Anglers also drop lines into the Belly River. The trail begins with a descent down to the valley floor. Look for scratches in the aspen bark where elk have rubbed to remove the velvet from their antlers.

As the trail undulates gently across the valley floor, it traverses aspen groves and open meadows blooming with lupine and paintbrush. At the pastoral Belly River Ranger Station, listed in 1986 on the National Register of Historic Places, you can envy the backcountry rangers who spend their summers staring at Gable Mountain's colorful strata, the spires of the Stoney Indian Peaks, and Mount Cleveland, the highest peak in the park.

Guides

In Many Glacier and St. Mary, options abound for guided hikes. The National Park Service leads hikes to various scenic destinations mid-June through mid-September, including full-day hikes to Grinnell Glacier and Iceberg Lake in Many Glacier. Some trips combine with boat tours to cross Swiftcurrent and Josephine Lakes. Although park naturalist hikes are free, you'll need to pay for the boat. The park's guided hikes are great for solo hikers to be in the company of others in bear country and to glean tidbits of natural history, but be prepared for hiking in very large groups—some upwards of 30 people in high season. For schedules, pick up a copy of *The Glacier Explorer* from the visitors centers, online (www.nps.gov/glac), at ranger stations, or hotel activity desks. For full-day hikes, pack along water, snacks, lunch, and extra clothes.

Glacier Guides (406/387-5555 or 800/521-7238, www.glacierguides.com) lead several types of day-hiking trips. While solo travelers can hook up with their Tuesday Hikes ($75 per person, July–Aug.) and Group Day Hikes ($375, 1–5 people, June–Sept.), those depart from their West Glacier office, more than two hours away. Their Custom Day Hikes ($450, up to 5 people) will depart from your lodge or campground in St. Mary or Many Glacier. Many of their favorite day hikes are in Many Glacier. All hikes require reservations and include guide service, deli lunch, and transportation to the trailhead. You bring a daypack with extra clothes, water bottle, bug spray, and sunscreen. The company also has three-, four-, and six-day backpacking trips that depart weekly ($135 per day, June–mid-Sept.)—some via St. Mary and Many Glacier trailheads.

BIKING

Bicycling the east side of Glacier Park is relegated to road biking as trails do not permit mountain bikes. No bike rentals are available, so bring your own.

St. Mary and Many Glacier park service campgrounds provide shared biker-hiker campsites on a first-come, first-serve basis for $5 per person. The sites have bear-resistant food storage containers and are held daily until 9 P.M. for cyclists.

Going-to-the-Sun Road

Bicyclists riding on Going-to-the-Sun Road have no restrictions heading westbound until reaching Sprague Creek Campground on the west side. Due to heavy traffic during July and August, riding earlier or later in the day is easier on the narrow, shoulderless road. See the *Going-to-the-Sun Road* chapter for details.

Blackfeet Highway

Cycling the Blackfeet Highway (Hwy. 89) from the Canadian border to St. Mary is easier than pedaling other roads in the area. The undulating road is wider, straighter, and has at least a bit of a shoulder. However, the wide open space means only one thing—high winds. Expect strong headwinds blowing mostly eastward. If you're heading the right direction, it will be a nice tailwind. Otherwise, you'll be cursing under your breath as you push against its bluster.

Riding south from St. Mary to East Glacier on Highway 89, however, is a different story. A wide thoroughfare with big shoulders climbs atop St. Mary Ridge, luring you into breathing comfortably with the width in spite of the huffing climb. But atop the ridge, the spacious road suddenly squeezes into a narrow, curvy ribbon with blind corners and little place to go when large vehicles hog the road. From a cycling perspective, it's a fun ride with the rolling terrain, but you'll find yourself nearly steering off the road while watching for vehicles coming up behind you. Blind corners have a tendency to make riders brake for safety and then curse the loss of momentum. To avoid the heavier traffic in high season, ride early or late in the day. Since the highway is open range, be prepared to brake; you may round a corner into cattle and may need to dodge cow pies.

Many Glacier Road

Bicycling Many Glacier Road is extremely picturesque. However, keep at least one eye on the road for potholes, cattle grates, and a few short gravel sections pockmarking the road. Also, be prepared for possible bear encounters, especially early or late in the day. While riding this road, some cyclists even whoop or holler to make noise to alert bears to their presence. With bears capable of running up to 40 mph, you won't be able to outbike a bear, so muster up all your bear country savvy when riding here.

TRAIL RIDING

Adjacent to the Many Glacier Hotel parking lot, **Swan Mountain Outfitters** (406/732-4203 or 877/888-5557 summer, 800/919-4416 winter, www.swanmountainoutfitters.com, early June–mid-Sept., $32–135) guides one- and two-hour rides departing several times daily for Josephine Lake and Cracker Flats. Half-day rides leave twice daily for Grinnell Lake's milky blue waters. Departing at 9 A.M., all-day rides (lunch not included) head through aspen parklands and wildflower meadows toward Poia Lake. Be aware that this is trail riding; the nose of one horse will be in the tail of another—sometimes in a long string of 15 horses. This is not the horse riding of the movies where you're galloping across Montana's prairies. However, the scenery is well worth a ride. Wear long pants and hiking boots or tennis shoes for these rides. Unfortunately, kids under eight are not allowed, and kids over eight pay the same rate as adults. Reservations are highly recommended.

BOATING

Power boating is restricted in Many Glacier. The public boat dock on **Swiftcurrent Lake** sits adjacent to the picnic area, but no motorized boats are allowed on the lake. Sans motors, only sailboats, kayaks, rowboats, and canoes ply the waters quietly. **St. Mary Lake** permits motorized craft with no horsepower limit as well as non-motorized boats such as canoes, kayaks, rowboats, and rafts. The boat launch sits at Rising Sun.

On the Blackfeet Reservation, you can launch onto **Lower St. Mary Lake** via the public boat ramp at Chewing Blackbones

Campground (milepost 37.3 on Hwy. 89). It's no longer a campground, but you can still access the boat ramp. Boating is also allowed on the reservation at **Duck Lake,** at milepost 29 on Duck Lake Road (Hwy. 464). Both lakes require a $20 Blackfeet recreation label, which you can purchase at St. Mary KOA (103 West Shore, 406/732-4122) or Montana's Duck Lake Lodge (milepost 32 on Duck Lake Rd., 406/338-5770) to affix to your boat. If you plan on fishing, your boat label is included in your tribal fishing permit.

No motorized boat rentals are available in St. Mary, Rising Sun, or Many Glacier. However, on Swiftcurrent Lake at the boat dock behind Many Glacier Hotel, **Glacier Park Boat Company** (406/732-4480 summers only, 406/257-2426, www.glacierparkboats.com, early June–mid-Sept., $14 per hour) rents rowboats, canoes, and kayaks with oars and lifejackets. Bring cash; no credit cards are accepted. On Lower St. Mary Lake, **St. Mary KOA** (106 West Shore, 406/732-4122 or 800/562-1504, www.goglacier.com; mid-May–early Oct.) rents rowboats and canoes ($10 per hour); you can launch right from the dock at the shallow inlet of St. Mary River.

KAYAKING AND CANOEING

High east-side winds deter many kayakers and canoers from the larger lakes. Instead, most paddlers head to more protected waters. Many Glacier's smaller lakes are less prone to kicking up big whitecaps. A popular kayak trip crosses **Swiftcurrent Lake** and paddles the connecting slow-moving Cataract Creek upstream to Lake Josephine, where a shoreline loop makes a wonderfully scenic tour. Launch this tour from the public boat dock adjacent to Many Glacier Picnic Area.

Rent canoes and kayaks at the boat dock behind the Many Glacier Hotel. **Glacier Park Boat Company** (406/732-4480 summers only, 406/257-2426, www.glacierparkboats.com, mid-June–mid-Sept., $14 per hour) rents boats for use on Swiftcurrent Lake. Paddles and lifejackets are included. Bring cash, as no credit cards are accepted. On Lower St. Mary Lake,

St. Mary KOA (106 West Shore, 406/732-4122 or 800/562-1504, www.goglacier.com; mid-May–early Oct.) rents canoes with paddles and lifejackets ($10 per hour).

FISHING

Glacier's east side is more noted for lake fishing than streams or rivers. Glacier's Red Eagle Lake has yielded state record trout, and Duck Lake on the Blackfeet Reservation claims a reputation for world-class fishing.

Inside Glacier, no license is required for fishing, although you must be aware of fishing regulations (for details, see the *Background* chapter). Outside park boundaries, visitors are on the Blackfeet Reservation and need a tribal fishing permit. Tribal fishing permits may be purchased at St. Mary KOA (103 West Shore, 406/732-4122) and at Duck Lake Lodge (milepost 32 on Hwy. 464, 406/338-5770, www.ducklakelodge.com).

St. Mary

St. Mary Lake doesn't support much in the way of good fishing with its raging winds. But it does have lake whitefish, brook trout, and rainbows. For better fishing, head instead to St. Mary River's deep channels below the lake for rainbow trout. The best fishing in the area requires a 7.5-mile hike to **Red Eagle Lake;** here a 16-pound state record native westslope cutthroat was caught. Those with a serious commitment and willpower hike in float tubes.

Many Glacier

With its number of lakes, the Many Glacier Valley offers lots of fishing holes. Grinnell, Josephine, Swiftcurrent, Red Rocks, Bullhead, Windmaker, and Ptarmigan Lakes all support varying trout populations, but don't be deceived into carrying your rod to Iceberg, Upper Grinnell, or Poia Lakes, which have no fish. Cracker Lake is closed to fishing. Sherburne Lake—a dam-controlled reservoir partly on tribal lands and partly in the park—supports northern pike. Cataract Creek between Josephine and Swiftcurrent Lakes contains brookies, but other creeks in the area don't offer much.

ST. MARY AND MANY GLACIER

Those willing to heft a backpack should hike through Ptarmigan Tunnel into the **Belly River** drainage (or hike from Chief Mountain Highway). Here, pools and riffles in the Belly and Mokowanis Rivers along with Elizabeth, Cosley, Glenns, and Mokowanis Lakes provide endless angling for arctic grayling and trout.

Duck Lake

Outside the park on Blackfeet tribal lands at 5,015 feet in elevation, Duck Lake (milepost 29 on Hwy. 464) attracts serious lake anglers year-round. One can easily spend a day of catch-and-release, pulling eight-pound rainbow trout from its waters. Some anglers commonly catch 10–12 pounders, and a rainbow or brown trout may reach 15 pounds! Although you can keep the fish from this tribally stocked and managed fishery, you may find your fishing over within an hour or so if you don't throw some back. The fishing is better from a boat or a float tube: Motorized boats are allowed with a 10 mph speed limit, and lots of float tubers launch from shore. In winter, the lake permits ice fishing. The lake is surrounded by tribal and private land, so be respectful of private property.

WATERSKIING

Waterskiing is not a big sport on Glacier's east side. But for die-hards, waterskiing is permitted on both upper and lower St. Mary Lake; however, brisk winds and cold waters inhibit the activity for most. All folks choosing to water-ski here wear wet suits or dry suits, as the water is extremely cold. On **Lower St. Mary Lake,** the public boat launch is at Chewing Blackbones Campground (milepost 37.3 on Hwy. 89). For Lower St. Mary, a tribal recreation label ($10 per year per person) and boat permit ($20 per year) are required for waterskiing. Purchase the permits at St. Mary KOA (103 West Shore, 406/732-4122). Duck Lake does not permit waterskiing.

WINDSURFING

Because St. Mary Lake kicks up good winds, it attracts a few skilled windsurfers, launching

from Rising Sun Picnic Area. (See the *Going-to-the-Sun Road* chapter for details.) Most serious windsurfers head instead for **Duck Lake** (seven miles north of St. Mary and three miles up Duck Lake Rd. #464), where winds blow more consistently—usually in the afternoon—and waters are warmer. Private land surrounds much the shoreline; be considerate of property here. Tribal recreation labels ($10 per person per year and $20 per sailboard per year) are required for windsurfing; purchase them at Duck Lake Lodge (milepost 32 on Hwy. 464, 406/338-5770, www.ducklakelodge.com).

ENTERTAINMENT
Park Naturalist Programs

Evening programs about natural history and wildlife are presented by park naturalists in Many Glacier Hotel, Many Glacier Campground Amphitheater, and St. Mary Visitor Center during summers. The free 45-minute programs run nightly at 8 P.M. in Many Glacier Hotel and the campground amphitheater and at 7:30 P.M. at St. Mary Visitor Center. Indoor programs include slide shows; outdoor programs feature park naturalists.

Native America Speaks

For more than 20 years, Glacier's naturalist programs have included the extremely well-liked Native America Speaks program. Once a week, the free 45-minute campground evening amphitheater shows feature members of the Blackfeet, Salish, and Kootenai tribes. Speakers use storytelling, humor, and music to share their culture and heritage. You'll walk away with a new appreciation of Glacier's Native American history.

Two acclaimed Native American programs draw standing-room-only crowds. At St. Mary Visitor Center's auditorium, the **Two Medicine Lake Dancers and Singers** demonstrate Blackfeet dances in full traditional regalia once a week during the summer. Tickets go fast for this popular show. At Many Glacier Hotel, Jack Gladstone, a Blackfeet, presents his multimedia **Legends of Glacier** show, blending slides, storytelling, and music into a walk

ONSTAGE WITH NATIVE AMERICANS

During summer months, Native Americans feature their talents around Glacier Park. Look for shows in park lodges, at campground amphitheaters, and in various Flathead Valley venues.

Renowned storytellers and performance artists of the Blackfeet, Salish, and Kootenai tribes share stories and legends from their history in the **Native America Speaks** program, free 45-minute presentations. Noted for his humorous storytelling, Curly Bear Wagner shares his expertise on Blackfeet culture, tradition, and heritage. Darrell Norman, a Blackfeet artist, narrates Blackfeet history. Blackfeet musicians, such as Jack Gladstone and Ernie Heavy Runner, convey legends and their heritage through original songs. You can catch the Native America Speaks series usually at the Apgar, Many Glacier, Rising Sun, and Two Medicine campground amphitheaters and Lake McDonald Lodge. Check *The Glacier Explorer* for the current times and days.

An award-winning and Grammy-nominated singer, songwriter, and storyteller, **Jack Gladstone** combines music and slides to create a narrative weaving Native American tradition with current cultural history. Gladstone packages a unique vision that gives insight into Blackfeet roots and Glacier's roots as sacred tribal land. Look for his **Legends of Glacier** (adults $5, kids 12 and under $2) performances at Many Glacier Hotel and Lake McDonald Lodge; check *The Glacier Explorer* for showtimes and dates.

At St. Mary Visitor Center, the **Two Medicine Lake Dancers and Singers** with Blackfeet school teacher Ray Croff stage Blackfeet dances in full regalia with narration by Joe McKay. The performances include traditional dances as well as jingle, fancy, and grass dances – each with different footwork, body movement, and costumes. For the finale, visitors can join in their Round Dance. This show packs out, so buy your tickets early (adults $6, kids 12 and under $2). Check *The Glacier Explorer* for current showtimes and dates.

through Glacier's history from the Blackfeet perspective. For show times and days, pick up the current copy of *The Glacier Explorer* at visitors centers or check online: www.nps/gov/glac. Tickets (adults $5, kids 12 and under free) for both shows help support the Native America Speaks program and the development of the St. Mary Visitor Center tipi encampment.

David Walburn Programs

Montana singer-songwriter-guitarist David Walburn (adults $7, kids six and under free) performs multimedia shows nightly in Many Glacier Hotel at 9 P.M. He entertains with live folk music, scenic photography, and stories in a series of rotating 90-minute shows. Celebrate the west's most famous explorers and their epic trip with Walburn's outstanding narrative **Lewis and Clark: West for America,** or catch his re-creation of homesteading in Alaska in **Cabin Song,** or the colorful regional history with **Montana: Life Under the Big Sky.** Check the sign in the hotel lobby for a current schedule.

Accommodations

St. Mary has access to Going-to-the-Sun Road and a modern luxury hotel; Many Glacier has location. While St. Mary is convenient for exploring Logan Pass and taking day trips to Many Glacier, Waterton, and Two Medicine, Many Glacier is the best place to be smack in the heart of hiking country. Here, you can park the car for a few days without getting back in it. In both locations, that 7 percent Montana bed tax will still find its way to your bill.

ST. MARY

❿ St. Mary Lodge and Resort (junction of Hwy. 89 and Going-to-the-Sun Rd., 406/732-4431 or 800/368-3689, www.stmarylodgeand resort.com, May–Sept.) is the biggest complex right in the center of town. It changed ownership in late 2007 to the Delaware North Company resorts. Rooms spanning family accommodations to luxury range $119–450 per night. The resort has three distinct luxury options ($250–450). Draping with flower baskets in high summer, their three-story, 48-roomed **Great Bear Lodge**) built in 2001 contains modern hotel comforts of satellite televisions, air-conditioning, wet bars, and private decks with stunning views on the top floor. The lodge's 13 suites also include fireplaces and Jacuzzis. Six two-bedroom **Pinnacle Cottages** with fully equipped kitchens, satellite television, river-rock fireplaces, and large decks look across St. Mary Valley with a peak skyline. Their luxury 700-square-foot **tipis** standing 27 feet tall include a queen bed, queen sofa bed, TV, fire pit, cedar wood floors, and private bathrooms with Jacuzzis. High-speed Internet is also available.

Less pricey rooms ($119–250) cluster in the resort's older lodges and smaller cabins. Recently upgraded rooms in the **West Lodge** include satellite television and air-conditioning. Older **East Lodge** rooms do not have either. The small, cozy **Glacier Cabins** each have kitchenettes and are great for families. Check the resort's website for packages—some that add golf, boat tours, fishing, and horseback riding. Although the resort surrounds itself mostly with parking lots rather than natural grounds, it provides utter convenience with shopping, restaurants, cafés, and a bar as part of the complex right at the park entrance.

Located 2.5 miles north of St. Mary, the **Glacier Trailhead Cabins** (milepost 34.4 on Hwy. 89, 406/732-4143 or 800/311-1041, www.glaciertrailheadcabins.com, mid-May–mid-Oct. $120–140) are quiet, removed from the bustle of town, and set back from the highway in aspens. The 12 plain smoke-free knotty pine log cabins built in 1999 maintain a silence without televisions and phones (a guest phone is available in the office). Each cabin has one or two queen beds with a private bathroom, electric heat, and a porch with a mountain view; one cabin is wheelchair accessible. Cook your own dinner at the community outdoor grill, where a covered kitchen area has sinks, a stove, picnic tables, and running water. St. Mary restaurants are five minutes away by car.

Two lodging options sit on a bluff above St. Mary with views into the park, where a five-minute walk connects to restaurants and shopping. The **Red Eagle Motel** (above Hwy. 89 just 0.5 mile north of Going-to-the-Sun Rd. and Hwy. 89 junction, 406/732-4453, www.redeaglemotel.com, May–Oct., $81–91) has the cheapest rooms in town. Its 23 rooms are plain and old, but face dramatic Napi Point. The third-generation family-owned **Johnson's of St. Mary** (0.5 mile north of Going-to-the-Sun Rd. and Hwy. 89 junction, 406/732-5565, www.johnsonsofstmary.com, May–late Sept.) added three cabins. The clean cabins come with fully equipped kitchens, private decks with great views, air-conditioning, and log beds with handmade quilts. Go for Single Shot or Flat Top cottages, which sleep two to four people ($75–90 for two people), as Glacier Cottage, a modular home that sleeps five, does not have the same charm nor views. None have phones or TVs. Johnson's Café is right next door.

Eight miles northeast of St. Mary, **Montana's Duck Lake Lodge** (milepost 32 on Hwy. 464, 406/338-5770, www.ducklakelodge.com, open year-round, $59–130) is a family-owned lodge mostly attracting anglers, hunters, and snowmobilers with Duck Lake one mile away and access to local Native American hunting and fishing guides. The rooms are simple: two twin beds with a shared bathroom and shower down the hall to a queen bed with in-room bathroom. West-facing rooms have views of Glacier. A great room has a guest phone, satellite television, fireplace, restaurant, and bar.

MANY GLACIER

(**Many Glacier Hotel** (milepost 11.5 on Many Glacier Rd., 406/892-2525, www.glacier parkinc.com, early June–late Sept., $135–255 double, $10 for each additional person) is the most popular of the park's historic lodges due to its stunning setting. Sitting on Swiftcurrent Lake with access to activities from boating and trail riding to red bus and boat tours, the lodge centers around its massive four-storied lobby with a large fireplace. The nonsmoking hotel rooms and suites facing lakeside stare at the Continental Divide's peaks. East-side rooms get the sunrise with a unique morning wake-up as the horses jangle to the corral.

From being the "Showplace of the Rockies," the hotel sadly slipped into disrepair, prompting Congress to fork over funds to renovate the National Landmark. An extensive five-year rehabilitation straightened the structure, repaired decks, and replaced windows. But bathrooms are small—many created from the original closets—with tiny sinks and skinny shower stalls. Some rooms have old-fashioned claw-foot tubs. The rooms have phones but no television, air-conditioning, or elevator access—even up to the fourth floor. A restaurant, lounge, convenience store, and gift shop are on-site. When the hotel opened in 1915, it was considered the epitome of luxury; today, that is hardly the case, but what the hotel lacks in amenities it makes up for in historical ambience, unbelievable scenery, and convenience to trailheads. Trails to

Cracker Lake, Grinnell Lake, Piegan Pass, and Grinnell Glacier depart from the hotel. Other trails depart from Swiftcurrent one mile away. Because of the renovation, this hotel has received lots of press, making reservations an absolute must.

At Many Glacier Road's terminus, **Swiftcurrent Motor Inn** (end of Many Glacier Rd., 406/892-2525, www.glacierparkinc.com, mid-June–mid-Sept., $80–124 double with private bath, $60–70 without bath, additional guests $10 each) has older cottages and a single-story motel. Units come with or without baths. For those without, a central comfort station and shower house awaits. It's similar to camping, especially with the lukewarm-to-cold shower, but with a bed, heat, walls, and a roof for inclement weather. The non-smoking rooms have no televisions, air-conditioning, or in-room phones. Pay phones are outside the camp store; the complex also has a laundry and restaurant. Historic charm isn't the lure, but rather its price and utter convenience. A stone's throw away are trailheads for Red Rocks and Bullhead Lakes, Granite Park Chalet, Swiftcurrent Pass and Lookout, Iceberg Lake, and Ptarmigan Tunnel.

CAMPING

While Many Glacier has only one park service campground with no hookups, St. Mary has both commercial campgrounds and a park service campground. The commercial campgrounds have flush toilets, hot showers, picnic tables, and hookups for electric, water, and sewer (and will add a 7 percent state tax to your bill) while the park service campgrounds are limited to flush toilets, dump stations, picnic tables, fire grates, and running water. Bring your own firewood for the park service campgrounds; collecting it is illegal within the park. In September after the campground water is turned off, you can camp primitively ($10, pit toilets only) through late October. If the park service campgrounds fill up, head to a commercial one in St. Mary, rather than up Going-to-the-Sun Road to Rising Sun, which usually fills up first.

St. Mary is convenient for exploring Going-to-the-Sun Road, and it works as a home base for day trips to Waterton, Many Glacier, and Two Medicine. However, if you envision parking the car, setting up a tent for a couple days, and hiking straight from the campground, then Many Glacier is where you need to be.

St. Mary

At St. Mary Lake's east end, but with no lake access, ◖ **St. Mary Campground** (milepost 0.9 on Going-to-the-Sun Rd., 406/888-7800, late May–late Sept., $23) has 183 sites—some in open meadows, others tucked between aspens. For the best views, the C loop sites stare at Divide and Red Eagle mountains, but in August heat, they can be hot. The campground can fit RVs up to 35 feet in 25 sites. Reservations here are highly recommended through the National Park Service Reservation System (877/444-6777, www.recreation.gov). This campground also opens late April–May for primitive camping ($10). A trail crosses St. Mary River on a wooden bridge to connect with the visitors center, St. Mary's restaurants, and shops (0.6 mile).

Away from the hubbub of St. Mary and one mile down a paved road, **St. Mary KOA** (106 West Shore, 406/732-4122 or 800/562-1504, www.goglacier.com; mid-May–early Oct., tents $24–30, RV hookups $24–49, cabins $65–95) sits on the St. Mary River and Lower St. Mary Lake in a huge meadow where elk often browse. Open, with views of surrounding peaks, the campground has little shade and can be quite windy, but it has the only swimming pool in the area. It rents canoes, kayaks, and paddleboats ($10 per hour), mountain bikes ($2.50 per hour), and cars for driving Going-to-the-Sun Road—a great option for RVers whose rigs are too big. In addition to the usual commercial campground amenities, it has a grocery store, espresso, outdoor hot tubs, splash park, putting green, laundry, gift shop, free Wi-Fi, playground, and the A-OK Grille (June–Aug.), which serves $2–6 sourdough pancake breakfasts and pizza ($6–15).

Sitting atop a bluff with premium RV sites having a gorgeous view of Glacier, the older **Johnson's Campground** (0.5 mile north of Going-to-the-Sun Rd. and Hwy. 89 junction, 406/732-4207, www.johnsonsofstmary.com, late Apr.–late Sept.) sprawls in a grassy setting broken up by chattering aspens just above St. Mary. With 75 tent sites ($23) plus 82 RV sites with hookups ($26–40)—some with fire pits—the campground can usually accommodate latecomers when park service campgrounds are full. The bathrooms are old, but amenities include a camp store, laundry, dump station, and 18-hole mini-golf. Both Sun Tours and the red buses stop at the campground, an easy solution to see Going-to-the-Sun Road for those with rigs too big. Restaurants and shops in St. Mary are a five-minute walk away.

Many Glacier

At the end of Many Glacier Road, ◖ **Many Glacier Campground** (406/888-7800, late May–late Sept., $20 per site) packs 110 shaded sites into a treed setting at the base of Grinnell Point. Because of the popularity of its location, it fills up early in high season. Plan to arrive by 11 A.M. to claim a site as they are all first-come, first-serve. Thirteen sites can accommodate RVs up to 35 feet. Here, trails depart for Red Rocks, Bullhead, and Iceberg Lakes as well as Ptarmigan Tunnel and Swiftcurrent Pass. From the picnic area, a five-minute walk down the road, trails depart to Josephine and Grinnell Lakes, Grinnell Glacier, and Piegan Pass. Across the parking lot at Swiftcurrent Motor Inn, you have access to a restaurant, laundry, hot showers, and a camp store. If bears frequent the campground, tent camping may be restricted, with only hard-sided vehicles allowed. Check www.nps.gov/glac or 406/888-7800 for status.

Backcountry Camping

From St. Mary, you can catch a series of backcountry campsites on the Continental Divide Trail to Cut Bank and Two Medicine. The most popular campsites sit on both ends of **Red Eagle Lake,** a fishing mecca. Hikers then continue southward over Triple Divide Pass to

Atlantic Creek or farther on to **Morningstar Lake.** The first campground is buggy in thick doghair timber, but the lake tucks under sunrise-catching cliffs housing mountain goats and a golden eagle nest.

Most of Many Glacier's spur valleys are reserved for day hiking only; however, **Cracker Lake** campground sits on a bluff above a turquoise lake at the base of Mt. Siyeh's monstrous face. North of Many Glacier via Ptarmigan Tunnel, The Belly houses seven gorgeous lakeshore backcountry campgrounds. **Elizabeth, Helen,** and **Cosley** are the most popular, but

all offer outstanding scenery and good fishing. Accessing the same lakes, Chief Mountain Customs leads first to **Gable Campground** hidden in aspens and surrounded by wildflower meadows near the Belly River Ranger Station.

Pick up permits ($5 per person per night; kids 8–18 $2.50; kids 7 and under free) at Many Glacier Ranger Station, St. Mary Visitor Center, or the Apgar Permit Office (406/888-7900). Permits must be picked up in person 24 hours in advance. A limited number can be reserved beginning in mid-April ($30). Check additional requirements online: www.nps.gov/glac.

Food

Because Many Glacier has only two restaurants, locals staying here for several days will drive to Babb (12 miles away) or St. Mary (21 miles away) to hit their favorite eateries. Nothing beats driving back in to Many Glacier at sunset with ample opportunities for wildlife-watching! Be aware that restaurants and grocery stores in Babb and St. Mary do not serve alcohol during Indian Days, a reservation-wide four-day celebration beginning the second Thursday in July. Other select days also prohibit alcohol sales, such as graduation in June. Because of their location in the park rather than on the reservation, the restaurants in Many Glacier can still serve beer, wine, and cocktails on those days.

RESTAURANTS
St. Mary

Located in St. Mary Lodge and Resort (junction of Going-to-the-Sun Rd. and Hwy. 89, 406/732-4431 or 800/368-3689, www.st marylodgeandresort.com, May–Sept.), the **C Snowgoose Grille** is the resort's headliner restaurant. Overlooking Divide Creek, the dining room (7 A.M.–10 P.M.) serves breakfast ($6–9), lunch ($6–13), and dinners ($16–31). During early and late seasons, the restaurant sometimes shortens its hours; call to confirm times in the shoulder season, and you'll

definitely need to make reservations for dinner in high season. Dinner specialties feature prime rib, buffalo steaks, and St. Mary whitefish. Finish off with the requisite huckleberry cheesecake. After dinner, cuddle up on country log furniture in front of the river-rock fireplace in the **Mountain Lounge** next door or on warm days sit on the deck overlooking Divide Creek to watch the sunset. Try, if you dare, one of the martini concoctions ($8)—the Montini with chocolate or the Huckletini with huckleberry-infused vodka.

Also in the resort, **Curly Bear Café** (junction of Going-to-the-Sun Rd. and Hwy. 89, 406/732-4431, May–Sept., 11 A.M.–7 P.M.) is the best place to take the kids as it has the closest thing to a fast-food menu: buffalo burgers ($9.50), pizza ($3.50 for a slice), and hand-scooped ice-cream cones. During high season, hours for the pizza shop extend to 10 P.M. You can also order pizza to go ($10–18). Try the gourmet house specialties—buffalo chicken or puttanesca pizza.

The **C Park Café** (0.2 mile north of Hwy. 89 and Going-to-the-Sun Rd. junction, 406/732-4482, late May–Sept., 7 A.M.–10 P.M.) cranks out daily the best homemade fruit pies. Try the triple berry or peach ($3.75). If your heart is set on a particular pie, order it when you order dinner, in case they run out by the time you get around to dessert. The restaurant serves breakfast, lunch, and dinner with an eclectic menu all of its own: creative veggie meals, burgers, and southwest style. Most items range $7–13. Be ready for long waiting lines in high season, for they don't take reservations, and it's a favorite haunt of locals. (But grab a beer at the store next door while you wait, as no alcohol is served in the restaurant.) In early June and after Labor Day, it opens at 7:30 A.M. and closes at 7 P.M.

Four miles north of St. Mary in a bright purple building with the walls inside covered with license plates and bumper stickers, **❰ Two Sisters Café** (milepost 36 on Hwy. 89, 406/732-5535, late May–mid-Sept., 8 A.M.–10 P.M.) serves up great eclectic homemade fare for breakfast, lunch, and dinner. Most menu items range $7–20, with its St. Mary whitefish and Cajun grilled chicken dinners accompanied by corn on the cob and fresh baked bread. The Red burger and chili cheeseburger fly off the grill all day. Best of all, be sure to order a plate of the sweet potato fries. Montana microbrews and margaritas are available, too. For dessert, try the ice-cream sandwich, but share the monstrous thing with a friend. It's a popular place with waiting lines in high season.

For a different experience, **Johnson's World Famous Historic Restaurant** (a half-mile north of Hwy. 89 and Going-to-the-Sun Rd. junction, 406/732-5565, www.johnsonsofstmary.com, late May–late Sept., 7 A.M.–9 P.M.) serves up its daily specials family-style along with creative pricing for kids—they charge by age (adults $5–10, kids $0.50–0.75 per year to age 12). Located at Johnson's Resort of St. Mary, the small old-fashioned restaurant with red-checked tablecloths serves its eggs, bacon, and hash browns all on one big platter for the entire table. Lunch soup shows up in a large tureen; you ladle it yourself. Dinner features country foods with fried chicken on Sunday. On Sunday, lunch is replaced by the dinner menu starting at 11:30 A.M. No alcohol is served, and contrary to other Montana unlicensed restaurants that permit beer and wine to be brought in, Johnson's does not.

Babb

The **❰ Cattle Baron Supper Club** (junction of Hwy. 89 and Many Glacier Rd., 406/732-4033, or before 3 P.M. 406/732-4532, weekends only mid-May–mid-June, daily mid-June–Sept., 5–10 P.M.) ranks as the best place around to get a melt-in-your-mouth steak. Up the log spiral staircase in the Babb Bar, once known as the roughest bar in Montana, the restaurant serves dinners ($16–32) where the baked potato isn't the biggest thing on the plate. You'd better be ready to gorge, for steak cuts are humongous—16–20 ounces. Salads with homemade dressings, grilled veggies, baked bread yanked fresh from the oven, and potato accompany most meals. The log lodge gives tribute to Blackfeet history with painted wall stories, a sculpture of a buffalo jump, and table placemats that narrate the family history of the Blackfeet owners. In high season, you'll be glad you made reservations.

Many Glacier

Many Glacier has three nonsmoking restaurants, all operated by the same concessionaire. No reservations are accepted for any of them, so you may have to wait in high season for a table.

In Many Glacier Hotel, the **❰ Ptarmigan Dining Room** (milepost 11.6 on Many Glacier Rd., 406/892-2525, daily mid-June–mid-Sept.) doesn't have a bad seat in it. Known more for its views than its cuisine, the restaurant's massive two-story floor-to-ceiling windows look out on Swiftcurrent Lake, Grinnell Point, and Mount Wilbur. For the best views to watch bears while you eat, ask to sit near the north windows facing Altyn Mountain. Like all the park's historic hotels, breakfast (6:30–9:30 A.M., $11–14) is a multi-table spread of fruits, pastries, eggs, French toast, bacon, sausage, biscuits and gravy, pancakes, or à la carte. While the buffet has a breadth of selection and enough to feed hikers carbo-loading for a long day, lukewarm entrees lose their appeal, but you can get a waffle hot off the iron. The dining hall is also open for lunch (11:30 A.M.–2 P.M., $8–14) and dinner (5–9:30 P.M., $16–33), which themes around

Swiss and Continental styles. The restaurant also makes hiker lunches ($7–10); order these one day in advance.

For a lighter meal in the hotel, grab a sandwich at the **Swiss Room and Interlaken Lounge** (2–10 P.M. daily mid-June–mid-Sept., $8–14). Instead of sitting in the dark Swiss cutout motif lounge, you can order drinks and eat in the lobby just outside the bar with views of the sunset over the Continental Divide. The bar serves Montana microbrews along with wine and cocktails 11:30 A.M.–midnight.

At Swiftcurrent Motor Inn, **Italian Garden Ristorante** (milepost 12.5 on Many Glacier Rd., daily mid-June–mid-Sept.) is open for breakfast (6:30–10:30 A.M., $6–10), lunch (11 A.M.–3 P.M., $8–14), and dinner (5–9:30 P.M., $13–16). Breakfast and lunch menus are standard café fare in the restaurant; dinner menu is pasta and pizza. Montana microbrews and wines are available, but no cocktails. It's popular for families and because of its convenient location near the campground. The restaurant also makes hiker lunches ($7–10); order these one day in advance.

CAFFEINE

Located in St. Mary Lodge, the **Glacier Perk** (junction of Going-to-the-Sun Rd. and Hwy. 89, May–Sept., 406/732-4431, 8 A.M.–8 P.M.) is the place to grab an espresso before driving over Going-to-the-Sun Road. If temperatures outside are too hot, order it iced. Many folks enjoy the huckleberry fudge, too, although it's incredibly sweet.

GROCERIES

In Many Glacier, you'll find only two options for groceries—both convenience-type stores. In the basement of Many Glacier Hotel, **Heidi's Store** (406/892-2525, mid-June–mid-Sept., 8 A.M.–9 P.M.) sells hot dogs, coffee, pop, snacks, newspapers, beer, wine, and other convenience store items. Located at Swiftcurrent, the **Swiftcurrent Campstore** (milepost 12.5

on Many Glacier Rd., 406/892-2525, mid-June–mid-Sept., 7 A.M.–9 P.M.) carries groceries, camping and hiking supplies, T-shirts, gift items, newspapers, beer, wine, firewood, and ice. Hikers can put together a hiker lunch. The camp store sits handily right across the parking lot from Many Glacier Campground and adjacent to Swiftcurrent Motor Inn.

In St. Mary, you can stock up on supplies at two grocery stores on Highway 89. The largest grocery store, but by no means a supermarket as its sign says, the **Country Market** is open year round (summers 7 A.M.–10 P.M., off-season 9 A.M.–5 P.M.) just south of the Going-to-the-Sun Road junction. It has fresh produce, a bakery, butcher shop, beer, wine, and some fishing supplies. The **Park Grocery and Gift Shop** (0.2 mile north of Hwy. 89 and Going-to-the-Sun Rd. junction, 406/732-4482, late May–Sept.) carries a great selection of Montana microbrews along with convenience store items and some groceries. During high season, hours are usually 7:30 A.M.–10 P.M., but the store will open a half-hour later and close one hour earlier in early June and after Labor Day. Neither shop sells alcohol during Indian Days celebrations (second Thurs.–Sun. in July).

Located in Babb, **Thronson's General Store** (0.2 mile north of Hwy. 89 and Many Glacier Rd. junction, 9 A.M.–6 P.M. daily in summer, weekdays only in winter) stocks convenience store items but no beer or wine.

PICNICKING

Many Glacier's small picnic area (milepost 12.2 on Many Glacier Rd.) is a great place to sit with binoculars and scan for bears on Altyn Peak—even if you aren't picnicking. It's a popular picnic site and can be crowded in high season at lunchtime. If you want to roast marshmallows in one of the fire pits, bring your own firewood because gathering wood is prohibited. The picnic area is also one of the trailheads for hiking to Lake Josephine, Grinnell Lake, Piegan Pass, and Grinnell Glacier.

TWO MEDICINE AND EAST GLACIER

Quiet and removed, Glacier's southeast corner harbors a less-traveled wonderland. It's away from the harried corridor of Going-to-the-Sun Road with its endless line of cars. With no hotel in Two Medicine, you'll find trails far less clogged on day hikes than at Many Glacier. Just because it sees fewer people, however, does not make it less dramatic. For many locals, it's their favorite park locale.

A string of three lakes curves through the Two Medicine Valley below Rising Wolf—a red hulking monolith. Its sheer mass is larger than any other peak in the park. Even though glaciers vacated this area within the past 150 years, their footprints are left in swooping valleys, blue-laked cirques, and toothy spires. Two Medicine Lake—the park's highest road-accessible lake sitting a mile high in elevation—shimmers in a valley strewn with hiking trails.

Around the corner, the tiny burg of East Glacier buzzes in summer. Great Northern Railway's historic headliner hotel, Glacier Park Lodge, dominates the town with its immense Douglas fir lobby. Those coming by train taste the history as they step from the depot across a garden walkway to the hotel, framed by the mountains of Dancing Lady and Henry. Hiking, golf, Native American and red bus tours, horseback riding, and swimming delight guests. Yet at night, quiet stretches across the sky, broken only by the rumble of trains rolling by.

© BECKY LOMAX

HIGHLIGHTS

◖ Boat Tour: Hop on the historic *Sinopah* for the best way to see Two Medicine Lake. The boat has plied the waters here since 1927 and knows its way around (page 146).

◖ Looking Glass Hill-Browning Loop: Drive up the dramatic and sometimes scary Highway 49. The narrow, bumpy, curvy road lends stupendous views of Two Medicine Valley (page 148).

◖ Running Eagle Falls: Catch sight of water cascading from underground chutes. Named for Pitamakin, a Blackfeet woman warrior, the falls also has another name – Trick Falls. (page 150).

◖ Glacier Park Lodge: Walk the gardens leading up to the front door of the headliner hotel for the historic chain of Great Northern park hostelries. Lounge in its massive lobby held up by three-story Douglas firs (page 150).

◖ Museum of the Plains Indian: Sample Blackfeet history and culture in Browning at this museum crammed with intricate beadwork. Local artisan crafts also fill the gift shop (page 151).

◖ Scenic Point: Hike high above Two Medicine Lake to a top-of-the-world view. Stare across the plains to the Sweet Grass Hills, spy the tiny towns of East Glacier and Browning, and maybe if it's clear enough, you'll see Minneapolis (page 152).

◖ Dawson-Pitamakin Loop: Skitter on a narrow trail along the Continental Divide thousands of feet above blue lakes and green forested valleys. Bighorn sheep summer on the high passes here (page 153).

◖ North American Indian Days: Join the Blackfeet celebration for four days. Visitors are welcome to attend the colorful early July festival in Browning (page 157).

LOOK FOR ◖ TO FIND RECOMMENDED SIGHTS, ACTIVITIES, DINING, AND LODGING.

TWO MEDICINE AND EAST GLACIER

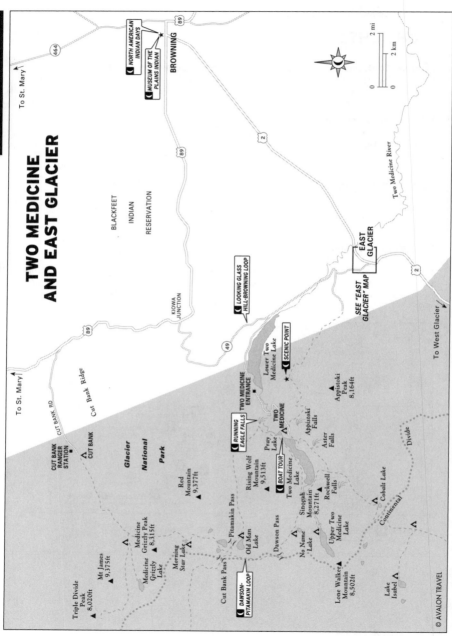

To St. Mary

464

89

NORTH AMERICAN INDIAN DAYS

MUSEUM OF THE PLAINS INDIAN

BROWNING

89

2

2 mi

2 km

0

0

BLACKFEET

INDIAN

RESERVATION

Two Medicine River

KIOWA JUNCTION

89

LOOKING GLASS HILL–BROWNING LOOP

EAST GLACIER

49

SEE "EAST GLACIER" MAP

To West Glacier

Lower Two Medicine Lake

SCENIC POINT

To St. Mary

CUT BANK RD.

Cut Bank Ridge

CUT BANK RANGER STATION

CUT BANK

Glacier

National

Park

Red Mountain 9,377ft

Pitamakin Pass

TWO MEDICINE ENTRANCE

RUNNING EAGLE FALLS

Pray Lake

TWO MEDICINE

Appistoki Falls

Aster Falls

Appistoki Peak 8,164ft

Rising Wolf Mountain 9,513ft

BOAT TOUR

Two Medicine Lake

Sinopah Mountain 8,271ft

Rockwell Falls

Cobalt Lake

Continental Divide

Triple Divide Peak 8,020ft

Mt James 9,375ft

Medicine Grizzly Peak 8,315ft

Medicine Grizzly Lake

Morning Star Lake

Cut Bank Pass

Old Man Lake

Dawson Pass

No Name Lake

Upper Two Medicine Lake

Lone Walker Mountain 8,502ft

Lake Isabel

DAWSON–PITAMAKIN LOOP

© AVALON TRAVEL

BLACKFEET NATION

Bordering Glacier National Park on the east side, Blackfeet tribal lands extend from the Canadian border past East Glacier, covering 1.5 million acres. About half of the tribe's 15,000 members live on the reservation.

Originally from north of the Great Lakes, the Blackfeet are related by language to the Algonquin tribes. As Europeans landed in North America in the 1600s, the Blackfeet were one of the first tribes to move westward, adopting a nomadic lifestyle hunting buffalo in Saskatchewan, Alberta, and Montana. Small bands, each led by a chief, met for summer medicine lodge or sun dance rituals and separated for winter.

The loose Blackfeet Confederacy contained three tribes: the **North Blackfeet** and **Bloods** gravitated into Alberta, and the **Piegan** to Montana. All three hunted using buffalo jumps, lighting fires to stampede bison over a cliff. ("Siksika," or Blackfeet, may have referred to moccasins ash-darkened from these prairie fires.) When the Blackfeet acquired horses in the 1700s from the Kootenai, Flathead, and Nez Perce and guns from French fur traders, their hunting methods altered.

The 1800s brought devastating misery to the Blackfeet. A smallpox epidemic in 1837 killed 6,000 people, wiping out two-thirds of the population. Buffalo herds declined, leading to Starvation Winter in 1884, when 600 Blackfeet died. By mid-century, the first treaty with the U.S. government defined Blackfeet territory as two-thirds of eastern Montana starting at the Continental Divide. White settlers arrived, rankling the Blackfeet, who raided settlements. To squelch hostilities, the U.S. Army sent Colonel E. M. Baker in 1870 to eradicate the raid leader Mountain Chief. But, Baker mistakenly attacked Heavy Runner's peaceful tribe, slaughtering 200 and capturing 140 women and children.

Tribal leaders, desperate to help their destitute people, bargained with the U.S. government for their survival. They sold off portions of the reservation in trade for tools, equipment, and cattle. Glacier Park from the Continental Divide to the eastern boundary was one of these trades: the U.S. government paid the Blackfeet a mere $1.5 million in 1896 for the land.

Today, the Blackfeet economy is based on some cattle ranching, but 90 percent of the tribe's income comes from oil and gas extraction. Browning, the center of Blackfeet culture, houses the small but outstanding **Museum of the Plains Indian,** which chronicles their history and displays amazing beadwork. The tribe celebrates **North American Indian Days** (second Thurs.-Sun. of July) and **Heart Butte Indian Days** (second Thurs.-Sun. of Aug.). Open to visitors, both celebrations include rodeos and powwows with dancing, singing, and drumming (406/338-7521, www.blackfeetnation.com).

HISTORY

Two Medicine acquired its name from Blackfeet legends. According to one story, two Piegan tribes planned to meet for a medicine ceremony in the valley. Failing to find each other, they both celebrated independently. In another version, two lodges for the Sun Dance sat on either side of Two Medicine Creek. Either way, the name stuck.

The 1896 land sale between the Blackfeet and the federal government included the Two Medicine area. Starving and nearly decimated as a tribe, the Blackfeet swapped part of their reservation land from the Continental Divide to the current reservation boundary for $1.5 million—a mere pittance considering what the parklands are worth.

In April 1891, Great Northern Railway began laying tracks from Cut Bank to Midvale (East Glacier) and over Marias Pass toward West Glacier. As railroad developer James J. Hill sought means to increase ridership on his new line, he spawned a grand plan: a lodge to greet eastern guests first arriving to Glacier and several chalets sprinkled in the park's most scenic spots for places to tour. For early visitors in 1911 debarking the train in Midvale, Two Medicine Lake was the first stop in Glacier's backcountry after a bumpy wagon ride. Originally a tipi enclave with canvas walls and wooden floors, the hugely successful camp prompted the railroad to add two log chalets—a dormitory and a dining hall. By 1915, guests arrived on horseback via trail, the first leg on the Inside Trail connecting to Cut Bank and St. Mary Chalets on Park Saddle Horse Company tours—a three-day trip costing $13.25.

In 1913, Great Northern's headliner hotel—the Glacier Park Lodge—finally welcomed arriving train guests, awed at the first glimpse of Glacier. Built on reservation land purchased from the Blackfeet, the posh lodge with a plunge pool in the basement erected its elegantly large lobby with 500–800-year-old Douglas firs sent from western Washington and Oregon. Rooms touted such high-class amenities as electric lights and steam heat. The nine-hole golf course followed 14 years later—on which employees were not allowed to play for fear of upsetting high-class tourists.

In 1929, Great Northern introduced the Empire Builder, named after J. J. Hill, as its modern train for the 2,200-mile Chicago–Seattle trip that packaged Glacier Park travel for its passengers. This is still the name for the Amtrak line here. It's the only U.S. train outside Alaska that stops regularly at a major national park.

© BECKY LOMAX

Glacier Park train depot, where the Empire Builder stops

In the wake of the Depression, World War II closures, and increasing auto traffic, the Two Medicine chalets met their demise and were torn down building by building until only the dining hall remained. It's now the Two Medicine store.

Exploring Two Medicine and East Glacier

ENTRANCE STATION

East Glacier sits outside park boundaries, but Two Medicine is within the park with an entrance station location approximately four miles up Two Medicine Road. It is staffed during daylight hours seven days a week in the summer. During shoulder seasons, staffing reduces to weekends only or not at all. It has a self-pay cash-only kiosk for when it is closed. If you don't have an annual pass, seven-day passes cost $25 per vehicle or $12 for individuals on foot, bicycles, or motorcycles. Maps and the biannual *Waterton-Glacier Guide* are available here.

Even though the Cut Bank Road enters the park, it lacks both an entrance station and self-pay kiosk.

SHUTTLES AND TOURS
Shuttles
The hiker shuttle operated by **Glacier Park, Inc.** (406/892-2525, www.glacierparkinc.com,

East Glacier map showing:
- To Two Medicine
- JACOBSON'S COTTAGES
- To Browning
- EAST GLACIER MOTEL AND CABINS
- WHISTLE STOP
- TRAVELER'S REST
- SEARS MOTEL
- BROWNIE'S HOSTEL/BROWNIE'S BAKERY AND DELI
- MOUNTAIN PINES MOTEL
- RANGER STATION
- **EAST GLACIER**
- 2
- BEAR TRACK TRAVEL CENTER
- POST OFFICE
- BLACKFOOT AVE
- 49
- GLACIER PARK LODGE GOLF COURSE
- WHISTLING SWAN
- MEADE ST
- WASHINGTON'S
- GLACIER AVE
- CIRCLE R MOTEL
- GLACIER PARK LODGE
- TRAIN DEPOT
- SERRANO'S/BACKPACKER'S INN
- BROWN HOUSE
- GLACIER PARK TRADING CO
- DAWSON AVE
- TWO MEDICINE GRILL
- VILLAGER DINING ROOM/BUZZ'S BREW STATION
- MONTANA AVE
- LAUNDERETTE
- DANCING BEARS INN
- LINDHE AVE
- To Marias Pass
- Y LAZY R RV PARK
- 0 100 yds
- 0 100 m
- © AVALON TRAVEL

$8–40 one way; kids 11 and under half-price) makes getting to trailheads easy. The east-side shuttle runs late May–September connecting East Glacier, Two Medicine, Cut Bank Road Junction, St. Mary, Many Glacier, and Waterton. At St. Mary Visitor Center, riders can link into the free Going-to-the-Sun Road shuttles running July–Labor Day. No shuttle runs directly from East Glacier to West Glacier via Highway 2. For trailheads at Marias Pass, for instance, you must drive yourself or hitch-hike, which is legal in Montana. From Glacier Park Lodge, daily shuttles ($11 round-trip) hook up with Two Medicine boat departure times. Ask for schedules at the hotel front desk.

While in theory the shuttle is a great way to access trailheads, consider where you are and how long it will take you to get to Logan Pass—three hours. And you won't start hiking

until 11:30 A.M. For the most efficient use of your time while staying in East Glacier, you're better off hiking in Two Medicine; then, move north to St. Mary or Many Glacier to hike trails in the park's core.

Flathead-Glacier Transportation (406/892-3390 or 800/829-7039; www.fgtrans.com) runs shuttles by reservation only between Glacier International Airport and East Glacier ($130 one-way).

Bus Tours

Historic **Red Bus** (406/892-2525, www.glacierparkinc.com, adults $40–80, kids 11 and under half-price) run from Glacier Park Lodge in East Glacier. Driven by storytelling jammer drivers who roll the canvas tops back when the weather permits, the vintage buses are not just a treat for their historic ambience, but for the whole-sky views. The 8.5-hour **Big**

Sky Circle Tour (mid-June–mid-Sept.) packs in the best of the park for those who have limited time to explore all its corners. Departing daily at 9 A.M., the tour travels over Marias Pass to Lake McDonald Lodge, then crosses Logan Pass on Going-to-the-Sun Road to St. Mary and back to the lodge. The three-hour **Two Medicine Tour** (June–Sept.) departs twice daily at 10 A.M. and 2:30 P.M. from the lake and the Blackfoot Reservation. For an excursion to Many Glacier and Waterton, the eight-hour **International Peace Park Tour** (mid-June–mid-Sept.) departs daily at 9:30 A.M. Prices do not include meals or park entrance fees. Reservations are required and can be made by phone or at the hotel front desk.

Departing East Glacier daily at 8 A.M., **Sun Tours** (406/226-9220 or 800/786-9220, www.glaciersuntours.com; June–Sept., adults $70, kids $20, meals and park entrance fees not included) drives 25-passenger air-conditioned buses with extra-large windows to catch the big views on Going-to-the-Sun Road. Tours travel through St. Mary to Logan Pass and back. Led by local guides who live on the reservation, the seven-hour tour highlights Glacier's connection with the Blackfeet. You'll get to know the background of peak names as well as the cultural history of the park. The guides, most of whom are excellent storytellers, also know about plants, wildlife, and geology. If you're staying in Browning, you can catch the tour there, departing at 8:30 A.M. Although you can call to hop on the day of the tour, you're better off planning at least 24 hours in advance. You can also stop in their East Glacier office on Highway 2 right across from the train depot.

◖ Boat Tour

The **Sinopah** (Glacier Park Boat Company, 406/257-2426, www.glacierparkboats.com, mid-June–early Sept., adults $11 round-trip, kids half-price) started service on Two Medicine Lake in 1927 and has never left its waters. The 45-foot, 49-passenger wooden boat cruises uplake four times daily for 45-minute tours (10:30 A.M. and 1, 3, and 5 P.M.) while the captain narrates a little history, trivia, and natural phenomenon. Two launches daily

The *Sinopah* that tours on Two Medicine Lake also acts as a hiker shuttle.

© BECKY LOMAX

also incorporate a short, guided hike to Twin Falls (0.9 mile one-way). For July–August, the boat company adds on a 9 A.M. hiker express. Purchase tickets (cash only) at the boat dock. To shorten the 10-mile round-trip Upper Two Medicine Lake hike to four miles, catch the boat both directions. For a three-mile jaunt, hike one way along the northern lakeshore through avalanche gullies under Rising Wolf's flanks and hop the boat back. You can pay (cash only) for one-way return rides upon boarding. At the end of the day, the boat collects all hikers waiting at the upper dock, even if it means extra trips.

SERVICES

Two Medicine has no gas station, but East Glacier has two: an Exxon at the Bear Track Travel Center at the east end of town on Highway 2 and Grizzly Gas on Highway 49 at the Sears Motel. There are ATMs at Glacier Park Trading Company and Glacier Park Lodge. The post office is in East Glacier (15 Blackfoot Avenue, 8:30 A.M.–noon and 1:30–5 P.M. weekdays only). The area's daily newspaper is the *Great Falls Tribune*.

A launderette (open 7 A.M.–9 P.M. daily) is in East Glacier at the west end of town on Highway 2. Another laundry is at Y Lazy R RV Park on Lindhe and Meade, and it offers coin-op showers available to drop-ins.

Some cell phones have reception in East Glacier. Internet access is available at Brownie's and Bear Track Travel Center.

The **Two Medicine Ranger Station** (406/888-7800, summers only, 8 A.M.–4:30 P.M. daily), at the terminus of Two Medicine Road at the campground junction, has current trail information and issues backcountry campsite permits. You can also pick up copies of *The Glacier Explorer* for park naturalist programs, fishing information, free non-topographical maps of trails in the area, and bear sightings. The ranger station plots bear sightings on a large wall map worth a look just for bear trivia. Rangers like to receive reports of bear sightings along trails or in the campground. The ranger station sells tribal conservation permits

($10 per person per year) for those hiking over Scenic Point to East Glacier.

The **East Glacier Ranger Station** (824 Hwy. 49, 406/888-7800) houses a small year-round staff, but the station doesn't maintain public hours. Rangers are often out working in the backcountry.

Rental Cars

From May–September, you can rent cars in East Glacier through Dollar Rent-A-Car at **Sears Motel** (1023 Hwy. 49, 406/226-4432 or 800/800-4000, www.dollar.com). Late April–September, **Glacier Park Trading Company** (314 Hwy. 2, 406/226-4433, summer 8 A.M.–9 P.M., winter 9 A.M.–8 P.M.) rents Avis cars (800/230-4898, www.avis.com).

Water

Since East Glacier draws its water from surface sources, both East Glacier and Browning struggle with water quality. When bacteria get into the water, all water must be boiled (five minutes) before drinking. To be safe, it's best just to drink bottled water in East Glacier, rather than tap water. All restaurants serve bottled water, so you don't have to worry—but ask just to be sure. Glacier Park Lodge heavily chlorinates its water (you'll taste it) to eliminate the bacteria.

Emergencies

In Glacier Park, contact a park ranger for emergencies (406/888-7800). You can also contact the **Two Medicine Ranger Station** (406/888-7800, summers only, 8 A.M.–4:30 P.M. daily), on Two Medicine Road at the campground junction. The nearest hospital is in Cut Bank—the Northern Rockies Medical Center (802 2nd St. E., 406/873-2251).

DRIVING TOURS
Two Medicine Road

Four miles north of East Glacier off Highway 49, Two Medicine Road heads up the Two Medicine Valley for 7.5 miles. It begins on the Blackfeet Reservation and winds through quaking aspen above Lower Two Medicine

TWO MEDICINE

Two Medicine Lake from summit of Mt. Sinopah

© BECKY LOMAX

Lake into the park. In September, the aspens turn bright yellow, almost emitting a light of their own. **Scenic Point** rises across the lake, and the red flanks of Rising Wolf hog the upper valley. You'll enter the park at 2.9 miles, crossing over a cattle guard, but you won't reach the entrance station until 4.1 miles. A few minutes past the entrance station (5.2 miles), stop for the short nature walk heading to **Running Eagle Falls.** As the road climbs into the Two Medicine Basin, look for blue camas, fleabane, paintbrush, and lupine. Once you cross the apex, the peaks of Two Medicine pop out: Sinopah, Lone Walker, and Rising Wolf. After passing the campground and picnic area entrance (7.1 miles), the road terminates in the parking lot at **Two Medicine Lake** where you can catch a boat tour on the lake or stop in the historic chalet, now a camp store selling ice-cream cones.

◖ Looking Glass Hill-Browning Loop

From East Glacier, drive Highway 49 north up Looking Glass Hill, an original part of the Blackfeet Highway. Because this section from Two Medicine Road to Kiowa Junction is closed in winter (Nov.–Apr.), this tour is a summer drive only. The shoulderless road with more curves than a snake is not ideal for trailers and large RVs, but they are permitted. Be aware, however, that wet downpours cause landslides; the road frequently closes for repairs, and you'll hit rough sections with chewed pavement. As the road climbs to a high vantage point above **Lower Two Medicine Lake,** it twists through aspen groves. Three miles past the Two Medicine junction you'll find unmarked pullouts overlooking the valley for great photo ops before descending to Kiowa Junction.

Drive slowly, for open range means no fences. Cattle wander willy-nilly where they please here. Often, you'll round a corner into cows standing smack in the middle of the road and may have to wait for them to move. They are not particularly speedy creatures, but they can dent your car with a good kick, so give them room. Because the road is narrow and curvy, take it slow. You'll have less chance of putting a cow imprint across your grille.

At Kiowa, you can choose the **Looking Glass-Browning** tour making a 49-mile scenic loop through the Blackfeet Reservation for grand views of peak panoramas from the plains. Take Highway 89 east toward Browning, stop at the Museum of the Plains Indian, and turn back to East Glacier on Highway 2 past the Blackfeet National Bison Preserve. From Kiowa, you can also continue north on the **Blackfeet Highway to St. Mary** (Hwy. 89) along the Rocky Mountain Front—a scenic, but narrow, curvy drive.

SIGHTS
Two Medicine Lake
The largest of three lakes, Two Medicine Lake is the highest road-accessible lake in Glacier, sitting almost one mile high in elevation. Its waters collect from snowmelt on peaks over 8,000 feet high, but devoid of glaciers. The lakes are all that remain of the monster thousand-foot-thick ice field that covered nearly 500,000 acres, flowing well out onto the prairie past Browning. To explore Two Medicine Lake, jump on the historic *Sinopah* tour boat for some good storytelling by Glacier Park Boat Company's captains. If waters are calm, rent a canoe to paddle its shoreline. Hike to Paradise Point for a swim in its chilly clear waters or fish for brook trout.

Family Peaks
Rich with Blackfeet history, the peaks in Two Medicine Valley tell a story. **Rising Wolf,** climbing straight out of the north shoreline to 9,573 feet, was named for Hugh Monroe, a Hudson Bay Company fur trapper who came to the Glacier area in the early 1800s. After living with the Piegans, he bargained with **Lone Walker,** the tribal chief, to marry his daughter. To see Lone Walker Mountain, look upvalley between Helen and Sinopah for what appears to be a low-angled pyramid but is actually 8,502 feet high. At Upper Two Medicine Lake, this peak sits above the lake's head. Rising Wolf married Lone Walker's daughter—**Sinopah,** the dramatic eroded pyramid directly across Two Medicine Lake at 8,271 feet.

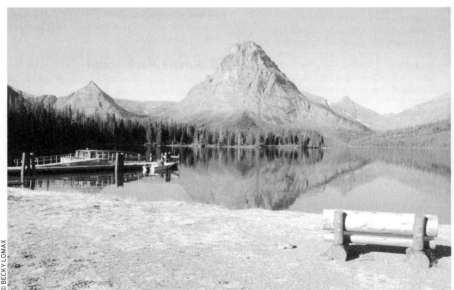

Mt. Sinopah sits across Two Medicine Lake from the tour boat dock.

© BECKY LOMAX

TWO MEDICINE

RISING WOLF

Without a doubt, the most prominent feature in Two Medicine Valley is the hulk of 9,513-foot **Rising Wolf Mountain.** It's named for the first European descendent to meet the Blackfeet. Born Hugh Monroe in Quebec, Canada, in 1798, the 16-year-old traveled west as an apprentice for the Hudson Bay Company.

With an intense interest in the Indians, he was sent to live with the Small Robes band of Piegans (a Blackfeet tribe) to learn their language and find beaver-trapping territory. The tribe's chief, **Lone Walker,** took a liking to the congenial Monroe. After several seasons with the Piegans, Monroe married **Sinopah,** Lone Walker's daughter, and lived permanently with them. (Lone Walker peak sits at the head of Upper Two Medicine Lake; Sinopah rises straight out of Two Medicine Lake opposite Rising Wolf.)

When officially admitted to the tribe, Monroe was ascribed the name Rising Wolf. Despite lack of written records, it is presumed that Monroe was the first European descendent to set eyes on St. Mary Lake and much of Glacier's eastern lands. He served as a guide and interpreter for territorial survey teams and early reconnaissance of Glacier Park. He later left Hudson Bay Company for the American Fur Company that established trading posts on the Marias River in Blackfeet country. Rising Wolf died in 1892, the same year Great Northern Railway laid tracks over Marias Pass.

While there is some discrepancy on Monroe's birthdate, it is apparent he lived to a ripe old age, even after losing sight in one eye in a fight with a Sioux. Many of Monroe's descendants still live on the Blackfeet Reservation.

Two Medicine Chalets

All that remains of historic Two Medicine Chalets is the dining hall, now operating as the Two Medicine Campstore and designated in 1987 as a National Historic Landmark. Built 1912–1913, the chalets replaced the original tipi camp for visitors. The log two-story chalet was once the hub of the small colony, the first stop on the Inside Trail horse trip with Park Saddle Company in the 1920s. The dining hall's most famous guest was Franklin Delano Roosevelt, who addressed the nation from here in an unofficial fireside chat in 1934.

◖ Running Eagle Falls

A short nature trail (0.6 mile round-trip) leads to Running Eagle Falls, also known as Trick Falls. In high runoff, water gushes over the top of the falls, spraying those standing nearby. But in lower flows, you can see the trick. Part of the falls runs underground and spits out through a cavern halfway down the falls' face. Running Eagle, the Blackfeet name for the falls, honors a female warrior named Pitamakin who had her vision quest here. She was renowned for stealing horses from the Kootenai but was eventually killed during a raid.

◖ Glacier Park Lodge

In East Glacier, Glacier Park Lodge stands as the headliner hotel for the historic chain of Great Northern hostelries built throughout Glacier. Set within the Blackfeet Reservation, the 155-room hotel built in 1915 started its life as a grand hotel providing visitors the first taste of Glacier. Since the advent of Going-to-the-Sun Road, additional avenues into the park stole some of the lodge's thunder. Today, the hotel is listed on the National Register of Historic Places. Even if you are not staying here, plan to walk the gardens leading up to the front door and lounge in its massive lobby held up by three-story Douglas firs. In the lobby, an excellent historic photo display chronicles the hotel's history.

Blackfeet Sentries

Blackfeet artist Jay Laber gives new life to garbage in what he calls "Reborn Rez Wrecks." Using farm tools, jewelry, hubcaps, and barbwire, he sculpted a not-to-be-missed sculpture series—Blackfeet Reservation Sentries—posted on the reservation's four boundaries. Each pair of life-size sentries rides atop horses. Posted in East Glacier, one pair guards the reservation's western entrance (0.2 mile west of town on Hwy. 2).

◖ Museum of the Plains Indian

Located in Browning, 12 miles from East Glacier, the Museum of the Plains Indian (junction of Hwy. 2 and 83, 406/338-2230, June–Sept. daily 9 A.M.–4:45 P.M., Oct.–May Mon.–Fri. 10 A.M.–4:30 P.M., adults $4, kids 6–12 $1, under 6 free, all ages free in winter) is a small but very informative center for Blackfeet culture and history. A multimedia five-screen show narrated by Vincent Price tells the story of the Blackfeet people, well worth the 20 minutes it takes to watch it. Displays cluster phenomenal beadwork, leather, tools, and clothing to tell the story of the Northern Plains Indians. Seeing the life-size beaded ceremonial costumes alone are worth the price of admission.

Recreation

HIKING

Hiking at Two Medicine is in a class by itself. Except for a few short hikes from the lake's upper boat dock, hikers here find solitude even on the most crowded hot summer days. For hikes on reservation land (those leaving directly from East Glacier or the latter half of the Scenic Point trail), a tribal recreation label is required. You can purchase the $10 annual permit at the Two Medicine Ranger Station or Bear Track Travel Center (Exxon gas station) in East Glacier.

With a maze of trail junctions breaking off of the north- and south-shore Two Medicine Lake trails, you'll find one of the park's non-topographical trail maps helpful. These are available at the ranger station and the Glacier Park Lodge activity desk. For longer hikes, such as the Dawson-Pitamakin Loop, tote a good topographical map: You can buy one in the Two Medicine Campstore.

Aster Park

- Distance: 3.8 miles round-trip
- Duration: 2 hours
- Elevation gain: 670 feet
- Effort: easy

- Trailhead: adjacent to Two Medicine boat dock

Beginning on the south shore trail, Aster Park is reached via a spur trail just past Aster Creek. About 1.2 miles up the trail, turn left at the signed junction and follow the trail past Aster Falls as it switchbacks up to a knoll. This overlook provides grand views of Two Medicine Lake and its northern peaks.

Twin Falls and Upper Two Medicine Lake

- Distance: 1.8–10 miles round-trip
- Duration: 1–5 hours
- Elevation gain: 0–350 feet
- Effort: easy
- Trailhead: Two Medicine Lake west boat dock or Pray Lake Bridge in Two Medicine Campground

Set in a subalpine bowl, Upper Two Medicine Lake is reached by a trail passing Twin Falls—a double flume of cascades. Taking the boat both ways on Two Medicine Lake makes the shortest hikes: Twin Falls, 1.8 miles round-trip; the lake, 4.4 miles. Taking the boat one way and hiking the remaining distance shortens the

LEAVE NO TRACE

To be a part of keeping Glacier pristine, visitors to this unique park need to take an active role in maintaining its well-being.

- **Plan ahead and prepare.** Hiking in Glacier's backcountry is inherently risky. Three miles here may be much harder than three miles through your neighborhood park back home. Choose appropriate routes for mileage and elevation gain with this in mind, and carry hiking essentials.

- **Travel and camp on durable surfaces.** In both frontcountry and backcountry campgrounds, camp in designated sites only. Protect fragile plants by staying on the trail, refusing to cut switchbacks, and walking single file on trails – even in the mud. If you must walk off the trail, step on rocks, snow, or dry grasses rather than wet soil and delicate plants.

- **Leave what you find.** Flowers, rocks, and goat fur tufts on shrubs are protected park resources, as are historical cultural items. For lunch stops and camping, sit on rocks or logs where you find them rather than moving them to accommodate your camp.

- **Properly dispose of waste.** Whatever you bring in, you must pack out. Pack out all garbage, including toilet paper. If toilets are not available, urinate on rocks, logs, gravel, or snow to protect soils and plants from salt-starved wildlife, and bury feces six-eight inches deep at least 200 feet from water.

- **Minimize campfire impacts.** Make fires in designated fire pits only, not on beaches. Use small wrist-size dead and downed wood, not live branches. Be aware that fires and firewood collecting are not permitted in many places in the park.

- **Respect wildlife.** Bring along binoculars, spotting scopes, and telephoto lenses to aid in watching wildlife. Keep your distance. Do not feed any wildlife, even ground squirrels. Once fed, they become more aggressive.

- **Be considerate of other visitors.**

For more Leave No Trace information, please visit www.LNT.org or call 303/442.8222.

---

hike to 7.2 miles. For the longest route, you can hike both up and back on the north shore trail or loop around Two Medicine Lake.

The trail climbs gently, passing the short spur trail to Twin Falls. After crossing avalanche gullies thick with huckleberries, you'll crest a prominent rock ledge to the lake. If you are eating lunch at the lake, help maintain the safety of those sleeping in the backcountry campground here by not eating in the sleeping sites. Sit in the cooking area to eat or hike up the north shoreline (which is impossible to do in early season high water).

◖ Scenic Point

- Distance: 6.2 miles round-trip
- Duration: 3–4 hours
- Elevation gain: 2,350 feet
- Effort: moderately strenuous
- Trailhead: milepost 6.9 on Two Medicine Road

Scenic Point is one short climb with big scenery. The trail launches up through a thick subalpine fir forest. A short side jaunt en route sneaks a peek at Appistoki Falls. As switchbacks line up like dominoes, stunted firs give way to dead silver, twisted limber pines. Broaching the ridge, the trail enters a seemingly barren alpine tundra. Only alpine bluebells and pink mats of several-hundred-year-old moss campion cower in crags.

The trail traverses across a talus slope, covered in early season with steep snows to be avoided. (You can climb a worn path that

© BECKY LOMAX

Scenic Point trail leads to mountaintop views of Two Medicine.

circumvents the snowfield.) The trail descends to Scenic Point. To reach the actual point above the trail, cut off at the sign, stepping on rocks to avoid crushing fragile alpine plants. Atop, you can swan dive several thousand feet straight down into Lower Two Medicine Lake. Return the way you came, or drop seven miles to East Glacier. You'll pass outside the park boundary, where cow pies buzz with flies. Tribal recreation permits are required for this option, available at the ranger station.

Rockwell Falls and Cobalt Lake

- Distance: 6.8–11.4 miles round-trip

- Duration: 4–5.5 hours

- Elevation gain: minimal to 1,400 feet

- Effort: easy to moderate

- Trailhead: adjacent to the Two Medicine boat dock

Follow the gentle south shore trail along Two Medicine Lake past beaver ponds and bear-scratched trees to Paradise Creek, where a swinging bridge makes you think of Indiana Jones movies, but it's not as scary. At 2.3 miles, turn left at the signed junction. The trail wanders through avalanche paths with uprooted trees shredded like toothpicks. At 3.4 miles, you reach Rockwell Falls. Spur trails explore the falls.

Continuing on to Cobalt Lake, the trail climbs up several switchbacks into an upper basin, crossing back and forth over the creek. The trail packs all of its elevation gain into the last two miles. Tucked in the uppermost corner of the basin, Cobalt Lake sits below talus slopes covered with mountain goats.

(Dawson-Pitamakin Loop

- Distance: 16.9 or 18.8 miles

- Duration: 7–9 hours

- Elevation gain: 2,935 feet

- Effort: strenuous

TWO MEDICINE

• Trailhead: Two Medicine Lake west boat dock or Pray Lake Bridge in Two Medicine Campground

Although this loop can be done from either direction, both with the same elevation gain up to 8,000 feet, the approach to Dawson Pass is much steeper than to Pitamakin Pass. It crams all of its elevation gain within three miles, while Pitamakin Pass sprawls it less steeply out over eight. So pick your poison based on your preference for uphill grunts and knee-pounding descents. If you catch the Two Medicine boat one direction or the other, you'll chop off 1.9 miles.

In its loop around Rising Wolf, the route actually crosses three passes: Pitamakin, Cut Bank, and Dawson, the latter two passes seeing frequent winds raging enough to force crawling. Starting toward Pitamakin, the trail crosses Dry Fork and follows it up to Old Man Lake (6.8 miles), a good fishing lake, before climbing to the pass (8.8 miles), where you'll often see bighorn sheep. With the narrow trail exposed high on a several-mile goat traverse between Cut Bank and Dawson (12.1 miles) passes, those with a fear of heights will be uncomfortable. For most, it's the best part of the trail, walking a tightrope between vertigo and soaring.

© BECKY LOMAX

the traverse between Dawson and Cut Bank passes

Medicine Grizzly Lake and Triple Divide Pass

• Distance: 12 or 14.4 miles round-trip

• Duration: 6–7.5 hours

• Elevation gain: 540 or 2,380 feet

• Effort: easy to strenuous

• Trailhead: terminus of Cut Bank Road

• Directions: Locate the signed Cut Bank Road six miles north of Kiowa Junction on Highway 89. Follow the narrow dirt road over cattle grates into the park and past the ranger station. The trailhead is about four miles up just before the campground.

Due to its location up the rough Cut Bank Road, many hikers are deterred. But it's a popular trail for anglers as Medicine Grizzly Lake harbors 12-inch rainbows. Check with the ranger station before leaving, as bear activity frequently closes the lake and its spur trail. The trail follows Atlantic Creek up a forested drainage to a signed junction at four miles. Turn right, climbing (0.6 mile) past the Atlantic Creek campground to a second junction. To head to Medicine Grizzly Lake, continue straight for 1.4 miles.

For Triple Divide Pass, the other trail bursts out of the trees, climbing up a rocky face below Mount James as it looks down on the lake. After winding into a large bowl, look for bighorn sheep, frequently browsing here. Tucked at the base of Triple Divide Peak, the pass actually stands on the split between the Saskatchewan and Missouri River drainages, beginning here as Hudson Bay Creek and Atlantic Creek.

Guides

The National Park Service guides free hikes mid-June through mid-September to a variety of destinations in Two Medicine: Upper Two Medicine Lake, Scenic Point, Dawson Pass, Rockwell Falls, and Cobalt Lake as well as a daily boat ride and hike to Twin Falls. (The hike is free, but you still need to pay for the boat ride.) Grab a copy of *The Glacier Explorer* from the ranger station for the current schedule.

Glacier Guides (406/387-5555 or 800/521-7238, www.glacierguides.com) will pick you up at the lodge, transport you to the trailhead, and bring along a deli lunch and snacks. You just need to bring your pack, sunscreen, bug juice, water, and extra clothes. Reservations are mandatory. Their Custom Day Hikes ($450, up to 5 people) will depart from East Glacier or Two Medicine. Solo travelers can also hook up with their Tuesday Hikes ($75 per person,

July–Aug.) and Group Day Hikes ($375, 1–5 people, June–Sept.), which depart from their West Glacier office, an hour from East Glacier. The guide service also has three-, four-, and six-day backpacking trips that depart weekly ($135 per day, June–mid-Sept.)—some on routes out of Two Medicine.

Shuttles

In Two Medicine, hikers use the tour boat as a shuttle uplake to prune miles off hikes and get farther into the backcountry faster. (See *Tours and Shuttles.*) Glacier Park, Inc. also runs a shuttle from Glacier Park Lodge to Two Medicine for hiking; the shuttles arrive in time to catch the boat across Two Medicine Lake.

BIKING

Bicycling around the park's southeast corner is usually restricted to narrow, curvy, shoulderless roadways. Although most drivers are fairly courteous toward bicyclists here, be prepared to have large RVs nearly shove you off the road, simply due to their size in comparison to the skimpy pavement. It's an area where you may encounter bears on the roadway, especially on Two Medicine Road; on Highway 49, you can round a corner into a small herd of cows, since the area is open range. For some reason, no matter which direction you're riding, a strong headwind always blasts. Since mountain biking is not permitted on trails within Glacier, riding is restricted to roadways. Families with youngsters should stick to the campground loops at Two Medicine Campground rather than riding the roadways. Most bicyclists out for the day ride from East Glacier to Two Medicine Lake and back.

For bicyclists, Two Medicine Campground has shared hiker-biker campsites for $5 per person. These are reserved until 9 P.M. for bikers and have bear-resistant food storage containers on-site.

TRAIL RIDING

Across the street from Glacier Park Lodge on Highway 49, **Glacier Gateway Outfitters** (0.4 mile north of Hwy. 2 and 49 junction,

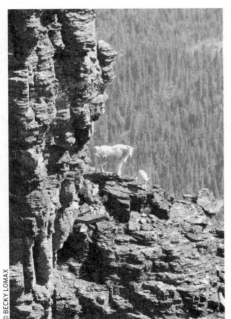

Mountain goats cling to steep cliffs on Sinopah.

© BECKY LOMAX

406/226-4408, June–Sept.) leads trail rides and cowboy-style horseback rides—ones that tour cross-country rather than riding single-file. Led by Native American guides, the tours roam outside Glacier Park on adjacent Blackfeet Reservation land. Rides wander along Two Medicine River Gorge through aspens and blooms of early-season shooting stars and late-summer lupine—all at the foot of the park's front range. Short rides (one-hour $25, two-hour $50) depart several times daily. Full-day rides ($175 per person with minimum of five people, bring your own lunch) depart at 9 A.M., and three-hour ($75) rides depart at 9 A.M. and 2 P.M. Wear long pants and sturdy shoes, such as hiking boots or tennis shoes. Kids must be at least seven years old and have some experience riding, but no special children's rates are offered. Reservations are recommended, especially in high season.

BOATING

Two Medicine is the highest lake you can drive to in the park; it's also one of the windiest. Boaters need to keep an eye on waves; if whitecaps pop up, consider getting off the lake. Two Medicine Road terminates at the public boat ramp, so it's easy to find. Hand-powered craft and motorized boats are allowed with 10 horsepower or less, but no jet skis, so the lake maintains a nice quiet. On calm days, kayakers and canoers tour the lake's shore. On Lower Two Medicine Lake, you won't see many boats. Lack of a boat ramp and no access trails preclude most people; it's hard to bushwhack carrying a kayak.

Glacier Park Boat Company (406/226-4467 summers only, 406/257-2426, www.glacierparkboats.com) rents canoes, kayaks, and small motorboats at the Two Medicine Boat Dock for $14–20 (cash only) per hour.

FISHING

Two Medicine River links together the three lakes by the same name with brook trout populating much of the waters. For fishing **Upper Two Medicine Lake,** hike two miles after taking the boat shuttle across

Two Medicine Lake. It's an attractive lake to fish, but its shoreline is brushy and the outlet clogged with downed timbers. Anglers in **Two Medicine Lake** may have more success tossing in a line from a boat rather than fishing from shore—especially because much of the shoreline is heavily timbered and brushy. On the valley's south side, Paradise Creek harbors some trout, but Aster and Apistoki Creeks are void, so don't bother dropping a line in here. On the dam-controlled **Lower Two Medicine Lake,** which is half in the park, half on the Blackfeet Reservation, only a few anglers go after the 10- to 12-inch rainbows and brookies here; difficult access with no trails or official boat ramp keeps most anglers away. Other area lakes—No Name and Old Man—support trout, but Cobalt is barren.

Licenses and Regulations

No fishing license is required in the park, but pick up park fishing regulations at the ranger station in Two Medicine. Outside the park on Lower Two Medicine Lake or Two Medicine River, you will need a tribal fishing permit. (See the *Background* chapter for details.) Purchase fishing licenses at Bear Track Travel Center (Exxon station in East Glacier, 20958 Hwy. 2, 406/226-5504, winter 7 A.M.–8 P.M., summer 7 A.M.–10 P.M.).

GOLF

Built in 1927, the **Glacier Park Lodge Golf Course** (406/892-2525, www.glacierparkinc .com, late May–early Oct.) is the oldest grass greens in Montana. The nine-hole course winds through aspen groves with views of Dancing Lady, Henry, Calf Robe, and Summit peaks. Don't be surprised if bears (or more commonly stray dogs) roam across the course. Because the course is on Blackfeet tribal lands, each of the nine holes is named after former Blackfeet Nation chiefs—Rising Wolf, Bad Marriage, Long Time Sleeps, and Stabs-By-Mistake. An 18-hole round costs $27. Clubs rent for $14–21 and power carts for $15–23. For tee times, call 406/226-5342 or the hotel front desk. The lodge often offers special spring and fall rates for golf-lodging packages; call or check the website for details.

A public, nine-hole pitch-and-putt miniature golf course covers half of the front lawn of Glacier Park Lodge. Pick up clubs and a souvenir ball ($8 per person) at the front desk. Ground squirrel holes add a challenge to the course.

CROSS-COUNTRY SKIING

Late December–April, **Two Medicine Road** (15 miles round-trip) makes a delightfully easy but long ski, with frozen Two Medicine Lake as the destination. Snow here piles up enough to bury the restrooms. While the going is not tough and the gentle terrain undulates except for one long hill, winds can scour the road free of snow in places, requiring skiers to take skis off and on. Headwinds also frequently blow both directions. Nevertheless, it's a stunning trip, with relatively little avalanche danger.

When snow permits, skiing **Looking Glass Hill** on Highway 49 is also popular. An eight-mile round-trip tour leads from the junction with Two Medicine Road to spectacular overlooks of Two Medicine Valley and Lake Creek drainage to Divide Mountain by St. Mary. Do not forget the camera on this trip! Sometimes winds blow the pavement bare, so be prepared to take skis off and put them on again.

No equipment rental is available in East Glacier; the nearest rentals are at the Izaak Walton Inn on Highway 2 and at Glacier Outdoor Center in West Glacier. Winter shuts down East Glacier and much of the park, so be prepared for trips here. Do not venture out without a complete pack full of emergency gear, ready for self-rescue.

ENTERTAINMENT

On summer evenings National Park Service naturalists present free 45-minute talks on natural history and wildlife in the Two Medicine Amphitheater, usually at 8 P.M. Once a week, the Native America Speaks program features storytellers who bring to life the history of local tribes and their involvement in Glacier. For a current schedule, pick up a copy of *The Glacier Explorer* at visitors centers and ranger stations.

Glacier Park Lodge sponsors entertainment from time to time—Native American speakers and entertainers as well as musicians, such as the Trapp Family Singers. Check the sign in the lobby near the front desk for the current schedule.

◖ North American Indian Days

Over four days beginning the second Thursday in July, North American Indian Days celebrates Blackfeet culture. Located behind the Museum of the Plains Indian, the powwow grounds (4th Ave. NW and Boundary St.) in Browning become home to tipis. Dancing, drumming, singing, games, and sporting events draw tribes from the U.S. and Canada. Traditional costumes—especially those worn for fancy dances—are spectacular with feathered headdresses and beadwork. Non-native people are welcome to attend. It's one of the best ways to learn about the Blackfeet and their culture, and watching is free. For details on the powwow, call the Blackfeet Nation Planning Department (406/338-7406).

Casino

You can find gaming and slot machines on the Blackfeet Reservation. The new **Glacier Peaks Casino** (406/338-2274; 877/238-9946; www.glaciercash.com; 10 A.M. to 2 A.M.) sits adjacent to the Museum of the Plains Indians in Browning at the junction of Highways 2 and 89. The 33,000 square foot facility contains 400 slot machines, live poker, and a restaurant.

TWO MEDICINE

Accommodations

East Glacier is divided in half by the railroad tracks. On one side, historic Glacier Park Lodge and the golf course sit on Highway 49 followed by a compact motel strip—think very rustic here, not a highway mega-strip—which ends abruptly within one mile. On the south side of the tracks along Highway 2, East Glacier tucks several motels within a few-block radius of restaurants. All fill to the brim in high season, so reservations are highly recommended. Two Medicine has no lodging available, only a campground.

EAST GLACIER
Lodges and Cabins
Historic 【 **Glacier Park Lodge** (0.1 mile north on Hwy. 49, 406/892-2525, www .glacierparkinc.com, open late May–early Oct., until mid-June $129–179, after mid-June $140–299, chalet $349–449), sits outside the park boundary on Blackfeet tribal land right across from the train depot. It's the only historic lodge with an outdoor swimming pool (heated, but still chilly), golf course, and pitch-and-putt. Main lodge rooms are connected to rooms in the west wing via a scenic enclosed walkway off the gigantic lobby, where huge western red cedars hold aloft a several-story ceiling. The west rooms tend to be larger than rooms in the other historic park hotels. Get a room facing the mountains to enjoy the sunrises and sunsets casting orange glows. You may want to bring earplugs; rooms catch the rumble and clatter of passing trains. Lodge rooms, suites, and family rooms are available, along with a chalet. All rooms are nonsmoking. Expect rustic—tiny bathrooms converted from original closets, cantankerous hot water, and no television, air-conditioning, or elevator access—and you'll be delighted with the historical ambiance. Reservations are highly recommended in June and September, an absolute must in July and August.

A restaurant, lounge, snack shop, and gift shop sit off the lobby, and Remedies Day Spa offers massages for trail-weary muscles. Red bus tours depart from the hotel, and trail riding is across the street. Trails to Scenic Point and Firebrand Pass depart nearby, crossing reservation land before entering park boundaries. In the evening, Native American speakers often give fireside talks.

Built in 2004, 【 **Traveler's Rest Lodge** (0.3 mile east of Exxon station on Hwy. 2, 406/226-9143 summer, 406/378-2414 winter, www.travelersrestlodge.net, May–Sept., $105–125 double occupancy) has clean, roomy nonsmoking log mortise and tenon cabins with gas fireplaces and fully equipped kitchenettes on eight acres amid aspen trees. Each is positioned for its deck to gain privacy and views of the Bob Marshall Wilderness. The nicely decorated cabins sleeping 2–4 people in log-hewn beds have televisions and CD players but no phones. (One is available in the office.) Because of East Glacier's frequent "boil orders" for water, each cabin is equipped with five gallons of drinking water. In one of the cabins, the owners, Diane and Bob Scalese, have their engraving workshop. They are well-known artisans who design, craft, and engrave spurs, bits, belt buckles, and saddle silver.

Motels
East Glacier has seven small motels, some with cabins, and all with convenient access to restaurants and stores. Four small seasonal (May–Sept.) ones line Highway 49's motel strip north of Glacier Park Lodge. The area hops in high summer, but highway traffic virtually disappears at night. You can hear a bit of train noise even though the motels are shielded from the tracks by trees. Three other year-round motels sit in "downtown" East Glacier. While highway noise dwindles at night, train noise here does not. Bring earplugs for the trains. Advance reservations in high season are a wise idea.

Sitting right on Highway 2 across from the train depot, **Glacier Park Circle R Motel** (402 Hwy. 2 E., 406/226-9331, www.circlermotel

.com, open year-round, summer $48–89; late Sept.–June $62–68) just added more new rooms in 2007. Year-round, the motel rents 16 nonsmoking rooms with cable television and Internet hookups. The second-floor rooms have good views of Dancing Lady. One suite has a full kitchen and air-conditioning. In summer, the motel also opens its older smoking-permitted rooms.

A half block off of Highway 2, **Dancing Bears Inn** (40 Montana Ave., 406/226-4402, open year-round, summer $75–99; winter $50–55) sits one block off the highway and train. Rooms offer Internet access, air-conditioning, and cable television, and some have kitchenettes.

Guesthouses
Art aficionados may enjoy renting a room from a professional potter and sculptor at **The Brown House** (402 Washington St., 406/226-9385, www.glacierinfo.com, June–Sept., $55–65), which has three remodeled nonsmoking rooms, each furnished with antiques and having a private entrance and bath. The upstairs room has a view of the park's peaks. Originally a 1920s store, the building still has some of the fixtures from that era. The gift shop also sells the works of local artisans.

Hostels
For the budget-minded, East Glacier has two hostels open mid-May–September. **(Backpacker's Inn** (29 Dawson Ave., 406/226-9392) has three dorms, plus two cabins located in the backyard of Serrano's Mexican Restaurant—a little oasis in the middle of town. The buildings are the renovated original pre-fab cedar Sears and Roebuck 1920 homes. Beds in the dorm rooms are $12 per person per night; bring your own sleeping bag ($1 to rent a bag). The cabins with one queen bed and linens rent for $40. **Brownie's Hostel** (1020 Hwy. 49, 406/226-4426, www.brownieshostel.com) is in an old renovated two-story 1920s building on the Highway 49 motel strip. An easy six-block walk from the train station and adjacent to restaurants, the hostel has a fully equipped

communal kitchen and three dorms with beds ($13 per night for Hostelling International members; $16 for non-members). Private bedrooms are also available ($20–43). Cinnamon rolls scent the air in the morning from the downstairs bakery. It has a deli and convenience store with Internet access, too.

CAMPING
RVers requiring hookups will need to stay in East Glacier, for the park service campgrounds in Two Medicine and Cut Bank have no hookups. If these are full, check the *Marias Pass and Essex* chapter for alternatives, such as Summit (11 miles away) or Glacier Meadow RV Park (17 miles away).

Cut Bank
Located 19 miles north of East Glacier off Highway 89, **Cut Bank Campground** (406/888-7800, late May–late Sept., $10 per night) sits at the end of a five-mile potholed dirt road inside Glacier Park. Large RVs shouldn't attempt the rough access road. To locate the road, look for the campground sign six miles north of Kiowa Junction. The campground is rustic with only pit toilets, tables, and fire grates, but no running water. Atlantic Creek runs nearby, but you'll need to boil (for five minutes) or filter the water. Bring your own firewood; gathering is prohibited. With only 19 sites set in deep shade under large firs, it's a great place to escape crowds. The campground has fishing in Atlantic Creek and the trailhead to Medicine Grizzly Lake and Triple Divide Pass is nearby.

Two Medicine
Inside Glacier, **(Two Medicine Campground** (406/888-7800, late May–late Sept., $20) yields views of bears foraging on Rising Wolf Mountain, especially from the A and C loops. The campground is set back from Two Medicine Lake, surrounding the calmer waters of small Pray Lake, a good place for chilly swimming and fishing. With 99 sites, the campground fills up in high season, but often not as early in the day as those on Going-to-the-Sun

Two Medicine Campground surrounds smaller Pray Lake.

Road; try to claim a campsite by early afternoon as they are first-come, first-serve. Flush toilets, a dump station, picnic tables, and fire grates are provided—bring your own firewood. (Gathering it is prohibited.) The north shore trail departs right from the campground. A seven-minute walk or few-minute drive puts you at the boat tour and rental dock, and the Two Medicine Campstore can cover what you've forgotten. Only 13 sites can handle RVs up to 32 feet. In late September and October, the campground allows primitive camping ($10) with pit toilets and no running water.

Backcountry Camping

Two Medicine has plenty of backcountry campsites that work as good destinations for kids as well as connections on the Continental Divide Trail. For kids, chop off mileage with the boat and head to **Upper Two Medicine** or **Cobalt Lake.** Both **No Name** and **Old Man Lake** serve as campsites for backpacking the Dawson-Pitamakin Loop. Or drop from Pitamakin Pass to **Morningstar,** with its lake tucked against a cliff wall where golden eagles

nest and mountain goats cavort, continuing north on the Continental Divide Trail toward Cut Bank and St. Mary. Pick up permits ($5 per person per night; kids 8–18 $2.50; kids 7 and under free) 24 hours in advance in person at Two Medicine Ranger Station or the Apgar Permit Office (406/888-7900) or by reservation ($30). Check additional requirements online: www.nps.gov/glac.

East Glacier

A small campground set on three grassy acres, **Y Lazy R RV Park** (junction of Lindhe Ave. and Meade St., 406/226-5505, mid-May–Sept., tents $16, hookups $20) is two blocks off Highway 2. With only a few aspen trees, its open setting affords great views of surrounding mountains. Amenities include flush toilets, picnic tables, coin-op showers, dump station, and a large laundry. The campground sits an easy few-block walk from restaurants.

Browning

Located 2.25 miles west of Browning on a prairie wildflower knoll staring at Glacier's peaks, the **C Lodgepole Gallery and Tipi Village** (look for sign on Hwy. 89, 406/338-2787, www.blackfeetculturecamp.com, May–mid-Sept.) is different—and not just because a small herd of nearly extinct Spanish mustangs, the original Indian horse, runs free on the property (they're not for riding, just for watching). Ten traditional double-walled canvas tipis with a fire pit inside each serve as tents. Supplied wood heats the tipis on cooler nights. You bring your sleeping bag, air mattress, and flashlight; if you don't have them, you can rent them for $6 (the sleeping bags come with linen). A central bathhouse with flush toilets and hot showers services all the tipis. Overnight rates ($40 for first person in tipi, $15 each additional person, $7.50 for kids under 12) include a continental breakfast.

For guests staying at the tipi village, meals by reservation are also available in the dining hall (full American breakfast $12, continental breakfast $6, dinner $16–30). Traditional southern Blackfeet cuisine—gourmet buffalo, deer, and elk—puts a delicious twist on dinner. Owner Darrell Norman, a native Blackfeet artist, singer, and dancer, also teaches art classes in the adjacent gallery; you can learn to make your own drum or fetish. He also guides tours to buffalo jumps and medicine rocks.

Food

Because Two Medicine has no restaurants, campers must hit East Glacier to dine out. However, the drive between the two is short, and in the evening can be a good time to spot wildlife on the return drive. During special days like graduation and North American Indian Days on the Blackfeet Reservation, none of the restaurants or bars serve alcohol. The four-day celebration is usually scheduled beginning the second Thursday in July. During that time, all alcohol sales in restaurants, lounges, and grocery stores are banned on tribal lands—including all restaurants in East Glacier.

RESTAURANTS
East Glacier
In the historic Glacier Park Lodge, the **Great Northern Steak and Rib House** (on Hwy. 49 across from train depot, 406/892-2525, late May–late Sept.) has the best views compared with any restaurant in town. Ask to be seated near the west windows facing Dancing Lady Mountain: The sunrise smears it with pink and the sunset casts orange alpenglow across its face. The nonsmoking restaurant serves up three meals per day with a menu similar to all the park lodges. It has kids menus, too.

Breakfast (6:30–9:30 A.M., $11–14) has two options—a huge buffet or à la carte. The buffet stacks with fruit, pastries, eggs, sausage, bacon, French toast, and pancakes. While selections are broad and you won't walk away hungry, the mass-produced entrees are sometimes only lukewarm. Lunch is served 11:30 A.M.–2 P.M. ($8–14). With its western theme, dinners (5–9:30 P.M., $16–33) specialize in steak, chicken, and ribs. The restaurant doesn't take reservations, so high season can see waiting lines. You can also order hiker lunches ($7–10) one day in advance.

Adjacent to the restaurant, the **The Sunset Lounge** serves up Montana microbrews along with wines and cocktails with a terrific view of Dancing Lady and Mount Henry. If you need a television fix, this is the place to go. For a quick, light meal in a nonsmoking atmosphere, the appetizers and sandwiches ($8–14) are served 2–10 P.M., but the bar is open 11:30 A.M.–midnight.

Waiting lines on the front porch of **C Serrano's Mexican Restaurant** (29 Dawson Ave., 406/226-9293, May–Sept., daily 5–10 P.M.) attest to its tasty food. Most dinners run $8–16 with the made-from-scratch Veggie Delight and Colorado Plates topping the choices, and the chiles rellenos use freshly roasted chiles. Huge plate-loads of food pacify hungry hikers. The smoke-free building is the oldest house in East Glacier; you can eat inside in its cozy dining room with wooden booths or sit on the deck out back while watching the sunset. Either way, the margaritas here are easy to down.

Inexpensive **Two Medicine Grill** (316 Hwy. 2, 406/226-5572, open year-round, daily 6:30 A.M.–9 P.M., but closes Oct.–April at 7 P.M., $3.50–11) is a good place to grab a bagel breakfast sandwich, an espresso, or a buffalo burger. This small hole-in-the-wall diner was built in 1935 in Choteau and moved to East Glacier. They bake their own cinnamon rolls. Go for the hard ice cream and a wild huckleberry milkshake on hot days. To jaw with the owner Mark Howser, sit at one of the eight stools at the bar in front of the grill. Dinners feature favorite greasy spoon foods.

Run by the same owners of Brownie's (see *Groceries*), the **C Whistle Stop Restaurant** (0.5 mile north on Hwy. 49, 406/226-9292, June–Sept., 7 A.M.–9 P.M.) sits in a funky rickety-looking old building with outside seating in good weather. The breakfast specialty is stuffed French toast, which is crammed with huckleberries or hazelnut-vanilla filling ($7.25). For kids, the Grizzly Paw French toast is served with chocolate sauce. Sandwiches for lunch or dinner run $6–8. The house dinner features barbecue ribs and chicken in different styles and portions ($11–24) with beer and wine available.

With historic park photos on the dining room wall, the **C Glacier Village Restaurant** (304-308 Hwy. 2 E., 406/226-4464, June–Sept., daily 6:30 A.M.–9 P.M., $5–20), also known as the Villager Dining Room, is one place you can get vegetarian and low-fat foods. It's also known for home-baked pastries and utterly decadent desserts. The coffee bar concocts espressos and carries a broad tea selection. The restaurant serves breakfast, lunch, and dinners featuring local fish, buffalo, chicken, and beef with local berry sauces; you can also get hiker lunches to go.

© BECKY LOMAX

Two Medicine General Store used to be the dining hall for traveling horseback riders.

The restaurant is now run by the owners of Izaak Walton Inn.

GROCERIES

On the shore of Two Medicine Lake at the terminus of Two Medicine Road, **Two Medicine General Store** (406/892-2525, mid-June–mid-Sept. 7 A.M.–9 P.M.) now operates in what used to be the historic dining hall for Two Medicine Chalets. It sells limited groceries, camping and hiking supplies, newspapers, maps, gifts, books, beer, wine, ice, and ice cream. Hikers can build a trail lunch from convenience items sold here.

In East Glacier, three small stores sell groceries, but don't expect them to carry every brand available. Open year-round, **Glacier Park Trading Company** (314 Hwy. 2, 406/226-4433, summer 8 A.M.–9 P.M., winter 9 A.M.–8 P.M.) sells fresh veggies, dairy products, wine, meat, and staples. It also carries a broad selection of Montana microbrews. The deli makes sandwiches ($5–6), good for hiker lunches, and pizzas to go. On the east end of East Glacier and also open year-round, **Bear Track Travel Center** (Exxon station, 20958 Hwy. 2, 406/226-5504, winter 7 A.M.–8 P.M., summer 7 A.M.–10 P.M.) sells convenience store foods, ice, firewood, camping and fishing supplies, beer and wine, propane, and fishing licenses.

In the same building that houses a hostel and a grocery, **Brownie's Bakery and Deli** (0.5 mile north on Hwy. 49, 406/226-4426, 7 A.M.–9 P.M. June–Sept.) is an everything place—a bakery, a deli, a convenience store, an ice cream shop, an espresso stand, and an Internet café ($1.50 for 15 min.). It's a great place to pick up a deli sandwich ($6, a PBJ is only $4) for hiking or grab a light breakfast of muffins or bagels. Daily, the bakery churns out freshly baked cookies and brownies.

If you need a larger grocery store, you'll have to head to Browning, 12 miles east of East Glacier on Highway 2.

PICNIC AREA

Two Medicine has the only picnic area, adjacent to the campground. It sits in a scenic spot right on the shore of Two Medicine Lake amid cottonwoods with running water and flush toilets. Most of the sites have some trees, which provide a good windbreak on howling days and scant shade on hot days. Sites include a picnic table and fire grate, but bring your own firewood. (It's illegal to gather firewood here.)

MARIAS PASS AND ESSEX

The Theodore Roosevelt Highway (Highway 2) runs 2,119 miles from Minnesota to Washington; 57 of its miles border Glacier National Park. Here, small mountain enclaves are part of the charm. Both Marias Pass and Essex gained their notoriety through the railroad: Marias Pass as the route the railroad chose to cross the Continental Divide; Essex as a train community to work the tracks. The history of this Rocky Mountain corridor, as much as its scenery, adds to its appeal.

Running through John F. Stevens Canyon, the year-round highway accesses some of the wildest country around. With 1.5 million acres of the Bob Marshall Wilderness Complex to the south and Glacier's one million acres to the north, the road bisects the largest grizzly bear habitat in the Lower 48. The Wild and Scenic Middle Fork of the Flathead River races through the canyon, creating a playground for rafters, kayakers, and anglers. The canyon also draws mountain goats in search of minerals and bighorn sheep and elk for wintering. From this passageway, hikers also launch onto one of Glacier's more remote trails, while horseback riders, anglers, and hunters dive into the Bob Marshall Wilderness.

Backwoodsy and removed from the usual accoutrements of civilization, you won't find fast-food and chain stores here. You're in wild country, where services are few and far between.

© BECKY LOMAX

HIGHLIGHTS

◖ Marias Pass: Drive over the Continental Divide on one of the lowest passes through the Rockies. From the pass, peaks sweep up above 8,000 feet revealing remarkable geology (page 171).

◖ Lewis Overthrust Fault: Catapult back in time 65 million years ago to when the Lewis Overthrust pushed older rock on top of younger sediments. See this stone story in the cliff face along Summit and Little Dog mountains (page 171).

◖ Goat Lick: Mountain goats congregate here for its minerals during spring and early summer. Bring your binoculars to see the shaggy white beasts strutting across death-defying cliffs (page 171).

◖ Izaak Walton Inn: Stop for lunch at the historic inn that used to house Great Northern Railway workers. The hotel now attracts train aficionados, cross-country skiers, and those looking for something a bit different (page 172).

◖ Firebrand Pass: Climb uphill through wildflowers. Fields below the pass make you want to break out in songs from *The Sound of Music* (page 174).

◖ Stanton Lake and Grant Ridge Loop: Hike in the Great Bear Wilderness to one of the best panoramic views of the park's southern monoliths. You'll spot Stimson, Jackson, and St. Nicholas (page 176).

◖ Rafting and Kayaking: Float the Middle Fork of the Flathead River below the Goat Lick. You'll stare up at the nimble creatures cavorting along the cliffs (page 177).

◖ Autumn Creek Trail: Cross-country ski or snowshoe beneath the ramparts of Marias Pass. Elk Mountain and Little Dog make a dramatic backdrop for the trail winding through lodgepole forest (page 179).

LOOK FOR ◖ TO FIND RECOMMENDED SIGHTS, ACTIVITIES, DINING, AND LODGING.

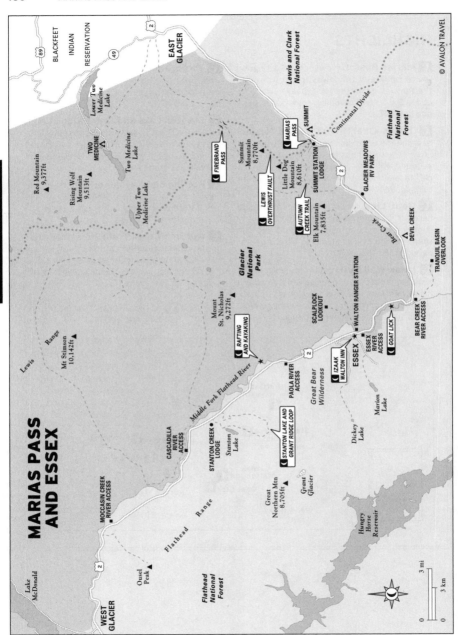

MARIAS PASS AND ESSEX

HISTORY
Marias Pass

When Lewis and Clark passed through Montana in 1805, they failed to find Marias Pass. They came within 25 miles, but swung south on the Missouri River to cross the Continental Divide on a much higher and more difficult pass. Lewis named the Marias River, christening it "Maria's River" after his cousin. The apostrophe got lost through history, much like the pass with the same name.

Reports of a "lost" pass filtered through the ranks of fur traders and mountain men. Government-funded expeditions went looking, but to no avail, while mountain men and Native Americans wandered through the real Marias Pass—yet "undiscovered." Rumors of the pass reached Great Northern Railroad developer J. J. Hill, prompting him to dispatch a railroad engineer named John F. Stevens and his Flathead guide Coonsa to see if the fable was true. While temperatures plummeted to 40 degrees below zero in December 1889, the pair traveled on rawhide snowshoes through deep snow. Unable to slog on, Coonsa stayed behind with a fire as Stevens ventured on solo. He found the lost pass, deeming it appropriate for the railroad crossing. Within two years, Hill shoved the railroad across the Continental Divide at Marias Pass in his push to complete his transcontinental railway.

Building a Highway

As auto travel claimed Americans, the demand for a road through John F. Stevens Canyon rose to a clamor. To transport an auto over the Continental Divide, you had to cough up $12.50 to put your car on a Great Northern Railway flatbed. While building Going-to-the-Sun Road dragged on for 20 years, the road over Marias Pass went through in a jiffy. Finished in 1930, the road over Marias Pass was simply much easier than chipping a route through cliffs over Logan Pass.

© BECKY LOMAX

MARIAS PASS AND ESSEX

railroad tracks at Firebrand trailhead

Lodges

In 1906 as one of its early depots, Great Northern Railway built Summit Station at Marias Pass. When Glacier Park Lodge and its depot in East Glacier attracted more tourists, Summit's use died. In 1985, the station was moved to its current location and converted into the Summit Station Lodge.

In 1939, Great Northern Railway constructed Izaak Walton Inn to house railroad workers who cleared the tracks of snow in winter. The railroad planned to convert it to guest lodging when the park service built a southern road entrance into Glacier. When the Depression and World War II sent park visitation plummeting, the park scrapped the south entrance. Today, Glacier's southern valleys remain remote bastions of wilderness, accessible only by trail, some only after fording the Middle Fork. The building eventually became an inn, but not under Great Northern Railway's umbrella.

Exploring Marias Pass and Essex

With 2.5 million acres of public lands surrounding U.S. Highway 2—Glacier National Park, Lewis and Clark National Forest, Flathead National Forest, and the Bob Marshall Wilderness Complex—only small strips of private parcels line the valley floor. The result is a necklace of tiny mountain communities, none barely large enough to warrant the title of "village." Truly, if you blink, you will miss them.

Seasonal Concerns

Highway 2 is considerably easier to maintain than Going-to-the-Sun Road. It is wider, more gradual, and for the most part, follows a fairly long, gentle 2,000-foot ascent from West Glacier to Marias Pass. However, even though Marias Pass is 1,500 feet lower than Logan Pass, the road still has its share of winter difficulties. While plows clear and sand the road frequently to keep it passable for winter travel, cornices thousands of feet above break loose, careening avalanches down across its path. Some winters the highway is closed for several days while road crews clear a path through ice, rock, and tree debris.

SHUTTLES AND TOURS

No hiker shuttles regularly run across Highway 2. You either have to drive yourself to trailheads or use your thumb (which is legal in Montana). By reservation, you can arrange for a shuttle with **Flathead-Glacier Transportation** (406/892-3390 or 800/829-7039, www.fgtrans.com). They accommodate backpackers hiking point-to-point trails, dropping you off at one trailhead and picking you up at another several days later ($36–130 one-way, depending on distance). The fee can be split among all people in your party. However, it's rather pricey for a round-trip day-hike shuttle. The company will also run a shuttle between Glacier International Airport and Izaak Walton Inn ($76 one-way).

The historic **red buses** run by Glacier Park,

Inc. (406/892-2525 www.glacierparkinc.com, mid-June–mid-Sept., adults $80, kids half-price) drive over both Marias and Logan Passes on their 8.5-hour loop. For $5-10 more, the buses will pick up riders at Glacier Meadows RV Park or Izaak Walton Inn for tours originating in East Glacier. For details, check the *Two Medicine and East Glacier* chapter.

SERVICES

This corridor through wild untamed wilderness is a road where the usual expectancies of civilization are not readily available. Since gas stations have all closed down on Highway 2 between East Glacier and West Glacier, you'll need to fill up in either of those towns before you leave.

While you can find some newspapers sold in the inns and restaurants along the highway, you'll need to head to East or West Glacier for ATMs, laundry, and anything resembling espresso. For hot showers ($5), you can pop in to Glacier Meadow RV Park. **The Half-Way House** (milepost 178, Essex, 406/888-5650) runs a tiny post office.

The nearest Internet services are also in East and West Glacier, although campers at Glacier Meadow RV Park have access to wireless Internet. Because of John F. Stevens Canyon and surrounding steep mountains, you'll find cell reception intermittent to nonexistent on Highway 2, but you can stop to use old-fashioned public pay telephones at Stanton Creek Lodge, Izaak Walton Inn, and Snow Slip Inn.

Even though Highway 2 lacks many services, public restrooms are plentiful. Most are vault toilets with no running water and are open spring–fall. Find these at all river access points, Walton Picnic Area, the Goat Lick, and Marias Pass.

For maps, guidebooks, and information on outdoor activities in the Great Bear Wilderness and the Bob Marshall, contact the **Hungry Horse Ranger Station** (10 Hungry Horse Dr. off Hwy. 2 at milepost 143.1, 406/387-3800;

PUBLIC LANDS: WHAT'S THE DIFFERENCE?

Many people are confused by the various types of public lands. In the greater Glacier ecosystem, national park lands border national forest and wilderness area. So what are these?

National parks, national forests, and wilderness areas are each managed differently with different purposes:

National parks fall under the U.S. Department of the Interior. Parks are set aside for their historical, geological, cultural, or biological significance, and geared toward public recreation. Hunting is not permitted, nor is picking wildflowers or berries for commercial use. Mining and logging are also taboo. Leases for developing recreation like ski resorts are not available. Generally, dogs are not allowed on trails; neither are mountain bikes. Permits are needed for backcountry camping.

National forests come under the U.S. Department of Agriculture. Their purpose is different. With permits, hunting, timber harvesting, and commercial berry picking are generally allowed. National forest land is leased for recreational development, such as ski areas. Your pooch can go with you on hikes; you can mountain bike as long as no special designation says otherwise. Permits are not needed for backcountry camping.

Wilderness areas are administered usually by the national forest that contains the wilderness boundaries. Two concepts set wilderness apart: no mechanical transports and no permanent human inhabitants. Wilderness areas do not have roads inside them. While hunting is permitted and Fido can go along on the trail, mountain biking is not allowed. Permits are not needed for backcountry camping.

www.fs.fed.us/r1/flathead) nine miles west of West Glacier. It is the place for information on river rafting, fishing, hiking, hunting, and horse packing in the national forest. For Lewis and Clark National Forest information, call the Rocky Mountain Ranger Station in Choteau (1102 Main Ave. NW, 406/466-5341, www.fs.fed.us/r1/lewisclark).

Emergencies

If the emergency permits a choice, most people head to the larger hospitals in Flathead Valley 35 minutes from West Glacier—Kalispell Regional Medical Center (310 Sunny View Lane, Kalispell, 406/752-5111) and North Valley Hospital (1600 Hospital Way, Whitefish, 406/863-3631). The nearest east-side and smaller hospital is the Northern Rockies Medical Center (802 2nd St. E., Cut Bank, 406/873-2251) 46 miles from East Glacier. For river emergencies along the Middle Fork of the Flathead, just get to a phone and call 911.

The **Walton Ranger Station** (milepost 180.5, 406/888-7800), at Walton on the southernmost tip of Glacier National Park, is adjacent to the Walton Picnic Area and the trailheads to Scalplock, Ole Creek, and the wild Nyack Loop. The station is staffed only in summer, and not full time, as the rangers here patrol miles of backcountry trails. If you need assistance, use the pay phone at Izaak Walton Inn (0.8 mile west of the Walton Ranger Station) to call Glacier Park Headquarters (406/888-7800).

DRIVING TOUR
Highway 2

After driving the dramatic Going-to-the-Sun Road, most visitors are less than impressed with this southern highway. You can drive the highway from East Glacier to West Glacier in a little over an hour. Locals use the road as a faster route across the Continental Divide when too many cars clog Going-to-the-Sun Road. All large RVs and trailers use it as they are precluded from driving Going-to-the-Sun

BOB MARSHALL WILDERNESS COMPLEX

The largest wilderness area in Montana, the **Bob Marshall Wilderness Complex** straddles 1.5 million acres along 110 miles of the Continental Divide. It harbors a huge ungulate population of deer, elk, moose, mountain goats, and bighorn sheep. They feed predators like lynx, grizzlies, black bears, mountain lions, and wolves. Over 1,000 miles of trails crisscross its ranges with peaks reaching 9,000 feet high. The 1,000-foot-high Chinese Wall escarpment runs for 22 miles along on the Continental Divide.

The complex is named for Bob Marshall, a young forester who became a local legend in 1925 with marathon 30-mile mountain treks around the Missoula area. Later, he penned *The Problem of Wilderness,* a treatise defining principles that would shape the movement to preserve America's wilds. In a one-man crusade as the Forest Service's Lands Division chief, he placed 5.4 million acres of vulnerable lands under wilderness protection. Along with Aldo Leopold and others, he launched the Wilderness Society in 1935, but died four years later at age 38.

In 1941, the South Fork, Pentagon, and Sun River areas south of Glacier were set aside as primitive zones. But finally after 66 drafts, the 1964 Wilderness Act protected them from development. As part of the act, the three primitive zone areas combined to create the one-million-acre **Bob Marshall Wilderness.**

After lobbying by an unprecedented citizen group led by a hardware store owner from Lincoln, the adjacent **Scapegoat Wilderness** added 239,936 acres to the south in 1972. Scapegoat houses 50 miles of the 3,100-mile-long Continental Divide Trail.

Six years later, a third wilderness was added to the complex – the **Great Bear Wilderness,** adjoining its 286,700 acres of land to the northwest. Tucked between Hungry Horse Reservoir and Glacier National Park, the Great Bear houses 300 miles of trail and tops out at 8,700 feet on Great Northern, the sweeping peak seen from Flathead Valley.

Together these three wilderness areas along with Glacier Park comprise 2.5 million acres of habitat for threatened species such as grizzly bears, lynx, and wolves. The wilderness complex, which crosses into four national forests, is managed jointly by Flathead, Lewis and Clark, Lolo, and Helena National Forests.

Road. In spite of its use as a year-round thoroughfare, it still is a scenic highway. Drive it from either direction: from East or West Glacier.

Public flush-toilet restrooms are few and far between on this highway. Pit and vault toilets, however, are available at Marias Pass, the Goat Lick, Walton Picnic Area, and all river accesses. Usually, these are open late spring through fall; in winter, you're out of luck, unless you stop at Izaak Walton Inn.

Montana has an oddity on its highways—white crosses marking fatalities. One cross equals one traffic fatality. Begun in 1953, the American Legion–sponsored program operates in conjunction with the Montana Department of Transportation to use the crosses as safety reminders. An estimated 2,000 sobering crosses line the state's highways—several on this highway.

SIGHTS

Highway 2 sights are listed here from East Glacier to West Glacier.

Lewis and Clark National Forest

From just south of East Glacier to the Continental Divide, Highway 2 passes through the Lewis and Clark National Forest. Its 1.7 million acres serve as the headwaters for the mighty Missouri River. High prairies at 4,500 feet in elevation climb up to Rocky Mountain Peak at 9,362 feet along the Rocky Mountain Front in an extremely diverse ecosystem that harbors species like lynx and grizzly bears. Around milepost 198, you'll get good views south of 46,000 burned acres from the 2007 Skyland Fire.

◖ Marias Pass   *mile* 197.9

At 5,220 feet, Marias Pass (milepost 197.9) is the lowest Continental Divide saddle north of New Mexico. Two monuments mark the pass: A statue of John F. Stevens commemorates his discovery of the passage, and a tall obelisk stands in memory of Theodore Roosevelt for whom the highway is named. Legend has it that he visited Many Glacier in 1910, but no official records indicate so. The 3,100-mile Continental Divide Trail crosses into Glacier National Park here where hikers and skiers launch onto Autumn Creek Trail. If signs and the monuments weren't here, you'd be hard pressed to realize you were crossing the Continental Divide, with the area's broad flat forest.

◖ Lewis Overthrust Fault   *mile* 198

Opposite Marias Pass, the Lewis Overthrust Fault shoved older 1.6-billion-year-old rocks on top of 80-million-year-old stones. This fault exposed some of the oldest sediments in the world—ancient Precambrian rocks that formed as Belt Sea sediments solidified. On the face of Summit and Little Dog Peaks, look for an obvious upward line where the younger Cretaceous rock from the dinosaur age shows up as black or brown. This is the site where in the 1890s geologists discovered the Lewis Overthrust Fault, which extends into Canada and sets Glacier apart as a World Heritage Site.

Silver Stairs Falls   188.2

Tumbling thousands of feet from Tranquil Basin, an unmarked and unsigned pullout on the highway's south side stares up at Silver Stairs Falls (milepost 188.2). The waterfall cascades down a series of stairsteps created from eroding sedimentary layers. In June and July, water rages down in torrents, but by late August it slows to a trickle. You can catch quick views with a drive-by, but with alder and brush surrounding the falls, you'll get a better view by stopping.

◖ Goat Lick   182.6

Much of Glacier National Park's wildlife tends to be mineral deficient. Because their bodies crave minerals from their winter-deprived condition, during spring and early summer mountain goats congregate at the Goat Lick (milepost 182.6). The lick is actually a huge mass of gray rock cliffs, an exposed fault containing salts like calcium, magnesium, and potassium. Goats hop sure-footed along the steep cliff faces as if they were on flat land to slurp the minerals. Located approximately three miles south of Essex, the well-marked overlook has a couple of viewing areas with interpretive signs. Bring your binoculars for better viewing.

Bob Marshall Wilderness Complex

While Glacier rises to the north of the highway, to the south the Bob Marshall Wilderness Complex spans nearly 1.5 million acres. It actually comprises three wilderness areas: The

© BECKY LOMAX

Dickey Lake in the Great Bear Wilderness

MARIAS PASS AND ESSEX

Bob (as locals call it), the Great Bear, and the Scapegoat. The Great Bear is the section bordering Highway 2. The Bob Marshall was one of the country's first wilderness areas, dedicated in 1964 concurrent with the Wilderness Act. Scapegoat was added in 1972 and Great Bear six years later. While roads do not enter the wilderness areas and mechanized vehicles are prohibited (no mountain bikes or snowmobiles), a plethora of trails lead off Highway 2. Short day hikes access the Great Bear, while longer overnight treks reach The Bob, a world-class area for horse packing, fishing, and big-game hunting.

◖ Izaak Walton Inn

Listed on the National Register of Historic Places, Izaak Walton Inn (milepost 179.7) sits opposite the southernmost point of Glacier National Park at Essex. The hotel stands adjacent to the train tracks, luring train aficionados, cross-country skiers, and those looking for something a bit different, like sleeping in a renovated caboose. Loaded with historical photos and memorabilia, the inn makes you feel almost like you've been transported back to a different era. In the downstairs bar, check out photos of avalanches burying the railroad tracks. Eat lunch on Great Northern Railway plates in the small dining room, and cozy up to the warm lobby fire.

Mount St. Nicholas

The toothy 9,376-foot spire of St. Nicholas is easy to pick out on the skyline—especially rimed with winter snow. Look for a notched spire with precipitous cliffs on its southern face. Grab good views of this forbidding-looking peak driving eastward on Highway 2. For more in-your-face views of it, hike Grant Ridge Loop counter-clockwise or climb to Scalplock Lookout.

John F. Stevens Canyon

Named for the Great Northern Railway engineer who verified the feasibility of Marias Pass as a railroad route, John F. Stevens Canyon begins just west of the pass and follows Bear Creek

At the Izaak Walton Inn, you can sleep in a caboose!

© BECKY LOMAX

© BECKY LOMAX

MARIAS PASS AND ESSEX

beargrass in front of Grant Glacier in the Great Bear Wilderness

and the Middle Fork of the Flathead until its terminus near West Glacier. Highway 2 and the railroad traverse the canyon's entire 40-mile distance. In places, the canyon broadens into wide valleys; in others it tightens up into narrow channels, frothing with wild waters. Although its more dramatic sections are seen best from a raft or kayak on the river, several highway pullouts still offer good photo ops.

Flathead National Forest

From the Continental Divide west past Flathead Valley and extending 120 miles south of the Canadian border, Flathead National Forest is broken up by state and private land but still tallies up a healthy 2.3 million acres. Within its glaciated mountains, it has 2,600 miles of trails. Over 46 percent of the forest is designated wilderness area. Spruce, Douglas fir, lodgepole, larch, and pine cover its slopes—home to wolverines, grizzly bears, and wolves.

Middle Fork of the Flathead River

Draining Glacier National Park and the Bob Marshall Wilderness Complex, the Middle Fork of the Flathead River is no small tributary. Designated a Wild and Scenic River, its 95-mile length is known for some of the best white-water rafting and kayaking in Montana. Dropping at 35 feet per mile, the Great Bear section teems with Class III and IV rapids; the lower waters break up long scenic floats with Class II and III rapids with such names as Jaws and Bonecrusher. Hook up with one of the four West Glacier rafting companies to splash in its waves.

mile 155 · 157

Wintering Range

Belton Mountain, to the road's north (milepost 155–157), is quite a different ecosystem from the heavily forested south slopes. Fires, winds, and a dry exposure have minimized forest growth. Winds create a lower snowpack and south-facing slopes melt off early—both keys to making the area a prime wintering range for ungulates such as deer, elk, and bighorn sheep. Grizzly and black bears also forage on its slopes. Even in summer, it's worth a stop at one of the several pullouts to scan slopes with binoculars.

Recreation

HIKING

Highway 2 is one road where hiker shuttles are not available; you must get to trailheads on your own! Most of Glacier's trails on the south end are long valley hikes accessing little-used areas. Additional short hikes, mostly in the Great Bear Wilderness, fill out the options—especially for hikers with Fido. While trails within Glacier do not allow dogs, your canine friend can tag along on a leash in the wilderness areas. Be aware, however, that hiking with pets in bear country poses certain dilemmas; a dog will not protect you from a bear encounter.

While trails within Glacier National Park are well-signed and frequently maintained, trails in the wilderness areas are not; signs, if any, may be just a wooden trail number or name nailed to a tree—no mileages. Take a good topographical map, which you can purchase from the Hungry Horse Ranger Station (10 Hungry Horse Dr. off Hwy. 2 at milepost 143.1, 406/387-3800), and know how to read it! Be prepared to encounter deadfall, downed trees, and heavy brush. Trail crews in the national forests do not have the staff numbers of the national park trail crews; it takes them longer to get to damaged or buried trails. Contrary to Glacier, bear warning signage does not exist except in extreme cases. Make noise and take precautions in bear country.

Hikes are listed here from east to west on Highway 2.

🄲 Firebrand Pass

- Distance: 9.6 miles round-trip
- Duration: 4.5 hours
- Elevation gain: 2,210 feet
- Effort: moderate

- Trailhead: at milepost 203 on Highway 2

From the trailhead, the path wanders by beaver ponds, crosses into Glacier Park, passes the old Lubec ranger station site, and follows Coonsa Creek northward. At 1.4 miles, turn right at the Autumn Creek Trail junction and ascend gently through aspens and meadows thick in July with valerian, lupine, paintbrush, and penstemon to another junction about one mile later. Take a left here, gaining elevation as the trail circumvents Calf Robe's lower slopes. Make noise, for this is prime bear country.

hiking on the Firebrand trail

© BECKY LOMAX

As the trail breaks out of the trees, you'll have views of Dancing Lady and East Glacier. The trail rounds Calf Robe into a hanging basin and then ascends to the pass, where you can look down Ole Creek and into Glacier's remote southern peaks. Scrambles up Calf Robe or Red Crow lend even better views, but don't go off trail unless you're ready to deal with steep scree hillsides.

Elk Mountain

- Distance: 7 miles round-trip
- Duration: 6 hours
- Elevation gain: 3,355 feet
- Effort: strenuous
- Trailhead: Turn north off Highway 2 at Fielding (milepost 192) and follow the dirt road #1066 about half a mile to the trailhead.

Hike up through private logged land to the railroad tracks and cross into Glacier Park. The trail starts off deceptively easy enough, but shortly after turning right at the junction near a ranger cabin, the trail climbs and climbs. Steep does come close to describing the pitch as it ascends to an open saddle. No wonder you have so much solitude here. From here, you can see the remainder of the trail, climbing sharply again across a talus slope to the summit.

From the top, among debris from what was once the lookout, the views make the grunt worthwhile. Panoramas both north and south line up peak tops for miles into Glacier's remote southern sector and the Bob Marshall Wilderness Complex. A knife ridge leads east toward the Continental Divide, and the view down Autumn Creek is dizzying.

Scalplock Lookout

- Distance: 9.4 miles round-trip
- Duration: 4.5 hours
- Elevation gain: 3,079 feet
- Effort: strenuous

- Trailhead: Walton Picnic Area (milepost 180.5)

This can be a gorgeous July hike, with bluebells in the high meadows, but be prepared for snow on top in June. Beginning in the Walton Picnic Area, the trail wanders along the Middle Fork of the Flathead in the first mile, crossing Ole Creek on a swinging bridge over a small gorge and ascending to the Ole Creek trail. Turn west on this trail for 0.4 mile to a second junction where the climb begins. In the remaining three miles, the trail ascends switchbacks at nearly 1,000 feet per mile.

Peek-a-boo views of the Middle Fork of the Flathead River are the only respite from the relentless ascent. Near the top, the trail breaks out of the trees to climb up a ridge flanked with wildflower meadows. At the top, Scalplock Lookout has a commanding view of the entire Middle Fork drainage with Mount St. Nicholas spire in your face.

Marion Lake

- Distance: 3.4 miles round-trip
- Duration: 2 hours
- Elevation gain: 1,810 feet
- Effort: short, but strenuous
- Trailhead: Turn south on the Dickey Lake Road (milepost 178.7) at Essex and follow the left fork 2.3 miles to the Flathead National Forest signed trailhead.

Due to the trail's popularity, it sees quite of bit of summer traffic, making it well worn and quite obvious to follow until you encounter heavy foliage. From the start, it taxes your lungs on its steep climb up Marion Creek Valley. You will encounter thick, heavy brush in the trail's midsection. Cowparsnip, nettles, elderberry, and false huckleberry nearly suffocate the trail. Make noise here to avoid surprising a bear.

You know you're nearing the lake when the trail assumes a more moderate pitch. Marion Lake sits in a photo-worthy glacial cirque surrounded by cliffs and the outlet congested

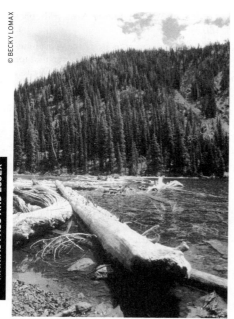

Marion Lake

with logs. Anglers should bring rods, for the lake harbors westslope cutthroat trout up to 12 inches.

Dickey Lake

- Distance: 4.8 miles round-trip
- Duration: 2.5 hours
- Elevation gain: 1,460 feet
- Effort: moderate
- Trailhead: Turn south on Dickey Lake Road (milepost 178.7) at Essex and follow the right fork three miles to an unmarked spur where the Flathead National Forest trail begins.

This short trail in the Great Bear Wilderness gives rather decent rewards for its efforts, and anglers will want to tote a fishing rod. After wading Dickey Creek, the forested trail climbs up a large bowl riddled with avalanche paths (translate into deadfall, limbs, or uprooted and downed trees). In places, thick brush chokes the path, but you can still follow it to the headwall near the basin's end. From here, a rock cairn, which may be buried in snow that hangs late in the season, marks the trail ascending steeply through false huckleberry bushes dangling with pale apricot blossoms into a hanging valley.

Upon reaching the upper basin, the trail pops out on the edge of Dickey Lake. The shallow tarn flanked by meadows and steep talus slopes is a scenic lunch spot. You'll most likely find solitude here. Anglers will enjoy fishing for cutthroats in the small lake.

◖ Stanton Lake and Grant Ridge Loop

- Distance: 2 miles round-trip or 10.2-mile loop
- Duration: 1 or 5 hours
- Elevation gain: 600 or 3,605 feet
- Effort: easy or strenuous
- Trailhead: Stanton Lake Trailhead on Highway 2 at mile marker 169.9 in the Flathead National Forest

An easy short hike plops hikers and anglers on the shores of Stanton Lake, or a longer strenuous loop explores the ultra-scenic Grant Ridge, both in the Great Bear Wilderness. From the trailhead, a steep grunt heads straight uphill. But never fear, for it levels out soon into a nice forested walk that leads into the basin cradling Stanton Lake. For a short hike to a well-traveled destination, stop here. Anglers should bring rods to fish for westslope cutthroat, rainbows, and mountain whitefish. Some maps show the trail continuing above Stanton Lake; however, that trail peters out promptly in willow bogs.

For the Grant Ridge Loop, take the left fork before the lake and ford the outlet creek. The trail climbs a forested hillside with peek-a-boo views of Great Northern, the highest peak in the Great Bear Wilderness. At the ridge top, follow a faint, intermittent trail a quarter mile south to a rocky outcrop overlooking Grant Peak and the waterfall springing from the glacier's snout. With views of Glacier's southern monoliths, the trail wanders north below the ridgeline before descending switchbacks to the highway a half mile from the starting point. Many hikers prefer to do this loop clockwise, staring at Grant and Great Northern during the ridgeline walk.

Ousel Peak

- Distance: 5.2 miles round-trip
- Duration: 3.5 hours
- Elevation gain: 3,260 feet
- Effort: very strenuous
- Trailhead: mile marker 159.6 on Highway 2 in the Flathead National Forest

Do the math: This trail gains well over 1,000 feet per mile and from the first minute makes no bones about heading straight uphill. If the uphill doesn't tax your lungs, the downhill will pound your knees. Nevertheless, the view from the top is outstanding and well worth the effort or pain. Sitting on the northern edge of the Great Bear Wilderness, the trail climbs through a forest canopy littered with various microclimates from wet seeps to dry, arid slopes. The path finally breaks out of the forest with glimpses of Glacier's peaks. At the top, remnants of the old lookout scatter across the hillside amid tiny yellow stonecrop. Look into Glacier to see Mounts Jackson and Stimson along with Harrison Glacier.

BIKING
Road Biking

Cross-country bicyclists use the Highway 2 to cross the Continental Divide when Going-to-the-Sun Road is not open. However, many use it also to make a big loop through and around Glacier (Going-to-the-Sun Road and Highways 89, 49, and 2). Compared to the rest of Glacier's roads, Highway 2 is definitely an easier ride, for it has shoulders in some sections and is a bit wider and less curvy. However, due to heavy traffic in summer, it can be downright dangerous with large rigs that nearly blow cyclists off the road. Tackle it only if you can handle riding with semis and RVs whipping by your elbows at 60 mph.

Be prepared for winds, especially at Marias Pass. They are usually blowing eastward, so those riding toward West Glacier encounter substantial headwinds. Also, be extra cautious in the five curvy miles east of West Glacier as severe turns reduce the visibility of drivers on the road. Even though no law requires a helmet, think twice about leaving your brain bucket off. Most drivers here are gawking at scenery or trying to spot wildlife rather than keeping their attention totally on the road.

Mountain Biking

Mountain bikes are not permitted on trails in the wilderness areas nor in Glacier Park. **Izaak Walton Inn** (290 Izaak Walton Inn Road, 406/888-5700, www.izaakwaltoninn.com, $20–25 per day with helmets) rents mountain bikes, which can be ridden on several dirt roads in the area.

◖ RAFTING AND KAYAKING

The **Middle Fork of the Flathead River** is the local hotspot for rafting and kayaking. No permits are needed; however, you'll need to take care about where you set up camp. In the Great Bear Wilderness, sites are not restricted, but in the lower section, private lands abut national forest land, much of it unmarked. To know where you can camp without infringing on private landowners, take a good river or topographical map along (contact Flathead National Forest, 406/755-5401; nearest ranger station is in Hungry Horse nine miles west of West Glacier, 406/387-3800). No camping is permitted on the north shore.

To access Great Bear Wilderness sections of the river (Class III and IV), you'll need to fly in to Schaeffer Meadows or pack in on a horse. Contact the U.S. Forest Service Hungry Horse Ranger Station (406/387-3800) for details on rafting and floating this upper wild section. The normal float season is mid-May through mid-July. During peak runoff in May, the trip can often be more challenging with several rapids becoming Class V and spring snow dumps chilling the air.

From the Bear Creek confluence to the confluence with the North Fork of the Flathead, river put-ins allow easy access from Highway 2: Bear Creek (milepost 185), Essex (milepost 180), Paola (milepost 175.2), Cascadilla (milepost 166), Moccasin Creek (milepost 160.5), and West Glacier (follow signs to the golf course). Between Bear Creek and Cascadilla, rapids rate Class III and IV. Waters flatten to a float trip from Cascadilla to Moccasin Creek, but be aware of deadly log jams. From Moccasin to West Glacier, rapids range mostly in Class II and III, with some IVs during June high water. To gauge your average float time in July, from Bear Creek to Cascadilla usually takes 6.5 hours and from Moccasin Creek to West Glacier 2.5 hours. If you're planning on rafting on your own, stop at the Hungry Horse Ranger Station nine miles west of West Glacier for maps, guidebooks, and information.

Rentals and Guides

Four local river companies operate out of West Glacier, all guiding half-day, full-day, and overnight trips on the Middle Fork of the Flathead: **Glacier Raft Company** (6 Going-to-the-Sun Road, 406/888-5454 or 800/235-6781, www.glacierraftco.com), **Great Northern Whitewater** (12127 Hwy. 2 E., 406/387-5340 or 800/735-7897, www.gnwhitewater.com), **Montana Raft Company** (11970 Hwy. 2 E., 406/387-5555 or 800/521-7238, www.glacierguides.com), and **Wild River Adventures** (11900 Hwy. 2 E., 406/387-9453 or 800/700-7056, www.riverwild.com). Some rent rafts and kayaks as well.

FISHING
Rivers and Streams

In Glacier Park, Ole, Park, Muir, Coal, and Nyack Creeks are closed to fishing. Anglers can drop lines in Summit, Railroad, and Badger Creeks, which flow from Marias Pass east through Lewis and Clark National Forest and onto the Blackfeet Reservation. **Badger Creek,** in particular, has a good reputation for rainbow trout. **Bear Creek,** good for westslope cutthroat, mountain whitefish, and some rainbow trout, drops west from Marias to its confluence with the Middle Fork of the Flathead River. The **Middle Fork** has plenty of river accesses for fishing: Bear Creek, Essex, Paola, Cascadilla, and Moccasin.

Lakes

Inside the park, good cutthroat trout fishing lakes such as Ole, Harrison, or Isabel usually require backpacking or fording the Middle Fork of the Flathead. It's actually easier to get to lakes in the Great Bear Wilderness on the south side of the highway. **Stanton Lake** is a quick destination with westslope cutthroat trout, mountain whitefish, and rainbow trout, but it's somewhat overfished because of its ease of access. Dickey and Marion Lakes also harbor cutthroat.

Guides

For guided fishing on Blackfeet Nation lands, contact **Blackfeet Fish and Wildlife** (406/338-7207, www.blackfeetfishandwildlife.com) for a list of licensed outfitters. From West Glacier, four fishing companies guide fly-fishing trips on the Middle Fork of the Flathead River: **Glacier Anglers** (Glacier Outdoor Center, 11957 Hwy. 2 E., 406/888-5454 or 800/235-6781, www.glacierraftco.com), **Glacier Guides** (11970 Hwy. 2 E., 406/387-5555 or 800/521-7238, www.glacierguides.com), **Montana Fly-fishing Guides** (Great Northern Whitewater, 12127 Hwy. 2 E., 406/387-5340 or 800/735-7897, www.gnwhitewater.com), and **Wild River Adventures** (11900 Hwy. 2 E., 406/387-9453 or 800/700-7056, www.riverwild.com).

Licenses and Regulations

Fishing regulations along Highway 2 vary depending on land ownership. Check carefully where you are before dropping a line into waters. The road passes through Blackfeet tribal lands, Glacier National Park, and national forests. For details on each of these permits, see the *Background* chapter. You can purchase Tribal fishing permits at Bear Track Travel Center (Exxon station in East Glacier, 20958 Hwy. 2, 406/226-5504, winter 7 A.M.–8 P.M., summer 7 A.M.–10 P.M.). For Montana State licenses, go to Glacier Outdoor Center in West Glacier (11957 Hwy. 2 East, 406/888-5454 or 800/235-6781, www.glacierraftco.com).

HUNTING

Hunting is illegal in Glacier National Park. But just south of Highway 2, the famed Bob Marshall Wilderness boasts world-renowned big-game hunting for bighorn sheep, elk, and black bear. East side grasslands are also famous for bird hunting. For hunting in the Bob Marshall Wilderness or in national forests, get regulations and license info from Montana Fish, Wildlife, and Parks (406/444-2535, www .fwp.m.ontana.gov). The Blackfeet Reservation (406/338-7207, www.blackfeetfishandwildlife .com) has separate regulations and licenses for tribal lands. Check also with each for names of licensed outfitters.

CROSS-COUNTRY SKIING AND SNOWSHOEING

In winter, ski and snowshoe routes off Highway 2 are popular for their ease of access. You'll find everything from groomed skate and classic skiing trails to snowmobile-packed tracks and off-piste break-your-own-trail treks.

Izaak Walton Inn

With 20 miles of track groomed for skate and classic skiing late November–mid-April, **Izaak Walton Inn** (290 Izaak Walton Inn Road, 406/888-5700, www.izaakwaltoninn.com) makes a great cross-country skiing destination at milepost 179.7 on Highway 2. At the inn, trails range from easy meanders to steep grunts. One short section of trail is lit for night skiing. Trail passes for skiing are $10 per day and are available to day visitors as well as inn guests. Although the area never feels crowded, its most popular time is Christmas through President's Day. Lessons ($20–45, depending on the number of skiers) are available from the

lodge as well as rentals ($20–25 for adults, $10 for kids), and the rentals can be taken elsewhere to use. The inn also rents snowshoes ($15) to venture into Glacier Park. With rates varying depending on the number of people, the inn also guides half-day snowshoe tours ($65 per person with two-person minimum) and full-day ski tours ($115 per person with two-person minimum, includes lunch and transportation to trailhead) in Glacier.

Autumn Creek Trail

One of the most popular ski trails in Glacier is Autumn Creek Trail at Marias Pass, which can be skied point-to-point if you set up a car shuttle or hitchhike, which is legal in Montana. The west trailhead sits at milepost 193.8 on Highway 2. Park across the highway; then ski up the railroad access road and across the tracks. The other trailhead is at Marias Pass, across Highway 2 from the parking lot

Izaak Walton Inn grooms trails for cross-country skiing.

© BECKY LOMAX

(milepost 197.9). Orange markers on trees denote the six-mile trail. Beginners will find more success in the Marias Pass section rather than the steep Autumn Creek section. Those seeking to avoid the narrow, steep 660-foot elevation drop downhill should begin on the west end and finish at the pass.

SNOWMOBILING

Snowmobilers gravitate to groomed and ungroomed roads in Lewis and Clark National Forest (406/791-7700) and Flathead National Forest (406/758-5204). The most popular snowmobiling is in the Marias Pass and Skyland/Challenge complex, both straddling the Continental Divide south of Highway 2. The Cut Bank Snowgoers and Flathead Snowmobile Association groom about 40 miles of trail here, which are open for snowmobiling December 1–May 15. Contact them via the Montana Snowmobile Association (406/788-2399, www.snowtana.com). Snow depths in both of these snowmobiling areas vary 150–250 inches. Some restrictions apply to the designated connecting trails, so get a good snowmobile map through Montana Snowmobile Association. The nearest rentals are in Flathead Valley.

ENTERTAINMENT

Every Labor Day Weekend, spiffed up and spit-shined classic cars descend on Stanton Creek Lodge for the annual **Show and Shine.** The event features evening parking lot dances, barbecues, live bands, and the car show. Call the Stanton Creek Lodge (406/888-5040 or 866/883-5040) for the current schedule and entry info.

Accommodations

Along Highway 2, lodging spans all spectrums: historic inns, rustic cabins, and dude ranches. Regardless of type, that 7 percent Montana State bed tax will find your bill here.

Lodges

Just west of Marias Pass on Highway 2, the **Summit Station Lodge** (197.3 on Hwy. 2, 406/226-4428, www.summitstationlodge .com, early June–late Sept.) is a historic 1906 train station converted into a lodge that stares up at the Continental Divide's Summit and Little Dog peaks. You can rent their upscale cabins ($195–295) nightly; the cozy non-smoking, air-conditioned log cabins with private bathrooms sleep one to five people and come with a continental breakfast. The lodge also has a fine-dining restaurant and bar on the premises. Partnering with local outfitters, the Summit Station arranges trail rides, cattle-drives, and multi-day mountain horsepacking trips. They also offer two- to seven-day all-inclusive fishing packages ($795–3,650) using licensed local guides.

Located at Essex and open year-round, **Izaak Walton Inn** (290 Izaak Walton Inn Rd., 406/888-5700, www.izaakwaltoninn .com, mid-June–mid-Sept. and mid-Dec.– Mar. $137–255 double occupancy, off-season rates drop to $117–235) is a cozy place to be. New owners who purchased the inn in 2006 improved it. From the lobby fireplace to the Dining Car Restaurant or the swinging seat on the porch, the nonsmoking inn is a place to unwind and relax. Rooms include continental breakfast and vary in sizes, although most bathrooms are fairly small. The inn maintains its historic ambience with no in-room televisions or phones; a pay phone is off the lobby. You'll have to walk the stairs here as no elevator services the building, but there is a sauna for aching muscles.

The inn also offers very unique lodging. A short walk over a footbridge above the railroad tracks leads to three cabooses, set alone in the trees and sleeping four in each. A three-night minimum ($690) is required (only two nights in winter) for the heated cabooses with kitchenettes and full bathrooms. In the same glen, six new log cabins with kitchens ($229–329) were built in 2008. They sleep up to six in bedrooms and lofts and include fully equipped kitchens.

To get good deals, check the inn's packages, which include skiing, rafting, and park sightseeing. It also hosts special weekends for railway fans. You can also arrive and depart by train as it's an Amtrak stop. With railroad tracks right outside the back door, you may sleep better with earplugs, for trains rumble by each night. The inn also grooms 20 miles of ski trails for skate and classic skiing in winter; in summer, they are hiking and mountain-biking trails. You can rent a car, skis, mountain bikes, snowshoes, ice skates, and kiddie sleds. In summer, red bus tours pick up riders here for an all-day loop around Going-to-the-Sun Road.

Motels

Several small motels dot Highway 2. Aptly named for its location halfway between East and West Glacier, **The Half-Way Motel** (milepost 178, Essex, 406/888-5650) is a very small family-run motel with only four large clean rooms ($65) with two queen beds, fridge, microwave, coffeemaker, and satellite TV. The motel also has a restaurant and a small general store. Bring earplugs for both highway and train noise seeps in, but you can sit on the deck to watch the hummingbirds and even rabbits. At milepost 173.8, **Glacier Haven Inn** (14305 Hwy. 2, 406/888-5720, www.glacierhaveninn .com, open year-round) has small clean motel rooms ($65–99) with two double beds and satellite TV. In summer, the rates include a breakfast buffet served Tuesdays–Sundays. Here, well-behaved pets are okay. A restaurant on the premises serves home-style meals in summer.

Cabins

Flathead National Forest (www.fs.fed.us/r1 /flathead/, 406/387-3809) rents two rustic cabins with three-night maximums. Both are accessible from Highway 2 and must be reserved (877/444-6777, www.recreation.gov). Decked out with propane, mattresses, and

kitchen utensils, the cabins are reasonably well-equipped and warm with either propane heat or woodstoves (wood is supplied). A seven-mile ski or snowmobile ride up Skyland Road (milepost 195.8 on Hwy. 2), tiny one-room **Challenge Cabin** (Dec.–Mar., $30 per night) sleeps six people stacked like sardines. A much larger two-bedroom cabin sleeping eight, **Zip's Place** (June–Mar., $50 per night) is found by turning off Highway 2 (milepost 191.9) and driving two miles, following signs. In winter, it requires a ski or snowshoe trip to reach the front door. Bring your own food and sleeping bags. Both are nonsmoking; neither permit pets.

Small simple rustic cabins, a restaurant, a bar, and a campground make up **Stanton Creek Lodge** (milepost 170 on Hwy. 2, 406/888-5040 or 866/883-5040, www.stanton creeklodge.com, open year-round). Six heated cabins vary in size ($69–99); all include linens and towels. The higher priced cabins, those open year-round, have satellite TV and private bathrooms; other cabins share a bathhouse, which is closed in winter. Trails to Stanton Lake and Grant Loop depart from here, and fishing on the Middle Fork River is easily accessible. Bring earplugs for highway and train noise.

The closest lodging to West Glacier, **Glacier Wilderness Resort** (milepost 163 on Hwy. 2, 406/888/5664, www.glacierwilderness resort.com, open year-round, $145–200) sits in a woodsy setting abutting the Great Bear Wilderness. With an indoor heated pool open year-round, their one- and two-bedroom log cabins that sleep four–six people come with fireplaces, satellite televisions, DVD/VCR, fully equipped kitchens, and private hot tubs. Summertime usually requires a five-night minimum; other seasons require a two-night minimum stay. In summer, you can use an outdoor picnic pavilion and walking trails. In winter, cross-country skiing and snowshoeing trails tour the property.

Dude Ranch

Located in Flathead National Forest adjacent to Glacier, **Bear Creek Ranch** (milepost

192, 406/226-4489, www.bearcreekranch .com, May–Sept.) is a dude ranch specializing in western horsemanship with lessons, rides, and cattle drives. Only six-day packages are offered, with lodging, three meals per day, and all ranch activities—horseback riding, hiking, and fishing—for one lump rate (adults $1,895, kids 5–15 $1,395). Accommodations are in five cabins with private baths or in the main lodge. The dining room serves buffet meals indoors and chuckwagon picnics outdoors. The ranch also leads five-day pack trips into the Bob Marshall Wilderness.

Bed-and-Breakfast

Located 1.5 miles from East Glacier, **Bison Creek Ranch B & B** (milepost 207.4, 20722 Hwy. 2, 406/226-4482 or 888/226-4482, mid-May–Sept., $54–95 for two people, $12 for each additional person) combines cabin stays with a continental breakfast. Rustic remodeled one- and two-bedroom Gandy Dancer cabins (built as bunkhouses for railroad repairmen) and two-bedroom A-frame chalets spread among firs and meadows. It appeals to those who want real quiet without phones or televisions (but with electricity and private baths), and the hot water may take a bit to get to your cabin. The rates include the Montana bed tax, making them an even better deal. A small fishing stream runs nearby, and a restaurant on-site serves western dinners.

CAMPING

Highway 2 has no drive-in national park campgrounds. But RVers and car campers will find two Forest Service campgrounds and a couple private campgrounds that will add on a 7 percent Montana bed tax. To camp in Glacier requires backpacking.

U.S. Forest Service Campgrounds

Two fairly small summer-only Forest Service campgrounds sit adjacent to Highway 2 tucked in doghair timbers for shade and monitored by campground hosts. Expect to find picnic tables (some wheelchair accessible), fire pits, vault toilets, drinking water, but no hookups.

COAL-NYACK LOOP

Remote doesn't come close to describing the Coal-Nyack Loop, an ancient Kootenai trail. A rough 38-mile trail encircles Mount Stimson, one of the six highest peaks in the park at 10,142 feet. Where other trails require camping in designated sites, the Coal-Nyack Loop is wild, with wilderness camping at large the modus operandi... which means, wherever you can find a flat place to sleep and abide by Leave No Trace principles. Bear resistant canisters are the way to carry food.

The loop is not a place for the faint of heart. Without bridges, creeks require fording, and there are plenty of them, for the mountains spew water in spring. Frequent avalanches splinter trees across trails. Thick brush cloaks routes. And the only access is via more trails or fording the Middle Fork of the Flathead River. Only those with experienced backcountry savvy should tackle the primitive isolation here. But for those heading out on foot or horseback, wilderness solitude awaits, for few intrepid souls tackle the loop.

Permits are required for backcountry camping in the Coal-Nyack Loop. Call 406/888-7800 or check for details online: www.nps.gov/glac.

You must also pack your own garbage away with you. Open only in summer, sites ($12) are first-come, first-serve, so get there by early afternoon in high season, especially if you want to nab one of the campsites farthest from the highway. Firewood is not available; you can collect it in the woods here. At Marias Pass, the **Summit Campground** (Lewis and Clark National Forest, 406/791-7700) has 17 sites. You can hop on to the Autumn Creek Trail across the highway and railroad tracks. At milepost 190, **Devil Creek Campground** (Flathead National Forest, 406/387-3800) has 14 sites, a few of which can handle up to 40-foot RVs. From the campground, a trail leads 5.9 miles up to Elk Lake or 8.2 miles to Moose Lake.

Private Campgrounds

Located 16 miles west of East Glacier between milepost 191 and 192, **◖ Glacier Meadow RV Park** (406/226-4479, www.glaciermeadow rvpark.com, mid-May–mid-Sept.) has 41 sites on a 58-acre meadow and forest setting with dump station, laundry, playground, full hook-ups, flush toilets, hot showers, and wireless Internet. The campground sits in full view of the highway, and all the sites are open, providing good satellite dish reception for those so inclined, but you'll not get much privacy from your neighbors. Hookups range $29–31, and tent sites are $20. In the evening and early morning, elk sometimes browse in the meadow here. You can hop the red bus tours heading over Logan Pass stop from here.

Located 16 miles east of West Glacier, **Stanton Creek Lodge** (milepost 170 on Hwy. 2, 406/888-5040 or 866/883-5040, www .stantoncreeklodge.com, open year-round) has tent ($15) and eight full-hookup RV ($24.50) sites adjacent to the highway and train. (Bring earplugs.) Amenities include flush toilets, hot showers, picnic tables, and fire pits. A full-service bar and restaurant is on-site. Walk a few minutes to the Stanton Lake and Grant Loop trailheads or 10 minutes to fishing. While you can camp here in winter surrounded by snow, the water is turned off—no flush toilets or hot showers.

Backcountry Camping

On Highway 2's north side, trails lead up Glacier's remote, rugged valleys. With multiple creek fords and primitive or undesignated campsites, the **Coal-Nyack Loop** keeps the wimps out. Its best campground—**Beaver Woman Lake**—sits in Martha's Basin in goat-watching terrain. Pick up permits ($5 per person per night; kids 8–18 $2.50; kids 7 and under free) in person at ranger stations, visitors centers, or the Apgar Permit Office (406/888-7900)

Stanton Lake in Great Bear Wilderness

24 hours in advance or by reservation beginning in mid-April ($30). Check additional requirements online: www.nps.gov/glac.

Backcountry camping on Forest Service land south of Highway 2 requires no special permit. Any destination works as long as you follow Leave No Trace ethics. Campsites are not maintained, nor designated. Overused campsites attest to the popularity of **Marion** and **Stanton Lakes**—short destinations good for anglers and families with young kids. **Tranquil Basin** ranks as one of the most scenic places for one–two nights. Call Hungry Horse Ranger Station (406/387-3800) for information.

Food

Restaurants along Highway 2 vary from old dives to fine dining. Off-season, don't be surprised if one is closed when its hours say otherwise—if fish are biting, owners will lock up.

FINE DINING

The **❰ Summit Station Lodge** (milepost 197.5, 406/226-4428, www.summitstationlodge.com, early June–late Sept., 5–9 P.M. daily, $12–35) opens its dining room nightly to the public for fine dining by Chef Xavier Simental. The menu changes weekly but has a smattering of Northern Italian pastas, steak, fish, chicken, and at least one vegetarian entree. Regional cuisine features Montana-raised bison and elk, sometimes prepared in traditional Blackfeet style. A fairly extensive wine list carries worldwide selections. Sip an after-dinner cocktail in the lounge, which stays open until 11 P.M.

Family Dining

At Izaak Walton Inn, the **❰ Dining Car Restaurant** (290 Izaak Walton Inn Rd., Essex, 406/888-5700, www.izaakwaltoninn.com, year-round, 7:30 A.M.–8 P.M. daily) serves up scrumptious meals on replicas of Great Northern Railway's historic dinnerware. (The gift shop sells the dishes, too!) The cozy restaurant is a great place to grab a huckleberry pancake breakfast before hiking or house lunch favorites like a buffalo burger or shredded pork wrap with red onion marmalade ($7–11). Enjoy a leisurely dinner ($11–24) of grilled rainbow trout with lemon-pepper pesto over a glass of wine as trains rumble past your window. You'll also find elk and Montana steak on the menu. They have a kid menu, too ($3.50–5). Be sure to head downstairs to the Flagstop Bar for a nightcap or at least to look at the historic photos of local railroad disasters.

Located 1.5 miles from East Glacier at milepost 207.4, **Bison Creek Ranch** (20722 Hwy. 2, 888/226-4482 or 406/226-4482, mid-May–Sept., daily 5–9 P.M., $8–18) has served up the

© BECKY LOMAX

Schauf family's western home cooking since the 1950s. House favorites include Edna's fried chicken and St. Mary Lake whitefish. Come hungry, for dinners are large, complete with salad bar, soups, rolls, veggie, potato, and ice cream. If anglers bring their own catch along, they'll cook it up for you.

Cafés

In the 30 miles between Essex and West Glacier, you'll pass three inexpensive cafés, good for post-hiking burgers. Lighter meals run $5–10; full dinners run up to $18. Open year round, **The Half-Way House** (milepost 178, Essex, 406/888-5650, Mon.–Sat., 8 A.M.–9 P.M. in summer, call for off-season hours) has a small restaurant featuring good portions of simple, tasty café fare and burgers favored by rangers and trail crews. Open Memorial–Labor Day weekend, the **Healthy Haven Cafe** (milepost 173.8, 406/888-5720, www.glacierhaveninn.com, Tues.–Sun., 8–11 A.M. and Tues.–Sat. 6–8 P.M.) serves breakfasts of homemade granolas, breads, and seasonal fresh fruit and home-style dinners of Alaska salmon, rib eye steak, and buffalo burgers. Open mid-May–Oct., **Stanton Creek Lodge** (milepost 170, 406/888-5040 or 866/883-5040, www.stantoncreeklodge.com, Wed.–Mon. 11 A.M.–7 P.M., bar stays open later on Fri. and Sat. nights) has a small lunch and dinner restaurant with a full service bar—a place to grab a burger-and-beer after hiking the Grant Ridge Loop. The funky restaurant is adorned with photos and T-shirts of their car rally winners; you can also sit outside on the small deck.

Bar

For a real taste of old funky Montana, stop at the **Snow Slip Inn** (milepost 191 on Hwy. 2, 406/226-9381, open year-round, 7 A.M.–midnight), six miles west of Marias Pass. The door may fall off its hinges, and the bartender may cuss at you, but you're in real Montana here, not a hybridized tourist place. The tiny bar and restaurant are permanently filled with smoke. Shoot pool while you wait for deep-fried bar food.

GROCERIES

Highway 2 lacks grocery stores, but the Half Way House near Essex (milepost 178, 406/888-5650) carries convenience store items: chips, pop, and a few staple groceries. To stock up for camping, you'll find seasonal grocery stores in East and West Glacier. Larger food markets are in Browning on the east side and Hungry Horse and Columbia Falls on the west.

PICNIC AREA

Only one designated picnic area is set aside on Highway 2, and that is **Walton** (milepost 180.5). Behind the Walton Ranger Station, the small picnic area clusters under thick trees adjacent to the Middle Fork River. Picnic tables, pit toilets, and fire pits are available, but you'll need to bring your own firewood; gathering wood is prohibited. It is, however, the trailhead for the Ole Creek Trail and Scalplock Lookout.

With six river accesses along the Middle Fork of the Flathead, there are plenty of additional places sans tables for picnicking at a scenic spot and soaking your feet in cold water.

WATERTON

For such a small park, Waterton Lakes National Park packs a punch. It houses rare plants found nowhere else and a plethora of wildlife that rivals its large northern sisters of Banff and Jasper. It sits on a nexus of major bird migration routes and weather systems. On the Continental Divide's east side, mountains literally collide with prairies. With no transitional foothills, eastern peaks plummet to grasslands—a phenomenon due to geological overthrusts that exposed the oldest sedimentary rock in the Canadian Rockies. Although active glaciers vacated Waterton's borders years ago, the results of ice gnawing on its landscape left lake pockets strewn through the park. A long glacier-gouged trough forms Upper Waterton Lake, the deepest lake in the Canadian Rockies and one that straddles the U.S.-Canadian border. The lake frequently kicks up with winds, giving credence to the park's ranking as the second windiest place in Alberta.

Dominated by the Prince of Wales Hotel and Waterton Lake, the park serves as a destination in itself as well as an entrance to Glacier's remote north country. On any summer day, the Waterton Townsite bustles with shoppers, bicyclists, backpackers, boaters, and campers. It's a quintessential Canadian mountain town that

HIGHLIGHTS

(Boat Tour: Hop aboard the historic MV *International* for a ride on the deepest lake in the Canadian Rockies. You'll float across the international boundary to Goat Haunt, U.S.A. (page 193).

(Chief Mountain: Spot this 9,080-foot sacred mountain of the Blackfeet from Chief Mountain Highway. Sitting in Glacier Park rather than Waterton, the mountain stands adjacent to Ninaki (the mother) and Papoose peeks up behind it (page 197).

(Prince of Wales Hotel: Drop in to the historic 1927 hotel sitting regally atop a knoll above the Waterton Townsite. Part of the chain of Swiss-style hostelries built by Great Northern Railway, the hotel maintains a decidedly British ambience with kilt-wearing bellhops and afternoon high tea (page 198).

(Goat Haunt, U.S.A.: Walk to the International Peace Park Pavilion. Accessible only by boat or on foot, Goat Haunt rests at Waterton Lake's southern end in Glacier Park – a launch pad to Glacier's remote northern trails (page 198).

(Cameron Lake: Rent a boat to paddle the lake, or walk the pathway along the west shore. The glacier-fed lake at Akamina Parkway's ter-

minus receives snowmelt from Herbst Glacier across the international boundary (page 199).

(Red Rock Canyon: Tread around a colorful mosaic of sediments. Argillites in striking reds and greens layer atop one another – evidence of its ancient inland sea origins (page 200).

(Maskinonge Lake: Focus your binoculars on unusual bird sightings here. Located on the axis of two migration flyways, Waterton is home to trumpeter swans, yellow-headed blackbirds, and Vaux's swifts (page 200).

(Bison Paddock: Drive through a paddock harboring majestic bison. In a tribute to the great wild herds that once roamed the prairies in vast numbers, Parks Canada maintains a small herd of these large mammals (page 200).

(Bear's Hump: Climb the short grunt up for a grand panoramic view. The trail gives you an eagle's-eye shot of Waterton Townsite and Waterton Lake (page 202).

(Carthew-Alderson: Cross over a high, windswept alpine pass on a scenic trail between Akamina Lake and the Waterton Townsite. You'll be wowed by the peaks and walk past blue icy jewels (page 203).

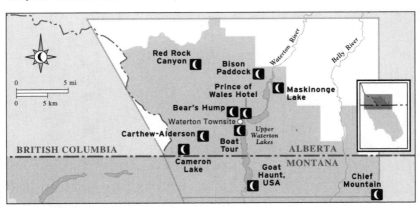

LOOK FOR **(** TO FIND RECOMMENDED SIGHTS, ACTIVITIES, DINING, AND LODGING.

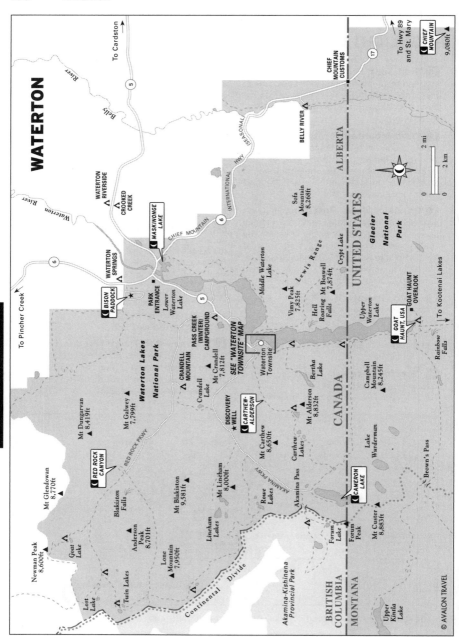

WATERTON

WATERTON

To Cardston →

To Pincher Creek →

To Hwy 89
and St. Mary

Belly River

Waterton River

Waterton River

Crooked Creek

WATERTON
RIVERSIDE

WATERTON
SPRINGS

MASKINONGE
LAKE

CHIEF MOUNTAIN

BISON
PADDOCK

PARK
ENTRANCE

Lower
Waterton
Lake

PASS CREEK
(WINTER)
CAMPGROUND

CRANDELL
MOUNTAIN

Crandell
Lake

Mt Crandell
7,812ft

DISCOVERY
WELL

CARTHEW-
ALDERSON

SEE "WATERTON
TOWNSITE" MAP

Waterton
Townsite

Middle Waterton
Lake

Vimy Peak
7,825ft

Hell
Roaring
Falls

Mt Boswell
7,874ft

Crypt Lake

Sofa
Mountain
8,266ft

BELLY RIVER

INTERNATIONAL HWY (SEASONAL)

CHIEF
MOUNTAIN
CUSTOMS

CHIEF
MOUNTAIN
9,080ft

Glacier

National

Park

Lewis Range

Upper
Waterton
Lake

Rainbow
Falls

GOAT HAUNT
OVERLOOK

GOAT
HAUNT, USA

To Kootenai Lakes →

UNITED STATES

ALBERTA

CANADA

Bertha
Lake

Mt Alderson
8,832ft

Carthew
Lakes

Campbell
Mountain
8,245ft

Lake
Warderman

Brown's Pass

Waterton Lakes

National Park

Mt Dungarvan
8,419ft

Mt Galwey
7,799ft

RED ROCK
CANYON

RED ROCK PKWY

Mt Glendowan
8,770ft

Newman Peak
8,600ft

Blakiston
Falls

Anderson
Peak
8,701ft

Mt Blakiston
9,581ft

Lone
Mountain
7,950ft

Mt Lineham
8,000ft

Lineham
Lakes

Rowe
Lakes

AKAMINA PKWY

Mt Carthew
8,650ft

Akamina Pass

Forum
Lake

Forum
Peak

CAMERON
LAKE

Mt Custer
8,883ft

Goat
Lake

Twin Lakes

Lost
Lake

Akamina-Kishinena
Provincial Park

Continental Divide

BRITISH
COLUMBIA

MONTANA

Upper Kintla
Lake

2 mi

2 km

0

0

© AVALON TRAVEL

KOOTENAI BROWN

John George "Kootenai" Brown was not only influential in the formation of Waterton Lakes National Park, but became the stuff of legend. Born in Ireland in 1839, he served with the British Army in India before coming to North America in 1861. With no money, he followed the Cariboo Gold Rush to Barkerville, B.C., where he mined gold. He spent it all, for he left with nothing several years later.

At 26 years old, he crossed the Continental Divide at South Kootenay Pass in what would become Waterton Lakes National Park. Called Kootenay Lakes at the time, he fell in love with the country and inherited his name through his close ties to the Kootenai Indians.

Local legend is full of Brown's escapades. When Blackfeet shot him in the back with an arrow, he reputedly pulled the arrow out himself and cleaned the wound with turpentine. In Montana, he spent 12 years as a trader, a pony express rider, a scout for Custer, and buffalo hunter. When buffalo became scarce, he hunted wolves. While he rode for the U.S. Army pony express, Chief Sitting Bull and the Sioux captured him, stripping and tying him to a stake while they debated his fate. He escaped in the middle of the night.

In 1869, he married and started a family with a Métis woman, Olivia Lyonnais. After being hauled into a Fort Benton court on murder charges and acquitted, he and his family packed off to Alberta. He built a cabin by Upper Waterton Lake, working as a guide, commercial fisherman, hunter, rancher, trader, and scout for the Rocky Mountain Rangers during the 1885 North-West Rebellion, the same year Olivia died. He later married Isabella, a Cree.

When Canada established the Kootenay Lake Forest Reserve in 1885, Brown became its first game warden and fisheries officer. In 1910, he was promoted to Forest Ranger in Charge. A year later, when Kootenay Lakes officially became Waterton Lakes, he stepped in as its first superintendent.

Kootenai Brown died in 1916 and is buried with his two wives along the entrance road to Waterton.

embodies what Banff used to be before booming commercialism. The MV *International* shuttles hikers and sightseers across Waterton Lake and the international boundary to Goat Haunt, U.S.A. Only two roads pierce the park's remarkable interior, both gateways to lakes, waterfalls, canyons, peaks, and wildlife.

HISTORY

In 1858, Lieutenant Thomas Blakiston, a European explorer, came to southern Alberta searching for a railroad route through the Canadian Rockies. He traveled to the large chain of Waterton Lakes, naming them for the British naturalist Charles Waterton, who never visited the area.

When the area became Kootenay Lakes Forest Park in 1895—Canada's fourth national park and the brainchild of Pincher Creek rancher F. W. Godsal—the legendary Kootenai Brown took the reins as its first game guardian and fisheries inspector. In 1911, he became Waterton's first superintendent, and the park's name officially changed to Waterton Lakes National Park.

Waterton produced Western Canada's first oil well in 1902. But within four years, the site closed down, the yield trickling to nothing. Meanwhile, an oil well near Cameron Falls produced one barrel a day and prompted building the Waterton Townsite. When oil riches dissipated in 1910, tourists arrived, fueled in part by Great Northern Railway's Glacier development. The Townsite sprouted cottages, a hotel, tennis courts, a golf course, packhorse outfitters, and boating.

In 1913, Great Northern Railway scouted Waterton for an appropriate hotel site, but World War I and a proposed dam in Waterton tabled its construction. Ironically, the

Prohibition in America prompted it to be built. Alcohol, after all, was still legal in Alberta, attracting scads of Montanans for thirst quenching. In 1927, the Prince of Wales Hotel finally opened on the wind-battered knoll above town and the 72-foot MV *International* launched its first sightseers up Waterton Lake.

Ecological Significance

For such a tiny park, Waterton is a nexus. The park sits on a narrow north–south wildlife corridor and the axis of two major bird migratory highways. Over 250 species of birds nest here or use the park's rich habitats for migration stopovers. It's one of the last places in North America where grizzly bears roam into the fringes of their original grassland habitat. Over 45 different habitats provide harbor for 10 species of amphibians and reptiles, 24 species of fish, and 60 species of mammals. Rare trumpeter swans nest here, as do Vaux's swifts.

Because Arctic and Pacific weather systems collide here, a breadth of vegetation abounds. With more than 1,370 plants, mosses, and lichens, Waterton houses more than half of Alberta's plant species, 179 which are considered rare, 22 found nowhere else in the province. Moonworts, a small fern, come in eight varieties here: one is found only in Waterton. The park's diminutive acreage has more plant diversity than the much larger Banff, Jasper, Kootenay, and Yoho parks combined! For such extremes and such rarities likewise contained in its sister park Glacier, the United Nations Educational, Scientific and Cultural Organization (UNESCO) named Waterton-Glacier a **Biosphere Reserve** and a **World Heritage Site.**

Exploring Waterton

Waterton's 52 square miles is tiny compared to Glacier. The Townsite sits at 4,200 feet in elevation, but surrounding peaks climb to 9,000 feet. While the Townsite houses about 100 people in winter, in summer it burgeons to nearly 2,000 residents. The park sees less than 400,000 annual visitors—about 20 percent of Glacier's crowds.

Waterton and Glacier span the 49th parallel (the international border), yet the parks are one connected system. Humans use one to access the other via Waterton Lake, and grizzly bears cross back and forth. In 1932 **Waterton-Glacier International Peace Park** was established—the world's first peace park. It celebrates the longest undefended border in the world at 5,525 miles.

PARK ENTRANCE

U.S. park passes are not valid in this Canadian park, although many Americans expect them to be. Even though Waterton-Glacier is an International Peace Park, no combined park pass is sold to date. To enter Waterton, you must purchase a separate Parks Canada day pass (adults CDN$7, youth 6–16 CDN$3.50, and seniors CDN$6, kids under 6 free, family or single-vehicle group CDN$17.50) valid until 4 P.M. the following day. You can also purchase year-long passes good for all Canadian National Parks (adults CDN$62, seniors CDN$53, youth 6–16 CDN$31.50, family or maximum per vehicle CDN$123). While the entrance gate is open 24/7 year round, it is only staffed early May–early October.

VISITORS CENTER

The **Waterton Lakes Visitor Information Center** (4.6 miles, 7.6 km south of the park entrance station on the park entrance road, 403/859-5133, early May–early Oct., daily 9 A.M.–5 P.M., June–Aug. open until 8 P.M.) sits across from the entrance road to Prince of Wales Hotel. It is the best stop for information, wilderness use permits, road conditions, fishing licenses, and maps. The trail to Bear's Hump departs from here. During months when the center is closed, you can get the

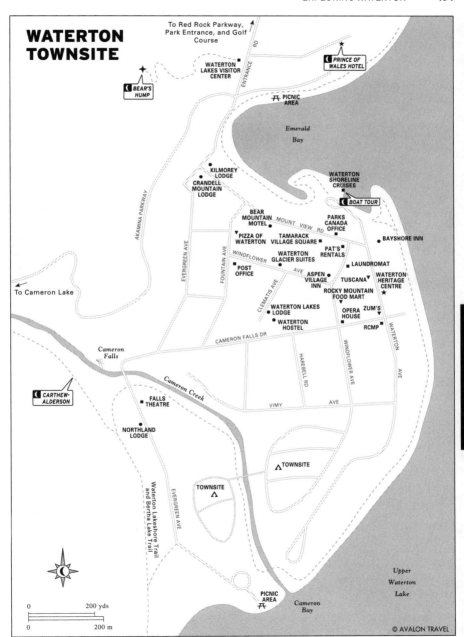

WATERTON TOWNSITE

To Red Rock Parkway, Park Entrance, and Golf Course

ENTRANCE RD

WATERTON LAKES VISITOR CENTER

BEAR'S HUMP

PRINCE OF WALES HOTEL

PICNIC AREA

Emerald Bay

AKAMINA PARKWAY

KILMOREY LODGE

CRANDELL MOUNTAIN LODGE

WATERTON SHORELINE CRUISES

BOAT TOUR

BEAR MOUNTAIN MOTEL

MOUNT VIEW RD

PARKS CANADA OFFICE

EVERGREEN AVE

FOUNTAIN AVE

PIZZA OF WATERTON

TAMARACK VILLAGE SQUARE

BAYSHORE INN

WINDFLOWER AVE

WATERTON GLACIER SUITES

PAT'S RENTALS

POST OFFICE

ASPEN VILLAGE INN

LAUNDROMAT

CLEMATIS AVE

TUSCANA

WATERTON HERITAGE CENTRE

To Cameron Lake

ROCKY MOUNTAIN FOOD MART

WATERTON LAKES LODGE

OPERA HOUSE

ZUM'S

WATERTON HOSTEL

RCMP

WATERTON AVE

CAMERON FALLS DR

Cameron Falls

HAREBELL RD

WINDFLOWER AVE

Cameron Creek

CARTHEW-ALDERSON

FALLS THEATRE

VIMY AVE

NORTHLAND LODGE

EVERGREEN AVE

Waterton Lakeshore Trail and Bertha Lake Trail

TOWNSITE

TOWNSITE

Upper Waterton Lake

PICNIC AREA

Cameron Bay

0   200 yds
0   200 m

© AVALON TRAVEL

WATERTON

Waterton Townsite and Waterton Lake

same information, licenses, and permits from the Parks Canada office (215 Mount View Rd., 403/859-2224, open year-round weekdays 8 A.M.–4 P.M.).

SHUTTLES AND TOURS
Shuttles

Getting between Glacier and Waterton by shuttle is complicated by the international border. From Glacier's east side, you can get to Waterton on the **Glacier Park, Inc.** shuttle (406/892-2525, www.glacierparkinc.com, $8–40 depending on distance, kids half-price). Originating at Glacier Park Lodge in East Glacier, the shuttle hits Two Medicine, Cut Bank Creek, St. Mary Visitor Center, Many Glacier Hotel, and Chief Mountain Customs before reaching the Prince of Wales Hotel. It runs once a day early June–late September with rates ($8–40 one-way) and departure times varying depending on your starting point. For the return connection between Waterton and Glacier, riders may not originate in Canada with GPI. Instead, you must use **Waterton Visitor Services** (Tamarack

Village Square, 214 Mount View Rd., 403/859-2378, www.hikewaterton.com, late May–early Oct.). They provide transportation (CDN$22 per person) by reservation to Chief Mountain Customs departing at 2:30 P.M. from Waterton. Walk through customs to the Chief Mountain parking lot, where you catch the GPI shuttle running down Glacier's east side.

Hikers can access Waterton trailheads via shuttles—by land or water. The **Crypt Lake Water Shuttle Service** (Waterton Shoreline Cruises, 403/859-2362, www.watertoncruise.com, mid-May–early Oct., daily, adults CDN$16 round-trip, kids CDN$8) departs from the marina daily at 10 A.M. for a 15-minute ride across Upper Waterton Lake to Crypt Landing, where the 10-mile (17.2-kilometer) round-trip trail begins. Watch your hiking time, for the return boats depart Crypt Landing at 4:15 (May and late Sept. only) or 5:30 P.M. (June–late Sept.). From late June–August, they add a 9 A.M. departure and a 4 P.M. return boat. No reservations are taken for this shuttle, so arrive at least 20 minutes before departure. The boat tour to **Goat Haunt** functions also as a hiker shuttle (June–mid-Sept., daily, adults round-trip CDN$32, kids CDN$10–16). It accesses trailheads in northern Glacier and provides transportation for those riding back to Waterton after hiking the shoreline trail to Goat Haunt. Buy your return ticket (half the round-trip rate) that morning before hiking down the lake. You can also pay in cash when you board in Goat Haunt. Hikers may catch an early boat and return on a later boat; just notify the ticket agent of your return intentions. Boats depart the Townsite at 10 A.M., 1 and 4 P.M.; boats depart Goat Haunt at 11:25 A.M., 2:25 and 5:25 P.M. Be aware of border regulations for hiking and using this shuttle. Starting in September, there is no 5:25 P.M. Goat Haunt pickup for hikers and backpackers as Canada Customs is closed.

Departing daily at 8:30 A.M. from Tamarack Village, the **Cameron Express** (Tamarack Village Square, 214 Mount View Rd., 403/859-2378, www.hikewaterton.com, late May–early Oct., CDN$12) shuttles hikers to the popular Carthew-Alderson trailhead for a point-to-point 11-mile (18-kilometer) hike back to the Townsite. Reservations are a good idea, especially in high season; you can make them with a credit card by phone. They'll also provide custom shuttles to other trailheads; ask for rates and details.

◖ Boat Tour

Waterton Shoreline Cruises (at the marina at the junction of Mount View Rd. and Waterton Ave., 403/859-2362, www.watertoncruise.com, May–early Oct., daily, adults round-trip CDN$32, kids CDN$10–16, kids three and under free) operates the historic MV *International* on Upper Waterton Lake. During the two-hour tour on the wooden 200-passenger boat cruising here since 1927, knowledgeable guides punctuate their patter with humor. For the best views, go for a sunny seat on the boat's top deck. If the weather is brisk, just bundle up. From June to mid-September, the boat docks for 30 minutes at Goat Haunt—time enough to walk to the International Peace Park Pavilion. Trips depart at 10 A.M., 1 and

4 P.M. June–mid-September. In May and after mid-September, they depart at 10 A.M. and 2:30 P.M. In high season, they add a 7 P.M. tour that stops only for 10 minutes in Goat Haunt. Because advanced reservations are only taken for large groups, in high season you should get to the dock early.

SERVICES

Gas up before you head north across the border—gas in Canada is more expensive than in the United States, usually around $0.50–0.80 per gallon more. Also, be aware that gas is sold by the liter in Canada rather than the gallon, so the price on the pump will look pretty darn good. To convert the price, remember 3.7 liters equals one gallon.

Pat's Gas Station (224 Mount View Road, 403/859-2266, www.watertoninfo.ab.ca) is much more than a place to gas up or buy propane for the RV. While Pat can magically perform minor car repairs, the shop's claim to fame is its rental line: surrey bikes (CDN$20 per hour), mountain bikes (CDN$8–11 per

MV *International* at Goat Haunt

hour, $35 per day), baby backpacks (CDN$10), and tennis rackets (CDN$3 per hour). You can even rent a scooter (CDN$80 per day). Pat's also sells food and convenience items as well as Cuban cigars, fishing tackle, park permits, and newspapers.

A launderette (301 Windflower Ave., 403/859-2460) is open during summer months daily 10 A.M.–8 P.M. The Townsite post office (102 Windflower Ave.) is open year-round Monday–Friday 8 A.M.–4:30 P.M. Remember: You must use Canadian postage stamps rather than U.S. stamps to post mail from Canada! ATMs are located at Pat's Gas Station, Tamarack Village Square, Rocky Mountain Food Mart, and the Prince of Wales Hotel. While keying in the dollar amount, remember that the ATM gives Canadian currency! *The Calgary Sun* carries regional, national, and international news, and a free newspaper, *The Boundary* (www.watertonboundary.com), published weekly mid-May through early September, carries the local Waterton news.

Waterton is not a place where you'll find Internet cafés and wireless access. In fact, most of the town still relies on old-fashioned dial-up. Plan for some good-size long distance phone charges if you're going to hook up. Cell phones can now get some service at the Townsite, but not in the rest of the park.

Shopping

Shopping in Waterton is a different experience. While a certain British flair marks some of the shops with bone china and Irish linens, souvenirs are decidedly Canadian with moose and traditional Royal Canadian Mounted Police decorating T-shirts. Most shops are open from May through September seven days a week; winter closes most. During shoulder seasons, hours are short, often 10 A.M.–5 P.M., but in high season, shops stay open into the evening (7–8 P.M.). Many stores and restaurants sell specialty Cuban cigars, unavailable in the United States. But remember, these cannot go back over the U.S. border.

If you need outdoor gear, **Tamarack Outdoor Outfitters** (Tamarack Village

A hiker relaxes on Avion Ridge in Waterton.

© BECKY LOMAX

Square, 214 Mount View Rd., 403/859-2378) can outfit you from head to toe with hiking, backpacking, and camping gear. The owners recently expanded their shop to 5,000 square feet. They carry good reputable brands, too, at reasonable prices. This is the best place to buy topographic maps for hiking. Chocoholics gravitate toward **Welch's Chocolate Shop** (corner of Cameron Falls Dr. and Windflower Ave., 403/859-2363), which stocks all kinds of international chocolates and makes its own fudge and candy.

Currency Exchange
In Waterton, most businesses, including restaurants, shops, and lodges will accept U.S. currency; however, return change will be given back in Canadian currency. For conversions, most businesses use the bank exchange rate, but some have their own policies. For the best exchange rates, use a credit card as much as possible. Waterton has no banks; the nearest banking services are in Cardston and Pincher Creek, but in Tamarack Village Square, **Waterton Visitor Services** (214 Mount View Rd., late May–early Oct., shoulder seasons 8 A.M.–6 P.M., high season 8 A.M.–8 P.M.) offers currency exchange.

Emergencies
For emergencies, contact the RCMP (202 Waterton Ave., 403/859-2244 or 403/653-4931) during summer months or Parks Canada Wardens (215 Mount View Rd., 403/859-2224) year-round. The nearest hospitals are 30 miles (50 km) away in Pincher Creek (403/627-3333) and Cardston (403/653-4411). To contact the park's one emergency ambulance, call 403/859-2636.

DRIVING TOURS
Chief Mountain Highway
The Chief Mountain International Highway provides a summer-only connection between Glacier and Waterton Parks. Its season and hours operate around the Canadian and U.S. customs stations at the border (open mid-May–Sept.; May and after Labor Day 9 A.M.–6 P.M., June–Labor Day 7 A.M.–10 P.M.). You may want to top off on gas in the United States since gas is generally more expensive in Canada. (The nearest gas is in Babb, MT, or Waterton Townsite.) The 30-mile road undulates over rolling aspen hills and beaver ponds as it curves around Chief Mountain, imposing alone on Glacier's northwest corner. A few unmarked pullouts offer good photo ops. Drive this open range carefully, for cows wander the road. Your car also may need a good cleaning if wet cow pies litter the road!

From the U.S. as the road rounds Chief Mountain, it enters Glacier Park. No entrance station is here; no payment is required. The road reaches the international border and Chief Mountain Customs at 18.6 miles. After customs, the road enters Alberta and Waterton Lakes National Park, but you won't reach a park entrance station until nearly at the Townsite. After the road crosses the Belly River, it briefly exits the park, crossing the Blood Indian Reserve (part of the Blackfoot family) before re-entering the park. Burn from the 1998 Sofa Mountain Fire lines both sides of the road. As you crest a big rise, stop at the overlook (28 miles, 45 km) to gaze at the Waterton Valley. For the descent, shift into second gear to avoid burning your brakes.

Park Entrance Road
The five-mile (eight-kilometer) road connecting the park entrance station with Waterton Townsite is worth a drive with a pair of binoculars. The park entrance road turns south off Highway 6, reaching the entrance station in less than half a mile. Linnet, Maskinonge, and Lower Waterton Lakes attract scads of birds as well as moose, bear, elk, and smaller wildlife. From the park entrance, you should stop at a picnic area along its route for wildlife-watching: Knight's Lake (0.6 mile, 0.9 kilometer), Hay Barn (2.5 miles, 4 km), and Marquis (4.1 miles, 6.5 km). The Waterton Lakes Visitor Information Center is 4.8 miles (7.7 km) from the entrance station.

AKAMINA-KISHINENA PROVINCIAL PARK

Where Waterton Lakes National Park meets the Continental Divide, Akamina-Kishinena Provincial Park sits to the west. It follows the international boundary of Montana's Glacier National Park to the North Fork of the Flathead River. This remote 27,000-acre park is accessible only on foot from Akamina Parkway in Waterton Lakes or trails from the end of a 68-mile (109-kilometer) dirt road that takes off 10 miles (16 km) south of Fernie, B.C.

The small park is part of the same narrow Rocky Mountain ecosystem that provides corridors for grizzly bears and wolves. Geologic wonders display themselves in Forum Peak's 1.3-billion-year-old sedimentary rocks, and rare plants like the pygmy poppy grow here.

From Waterton, hikers and mountain bikers can access the park via an old circa 1920 trail that connects the Cameron Valley to the North Fork of the Flathead Valley. To access Akamina-Kishinena, hike to Akamina Pass, the boundary between Waterton Park and Akamina-Kishinena. From here, you can mountain bike to Wall Lake or hike to Forum Lake.

Some Canadians want to expand Waterton Lakes National Park to include Akamina-Kishinena. The addition would not only increase the size of Waterton, but complete the "Crown of the Continent" ecosystem.

For more information, contact British Columbia Parks (205/489-8540, www.gov.bc.ca /bcparks).

Hikers access Akamina-Kishinena Provincial Park on the Akamina Pass.

Akamina Parkway

A 10-mile (16-kilometer) paved drive climbs above Waterton Townsite along the base of Crandell Mountain on Akamina Parkway. The road is open all year, although in winter only to Little Prairie. Just west of the Waterton Visitor Information Center, the signed Akamina Parkway turns off and begins climbing steeply from Waterton Townsite as it curves up above the Cameron Creek Gorge. It passes the **Oil City Historic Site** as well as trailheads to Crandell Lake, Lineham Falls, Rowe Lakes, Akamina Pass, and Forum Lake. For those looking to picnic along Cameron Creek, picnic tables, pit toilets, and shelters are at McNeally's (4 miles, 6.4 km) and Little Prairie (8.1 miles, 13 km). The road ends at **Cameron Lake.** On the return trip, shift into second gear for the steep descent back to the Townsite; you can always smell the brakes of those who forget.

Red Rocks Parkway

Red Rocks Parkway (May–Oct.) is self-descriptive, for the paved road ends at a red-rock canyon. Locate the signed turnoff on the park entrance road (2.2 miles, 3.5 km from the Townsite; 2.8 miles, 3.9 km from park entrance station). The 9.3-mile (15-kilometer) narrow road climbs through grasslands, squeezes through a canyon, and opens up into meadows along Blakiston Creek. Through the canyon, the road is quite narrow but passable for trailers and RVs. Bring your binoculars for wildlife-watching of bears and bighorn sheep. Crandell Mountain Campground (4.6 miles, 7.5 km) is accessed via this road. The parkway ends where a self-guided trail leads around **Red Rock Canyon.** To picnic along Red Rocks, you'll find tables, pit toilets, and shelters at three spots: Coppermine Creek (5 miles, 8 km), Dungarvan (8 miles, 13 km), and Red Rocks (9.3 miles, 15 km).

SIGHTS
◖ Chief Mountain

Located along Chief Mountain Highway, Chief Mountain rises up 9,080 feet abruptly from aspen parklands and prairies. It marks the northeasternmost peak in Glacier National Park. Legend tells of a young Flathead brave

WATERTON

© BECKY LOMAX

International Peace Park Pavilion at Goat Haunt

who carried a bison skull to its summit and remained there for four nights wrestling the Spirit of the Mountain. When he finally prevailed, the Spirit gave him a protection totem to keep him safe in battle and hunting.

◖ Prince of Wales Hotel

Designated a Canadian National Historic Site, the 122-foot-tall, four-story, 90-room Prince of Wales Hotel took more than a year to build. Constructed by Great Northern Railway as a link for the Glacier chain, the hotel opened its doors in 1927. Even if you are not staying here, drop in to see its massive lobby with floor-to-ceiling windows looking down Waterton Lake. Kilt-wearing bellhops haul luggage, and the lobby serves high tea in the afternoon. Walk out on the bluff for the best photographic views of Waterton Lake. But hold onto your hat; howling winds rage here!

Waterton Lake

Set in a north–south trough gouged by Pleistocene ice age glaciers, Waterton Lake is the deepest lake in the Canadian Rockies. (It's actually Upper Waterton Lake, which feeds Middle and Lower Waterton Lakes, but no one calls it that.) Its 487-foot depths hold 50-pound lake trout and tiny ice age relics—the opossum shrimp. Spanning the international boundary, the half-mile-wide and nearly seven-mile-long lake conveys visitors over its waters in the 1927 wooden MV *International*.

The U.S.-Canadian Border

For Waterton visitors, the border inside the park is an attraction. The long, straight swath is cleared every 20 years by the International Boundary Commission. The boat tour down Waterton Lake crosses this unnatural forest line en route to Goat Haunt, where visitors can debark and walk to the Peace Park Pavilion without going through customs. Hikers can also walk over the border swath on the Waterton Lake Trail.

◖ Goat Haunt, U.S.A.

A tiny seasonal enclave housing rangers, Goat Haunt, U.S.A., rests at Waterton Lake's southern end in Glacier National Park. Accessed only

Cameron Lake and Herbst Glacier

© BECKY LOMAX

WATERTON

© BECKY LOMAX

Cameron Falls is an easy walk from the Townsite Campground.

by boat or on foot, Goat Haunt sees hundreds of visitors per day in high season. Most arrive via the MV *International*. Walk the paved pathway to the International Peace Park Pavilion, where displays tell the story of the peace park. Trailheads depart to Goat Haunt Overlook, Kootenai Lakes, Rainbow Falls, and beyond.

🌙 Cameron Lake

Tucked in a glacial cirque at the terminus of Akamina Parkway, Cameron Lake reflects the steep slopes of Mount Custer. Look across the glacially-fed lake to Herbst Glacier: You're looking across the international boundary into Montana. Avalanches preen the slopes into good bear habitat. Rent a rowboat or canoe to paddle around the lake's shoreline, or saunter the pathway along the west shore watching for moose, shorebirds, and bears. From here, hikers climb the Carthew-Alderson trail to trek to the Townsite.

Waterton Heritage Centre

Waterton Heritage Centre (117 Waterton Ave., 403/859-2267, mid-May–Sept., 10 A.M.–6 P.M.) is a small museum housed in the old fire hall with displays on Waterton's natural and cultural history. Books—from hiking guides to coffee table picture books—are also sold here. Operated by the Waterton Natural History Association, the center also hosts summer geology, botany, wildlife, photography, and birding field trips and speakers. Evening presentations usually run $5; one-day field courses cost $20. All are taught by local experts.

Cameron Falls

Picturesque Cameron Falls sits on the edge of the Waterton Townsite on Evergreen Avenue. In June, water roars through its slots, but flows drop substantially by August. Several benches allow for gazing. Here, Cameron Creek has eroded a massive fold of the Waterton Formation, a 600-million-year-old rock layer. Short, steep 10-minute trails on both sides of the creek access viewpoints. Opt for the north side switchback trail for better views.

Waterton Townsite

A quaint little tourism town, Waterton Townsite sits in a dramatic location at the foot of Waterton Lake. Paved walking trails circumvent the town, connecting the few-block-long shopping district with the campground and picnic areas. It hums in summer with visitors riding surrey bikes, but quiets in winter under snows. You'll frequently see bighorn sheep and deer sitting on lawns.

◖ Red Rock Canyon

Red Rocks Parkway begins at Blakiston Creek and terminates at Red Rock Canyon, a colorful narrow gorge. Walk the 0.4-mile (0.7-kilometer) pathway up one side and down the other to take in all its hues. Iron-rich argillite sediments layer on top of each other, some turning red from oxidization, others remaining green. Evidence of the ancient Belt Sea, these sediments are some of the oldest exposed rock in the world, created between 800 million and 1.6 billion years ago. Look for sea evidence of mud cracks and ripple marks.

◖ Maskinonge Lake

Birders and wildlife-watchers migrate to Maskinonge Lake for its rich diversity. Located east of the park entrance, the aspen-rimmed lake attracts waterfowl, osprey, trumpeter swans, yellow-headed blackbirds, and kingfishers. Because Waterton sits on the axis of two migration flyways, it sees over 250 species of birds. The lake also attracts everything from huge Shiras moose weighing 1,500 pounds to muskrats, mink, and tiny vagrant shrews. When rare trumpeter swans nest in July and early August, some of the area is closed to protect their offspring. Don't forget to take your binoculars and spotting scopes!

◖ Bison Paddock

Once roaming the plains in vast numbers 150 years ago, wild bison have all but vanished from North America. On Highway 6, 1.2 miles (2 km) west of the park entrance road, the Bison Paddock contains a small herd. Bison weigh close to 2,000 pounds and look like shaggy cows. But don't be lured into thinking they are docile: They may look big, lunky, and dumb, but they are extremely unpredictable and aggressive. Drive on the narrow, roughly paved 2.5-mile loop through the grassland paddock; for safety, stay inside the car.

Discovery Well and Oil City

Located on the Akamina Parkway, two stops mark the sight of the Discovery Well, western Canada's first oil well, and its accompanying Townsite. The first is at 4.8 miles (8 km) up the road; it's the actual site of the first well from 1902. Continue on a bit to the original Townsite for **Oil City.** A short five-minute walk through the trees leads to the hotel foundation—all that remains of the 20-block city that was plotted out. Closed within four years, Oil City soon became a ghost town.

Recreation

HIKING

Waterton has well over 124 miles (200 km) of trails. Nearly two miles of walking trails—both paved and dirt—connect sights, restaurants, lodging facilities, the campground, and picnic areas in Waterton Townsite. From the marina to Cameron Bay, the trail follows the shoreline. Trails also connect to the Falls Theater, Cameron Falls, Bertha Lake and Waterton Lake trailheads, Emerald Bay, and Prince of Wales Hotel. Contrary to Glacier's backcountry rules, Waterton's trails permit dogs on a leash, but keep your pet under control and away from wildlife. You'll find updated trail reports on the Parks Canada website (www.pc.gc.ca, look under Waterton hiking for access). The visitors center also has trail closure and update info.

For hiking, you'll find the best Waterton topographical map at the visitors center. The Gem Trek Publishing map (CDN$9, 877/921-6277, www.gemtrek.com) not only includes roads, trails, and bike routes, but trail descriptions for easy, moderate, and strenuous hikes. It also includes the eastern end of Akamina-Kishinena Provincial Park and the Goat Haunt area of Glacier.

For those planning to camp in the backcountry, wilderness permits are necessary (CDN$10 per person per night, ages 16 and under free) for all of the nine designated backcountry campsites. Reservations are available for CDN$12 per trip 90 days in advance beginning April 1 each year. You can get permits and reservations at the Waterton Visitor Information Center (403/859-5133) or Waterton's Parks Canada office (403/859-5140).

Shuttles by water and land make for easy trailhead access. Waterton Shoreline Cruises (403/859-2362, www.watertoncruise.com) operates the Crypt Lake and Goat Haunt boats. Waterton Visitor Services (214 Mount View Rd., 403/859-2378, www.hikewaterton.com) operates the land shuttles.

Bertha Lake

- Distance: 7 miles (11.4 km) round-trip
- Duration: 3–4 hours
- Elevation gain: 1,480 feet
- Effort: 2 miles moderate, remainder strenuous
- Trailhead: southwest corner of Waterton Townsite off Evergreen Avenue

The trail starts as a signed interpretive path to Lower Bertha Falls. The path climbs gradually along the western shore of Waterton Lake to an overlook with views of Mount Cleveland, the highest peak in Glacier. At the junction, take the right fork and head across the dry open hillside to Lower Bertha Falls, where pounding waters crash through bedrock. For a destination, the falls is 4 miles (6.4 km) round-trip.

To continue to Bertha Lake, cross the bridge below the falls and climb incessant switchbacks up through a forested hillside beside Upper Bertha Falls, a larger sister of the lower falls. Soon, the trail crests a timbered knoll high above narrow Bertha Lake. The best view of the lake is here. To reach the shore, descend 0.1 mile to the campground near its outlet.

Waterton Lake Trail

- Distance: 8.7 miles (13 km) one-way
- Duration: 4–5 hours
- Elevation gain: minimal
- Effort: easy by elevation gain, moderate by length
- Trailhead: southwest corner of Waterton Townsite off Evergreen Avenue

Bordering the west lakeshore of Waterton Lake, the trail begins at the Bertha Lake Trailhead. After 1 mile (0.6 kilometer), the trails diverge, with the Waterton Lake Trail dropping in a quick steep descent to Bertha Bay Campground on the lakeshore. From here, the trail wanders through cottonwoods, subalpine firs, lodgepoles, and aspen. A few overlooks offer views of the lake.

The trail crosses the international boundary at 3.8 miles (6.1 km) before connecting to a well-signed maze of trails at the end of Waterton Lake. Follow signs to Goat Haunt and catch the MV *International* back to the Townsite. Before you leave in the morning, book your return trip with Waterton Shoreline Cruises. Bring your passport; you'll need it for customs in Goat Haunt. Only U.S. and Canadian citizens are permitted entry at Goat Haunt.

Crypt Lake

- Distance: 11.2 miles (17 km) round-trip

- Duration: 5–6 hours

- Elevation gain: 2,300 feet

- Effort: moderately strenuous

- Trailhead: Crypt Landing, accessible by boat from Waterton

Catch the water taxi operated daily by Waterton Shoreline Cruises to reach Crypt Landing. From Crypt Landing, the climb bolts up through a wooded hillside along Hellroaring Creek Valley. An alternate route leads to the edge of Hellroaring Creek and its waterfalls; you can take one route up and one down this short section. Soon, the trail passes Twin Falls and lodgepole pines give way to open meadows and boulder fields.

The trail appears to dead-end in a headwall. But, an iron ladder climbs up to a four-foot-high tunnel with an awkward walk or crawl. The tunnel emerges on a cliff with a steel cable for assistance in crossing. The trail breaks into a tight cirque housing Crypt Lake, which drains from an underwater channel. The international boundary crosses the lake's southern end. In a mad dash, hikers suddenly check their watches and all jump up to speed down the trail en masse to catch the return boat.

🔊 Bear's Hump

- Distance: 1.7 miles (2.8 km) round-trip

- Duration: 1.25 hours

- Elevation gain: 550 feet

- Effort: strenuous, but short

- Trailhead: Waterton Visitor Information Centre parking lot

The trail heads promptly uphill—piling on switchback after switchback in a vertical Thighmaster. At least it offers two benches en route for rest. Partially forested and thick with thimbleberry and virgin's bower, the hike is cool in early morning or late afternoon after the hump shades the east slope from the sun. The visitors center has a free interpretive guide to accompany the trail.

Topping out on the Bear's Hump, a rocky outcropping on Mount Crandell's ridge, the trail offers one of the best views of the Waterton Townsite, Prince of Wales Hotel, Waterton Lake, Glacier National Park, and the prairie. On top, three benches offer good spots to gaze at the scenery before you tackle the knee-pounding descent.

Lineham Ridge

- Distance: 10.6 miles (17.2 km) round-trip

- Duration: 6 hours

- Elevation gain: 3,116 feet

- Effort: strenuous

- Trailhead: Tamarack Trailhead 6.7 miles (10.9 km) up on Akamina Parkway

In early July, this trail bursts with wildflowers: yellow arnica, paintbrush, and purple lupine. The climb starts through thin forest broken by avalanche paths, following Rowe Creek. At 2.4 miles (3.9 km), you'll pass the junction to Lower Rowe Lake, a short 10-minute side trip. From here, the trail ascends to the base of a giant cirque. After crossing the creek, take the right fork to ascend around the basin.

As the trail swings around the cirque, it passes from subalpine wildflower meadows into alpine tundra. Red argillite colors the mountainside. From the ridge, Lineham Lakes appear below. At the saddle below Mt. Lineham, you can opt to climb off-trail east to the peak or continue on the rugged trail west up Lineham Ridge to look down Blakiston Creek.

Cameron Lakeshore

- Distance: 1.9 miles (3.2 km) round-trip

- Duration: 1 hour

- Elevation gain: none

- Effort: easy

- Trailhead: at the day-use facility at Cameron Lake

This short trail follows the lake's west shoreline to a wooden platform and small interpretive display called Grizzly Gardens, where trees are starting to cut the view. Although the trail is flat, watch your footing on tree roots. Several points reach the shoreline for photos of Mount Custer and Herbst Glacier. At the trail's terminus, scan the avalanche slopes for grizzly bears feeding on glacier lilies. Do not continue farther; bears depend on quiet here for denning, feeding, and cub rearing.

◖ Carthew-Alderson

- Distance: 11.8 miles (18 km) one-way

- Duration: 6 hours

- Elevation gain: 1,440 feet

- Effort: moderately strenuous

- Trailhead: behind day-use facility at Cameron Lake

Catch the Cameron Express hiker shuttle to Cameron Lake. One of the most popular hikes in Waterton, the trail climbs 4.5 miles to Carthew Summit, where alpine tundra stretches along a windswept ridge. Be prepared for strong winds here, even on a sunny summer day. Some winds may even force you to crawl over the pass. Views span deep into Glacier's interior.

The descent is a knee-pounder, dropping over 3,000 feet in elevation. From the summit, the trail passes by several high tarns, sometimes flanked with snowfields well into July. The path drops along a cliff wall, before reaching Alderson Lake. Once you depart the lake, only peek-a-boo views of avalanche chutes break out from the thick timber en route to Cameron Falls at Waterton Townsite.

Akamina Ridge via Wall and Forum Lakes

- Distance: Akamina Ridge Loop 11.4 miles (18.3 km)

- Forum Lake 5.4 miles round-trip (8.8 km)

- Wall Lake 6.4 miles (10.4 km)

- Duration: 6–7 hours

WATERTON

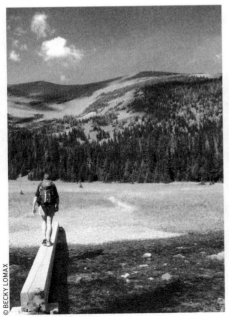

© BECKY LOMAX

Lineham Ridge trail

- Elevation gain: 3,199 feet
- Effort: strenuous
- Trailhead: Akamina Pass Trailhead 9.2 miles (14.8 km) up Akamina Parkway

This hike begins in Waterton Park, but within one mile reaches low, forested Akamina Pass where it crosses over the Continental Divide and into Akamina-Kishinena Provincial Park. Continue 0.4 miles (0.7 km) to the Forum Lake junction, turning left (Wall Lake is to the right and the way you will return). The trail climbs to the snowmelt-fed Forum Lake, surrounded by steep talus and larch slopes. From the lake, follow the rough, unmaintained trail that ascends the western ridge up through a 16-foot rock band where you'll need to use your hands for climbing. Once above the band, the ridge walk begins.

The Akamina Ridge walk is truly spectacular. Rolling over peaks and knolls, the alpine tundra is devoid of trees, but rampant with miniature plants like pink moss campion struggling to survive. To the south, Glacier's remote Kintla Peak stands with Agassiz Glacier in your face while a sea of peaks stretches in all directions. The trail continues along the ridge for three miles before taking a steep drop back into forest to Wall Lake, a dramatic cirque tucked against abrupt limestone walls. From Wall Lake, hike 1.8 miles (3 km) back to the Forum Lake junction and return to the trailhead over Akamina Pass.

Blakiston Falls

- Distance: 1.2 miles (2 km) round-trip
- Duration: 45 minutes
- Elevation gain: minimal
- Effort: easy
- Trailhead: end of Red Rocks Parkway

Turn left just after you cross Red Rocks Creek. Then across Bauerman Creek, look for the hiker trailhead and walk through a coniferous forest. Blakiston Creek tumbles below the trail, and Mount Blakiston peeks into

Hiking Akamina Ridge above Wall Lake yields views of Waterton and Glacier.

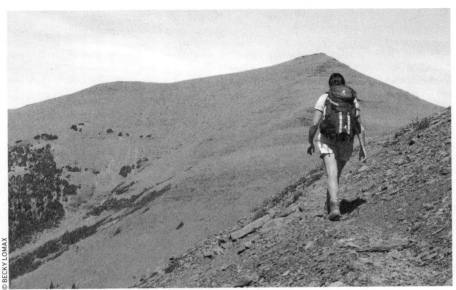

© BECKY LOMAX

hiking on Avion Ridge, along the Waterton Park boundary

view from time to time. At Blakiston Falls, a wooden deck conveniently makes for easy observation of the tumbling falls.

Avion Ridge and Goat Lake

- Distance: Avion Ridge Loop 14 miles (22.5 km)
- Goat Lake 7.8 miles (12.6 km) round-trip
- Duration: 4 hours
- Elevation gain: 1,750 feet
- Effort: moderately strenuous
- Trailhead: at end of Red Rocks Parkway

The Avion Ridge Loop begins and ends on the Snowshoe Trail, an old overgrown roadway that permits bicycles. It's easiest done clockwise, but some hikers prefer the vertical ascent via Goat Lake in favor of a less steep descent. At 2.4 miles (4 km) up the Snowshoe Trail, you'll reach the Goat Lake junction. Those heading to Goat Lake abruptly climb a relentless uphill into the hanging valley above to Goat Lake, known for its rainbow trout.

For Avion Ridge Loop, continue up the Snowshoe Trail from the Goat Lake junction. At 5.1 miles (8.2 km), you'll reach the Snowshoe Warden Cabin and campsites. Take the trail heading north toward Lost Lake and climb to Avion Ridge. A five-mile unmaintained trail ascends the ridgeline through larch before popping out of the trees on a barren, windswept ridge. The trail circles above a cirque right on the boundary line of Waterton National Park (you'll see signs). Endless peaks parade in all directions. As the trail swings north, it descends to a saddle, traverses a steep sidehill, and reaches a pass above Goat Lake. A knee-pounding descent through wildflower meadows plummets to the lake and then to the Snowshoe Trail junction. Turn left to return to the trailhead.

Rainbow Falls

- Distance: 1.4 miles round-trip
- Duration: 1 hour
- Elevation gain: minimal
- Effort: easy

- Trailhead: behind ranger station at Goat Haunt in Glacier National Park

Rainbow Falls is one option for a short hike from the boat tour on Waterton Lake. (Check with Waterton Shoreline Cruises for a schedule and book a return boat that allows enough time to complete your hike. Take passports to pass through customs in Goat Haunt.)

Follow the paved trail to the first junction, taking the right fork onto dirt. The trail wanders through thick forests, mosquito-filled in early summer. Just before reaching Waterton River, take a left turn at the signed junction, heading up the east bank toward Rainbow Falls. The falls is actually a series of cascades cutting troughs in bedrock, but a great place to sit.

Goat Haunt Overlook

- Distance: 2 miles (3.2 km) round-trip
- Duration: 2 hours
- Elevation gain: 844 feet
- Effort: very strenuous
- Trailhead: behind ranger station at Goat Haunt in Glacier National Park

Goat Haunt Overlook is another option for a short hike from the boat tour on Waterton Lake. (Check with Waterton Shoreline Cruises for a schedule and book a return boat that allows enough time to complete your hike. Take passports to pass through customs in Goat Haunt.)

Follow the paved trail past the first right-hand turn to a dirt trail and hike 0.1 mile on the Continental Divide Trail heading south toward Fifty Mountain. At the signed junction, turn left. The trail climbs gently for a few hundred feet before it turns steep straight uphill. It's a grunt, but the view is well worth the climb. At the overlook, you can flop on a conveniently placed log to eat lunch and gander downlake to the Waterton Townsite and Prince of Wales Hotel.

Kootenai Lakes

- Distance: 5.6 miles (9 km) round-trip
- Duration: 3–3.5 hours
- Elevation gain: minimal
- Effort: easy
- Trailhead: behind ranger station at Goat Haunt in Glacier National Park

Kootenai Lakes attracts hikers for its often-seen moose and sometimes-seen nesting trumpeter swans. Access is via the tour boat. (Check with Waterton Shoreline Cruises for a schedule and book a return boat that allows enough time to complete your hike. Take passports to pass through customs in Goat Haunt.)

At Goat Haunt, follow the paved trail past the first right-hand turn and hike on the Continental Divide Trail heading south toward Fifty Mountain. The trail wanders through old growth forest. At 2.5 miles (4 km), take the right junction toward the campground. If you eat lunch here, do so on the beach or in the cook area and protect the cleanliness of the tenting sites for those sleeping in bear country.

International Peace Park Guided Hike

Twice a week during July and August, Park Service interpretive rangers from Waterton and Glacier jointly lead the International Peace Park Hike. The 14-kilometer (8.7 mile) hike leaves at 10 A.M. from the Bertha Lake Trailhead usually on Wednesdays and Saturdays. Bring a sack lunch, water, and extra clothes, and wear sturdy walking shoes. You'll stop at the boundary for a hands-across-the-border ceremony and photos before hiking to Goat Haunt and returning by boat to the Townsite by 6 P.M. Group size is limited to 35, so you'll need to pre-register at the Waterton Lakes Visitor Information Center (403/859-5133) or Glacier's St. Mary Visitor Center (406/732-7750). It's free, but you'll need to pay for the boat ride and make reservations through Waterton Shoreline Tours.

Guides

Two guide companies operate in Waterton, both offering custom hikes with interpretive services by reservation only. Rates vary depending on length and number of people; boat shuttle costs are extra. Bring your own trail snacks, lunches, and water.

Brian and Lauren Baker, longtime Waterton folks who run the outdoor gear shop, arrange guides through **Waterton Outdoor Adventures** (Tamarack Village Square, 214 Mount View Rd., 403/859-2379, www.hike waterton.com, late May–early Oct.). In general, a day hike for three people starts at CDN$75 per person and includes ground transportation to the trailhead.

Beth Russell-Towe offers guiding services through her shop, **Trail of the Great Bear** (114 Waterton Ave., 403/859-2663 or 800/215-2395, www.trailofthegreatbear.com, $50–400). She specializes in linking up local expert naturalists for hikes or adventures in geology, botany, or wildlife.

BIKING

All roadways in Waterton offer good bicycling. Particular favorites are Akamina and Red Rocks Parkways. Neither have big shoulders, and both narrow up tightly in spots, so be prepared to ride with cars at your elbows and encounter bears on both roads.

In addition to roadways, four trails in Waterton National Park permit bicycles. However, Parks Canada levies heavy fines up to CDN$2,000 for riding on sidewalks, grass, or trails designated for hiking only. For campers traveling by bicycle, both the Townsite and Crandell Mountain Campgrounds have bear-resistant food storage facilities.

Alberta law requires kids under 18 to wear a helmet while bicycling. Given the narrow roads and the fact that most drivers are gaping at the scenery or looking for bears and that winds can be strong enough to knock you off your bike, it's a wise idea for all ages to wear helmets.

Bike Trails

Four trails in Waterton permit bikes. For these, mountain bikes are best in handling the trail rubble, roots, and terrain. For current trail conditions, check with the visitors center.

Departing from 8.4 miles (14 km) up the Akamina Parkway, **Akamina Pass Trail** is a wide, but stiff and steep 0.8-mile (1.3-kilometer) climb on a forested trail. Even though the pass offers no great scenery, it's the Continental Divide and marks the boundary of Waterton National Park and Akamina-Kishinena Provincial Park as well as Alberta and British Columbia. After crossing the pass, you can continue riding to Wall Lake—adding another 4.8 miles (8 km) round-trip.

Beginning at the end of Red Rocks Parkway, the **Snowshoe Trail** rides 9.8 miles (16.4 km) round-trip along Bauerman Creek to the Snowshoe Warden Cabin. An abandoned fire road, with a fairly wide berth, the trail has some steep sections and creek fords for spice. Bikes are prohibited on the side trails. Hikers with a little savvy here do biking-hiking trips—bicycling to the Snowshoe cabin, then hiking to Lost or Twin Lakes.

Leaving Chief Mountain Highway less than half a mile from the Highway 5 junction, the 12.6-mile (21-kilometer) round-trip **Wishbone Trail** starts off wide and easy on an old wagon road through aspen parklands, but about halfway it narrows and becomes overgrown. At 4.9 miles (8.2 km), you'll pass the Vimy Trail (hiking only) junction just before traversing above the Lower Waterton Lake shoreline.

The most challenging ride is the 12.6 mile (21-kilometer) **Crandell Mountain Loop,** combining trails to circle the massive mountain. Be prepared to encounter rough terrain and washouts. You can start at three different trailheads: Crandell Lake Trailhead 3.6 miles (6 km) up Akamina Parkway, 3.6 miles (6 km) up Red Rocks Parkway on the Crandell Campground turnoff, or Waterton Townsite.

Rentals

Pat's Gas Station (224 Mount View Rd., 403/859-2266, www.watertoninfo.ab.ca) rents mountain bikes by the hour (CDN$8–11) or full day (CDN$34). The shop also carries full

WATERTON

suspension mountain bikes (CDN$45), helmets (free with rentals; otherwise CDN$10), and cycle trailers (CDN$25) for baby hauling. You'll see Pat's famous two-person four-wheel surrey bikes tootling around the Townsite (CDN$20 per hour); they're fun for a spin, but stick to the Townsite roads!

TRAIL RIDING

Horseback riding is available daily through **Alpine Stables** (2.4 miles, 4 km from park entrance on park entrance road, 403/859-2462, www.alpinestables.com, May–Sept., 9 A.M.–5 P.M.). Guided hourly rides (CDN$30) leave daily on the hour until 4 P.M., touring on open grasslands with big views of surrounding Waterton peaks. During shoulder seasons, the first ride starts at 10 A.M. With small saddles, the stables can take kids as young as four years old. You can either reserve a spot or simply show up about 20 minutes early. Wear long pants and tennis shoes or boots. For 90-minute rides (CDN$40), departures are at 3:30 and 5 P.M. Two-hour rides through wildlife habitat (CDN$50) leave at 10 A.M. and 1 and 5 P.M. Three- and four-hour rides (CDN$70–85) depart at 1:30 P.M. heading to the bison paddock. For longer rides of up to eight hours (CDN$135), you'll need to bring your own lunch and be ready to leave at 9 or 10 A.M. If you're traveling with your own equine, Alpine Stables will board your horse (CDN$9 per night, including feed).

BOATING

Motorized boats are permitted on only two lakes: **Upper and Middle Waterton Lakes.** Jet skis are banned. You can launch boats on ramps at Linnet Lake Picnic Area (0.7 mile, 1.1 kilometer from the Townsite on the park entrance road) on Middle Waterton Lake or the marina on Upper Waterton Lake. The marina sells gas and also has overnight mooring services operated by Waterton Shoreline Cruises (403/859-2362).

Boaters are not permitted to camp in their watercraft, but two wilderness campsites are accessible by boat—Bertha Bay and Boundary

Creek. Permits are required for these (CDN$10 per person per night; kids 16 and under free). Reservations are available for CDN$12 per trip 90 days in advance beginning April 1 each year. Both permits and reservations are available at the Waterton Visitor Information Center or Waterton's Parks Canada office. Goat Haunt also permits camping, but you need to get a permit in Glacier Park.

KAYAKING AND CANOEING

Canoeing, kayaking, and rowing are perfect activities for many of Waterton's road-accessible lakes. However, be aware that winds are common here with an average speed of 20 mph on Waterton Lake.

Waterton Lakes

A few paddlers tackle Upper Waterton Lake; those who hug shorelines because of the wind. With less hefty gales, more kayakers and canoers gravitate toward Middle Waterton Lake, the Dardanelles (the waterway connecting the two lakes), and Lower Waterton Lake for exceptional wildlife-watching and birding. Hay Barn and Marquis Picnic Areas are the most popular put-ins for paddling these sections.

Cameron Lake

Cameron Lake is an ideal spot for sea-kayaking, canoeing, and rowing. Winds are often less cantankerous here than at Waterton Lakes and the views equally as tantalizing. Do not beach or hike on the slopes surrounding the southern half of the lake; this is prime grizzly bear habitat. Canoes, paddleboats, and rowboat rentals (403/859-2396, mid-June–Aug., 7:30 A.M.–7:30 P.M., CDN$20–25 per hour, cash only) are available at the lakeshore. Life jackets and paddles are included in the rates.

FISHING

As in Glacier, fish are no longer stocked in Waterton Lakes National Park; however, introduced species still populate waterways: arctic grayling, British Columbia and Yellowstone cutthroat, and rainbow, eastern brook, and brown trout. Seventeen species of native fish—bull trout, ling, lake chub, deepwater sculpin, northern pike, pygmy whitefish, and spottail shiner, to name a few—still harbor here.

In **Waterton Lake,** catch rainbow trout, whitefish, and pike. Fish feed here on the tiny opossum shrimp, a crustacean that is a relic descended from pre–ice age days. The record lake trout caught in Waterton Lake was 51 pounds. Some hiking destinations, like **Goat Lake,** have good rainbow trout fishing.

Season

Four waterways are open year-round for fishing: the Dardanelles, Lower Waterton Lake, Waterton River, and Maskinonge Lake. One river is closed year-round—the North Fork of the Belly River. From late May through early September, anglers may fish Upper and Middle Waterton Lakes, Crandell Lake, Cameron Lake, Cameron Creek, and Akamina Lake. Blakiston Creek limits fishing to late June through early September. Beyond that, the general fishing season is late June through the end of October.

Regulations

Waterton Park requires a fishing permit (daily CDN$10, annual CDN$34.50) to fish within park boundaries. Purchase one at the visitors center, Parks Canada office, campground kiosks, Cameron Lake boat rentals, or Pat's Gas Station. The license is valid in all Canadian mountain parks. Kids under 16 can either purchase their own permit to catch a full limit or share limits with an adult. Check for species limits when you purchase fishing licenses. In general, native species—bull trout, kokanee, and cutthroat (those caught in the three Waterton Lakes)—are catch-and-release only. You may, however, keep two fish of introduced species: arctic grayling, rainbows, brown trout, brookies, lake trout, northern pike, mountain whitefish, lake whitefish, and cutthroat caught elsewhere than the three Waterton lakes.

Lead weights less than 50 grams (1.75 oz.) are not permitted due to contamination of waterfowl. As in Glacier, bull trout are a protected species in Waterton. Follow the adage, "No black, put it back."

WATERSKIING

Waterskiing is permitted only on Upper and Middle Waterton Lakes; however, most waterskiers gravitate to the middle lake. It's more sheltered and less windy than its upper sister. You'll find boat ramps at Linnet Lake Picnic Area (0.7 mile, 1.1 km from the Townsite on the park entrance road) on Middle Waterton Lake or the marina on Upper Waterton Lake. Because the water is extremely cold, water-skiers wear dry suits or full wet suits here. Floating debris—logs, sticks, and branches—is common; keep your eyes open for these hazards. Waterton has no water-ski boat or ski rental service.

WINDSURFING

It's a rare day when Waterton doesn't see wind. Winds don't just blow here; they gust and howl. For traveling windsurfers with their own gear (no rental gear is available in Waterton), Upper Waterton Lake is the best place to catch some waves with consistent wind. The glacier-fed lake, however, is freezing cold. Wear a wet or dry suit to prevent hypothermia. To windsurf here, you should know how to water start and self-rescue; it's not a place for beginners. For the best launching on the upper lake, head to the picnic shelters on Waterton Avenue one block west of Vimy Avenue. For safety, check the current weather report at the Waterton Visitor Information Center before launching into a big wind.

SCUBA DIVING

Scuba divers go after a spot in Emerald Bay, where a sunken circa 1900 paddle steamer, *The Gertrude,* provides exploration at a 65-foot (20-meter) depth. For the clearest waters, early spring and fall are best for scuba diving here. Just remember that historic artifacts, which include anything on the wreck, are protected by the park; leave all things where you find them. Bring your own gear, as the nearest scuba shop for rentals and repairs is 78 miles (130 km) east in Lethbridge.

GOLF

Focusing on your putting can be difficult with huge scenery. Not only are sand traps a hazard, but sometimes grizzly bears are too. Located 1.7 miles (3 km) from the Townsite, the 18-hole **Waterton Golf Course** is an original Stanley Thompson design like the Banff Springs and Jasper courses—rolling fairways bordered with aspens. The dawn-to-dusk course charges CDN$39 for 18 holes. A full pro shop rents golf carts (CDN$32) and clubs (CDN$7–20), and a licensed clubhouse keeps guests fed and watered on its patio with outstanding views. For tee times, call 403/859-2114. Many of Waterton's hotels offer golf packages in May and after mid-September.

TENNIS

Four hard-surface public tennis courts are smack in the Townsite Center on Cameron Falls Drive between Harebell Drive and Windflower Avenue. **Pat's Gas Station** (224 Mount View Rd., 403/859-2266) rents tennis rackets for $3 per hour. The free courts are available on a first-come, first-serve basis. Limit playing time to 30 minutes when other players are waiting. The outdoor courts are unlit at night and snow-covered in winter.

CROSS-COUNTRY SKIING AND SNOWSHOEING

In winter, when heavy snows render many of the roads impassable by vehicle, the parkways become ideal cross-country ski trails. Alternatively, ski along Waterton Lake or on the lake after it freezes. With less than 100 residents wintering in Waterton, services are minimal, so plan on bringing skis and snowshoes. The park does not permit snowmobiles, so a quiet backcountry winter experience is guaranteed. Also, dogs are not permitted on the park's groomed ski trails, which helps maintain the tracks in good condition for gliding.

Waterton is a land of winter extremes. It records the highest precipitation levels in Alberta, much of it in snowfall. It also records winter winds over 60 miles per hour, which can plummet wind chills. With winter chinooks, the park is also one of Alberta's warmest areas with an average of 28 days above freezing. With this diversity, you can expect all types of snow—from dry, light powder to heavy, wet glop—and conditions that change within an hour. Most cross-country skiers here sacrifice a bit of speed for reliable glide by using waxless skis.

Two designated ski trails are marked and track-set for weekends: **Cameron** and **Dipper Ski Trails,** both off Akamina Parkway, which is plowed to the trailheads at Little Prairie. Other trails such as Crandell Lake, Rowe Trail, and Akamina Pass are popular trails, but skiers should be prepared with rescue beacons, probes, and shovels for avalanche travel. Contact the Waterton Parks Canada office (403/859-2224) for details.

ENTERTAINMENT

During summer months, Parks Canada offers evening slide shows and indoor programs at the Townsite Falls Theater (across Evergreen Ave. from Cameron Falls) and Crandell Mountain Campground. Varying programs cover wildlife, ecology, and geology. Contact 403/859-2445 for current schedule. Schedules are also posted in the visitors center and campgrounds.

The **Waterton Opera House** (309 Windflower Ave., 403/859-2466), which shows movies rather than staging operas, opens during summer months only. Shows change regularly, but don't expect to see world premieres at this tiny outpost.

Waterton celebrates festivals. For 10 days in late June, the **Waterton Wildflower Festival** (800/215-2395, www.watertonwildflowers.com) pulls together hikes, art shows, photography courses, watercolor painting workshops, drawing classes, slide shows, and free evening lectures in a tribute to the park's rare and diverse wildflowers. Some events are single-day programs lasting two hours; others are multi-day. All are taught by regional experts. Course fees range CDN$25–99, but several are free. Call or stop in Trail of the Great Bear shop on Waterton Avenue to register. In late September, the town celebrates the **Waterton Wildlife Festival,** which includes the International Wildlife Film Festival and special wildlife-watching excursions in the field. Check with **Waterton Outdoor Adventures** (Tamarack Village Square, 214 Mount View Rd., 403/859-2379, www.hikewaterton.com) for current program and costs.

Accommodations

In Waterton, everything is within walking distance, with the compact town less than a mile across. You're not far from restaurants, shopping, boat tours, hiking, tennis, or movies no matter where you stay. While the town bustles in summer, in winter only a few services and hotels remain open. All accommodations add a 5 percent provincial hotel tax and 7 percent Goods and Services Tax on to your rates; together, those add up, so don't be surprised that your final room bill tallies higher than you might have expected. Many of the hotels offer golf, seasonal activity packages, and specials; ask or check their websites for current deals. You'll get better deals in Waterton in the off-season (May–early June, late Sept.–Oct., winter) when most lodging properties drop their room rates substantially, making travel cheaper at a crowd-free time. Most hotels do not have Internet services for guests.

Lodges and Inns

Located on a bluff above Waterton Lake and the Townsite, historic **(Prince of Wales Hotel** (4.6 miles, 7.6 km south of park entrance station across from the visitors center, 406/892-2525, www.glacierparkinc.com, early June–mid-Sept., CDN$265–345, rates for two people, additional CDN$15 each, suites $799) is a four-storied wonder, and yes, it is named for Prince Edward. Its lobby with floor to ceiling windows swings with large rustic chandeliers. Lake-view rooms and suites allow you to shower with a view into Glacier Park while mountain-view rooms lend to spying bighorn sheep on Crandell Mountain. But in spite of its grand facade, the building is old, creaky, and thin walled, and the upper stories seem to sway in high winds. Be prepared for tiny

sinks and small bathrooms—many installed in what were once closets. All nonsmoking, rooms have phones, but no television nor air-conditioning. An elevator accesses upper floors but requires a bellhop to run, so it is not available at all hours—nor does it always work. If you're on one of the top floors, you'll get a workout climbing to your room, but the view is stunning. Before late June, you can get rooms for CDN$179–219 and suites for $599. A restaurant, gift shop selling English bone china and Waterford crystal, and lounge surround the lobby. A 5-minute drive or 20-minute walk down a trail accesses the town for boat tours, shopping, bicycle rentals, and restaurants. Reservations are required.

Tucked under the trees on Emerald Bay, **(Kilmorey Lodge** (117 Mount View Rd.,

historic Prince of Wales Hotel

© BECKY LOMAX

WATERTON

WHAT IS GST?

In Canada, a GST/HST (Goods and Services Tax/Harmonized Sales Tax) is applied to lodging, restaurants, souvenirs, and services. Visitors from outside Canada can claim a refund of the GST on some goods and services and under certain conditions. You'll need to keep your original receipts to apply for your refund. (Credit card slips and photocopies are not acceptable.)

To qualify for a GST refund, you must:

• not be a Canadian resident

• purchase eligible goods for personal use

• purchase eligible short-term accommodations

• have paid GST/HST on your purchases

• have Proof of Export for the eligible goods you purchased in Canada (receipts must be validated by customs officials at border crossings or airports)

• have a total purchase amount (before taxes) of at least CDN$200

• have each receipt for eligible goods showing

a minimum total purchase amount (before taxes) of CDN$50

• remove the goods from Canada within 60 days of the date you bought them

In short, GST paid on camping fees and hotel rooms can be refunded, provided your stay was less than one month and criteria listed above are satisfied. However, GST paid on meals and beverages consumed in Canada and RV or trailer rentals are not refundable, but you can get the GST paid on hard goods (souvenirs, books, gifts, clothing) refunded. In general, the following are not eligible for a tax refund: tobacco products, entertainment, transportation, gas, rentals, parking, services (dry cleaning, car repairs, guiding), and medical expenses.

For more details, call 800/668-4748 (in Canada) or 902/432-5608 (from outside Canada). You can also check online and download a refund application: www.cra-arc.gc.ca/tax /nonresidents/visitors/tax-e.html. While in Waterton, pick up tax refund forms at **Waterton Visitor Services** at Tamarack Village Square (214 Mount View Rd.).

403/859-2334 or 888/859-8669, www.kilmoreylodge.com, mid-May–mid-Oct. CDN$129–252, winter rates CDN$99–196) has small rooms where the bed fills 90 percent of the space, but the cozy log inn is loaded with country ambience. The halls even creak. Open year-round, its 23 unique rooms furnished with antiques and down comforters match the 1920s era of the lodge's narrow hallways lined with historic photos. With no in-room phones nor televisions, the atmosphere is quiet and relaxed. With no air-conditioning, rooms are equipped with fans, but with cool evening temperatures in Waterton, they mostly go unused. The lodge also houses the best restaurant in Waterton—the Lamp Post Dining Room—as well as a small outdoor café in summer. In winter, a fire blazes in the Ram's Head Lounge's

river rock fireplace; in summer, its deck opens for shaded seating.

The 17-room year-round country-style **Crandell Mountain Lodge** (102 Mount View Rd., 403/859-2288 or 866/859-2288, www .crandellmountainlodge.com, June–mid-Sept. CDN$139–159, mid-Sept.–May CDN$99–109) almost gets lost beneath its namesake peak. The two-story circa 1940 inn has a variety of country theme rooms—all nonsmoking—from standards to three-room suites with full kitchens and fireplaces. In a private garden area, a huge deck with a barbecue and lounge chairs begs for afternoon relaxation.

Modern, large, and loaded with amenities such as free use of the Waterton Spa and Recreation Center's salt-water pool and facilities, **Waterton Lakes Resort** (end of Clematis

Ave., 403/859-2151 or 888/985-6343, www
.watertonlakeslodge.com, open mid-May–
mid-Oct., CDN$174–219) has 80 air-condi-
tioned all nonsmoking standard and deluxe
rooms as well as kitchenettes and suites.
Accommodations are spread throughout 11
themed chalet buildings sitting adjacent to
each other on four acres. While some rooms
have fireplaces and jetted tubs, all rooms have
televisions, VCRs, dial-up Internet, coffeemak-
ers, and phones. A restaurant, lounge, and café
complete the scene.

Motels
Right on Waterton Lake, **The Bayshore** (junction of Mount View Rd. and Waterton Ave.,
summers 403/859-2211 or 888/527-9555, winters 604/708-9965, www.bayshoreinn.com,
late April–mid-Oct., CDN$174–249) lakeside
rooms have prime views from private balconies
that make up for its room decor reminiscent
of chain hotels. The nonsmoking complex has
restaurants, a lounge, a saloon, a hot tub, gift
shop, and ice cream shop on site and sits adjacent to the marina, shopping, and additional
restaurants. The Townsite Loop trail system
passes between the inn and the lake.

The **Aspen Village Inn** (111 Windflower
Ave., 403/859-2255 or 888/859-8669, www
.aspenvillageinn.com, May–early Oct.,
CDN$154–270) has both comfortable stan-
dard hotel rooms and suites with kitchens in
its modern two-story Windflower and Aspen
buildings, where decks hang with colorful
flower boxes. Rooms have satellite televisions.
Bright cottages accommodating two–eight
people are great for families, and extras include
a playground, outdoor barbecue picnic area,
and Jacuzzi. Surrounded by mowed lawns, the
large red-metal roofed complex (you won't get
lost trying to find it!) is centrally located right
in the heart of the Townsite.

Open year-round, the **C Waterton Glacier
Suites** (107 Windflower Ave., 403/859-2004
or 866/621-3330, www.watertonsuites.com,
mid-June–mid-Sept., CDN$199–279; win-
ter CDN$139–209) has 26 modern clean and
spacious units with balconies, refrigerators,

microwaves, satellite televisions, air-conditioning, and whirlpool tubs. Some rooms have
fireplaces, and all have mountain views. Most
guests rave about friendly service here. A quick
two-block walk reaches restaurants, shopping,
and the tour boat, and it's easy to find on your
return: look for the turquoise roof.

If you're looking for really affordable, your
answer is the **Bear Mountain Motel** (208
Mount View Rd., 403/859-2366, www.bear
mountainmotel.com, mid-May–mid-Oct.,
CDN$89–140). New owners purchased the
circa 1960 wood-and-masonry motel in 2004
and revamped the 36 nonsmoking rooms.
Small bathrooms are still the same, but new
carpets, beds, linens, and paint upgraded the
accommodations of the one-, two-, and three-
bedroom suites, several with small kitchenettes. Rooms have no phones. Pay phones are
near the office.

Bed-and-Breakfast
For park history buffs, the **Northland Lodge**
(408 Evergreen Ave., 403/859-2353, www
.northlandlodgecanada.com, mid-May–mid-
October, CDN$109–210) carries a certain at-
traction. Louis Hill, builder of the Prince of
Wales Hotel and many of Glacier Park's historic hotels, constructed the Swiss-style lodge
as his private residence circa 1948, although
he never had time to live there. The lodge only
has nine rooms (two with a shared bath and
the rest with private baths), split between three
levels. A large balcony is great for soaking up
views with complimentary coffee and homemade muffins with Saskatoon berry jam in the
morning. Cameron Falls is a short half-block
walk away, as is the trailhead to Bertha Falls
and Lake. A 10-minute walk puts you in the
heart of shopping and restaurants, or you can
hop on the 20-minute more scenic Townsite
Loop trail just across the street.

Hostel
The **Hostelling International Waterton**
(corner Cameron Falls and Windflower Ave.,
403/859-2151, www.hihostels.ca, May–Sept.)
is connected to Waterton Lake Resort, so

hostelers have access to the saltwater pool, hot tub, sauna, and steam room. Internet access is available as well as laundry facilities and shared kitchen. The year-round hostel has 21 beds in six rooms; dorm beds are CDN$35 per nonmember, but Hostelling International Members (CDN$35 memberships, www.hi hostels.com) get about a 10 percent discount in rates. Check-in is at 4 P.M. and check out is at 11 A.M. Linens are provided; sleeping bags are not permitted.

CAMPING
Inside the Park

Waterton Park campgrounds have flush toilets, drinking water, kitchen shelters, and bear-resistant food storage lockers. Some sites have fire rings, and firewood is supplied, but you pay $8 per site for a burning permit in addition to your campground fee.

Smack in the middle of the Waterton Townsite, it's hard to feel like you're camping here with mowed lawn sites; however, the **《 Waterton Townsite Campground** (403/859-2224, www.pc.gc.ca, mid-Apr.–mid-Oct., unserviced sites CDN$21–25.50, full hookups CDN$35.50) sits on prime real estate with gorgeous views. The 238-site campground borders the Townsite Loop trail and the beach. A few trees shade some sites, but most are open, offering little privacy. Go for the most scenic unserviced spots in the G loop—sites 26–46, but be prepared for strong winds. For more sheltered scenery, go for the Cameron Creek E loop sites (even numbers 2–16). Kitchen shelters are the only place where fires are permitted here, but the campground includes hot showers, a dump station, and the trailheads to Bertha Lake and Waterton Lakeshore are within a few minutes' walk. In July and August, the campground fills early; plan on arriving by noon to claim a site, or make reservations (CDN$11 nonrefundable processing fee) starting in early April through the National Parks Canada Campground Reservation Service (877/737-3783, www.pc camping.ca). In early or late season, you'll have your pick of sites without a reservation; off-season the campground is virtually empty.

On the opposite side of Crandell Mountain from the Townsite and 3.8 miles (6 km) up the Red Rocks Parkway, **《 Crandell Mountain Campground** (403/859-2224 www.pc.gc.ca, mid-May–early Sept., CDN$21) nestles in the woods along Blakiston Creek. With its sites deep in trees, the campground has a remote feel with trees and brush providing some privacy between sites. Sometimes you can see bear and moose nearby on Blakiston Creek. Its 129 sites offer no hookups; however, a dump station is available. An easy walk to Crandell Lake (5 km, 3.1 miles round-trip) departs from here. The campground takes no reservations, so plan on claiming your site by midday in July and August. A, B, C, and D loops sit in thicker trees; E, F, G, and H loops are more open with views of surrounding peaks. A quick 10-minute drive puts you at the end of Red Rocks Parkway, where trailheads lead to Blakiston Falls and Goat Lake.

On Chief Mountain Highway and 17 miles (26 km) from Waterton Townsite, the **Belly River Campground** (www.pc.gc.ca, mid-May–early Sept., CDN$15) has 24 pleasant sites in aspen groves with hand-pumped well water and some pit toilets in addition to the flush toilets. Some sites are shaded; some are open, but not much in the way of views meets the eye. It is, however, a good site for wildlife-watching and birding, and the closest campground to Chief Mountain Customs for those who want to shoot across the boundary first thing in the morning. A short trail leads up the Belly River but dead-ends just before the international boundary.

In winter when all other campsites have closed, free sites are available at **Pass Creek Winter Campground** (403/859-2224, www .pc.gc.ca, mid-Oct.–mid-Apr.). Located on the entrance road 3.1 miles (5 km) from the Townsite, the eight sites offer primitive camping with only a pit toilet and a woodstove in the kitchen shelter. Water from the creek may be boiled or purified for use.

Backcountry Camping

Waterton has nine backcountry campgrounds (called "wilderness campsites"). Some backpackers break up the Avion Ridge traverse with stays at **Snowshoe** and **Goat Lake**. But **Twin Lakes** and **Lost Lake** put you farther away from day hikers. Required permits ($9.80 per person per night; kids 16 and under free) are available at the visitors center (403/859-5133) in person 24 hours in advance or by reservation ($11.70) up to 90 days in advance.

Outside the Park

Just outside the park boundary, three private campgrounds can handle the overload when park campgrounds are full. On the Highway 6 to Pincher Creek, **Waterton Springs Campground** (1.5 miles or 2.5 km north of the park entrance road, 403/859-2247 or 866/859-2247, www.watertonspringscamping.com, late Apr.–early Oct.) has 70 full-hookup unshaded, dusty parking lot-type sites (CDN$29) and 75 partial hookups (CDN$23–29) and tent (CDN$18) sites set around small ponds and a creek in a rough aspen parkland—both away from the highway. Amenities include showers, flush toilets, picnic tables, launderette, camp store, Internet access, outdoor pool, playground, and fire grates.

Waterton Riverside Campground (3.2 miles, 5.2 km east of park entrance road, 403/653-2888, June–mid-Sept., hookups CDN$25, tents CDN$20) has 65 sites with running water, flush toilets, showers, playground, and a central fire pit. Locate the campground 0.6 mile (1 kilometer) down a dirt road; set far back in aspen parklands, the treed campground is very quiet. The owners do not take reservations, so an earlier arrival in high season is advisable. You can canoe and swim on the Waterton River, which runs adjacent to the campground.

Operated by Waterton Natural History Association, **Crooked Creek Campground** (3.8 miles, 6 km east of park entrance road, 403/653-1100, mid-May–early Sept., hookups CDN$24–28, tents CDN$17) has 43 sites set adjacent to the highway. Amenities include flush toilets, running water, kitchen shelter, dump station, firewood, power & water hookups, and a new shower-restroom and launderette facility. Reservations are accepted.

Food

Most restaurants in the Townsite cluster along Waterton Avenue and spill over to Windflower Avenue. While most of the hotel dining rooms cater to fine dining, the town has several worthy places to grab a meal without dropping an exorbitant pile of cash. You'll also find your final bill jacked up a bit in price by the GST (Goods and Services Tax).

RESTAURANTS

With the exception of the Prince of Wales Hotel, all of the restaurants congregate within a few blocks in the Waterton Townsite. In off seasons (Sept.–mid-June), many may shorten their hours or days or simply close if no one seems to be around. Call to check.

Located in the Prince of Wales Hotel, the **Royal Stewart Dining Room** (406/892-2525, early June–mid-Sept.) looks out its massive floor-to-ceiling windows down Waterton Lake. The nonsmoking restaurant's claim to fame is its view more than its service or culinary uniqueness. As in all of the park's historic hotels, breakfast (6:30–9:30 A.M., CDN$11–14) is a huge buffet spread of fruits, pastries, and mass-produced hot items. If you're not hungry enough for the buffet, you can order à la carte. The dining hall is also open for lunch (11:30 A.M.–2 P.M., CDN$8–14) and dinners (5–9:30 P.M., CDN$16–33), which carry the hotel's British theme into its cuisine with English and Canadian dishes. No reservations

WATERTON

are accepted for groups fewer than 12 people, so you may have a waiting line in high season. The restaurant also makes hiker lunches (CDN$8–10); order these one day in advance.

The British atmosphere of the Prince of Wales Hotel goes into full swing with **Valerie's Tea Room** (406/892-2525, early June–mid-Sept.) in the hotel lobby where huge windows overlook Waterton Lake. Afternoon tea—more or less a full sugarfest meal of desserts—is served 2–5 P.M. Homemade pastries, scones, fruits, and berries stack on multi-tiered serving dishes, and Devonshire cream comes on the side. You can go American with coffee rather than tea, if you prefer. It's a unique experience, but more mood than anything else for the price (CDN$37 adults, $10 kids). Reservations are a good idea. If you partake in high tea, you may be too full to need evening dinner.

If you're not staying at the hotel, at least drop by for a drink to enjoy the sweeping views. The tiny nonsmoking **Windsor Lounge** (406/892-2525, early June–mid-Sept.) is a gorgeous cozy place to sit in front of the window looking down Waterton Lake. You can also order drinks for the lobby if you prefer sitting by the larger windows. A bar menu (appetizers and sandwiches) is available (2–10 P.M., US$8–14). Beer, wine, and cocktails are served 11:30 A.M.–midnight.

Kilmorey Lodge houses the ◖ **Lamp Post Dining Room** (117 Mount View Rd., 403/859-2334 or 888/859-8669, www.kilmorey lodge .com, open daily year-round, 7:30 A.M.–10 P.M.), hands down the best fine dining in Waterton. Reservations are highly recommended. The restaurant specializes in eclectic flavors from East India to coastal delights. For breakfast (CDN$6–10), try saskatoon berry jam on your toast (take a jar of jam home, too, for CDN$6). For lunch, test the wild game chili (CDN$11). Dinners (CDN$17–39) are scrumptious with buffalo tenderloins or Alberta beef steaks. In case you haven't had your fill of saskatoons, save room for saskatoon berry pie (CDN$6). An extensive wine list specializes in a broad selection from British Columbia as well as imported wines from around the world.

For the same yummy fare but in a more relaxed setting, Kilmorey's **Ram's Head Lounge** (7:30 A.M.–10 P.M.) has cozy eating in front of the fieldstone fireplace in winter and alfresco on the smoke-free patio in summer. The lounge serves the same menu as the dining room and has a small, reasonably priced bar as well.

Located in the Bayshore Inn, the **Kootenai Brown Dining Room** (junction of Mount View Rd. and Waterton Ave., 403/859-2211 or 888/527-9555, daily late Apr.–mid-Oct., 7 AM–10 P.M.) has mostly the view going for it as the restaurant sits right on Waterton Lake. Full breakfasts run CDN$8–12, and lunch (CDN$8–15) features salads, wraps, burgers, pizza, and pasta. The chef combines steaks, chicken, fish, and pasta dinners (CDN$19–38) with a chef's choice wine recommendation to accompany each dish. The restaurant also makes hiker lunches to go (CDN$11).

Also part of the Bayshore complex, but not nearly as pricey as the dining room, the **Glacier Café** (7 A.M.–10 P.M.) serves lighter meals for breakfast, lunch, and dinner (CDN$5–12): croissants and lattes to burgers, calzones, and a huge selection of dessert goodies. If you prefer people-watching while you eat, the café has a shaded sidewalk deck.

For pasta, head to ◖ **Tuscana Ristorante** (110 Waterton Ave., 403/859-2236, www .tuscana.ca, daily May–Sept., 11 A.M.–11 P.M.), which has both indoor and covered outdoor seating. It serves all the basic pastas and lasagnas as well as a few more interesting concoctions with their handmade meatballs. Lunch pastas range CDN$10–13, while dinner specials bump up to CDN$16–21. Chicken, fish, and veal specialty entrees bump up as high as CDN$26. Wines hail from Canada, Argentina, France, Australia, and New Zealand. Reservations are highly recommended for dinner in high season.

Tucked in a small house, ◖ **Pizza of Waterton** (103 Fountain Ave., 403/859-2660, May–Oct., daily noon–10 P.M., CDN$13–22) is known for creative hand-crafted pizzas and huge calzones. It also has big salads and a good selection of Canadian microbrews to accompany pizzas, which you can feast on inside the homey restaurant or outside on the deck watching bighorn sheep browse through town. For an easy take-out dinner while camping at the Townsite, order a pizza to go.

For a buffalo burger (CDN$7) with friendly service, head to **(Zum's Eatery and Mercantile** (116 Waterton Ave., 403/859-2388, daily May–Sept.). Its broad menu makes it a great place to take the family for breakfast and lunch, where entrees range CDN$5–16. Dinners, which specialize in schnitzel, bratwurst, fish, steaks, and chicken are a little more pricey (CDN$16–33), but sometimes you can still order off the lunch menu. Shaded outside seating along the sidewalk allows for people-watching. To satisfy your sweet cravings, order the wildberry pie (CDN$5), a yummy combination of raspberries, blueberries, blackberries, rhubarb, and apple.

CAFFEINE

Over the past few years, espresso shops have boomed in Waterton. Even several of the traditional long-time restaurants have added espresso machines. Although it may be the tiniest place to order a latte, the **(Waterton Bagel & Coffee Shop** (309 Windflower Ave., 403/859-2466, May–Oct., 7:30 A.M.–10 P.M.) answers the need for a caffeine fix well! Along with a full espresso menu, it serves smoothies, juices, biscotti, bagels, and muffins. The diminutive shop only seats a couple of people on stools, but you can grab a bagel with cream cheese and head one block away to the beach to eat.

GROCERIES

While several locations in town carry convenience foods (Pat's Gas Station and the Tamarack Village, both on Mount View Rd.), only one grocery store—**Rocky Mountain Food Mart** (307 Windflower Ave., May–Sept., daily 8 A.M.–8 P.M.)—stocks a full line with produce, meats, dairy, deli, and a bakery. However, it is small, so expect limited brands. It also carries ice, firewood, and camping supplies.

WATERTON

FLATHEAD VALLEY

The Flathead Valley is an outdoor paradise. Surrounded by mountain ranges and abundant lakes, back doors open on fishing, skiing, hiking, hunting, biking, and boating. Surrounded by 2.5 million acres of wilderness and national parklands, there's no shortage of space to get away from it all and play outdoors. One of the country's largest national forests fringes the valley floor, which is dotted with oodles of lakes including the largest freshwater lake west of the Mississippi. Summer brings on flat-water kayaking and floating lazy rivers. Anglers drop lines from drift boats. Golfers hit the links. Hikers climb to wildflower-strewn heights with huge views of the vast valley.

Sadly, strip-mall culture has made some inroads into the valley, paving once pastoral farmlands. Housing developments sprout between towns blending the borders of one with another. Aspen-wannabes throw multimillion-dollar mansions up on hillsides. But an underlying culture remains—one where ripped Carhartts and a duct-taped jacket rank as fashion. Rather than hit the nine-to-five office hours, lots of folks here work seasonally—in Glacier or Flathead National Forest in summer, and ski areas in winter.

When snows fall, logging roads and golf courses convert to ski and snowshoe trails, while two alpine ski areas rack up the vertical for skiers and snowboarders. Many in the

HIGHLIGHTS

◖ Flathead Lake: Sail its blue waters or drive around its perimeter. The largest freshwater lake west of the Mississippi draws waters from as far north as Canada (page 222).

◖ Whitefish Lake: Cool off on hot summer days in a lake hopping with water-skiers and anglers. Three parks and a marina provide different access options (page 223).

◖ Mount Aeneas: Hike the short trail up the highest peak in Jewel Basin. From the summit, you'll stare into the Great Bear Wilderness and down on Flathead Lake (page 224).

◖ Danny On Trail: Ride a chairlift up to hike down the most popular trail in the Flathead. It's a romp through mounds of wildflowers with stunning views of Glacier Park (page 225).

◖ Whitefish Mountain Resort: Step into skis for this winter wonderland or ride its summer lift to huckleberry picking. From the top, you'll see one of the best panoramas of Glacier (page 230).

LOOK FOR ◖ TO FIND RECOMMENDED SIGHTS, ACTIVITIES, DINING, AND LODGING.

valley adhere to the six-inch rule: If six inches or more of snow falls, call in late for work.

HISTORY

Originally the home of the Flathead, Salish, and Kootenai Indians, the Flathead Valley saw its first European descendent—famed explorer David Thompson—in 1809. Within 40 years, trappers, homesteaders, and ranchers edged their way into the valley. By the end of the century, Great Northern Railway laid tracks through the Flathead, prompting Kalispell to be plotted for township in 1890, in theory to become the next St. Paul.

Growing with ranchers, farmers, and timber harvesters, the Flathead soon sprouted other towns clustered around its lakes and rivers. In 1901, Great Northern rerouted its railroad tracks through Whitefish to access Canadian coal, catapulting the tiny Whitefish lakefront community into a train town. The mid-1900s saw tremendous change in the Flathead with the construction of the Hungry Horse dam spawning an aluminum plant, Plum Creek Timber Company, and Big Mountain Ski Resort growing. Today, while original valley ranching, farming, and timber still support many families, part of the Flathead economy for its estimated 87,000 residents comes from technology industries and tourism.

FLATHEAD VALLEY

© AVALON TRAVEL

Exploring Flathead Valley

Flathead Valley centers around four main towns: Kalispell, Whitefish, Columbia Falls, and Bigfork. Each has its own draw, brought on by seasonal recreation in each area.

Outside the four main towns, small burgs dot Flathead Lake's shoreline. Lakeside buzzes with summer water fun and serves as the launching point to reach Blacktail Mountain Ski Area in winter. Somers is a blink-and-miss-it town, but popular for its marina.

Kalispell

The nucleus of Flathead Valley with three golf courses, restaurants, and shopping, the area's largest town has moved beyond its cow town past. In historic downtown Kalispell, you can tour the pre-1900s Conrad Mansion, but also peruse 20 art hotspots identified by yellow and red banners. In August, catch the Northwest Montana Fair and Rodeo, and in October, join in the Glacier Jazz Stampede. Kalispell sits 9 miles from the airport and 34 miles from Glacier.

Whitefish

The recreation capital of Flathead Valley, Whitefish packs in summer with boating in Whitefish Lake and golf at the valley's only 36-hole course. In winter, skiing becomes the passion at Whitefish Mountain Resort. Surrounded by rampant new housing developments, downtown Whitefish fits compactly into several square blocks with boutiques, restaurants, art galleries, and theaters. It sits 11 miles from the airport and 27 miles from Glacier.

Columbia Falls

The gateway to Glacier, Columbia Falls never had a falls of its own until the town built one just off Highway 2. Recently, the town has boomed with new restaurants in its downtown area, upgrading its dining quality. Beside its newly rebuilt public outdoor swimming pool, Columbia Falls is home to Big Sky Waterslides. It sits 8 miles from the airport and 18 miles from Glacier.

© BECKY LOMAX

FLATHEAD VALLEY

Great Northern Locomotive #181 sits in Whitefish as a tribute to train history.

HUCKLEBERRY MANIA

The huckleberry – a small dark purple berry about the size of your little fingertip – resembles a blueberry, but it's much sweeter and more flavorful. It grows only in the wild on low deciduous bushes with leaves turning red in fall. Growing mostly at elevations above 4,000 feet, they ripen late July–September.

The berry has yet to be successfully cultivated. Outside the park, around Hungry Horse, and in Flathead Valley, you'll find berry stands selling hucks that have been picked by commercial permit in national forests or private lands. Expect to pay about $35-40 per gallon of the precious purple gems. (Now you know why huckleberry pie is so expensive!) Be careful when purchasing berries early in the summer from fruit stands, as you may be buying frozen berries from last year rather than fresh-picked ones. The frozen berries are still yummy, but a little softer when they thaw. Fresh ones usually hit the stands in late July.

You can pick your own huckleberries to eat – no permit needed. You'll find them on many hikes in Flathead National Forest and the park. While locals all have their secret stashes in Flathead National Forest and aren't about to divulge their prized secrets, you can usually find good huckleberry picking on Big Mountain at Whitefish Mountain Resort. Glacier Park rules permit plucking a few berries to eat, but harvesting for commercial purposes is not allowed.

Two mammals crave the berries: bears and humans. High in vitamin C, the berries are not only healthy and low in fat, but they enliven any pastry, pie, sauce, or fruit concoction. They're wonderful in smoothies and delightful on pancakes. And you'll find them here in everything, from ice cream to beer.

What huckleberry products are out there? Just about anything! Syrup, jam, and jellies top everyone's favorites. Hucks also flavor and scent chocolates, honey, cocoa, barbecue sauce, tea, salad dressing, ice cream toppings, a daiquiri mix, lotion, lip balm, bubble bath, shampoo, soap, and more.

One word of advice: Avoid using huckleberry shampoo before hiking in bear country!

Bigfork

A summer resort town, Bigfork combines easy access to the Swan Mountains with boating on Flathead Lake. Bigfork Summer Playhouse dominates the town, packing restaurants before nightly shows. Quaint shops and art galleries fill its several-block-long village, and its one-lane steel bridge crosses the Swan River. In early June, the town hops with the Bigfork Whitewater Festival, when kayakers shoot the Swan's Wild Mile. It sits 26 miles from the airport and 40 miles from Glacier.

VISITORS CENTERS

One of the easiest ways to grab additional information on the Flathead is to contact visitors centers. Flathead Valley has six: **Flathead Valley Convention and Visitors Bureau** (800/543-3105, www.montanasflatheadvalley.com), **Kalispell Chamber of Commerce** (15 Depot Park, 406/758-2800, www.kalispellchamber.com), **Whitefish Chamber of Commerce** (520 E. 2nd St., 406/862-3501, www.whitefishchamber.com), **Columbia Falls Chamber of Commerce** (233 13th St. E., 406/892-2072, www.columbiafallschamber.com), **Bigfork Chamber of Commerce** (Olde Town Center, 406/837-5888, www.bigfork.org), and **Lakeside Chamber of Commerce** (406/844-3715, www.lakesidechamber.com).

SIGHTS
(Flathead Lake

Stretching 28 miles long and 15 miles wide, Flathead Lake is the largest freshwater lake west of the Mississippi. Its 188 square miles, six state parks, islands, deep fishing waters, and wildlife refuges make it a summer playland. Highways encircle the lake, popping at 13 different points in to public lake accesses.

The southern half of the lake falls inside the Flathead Indian Reservation, home to the Salish and Kootenai tribes.

Catch boat tours on Flathead Lake from Bigfork. But just a warning: If nasty weather prevails, launches will cancel. **Questa Sailing Charters** (150 Flathead Lake Lodge, 406/837-5569, mid-June–Sept.) launch from Flathead Lake Lodge's dock. Two 51-foot 1928–1929 Q class sloops each carry 12 passengers. On the beautifully restored 1928 and 1929 boats, trips ($39–44, ask for special senior and kids 12 and under rates) depart daily at 1:30 P.M. At 7 P.M., the popular adults-only sunset cruise includes complimentary wine and beverages.

To see bighorn sheep, osprey, eagles, and Native American pictographs, charter a **Wild Horse Island Boat Tour** from Pointer Cruises (452 Grand Dr., Bigfork, 406/837-5617, May–Nov., $85 per hour) to visit the lake's largest island, state park, and wildlife refuge that houses more than 75 species of birds. The boat holds up to nine guests; bring your own food and drinks. A four-hour tour circles the island, but the seven-hour tour allows time to hike it to see wildlife.

◖ Whitefish Lake

The 3,315-acre lake in Whitefish buzzes in summer. Anglers hit the lake in early morning and evening, while midday turns into a frenzy of water-skiers, jet-skiers, party barges, kayakers, and canoers. Swimmers cool off at Whitefish State Park, City Beach, and Les Mason Park. In winter when ice covers the lake, hockey players make their own rinks and anglers ice fish.

Flathead River

Outside Hungry Horse, the South, Middle, and North Forks of the Flathead River converge. From here, the Flathead River snakes 55 miles across the valley to Flathead Lake. Seven river accesses allow places for anglers, canoers, and floaters to hop onto its meandering pace. Toward Flathead Lake, the river takes several sharp S turns in sloughs and estuaries, bird habitat for ospreys and waterfowl.

© BECKY LOMAX

City Beach at Whitefish Lake is a popular summer swimming area.

Whitefish Mountain Resort

Skiers and snowboarders flock to Whitefish Mountain Resort's 3,000 acres in winter. Twelve lifts access on average 300 inches of snow per year. Snow ghosts—ice-encrusted bent firs—compete with the view of Glacier National Park from the mountain's 6,817-foot summit. In summer, scenic lift rides, mountain biking, hiking, and huckleberry picking lure visitors.

Museums

In Kalispell, the historic Victorian **Conrad Mansion** (between 3rd St. and 4th St. on Woodland Ave., 406/755-2166, www.conrad mansion.com, May 15–Oct. 15, Tues.–Sun. 10 A.M.–5 P.M., adults $8, seniors $7, kids $3) preserves 26 rooms with their original 1895 furniture. Vintage clothing and toys recall the days of rummaging through Grandma's attic.

Also in Kalispell, the **Hockaday Museum of Art** (302 2nd Ave. E., 406/755-5268, www.hockadayartmuseum.org, Tues.–Sat. 10 A.M.–5 P.M. and Sun. noon–4 P.M., summer weekday hours extend to 6 P.M., adults $5, seniors $4, kids $1, under six free) features Montana pottery, jewelry, and paintings—particularly Native Americans and Glacier Park artists. A children's Discovery Gallery has creative hands-on exhibits for kids.

Atop Big Mountain, the **USFS Summit Nature Center** (406/862-2900, www.ski whitefish.com, mid-June–Labor Day, daily 10 A.M.–5 P.M., free) requires a hike or Whitefish Mountain Resort lift ride ($8–12) to reach its exhibits, but it may be the only place you can touch a grizzly bear! Free guided flower walks (July–Aug.) depart daily at 11 A.M. and 3 P.M., and there's a Junior Ranger program for kids.

Recreation

The Flathead Valley is a four-season recreation mecca. Lakes draw summertime paddlers and swimmers; fall lures hunters; ski resorts cater to powderhounds; and spring explodes with hiking.

HIKING

Since Flathead National Forest surrounds Flathead Valley, hikers have no shortage of trails within spitting distance of the back porch. Most trails are multi-use, permitting mountain bikes and motor bikes, but a few—such as the Jewel Basin trails or the Danny On Memorial Trail on Big Mountain—limit use to hikers.

In the Swan Mountains, **Jewel Basin** holds 50 miles of hiking paths. Open for hiking June–October, depending on snow, the 15,349-acre hiker-only area is called The Jewel, for 27 alpine fishing lakes sparkle in its basins. Paths tromp across huckleberry meadows and high ridges with top-of-the-world views. Fido can go on a leash. It's extremely popular: July

Fourth weekend sees 200 people per day. Trail signage is scanty, so find maps in local sports shops or contact Flathead National Forest (406/758-5200, www.fs.fed.us/r1/flathead) or Swan Lake Ranger Station (200 Ranger Station Rd., Bigfork, 406/837-7500).

A seven-mile narrow curvy dirt road climbs up to 5,717 feet off the valley floor to The Jewel. Leave low-clearance vehicles and trailers behind as it's riddled with washboards, rollers, and limited turnouts. To reach the Camp Misery Trailhead with its less-than-inspiring name, catch the Swan Highway (Hwy. 83) two miles north of Bigfork. Follow it to Echo Lake Road and head north approximately three miles to the Jewel Basin Road (#5392).

◖ Mount Aeneas

- Distance: 5.9-mile loop
- Duration: 3 hours
- Elevation gain: 1,811 feet

- Effort: moderately strenuous
- Trailhead: Camp Misery Trailhead in Jewel Basin

Mount Aeneas, at 7,528 feet, is the highest peak in The Jewel and offers big views for little work, but don't expect solitude at the summit. From the top, you'll see Flathead Lake, Glacier National Park, the Bob Marshall Wilderness Complex, and the Swan Mountains. A lot of scenery for a short hike! Combined with Picnic Lakes, the trail loops on a ridge and through a lake basin.

Begin hiking up trail #717, a wide road-bed. In 1.5 miles, the trail reaches a four-way junction—stay on #717 heading uphill. After a few switchbacks, you'll pass an ugly micro-wave tower before waltzing with the mountain goats along an arête to the summit. From the summit, drop down through the Picnic Lakes Basin. At the lakes, hook onto #392, then right onto #68, and left onto #8. (At 1.7 miles from Camp Misery, Picnic Lakes makes a good tiny kid destination—just reverse the route.)

Birch Lake

- Distance: 6 miles round-trip
- Duration: 3 hours
- Elevation gain: 800 feet
- Effort: moderate
- Trailhead: Camp Misery Trailhead in Jewel Basin

A short hop over a ridge along with a skip down a trail plops hikers on the banks of Birch Lake—a great destination for kids. Swim in the lake's west end, but don't expect balmy waters. This clear snowmelt pond retains its chill even in August. For those with more gumption, another 2.5 miles sets hikers on the boulder shoreline of Crater Lake.

Begin hiking up the broad roadway of trail #717 to the four-way junction. Take the right fork on #7. The trail curves around the lower flanks of Mount Aeneas as it descends to Birch Lake. (You'll have to hike up this on the way

out!) A trail circles the lake, but the best place to plunk yourself is on its obvious peninsula.

◖ Danny On Trail

- Distance: 4 miles one-way
- Duration: 2 hours
- Elevation gain: 2,400 feet
- Effort: moderate
- Trailhead: next to the Chalet at Whitefish Mountain Resort
- Directions: drive seven miles north of Whitefish following signs

The Danny On Trail chocks up over 14,000 hikers annually. At Big Mountain's summit, the USFS Nature Center provides interpretive resources for the trail. Catch the chairlift up to hike down ($8–12), or hike up and take the chair ride down free. While you can hike with

© BECKY LOMAX

FLATHEAD VALLEY

Danny On Trail on Big Mountain

your pooch on a leash here, Fido may not ride up or down the chairlift.

After beginning in Whitefish Mountain Resort Village, the trail switchbacks up through a forested slope and crosses ski runs as it sweeps around the mountain. Valerian and penstemon bloom in July; huckleberries scent the air in later summer. Junctions to Flower Point are well-marked: stay left at both to go directly to the top. (Loop through Flower Point for a 5.6-mile hike.) At the East Rim junction, turn left for a gentle, scenic loop before the final steep ascent. Panoramas at the top span Glacier Park to Flathead Lake.

BIKING

Oodles of two-lane highways and paved country lanes tie into long loops around Flathead Lake or short farmland tours for roadies, while single-track and dirt-road choices swamp mountain bikers. For itineraries to suit your palate and abilities, check Glacier Cyclery's website (www.glaciercyclery.com) for popular bike routes.

For single-track mountain biking, **Whitefish Mountain Resort** (end of Big Mountain Rd., Whitefish, 406/862-2900, www.skiwhitefish .com, mid-June–mid-Sept.) hauls bikes and riders up its chairlift for $8–24, depending on the numbers of rides down you want. Although the grade isn't steep, hairpin turns and natural obstacles chuck the trail in the have-some-experience-first category. Their new Runaway Train trail is for experienced downhillers. Rent bikes (adults $39–46, kids $16–19, all with helmets) at Whitefish Mountain Resort's rental shop.

Rentals

For scads of information on where to bike, **Glacier Cyclery** (326 E. 2nd St., Whitefish, 406/862-6466, www.glaciercyclery.com) is one of the best places to go. The shop rents touring bikes, roadies, and mountain bikes ($29–39 per day, $149–189 weekly), all with helmets. They can also equip you with car racks ($15 per day), Burleys ($24 per day), and strollers ($79 per week). **Mountain Mike's** (417 Bridge St., Bigfork, 406/837-2453, late

Apr.–early Oct. Mon.–Sat. 8 A.M.–4 P.M.) rents kid and adult mountain bikes ($30 including helmet), convenient for touring Swan Valley. You can also hire a guide ($40 per person, reservations required) for half-day dirt-road or single-track tours. Cross your fingers that you won't need a repair shop, but if you do, you'll find several throughout the valley in the phone book.

BOATING

Flathead Valley has a plethora of lakes for boating; the two largest are Flathead and Whitefish Lakes. Both have several launch sites and rentals available. Expect to pay hourly rates of $50–70 for jet skis, $60–90 for water-ski boats, and $75–100 for pontoon fishing boats and party barges. In addition to your rental fee, you'll need to pay for the gas used. Hand-propelled craft like canoes, kayaks, and rowboats usually run $10–20 per hour.

Flathead Lake

On Flathead Lake's north end, three communities—Bigfork, Somers, and Lakeside—service boaters with marinas usually open May–October. For launching boats, Flathead Lake has 13 public accesses, six of which are state parks ($5 per day use fee) maintained by Montana Fish, Wildlife, and Parks (406/752-5501, www.fwp.state.mt.us.). Boat rentals are available in four locations: **Wild Wave Watercraft** (7125 Hwy. 93 S., Lakeside, 406/844-2400 or 406/257-2627), **Flathead Boat Rentals** (5417 Hwy. 93 S., Somers, 406/857-3334), **Bigfork Marina and Boat Center** (100 Parkway Ave., Bigfork, 406/837-4224), and **Marina Cay Resort** (180 Vista Ln., Bigfork, 406/837-5861, www.marina cay.com).

Whitefish Lake

For launching boats, you'll find public ramps at Whitefish Lake State Park ($5 per day use fee) and City Beach ($4 launch fee). For rentals, mooring, and fuel service, **Whitefish Lake Lodge Marina** (1390 Wisconsin Ave., 406/862-9283, mid-May–Sept.) is the only option.

WATERSKIING

Most vacationers don't come to the Flathead solely for waterskiing. Compared to other waters, glacial-fed lakes are downright cold. But locals do water-ski on Whitefish Lake and Flathead Lake as well as smaller valley lakes, particularly in July and August. The marinas listed under *Boating* rent water-ski boats and gear ($60–90 per hour, plus gas).

KAYAKING AND CANOEING

White-water kayakers wearing wet suits in freezing cold water gravitate to the Swan River outside Bigfork. For Class IV–V rapids, the **Swan River Wild Mile,** a short 1.25-mile stretch that drops 100 feet below Bigfork Dam, sees its best water May–July and Wednesday nights during the summer when the dam releases flows. For sea-kayaking and canoeing, head to ambling stretches of the Flathead and Whitefish Rivers as well as the larger lakes—good any time of year until they freeze.

Rentals and Guides

You can rent kayaks to take to Glacier from all of these companies. Many of Flathead's kayak rental companies operate out of private homes, without keeping "shop hours," so call to make reservations. Life jackets, paddles, and spray skirts are included in rates. Half-day canoe or sea-kayak rentals run $25–55; full-day rentals are $35–75. Most renters choose the company by their location.

Whitefish Sea Kayaking (406/862-3513, wfseakayak@yahoo.com, year-round) rents single and double sea-kayaks, and for $12 they'll deliver the kayaks to Whitefish Lake. If you want to float Whitefish River, they'll also pick you up down the river ($12). They also guide half-day ($60) and full-day ($80, bring your own lunch) trips on Whitefish and Flathead Lakes.

A bit hard to locate, so call for directions, **Silver Moon Kayak** (1215 N. Somers Rd., Kalispell, 406/752-3724, www.silvermoonkayak.com, May–Sept., Tues.–Sat., 9 A.M.–6 P.M., call for winter hours) is convenient for Flathead River or Lake trips. Rental rates include foam blocks and straps for transporting. White-water kayaks are $40 per day.

Kayaking on Whitefish Lake is popular until the lake freezes.

© BECKY LOMAX

FLATHEAD VALLEY

Silver Moon guides lead two-hour ($45) to full-day tours ($95–115, including lunch and rental); their specialty trip is Paddle by Moonlight (June–Sept.; call for dates, $90).

FISHING

Lakes, estuaries, and rivers abound for fishing here. You'll need a Montana State license to fish in all of them. See the *Background* chapter for details.

Flathead Valley is sliced by the **Flathead River,** a giant highway for migrating fish. Because of dam control and cold glacial water, do not expect blue-ribbon trout fishing. But neither does the river see lots of fishing pressure. It carries many nonnative species—especially northern pike lurking in larger southern sloughs. Seven river accesses offer places to fish and to launch boats downstream: Blankenship Bridge, the Highway 2 bridge at Hungry Horse, a spur road at Bad Rock Canyon's west end, Kokanee Bend, Pressentine Bar, the old Steel Bridge, and the Stillwater mouth. Most anglers hit the stretch between Columbia Falls and the Old Steel Bridge in Kalispell.

Flathead Lake teems with cutthroat, giant trophy lake trout, mountain and lake whitefish, largemouth bass, bull trout, and yellow perch. It's good for all types of fishing: bait to lure, fly-fishing to trolling. The southern half of the lake is on Salish and Kootenai tribal lands; fishing here requires a tribal recreation label (Flathead Indian Reservation, 406/675-2700, $10 per year) available at small town businesses surrounding the southern shore.

Whitefish Lake draws anglers for its lake trout and whitefish. During winter, some anglers ice fish. Northern pike, lake trout, and kokanee are common, and it is regularly stocked with westslope cutthroat trout.

Fly Shops and Guides

Hit up fly-fishing shops in the Flathead for locally made hand-tied flies and tackle as well as advice on where fish are biting. Most of the following shops also offer guide services that range $250–450 for two people from half to full days. Rates usually do not include Montana fishing licenses.

Lakestream Flyshop (334 Central Ave., Whitefish, 406/862-1298, www.lakestream .com) guides fly-fishing trips on a private lake. **Stumptown Anglers** (5790 Hwy. 93 S., Whitefish, 406/862-4554, www.stump townanglers.com) guides trips on five different northwest Montana rivers, including the Flathead. **Arends Fly Shop** (7356 Hwy. 2 E., Columbia Falls, 406/892-2033, www .montanaflies.com) hits the south and main forks of the Flathead River. For guided fishing on Flathead Lake and Swan River, head to **Two River Gear** (603 Electric Ave., Bigfork, 406/837-3474).

Montana has no shortage of independent fly-fishing guide services operating unattached to shops. You can find them in the phone book or through the Internet. Be sure the guide service is licensed with the state before hiring them.

Charter Fishing

Charter fishing services on Flathead Lake operate May–September. Expect rates to range $300–700 per day, depending on duration and number of people. Located at Marina Cay in Bigfork, **A Able Fishing and Tours** (406/257-5214 or 800/231-5214, www.aablefishing.com) guides fishing trips on Flathead Lake with "Shorty," who guarantees fish! Other charter services also operate on Flathead Lake; locate them in the phone book.

HUNTING

With Flathead Valley surrounded by Flathead National Forest, it is popular for hunting—big game and birds. Get hunting regulations, seasons, and license info from Montana Fish, Wildlife, and Parks (406/444-2535, www .fwp.m.ontana.gov).

GOLF

Golf Digest rated Flathead Valley as one of the world's 50 greatest golf destinations—not just because the scenery is good and the prices are reasonable, but because of nine championship courses. With over 16 hours of daylight

© BECKY LOMAX

golfing at Whitefish Lake Golf Course, a city-owned 36-hole course

in early summer, courses open from dawn to dusk, adjusting tee times as daylight drops. Depending on snows, most courses are open April–October.

For playing 18 holes, expect to pay $37–90 during the day, depending on the course. Rates in April, May, and October and daily after 3 P.M. drop to $25–55. Club rentals range $14–30 and carts $15–28.

One of the best resources for Flathead golf is www.golfmontana.net, where you can get stats for all the local courses. A central number (800/392-9795) will get you guaranteed advanced reservations and golf packages. With a two-day advance reservation, you'll get the same rate the golf course offers. For guaranteed reservations with less notice, rates run $5 higher than if you call the golf courses direct and take what's available.

Courses

Six courses—all with rentals, pro shops, restaurants, and lounges—sprawl across the northern Flathead. With the highest greens fees, **Eagle Bend Golf Course** (279 Eagle Bend Dr., Bigfork, 406/837-7310 or 800/255-5641, www.golfmt.com) is ranked in the top 50 public courses in the country. The challenging 27-hole course is a Jack Nicklaus design with big variety in its hole layouts. From different tees, you can see Flathead Lake, Swan Mountains, and Glacier Park; osprey fly overhead. With cheaper greens fees, the city-owned **Whitefish Lake Golf Course** (1200 Hwy. 93 N., Whitefish, 406/862-4000, www.golfwhitefish.com) is Montana's only 36-hole course. The north course tours through large cedars and firs; the south course runs past Lost Loon Lake. Both have grand views of Big Mountain.

Meadow Lake Golf Course (490 St. Andrews Dr., Columbia Falls, 406/892-2111 or 800/321-4653, www.meadowlakegolf.com) weaves its 18 holes through the woods with some tight fairways and lots of adjacent houses. A couple of ponds and a creek separate the fairways, and some trees shade the course. **Big Mountain Golf Course** (3230 Hwy. 93 N., Kalispell, 406/751-1950, www.golfmt.com) is a Scottish links–style course. Since its 18 holes sit mid-valley with few trees, views open up to Big Mountain and Glacier Park. The Stillwater River runs adjacent to the back nine.

Village Greens (500 Palmer Drive, Kalispell, 406/752-4666, www.montanagolf.com) surrounds its bent-grass greens with a few trees, ponds, and some houses. The 18 holes afford a pleasant place to play on one of the easier courses here. **Buffalo Hill** (1176 N. Main St., Kalispell, 406/756-4530, www.golfbuffalo.com) combines an older course with a newer course for 27 holes. The older Cameron Nine abuts the highway; the newer 18-hole course is moderately difficult with a lot of terrain variety.

SKIING
◖ Whitefish Mountain Resort

Located seven miles from town, Whitefish Mountain Ski Resort (end of Big Mountain Rd., 406/862-2900, www.skiwhitefish.com,

early Dec.–early Apr. 9 a.m.–4:00 p.m., adults $56, kids 7–18 $30–46, 6 and under free) lives up to its former name of Big Mountain with 3,000 acres of skiing terrain, 2,400 feet of vertical, 12 lifts, and 91 named runs. Big bowls, glades, and long cruisers head 360 degrees off the summit; you can even find good tree skiing in the mountain's famous fog.

The resort's village contains restaurants, shops, rental gear ($15–35 per day), ski school, day care, and lodging from economy to upscale condos. You can also get deals on lift tickets: early and late season rates, lodging-lift packages, and multiple day passes, some of which must be purchased before the season starts. Call or check online for these.

In summer (mid-June–mid-Sept.), the resort runs its lift for sightseeing ($8–12 for single rides, kids 6 and under and seniors 70+ free). It also offers mountain biking, festivals, concerts, and Walk in the Treetops ($54, age 10

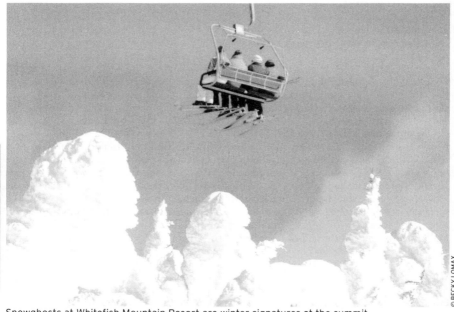

Snowghosts at Whitefish Mountain Resort are winter signatures at the summit.

and 54-inch height minimum), a boardwalk tour through the tree canopy 70 feet up in the air (you're clipped in with a safety harness).

Valhalla Adventures

For those looking for powder skiing in the backcountry, **Valhalla Adventures** (406/862-2369; www.valhallaadv.com; day trips $200 pp; overnight tours $300–950 pp) leads cat-ski tours just north of Whitefish on Stryker Ridge. A cozy backcountry yurt provides a warm lunch spot or overnight accommodations with gourmet meals.

CROSS-COUNTRY SKIING

Several small cross-country ski areas dot Flathead Valley. In addition to trails on Blacktail Mountain, four other areas groom trails for Nordic skiing usually between mid-December and March.

In Whitefish at the golf course on Highway 93 North, **Glacier Nordic Center** grooms 7.5 miles daily for skate and classic skiing ($5). On-site, the Outback Ski Shack (406/892-9498) rents both skate and classic gear ($10–18) and teaches lessons in both disciplines ($30).

SNOWMOBILING

The Flathead Valley is surrounded by 200 miles of groomed snowmobile trails (Dec.–mid-April, but some trails close April 1). Flathead Valley Snowmobile Association (406/756-3703 or www.snowtana.com for Montana Snowmobile Association) maintains the grooming on nine popular trails near Whitefish, Columbia Falls, and Bigfork. For those striking out on their own, be sure to check conditions with Glacier Country Avalanche Center (406/257-8402 or 800/526-5239, www.glacieravalanche.org).

Rentals are available at **Extreme Motorsports** (803 Spokane Ave., Whitefish, 406/862-8594) and **J & L Rentals** (5410 Hwy. 2 W., Columbia Falls, 406/892-7666, www.jandlrvrentals.com). Expect to pay around $175–195 per day for renting a snowmobile (helmets included); snowmobile suits, boots, and gloves are extra. To hire a J & L guide costs $130 per day.

ENTERTAINMENT AND EVENTS
Theaters

In Bigfork, the **Bigfork Summer Playhouse** (526 Electric Ave., 406/837-4886, www.bigforksummerplayhouse.com, mid-May–late Aug., $19–25 adults, $14 kids) presents five shows in repertory during each summer, from Broadway musical favorites to comedies. In Whitefish, **Whitefish Theater Company** (1 Central Ave., 406/862-5371, www.whitefishtheaterco.org) sponsors plays, concerts, speakers, and art films in the O'Shaughnessey Center. Broadway veterans formed the acclaimed **Alpine Theater Project** (406/862-7469, Whitefish, www.alpinetheatreproject.org), which produces plays during the summer at Whitefish Performing Arts Center. Beloved musicals, classic comedies, and first-run plays highlight its summer schedule along with *An Evening With* big names like John Lithgow, Olympia Dukakis, and Henry Winkler.

While we may be on the dark side of the moon regarding lots of things, you can actually catch a just-released blockbuster movie in the Flathead—but don't expect a hotbed of foreign, independent, or avant garde films. Whitefish has one movie theater, **Mountain Cinema** (Mountain Mall on Hwy. 93, 406/862-3130). In Kalispell, you'll find 14 movies showing at **Stadium 14** (185 Hutton Ranch Road, 406/752-7800, www.signaturetheatres.com). One of three remaining drive-in theaters in Montana, **Midway Drive-in** (3115 Hwy. 40 W., Columbia Falls, 406/892-4515) is open only during summer months. In June and early July, when the skies don't darken until 11 P.M., shows do not begin until very late; by August, they can start around 9:30 P.M.

Rodeos and Fairs

Located mid-valley between Whitefish and Kalispell, **Majestic Valley Arena** (3630 Hwy. 93 N., 406/755-5366, www.majesticvalleyarena.com) is the hub for big events: concerts, rodeos, equestrian competitions and expositions, and trade shows. Special attractions include calf-roping, pro-rodeos, and horse jumping. For cowpoke wannabes, the annual **Northwest Montana Fair and Rodeo** opens in mid-August at the Flathead County Fairgrounds (265 N. Meridian, Kalispell, 406/758-5810). The five-day, six-night event features PRCA Rodeos, fireworks, animal and produce exhibits, pari-mutuel horse racing, team penning, musical concerts, and livestock sales.

Events

The annual **Glacier Jazz Stampede** (406/862-3814 or 888/888-2308, www.glacierjazz stampede.com) is for those who love traditional jazz, swing, ragtime, Dixieland, and big-band sounds. The October event crams four days with 12–14 bands from across the U.S. and Canada, pounding out nearly nonstop music in four different Kalispell venues. Bands, schedules, and ticket prices vary yearly for each event, but you can order an "all event" ticket ($60–65) online.

Attracting hundreds of spectators even in soggy weather, the **Bigfork Whitewater Festival** (406/837-5888, www.bigfork.org) runs kayakers down the Class IV Wild Mile of the Swan River at the peak of spring run-off. Traditionally held for two days over Memorial Day Weekend, competitions run the gamut from slalom to boater cross. Local pubs and restaurants party with nightly entertainment.

In the doldrums of winter, Whitefish celebrates its wacky **Winter Carnival** (406/862-3501 or 877/862-3548, www .whitefishchamber.org), a three-day spree of ski races, ice hockey, penguin plunge, a fig-ure-skating show, torchlight parade, ski jor-ing, and snow skate jam held the first weekend in February. Hundreds of people line the few blocks of downtown Whitefish for an old-fashioned, drive-the-old-tractor-down-main-street parade disrupted by raucous Yetis and Viking women.

Art events abound in the Flathead.

The Whitefish Winter Carnival parade draws thousands to see the wackiness.

© BECKY LOMAX

Yetis show up for Whitefish Winter Carnival to kidnap the Queen of the Snows.

Whitefish hosts their **Gallery Nights** on the first Thursday of each month, May–October, and their three-day **Huckleberry Days** art festival in mid-August in Credit Union Park. Kalispell celebrates their three-day **Arts in the Park** in late July in Depot Park and a late-November **Art Walk** through downtown galleries. The **Bigfork Festival of the Arts** takes place in early August on the town's main street. Check with respective chambers of commerce for current schedules.

Casinos

While gambling is legal in Montana, casinos haven't rocketed to Las Vegas style—or even to the level of those found on some Native American reservations. Here, most bars have a few slot machines squirreled away in a corner; some even run a card table or two. In a twist to the usual gas station–convenience mart, some gas chains add small, dark, and smoky casinos featuring gaming machines and poker tables.

Accommodations

You'll find everything from motels to guest ranches in Flathead Valley, but most of the chain hotels congregate in Kalispell. Find complete lists through the area visitors bureaus and chambers of commerce. Contrary to the rustic nature of Glacier Park's lodges, you'll find most accommodations with the exception of B and B's here have Internet, televisions, air-conditioning, and modern amenities. You can also rent homes—nightly, weekly, and long-term. Two reputable property management companies offer short-term rentals: Hideaway Resorts (406/862-5500 or 888/836-5500, www.hideawayresorts.com) and Lakeshore Rentals (406/863-9337 or 877/817-3012, www.lakeshorerentals.net).

All accommodations listed here are open year-round unless noted otherwise. When making reservations, be sure to ask about golf or ski packages, as many places offer good deals in season—even independent motels. Rates vary according to season; the ranges listed reflect the low rates of the off-season and high rates of peak seasons. However, what is considered high and low season varies with location: summer is high season valley-wide, but in winter, it's high season in Whitefish. Fall and spring are off seasons. A 7 percent Montana State bed tax will be added to your bill. In Whitefish, an additional 2 percent resort tax will also be added.

MOTELS AND LODGES

Scattered throughout Flathead Valley, you can find most major low end to moderately priced chain hotels congregated mostly in Kalispell, Whitefish, and Columbia Falls.

Bigfork

The town's most reasonably priced lodging is **Timbers Motel** (8540 Hwy. 35 S., 406/837-6200 or 800/821-4546, www.timbersmotel.com $58–144), which puts you within a five-minute drive to Eagle Bend Golf Course and just a couple minutes from the Bigfork Summer Playhouse. It sits on a small knoll on, but above the highway; however, traffic on this highway slows substantially at night.

Right in downtown Bigfork, **Bridge Street Cottages** (309 Bridge St., 406/837-2785 or 888/264-4974, www.bridgestreetcottages.com) offers higher-end lodging with a three-night minimum stay. Four of the units sit right on the Swan River. Surrounded by small perennial gardens, these well-furnished, well-kept one-bedroom cottages built in 2004 come with Internet access, cable television, air-conditioning, and come with fully equipped kitchens ($115–325 per night). Suites ($85–185) are smaller with just a fridge and microwave.

Columbia Falls

Columbia Falls is the closest town to Glacier, but with minimal lodging. Good for those on a budget, two motels sit near the waterslide and Flathead River. **Glacier Gateway Inn** (300 Hwy. 2 E., 406/892-4341, www.glaciergateway.com, $40–80) has an indoor pool and hot tub, wireless Internet, and free continental breakfast. **Glacier Mountain Shadows** (7285 Hwy. 2 E., 406/892-7686, www.glacierparkmotelandcampground.com, $105–150) is a renovated nonsmoking motel with an outdoor pool and indoor hot tubs, kitchenettes, wireless Internet, and free bagel bar breakfast.

Kalispell

Right in downtown Kalispell's shopping district, the historic ◖ **Kalispell Grand Hotel** (100 Main St., 406/755-8100 or 800/858-7422, www.kalispellgrand.com, $73–140) makes you take a leap back in time. Walking in the lobby, you're greeted by a tin ceiling, ornate pump organ, and the original wide, oak banister stairway. Renovated rooms have smaller bathrooms with showers rather than tubs. Although the ambience harkens back to 1912, when the hotel opened with a room costing $2, its modern amenities now include an elevator, high speed Internet, air-conditioning, and televisions. In the afternoon, pick up home-baked cookies in the lobby.

BED-AND-BREAKFASTS
Bigfork
A short 3.5 miles south of Bigfork puts you at **Candlewycke Inn Bed & Breakfast** (311 Aero Lane, 406/837-6406 or 888/617-8805, www.candlewyckeinn.com, $135–185). On 10 acres, the nonsmoking cedar-and-log inn serving a full breakfast in the morning has five folk-art-themed rooms with pillow-top beds and private baths, some with Jacuzzi tubs. Discounts are given for three or more nights. Walk on trails around the property, cross-country ski in winter, or lounge on the massive decks or in the outdoor hot tub.

Columbia Falls
On 10 quiet acres 10 minutes from town, **Bad Rock Bed and Breakfast** (480 Bad Rock Dr., 406/892-2829 or 888/892-2829, www.badrock.com, $115–250) opens its doors to guests with four log cabins surrounding a river-rock and log-frame house. Cabin rooms have hand-crafted log furniture, while the three house rooms are decorated in different styles. All have private baths. Breakfast is a large Montana-style affair, sometimes featuring Belgian waffles heaped with strawberries.

Whitefish
A short walk to restaurants and nightlife in downtown Whitefish, the circa 1920 **Garden Wall Inn** (504 Spokane Ave., 406/862-3440 or 888/530-1700, www.gardenwallinn.com, $135–185, suite $235) is furnished with antiques inside, while a perennial garden blooms outside. It's an extension of Glacier Park, with historic photos and picture books in the living room, and if the weather deteriorates, you can curl up in front of a real fire in the glazed brick fireplace. Five guest rooms each have private baths—some with oversized claw-foot tubs. In the morning, awake to a coffee or tea tray delivered to your room before heading to the dining room for a breakfast of treats like huckleberry-pear crepes.

A five-minute drive from downtown and 10 minutes from the ski resort, **Hidden Moose Lodge** (1735 E. Lakeshore Dr., 406/862-6516 or 888/733-6667, www.hiddenmooselodge.com, $99–199) provides three styles of upscale Montana-outdoors themed rooms with private decks and baths: lodge rooms, Jacuzzi rooms, and a suite. A great room centers around a large river-rock fireplace, and decks face the woods. Amenities include an outdoor hot tub, wireless Internet, air-conditioning, cable-TV, mini-fridge, and complimentary evening beverages. Breakfast is big with Hidden Moose chorizo quiche being one of the favorite entrees.

RESORTS
During the high season (winter for ski resorts, summer for golf, beach, and ranches), all resorts charge premium rates, but you can get great deals during their low seasons or off-seasons.

Ski and Golf
At the valley's north end, **Whitefish Mountain Resort** (406/862-2900 or 800/858-5439, www.skiwhitefish.com) has all lodging options—motels and condos ($60–699 per night) and vacation homes ($100–2,100 per night). Winter sees the highest rates as all restaurants and shops are open for the ski and snowboard season and all lifts operate. Summer has moderate prices when some restaurants open and one lift to the summit runs for hiking and mountain biking. Fall and spring are very inexpensive, but no lifts, shops, nor restaurants are open. Kandahar Lodge has the best reputation for upscale accommodations with an outstanding gourmet restaurant; for budget lodging, ask about the Hibernation House.

In Whitefish, one mile from downtown restaurants and nightlife, **Grouse Mountain Lodge** (Hwy. 93 and Fairway Dr., 406/862-3000 or 800/321-8822, www.grousemountainlodge.com, $99–259) sits its modern hotel rooms right on a 36-hole golf course that converts in winter to groomed Nordic skiing trails. It has an indoor pool and outdoor hot tubs, a restaurant, DSL and wireless Internet, and comfortable lobby with its huge river-rock fireplace. Rooms come in seven configurations all with private baths—from a basic hotel room to a high-end room with oversized shower sporting multiple water heads. For accessing town, the airport, or ski resort, a complimentary shuttle bops you quickly to your destination, and Montana Adventure Company located in the lobby books activities—skiing to Glacier Park tours.

Outside Columbia Falls among big trees, **Meadow Lake Resort** (100 St. Andrews Dr., 406/892-8700 or 800/321-4653, www .meadowlake.com) sits on an 18-hole golf course with a restaurant, indoor and outdoor swimming pools and spas, and tennis courts. For lodging, the resort has 24 modern hotel rooms ($139–189), one- or two-bedroom condos with fully equipped kitchens and private decks ($139–365), and vacation homes ($160–620). In winter, the resort provides a ski shuttle to Whitefish Mountain Resort. The on-site concierge books activities—white-water rafting, scenic boat cruises, and horseback riding—and to free up time for adults, Troop Meadow Lake supervises the kids for swimming, movie night, arts and crafts, and outdoor activities.

Waterfront

With a two-story lobby draped with a giant wrought-iron chandelier and river-rock fireplace, **C The Lodge at Whitefish Lake** (1380 Wisconsin Ave., 406/863-4000 or 877/887-4026, www.lodgeatwhitefishlake.com, $125–1,044) opened in late 2005 with more upscale furnishings than other valley hotels. Spacious balconied suites and condos (two- and three-bedroom $269–604) vary in size with fireplaces, slate floors, granite countertops, refrigerators, both tubs and walk-in showers, and high-speed Internet. Their premier rooms overlook the lake facing sunsets; upstairs north rooms have mountain views. The lodge has a private beachfront on Whitefish Lake, outdoor pool and hot tub, full-service marina, boat rentals, art gallery, gift shops, day spa,

restaurant, and lounge. Golf and skiing are both within a 7- to 10-minute drive.

On Flathead Lake, **Marina Cay Resort** (180 Vista Ln., Bigfork, 406/837-5861 or 800/433-6516, www.marinacay.com) has courtyard and waterfront suites ($89–139) and two- and three-bedroom condos ($139–389) along with restaurants, seasonal outdoor pool and hot tub, and marina with boat rentals. You can easily walk seven minutes to downtown Bigfork's shops and restaurants. Eagle Bend Golf Course is a five-minute drive away, and the closest hiking trails are in Jewel Basin.

Guest Ranches

C Averill's Flathead Lake Lodge (Flathead Lake Lodge Rd., Bigfork, 406/837-4391, www .averills.com, June–Labor Day) is a family-owned working dude ranch on 2,000 acres. Lodging, meals, and activities all wrap up in one big price for 7 or 14 days: per week rates run adults $3,143, kids–teens $1,309–2,345, and infants $168. With horseback riding, fishing, swimming, waterskiing, tennis, and sailing, the ranch centers around the classy log lodge and cabins. You can park the car and dive into vacation mode for several days, as the ranch coordinates the activities.

The new **Bar W Guest Ranch** (2875 Hwy. 93 W., Whitefish, 409/863-9099 or 866/828-2900, www.thebarw.com) houses guests in its 6,200-square-foot western lodge and cabin suites adjacent to a small lake and Spencer Mountain. Ranch activities pile on trail rides, rodeos, cookouts, boating, archery, hiking, fishing, and campfires. Three-, four-, and six-night packages include all meals, lodging, and ranch activities (adults $592–3,150, kids $450–1,200). If you're looking for a deal, hit fall, spring, or winter for lower rates.

CAMPING

In Flathead Valley, state parks for camping tend to cluster around lake shores with drinking water, picnic tables, and flush toilets, but no hookups. Conversely, most private commercial campgrounds have full hookups, laundry, hot showers, dump stations, and camp stores, and will accommodate large RVs with pullouts as well as tents. Commercial campgrounds add a 7 percent Montana bed tax to your bill, and Whitefish private campgrounds add another 2 percent resort tax. Most will give 10 percent discounts to AAA, Woodall's, and Good Sam members.

Bigfork

Located on Flathead Lake, **Wayfarer's State Park** (0.5 mile south of Bigfork on Hwy. 35, 406/837-4196, www.fwp.state.mt.us, May–Sept., $15) is great for boating and fishing. The park is one of the lake's largest campgrounds with 30 sites on 68 acres, a boat ramp, a swimming area, and 1.5 miles of hiking trails. Pets are allowed on a leash. Campground amenities include firewood, fire grill, flush and vault toilets, showers, picnic tables, and drinking water.

Columbia Falls

Three private campgrounds string along Highway 2 between Columbia Falls and Whitefish, all with Glacier Park 16–23 minutes away. All sit right on the highway, so be prepared for road noise. The closest golf course is Meadow Lake; the closest grocery stores are in Columbia Falls. These all have flush toilets, hot showers, dump stations, and laundries for about the same rates: tents $10–16, RV hookups $26–35.

With 35 sites in a grassy setting surrounded by trees right in town, **Columbia Falls RV Park** (103 Hwy. 2 E., 406/892-1122 or 888/401-7268, www.columbiafallsrvpark .com, May–Oct.) is the closest to Glacier and one mile from the water slides, an outdoor community swimming pool, and grocery stores. A few-block walk puts you at restaurants in town. **Glacier Peaks RV Park** (3185 Hwy. 40, 406/892-2133 or 800/268-4849, open all year) is easy to spot with its flower-painted VW bug and trailer as a sign. Under partial-shade, 60 grassy sites sprawl adjacent to a summer outdoor drive-in theater. With its location at the junction of Montana Highway 40 and U.S. Highway 2, driving access is quick

to Columbia Falls, Whitefish, and Kalispell. The campground also has cable, phone, computer lines, and a playground. **Mountain View RV Park** (3621 Hwy. 40, 406/892-2500, mid-Apr.–early Oct.) is the newest campground built in 2006; small trees are still growing up between sites (think views!). Located midway between Columbia Falls (two miles) and Whitefish (three miles), the park offers high-speed Internet and a playground.

Kalispell

Quite a few year-round commercial campgrounds scatter in Kalispell, all within 30–40 minutes from Glacier and 15–20 minutes to Flathead Lake. Golf courses (Eagle Bend, Village Greens, Buffalo Hills) are within five miles, along with shopping, box stores, and restaurants. The following all have comparable rates: tents $15–19; RV hookups $24–28. Standard amenities include flush toilets, hot showers, dump stations, laundries, picnic tables, and firepits.

The nearest to Glacier, **Rocky Mountain "Hi" RV Park and Campground** (825 Helena Flats, 406/755-9573 or 800/968-5637, www .glaciercamping.com) sits adjacent to a spring-fed creek with 98 grassy sites tucked between large fir trees—a few with Swan Mountain views. Because it's back from the highway, you'll hear less road noise. With swimming, fishing, and canoeing in a wide creek and a playground on-site, it's a good campground for kids. They also have cable TV hookups and a remodeled laundry facility.

Convenient to downtown Kalispell (a seven-minute drive), two RV parks sit adjacent to the noisy Highway 35 truck route; however, each has something more to recommend it. **Glacier Pines RV Park** (1850 Hwy. 35, 406/752-2760 or 800/533-4029, www.glacier pines.com) has grassy sites under large trees with a seasonal outdoor heated swimming pool. Additional amenities include modem hookups, camp store, and horseshoe pits. **Spruce Park on the River** (1985 Hwy. 35, 406/752-6321 or 888/752-6321, www.spruce parkrv.com) accommodates 100 RVs and 60

FLATHEAD VALLEY

tents in shaded sites. The park sits right on the Flathead River, so you can fish from the campground. Additional amenities include cable TV hookup, playground, pet walks, and you can wash your RV here.

Whitefish

Within 30–35 minutes from West Glacier, campers have three options in Whitefish for campgrounds—all with extremely different environments. Golf sits within a 5–10 minute drive as are shopping and restaurants in town; Whitefish Mountain Resort is a 15-minute drive up the hill.

Set in deep woods right on Whitefish Lake, **Whitefish Lake State Park** (one mile west of Whitefish on Hwy. 93, then one mile north following signs, 406/862-3991, www.fwp .state.mt.us, May–Sept., $15 per site) is perfect for swimming and launching boats, but not particularly for sleeping as the train tracks cross the park with nearly 30 trains per day rumbling along and tooting their horns as they enter town. With a good set of earplugs, you can survive the night. Amenities include flush toilets, picnic tables, fire pits, firewood, and running water.

Whitefish has two commercial campgrounds—both with flush toilets, hot showers, picnic tables, fire pits, and dump stations. Located conveniently behind the Cheap Sleep Motel, **Whitefish RV Park** (6400 Hwy. 93 S., 406/862-7275, www .whitefishrvpark.com, open year round, $30–34) is a short five-minute walk to shopping, theaters, restaurants, and the winter bus to the ski area. With 57 grassy sites separated by small trees, it is sheltered from some of the highway noise. Extra amenities include playground, laundry, and cable TV hookups. Sitting two miles south of town, **Whitefish KOA** (5121 Hwy. 93 S., 406/862-4242, www.glacierparkkoa.com, mid-Apr.–mid-Oct., RV hookups $30–60, tents $20–36,) sits on 33 acres shielded from the highway by thick forest—much more quiet than the other two Whitefish campgrounds. The outdoor pool attracts kids while oldsters gravitate to the adults-only hot tub. A full-service restaurant serves nightly barbecues, sandwiches, and pizza. Other amenities include a camp store, wireless and high-speed Internet, a game room, free mini-golf, free continental breakfast, and bike rentals.

Food

Dining in the Flathead Valley is a casual affair, even in the priciest restaurants. Don't bother with a suit and tie or fancy dinner dress; even in fine establishments, relaxed attire is common. Check the phone book for options: You'll find Mexican to Japanese, country cafés to steak houses.

BIGFORK

For a tiny town, Bigfork packs in the tasty restaurants, most of which are in downtown within two blocks walking distance of the theater. On performance nights at the theater, you won't get in a restaurant for dinner unless you make reservations. While in Bigfork, pick up oversized chocolate-chip cookies for

your hiking lunch at **Brookies Cookies** (191 Mill St., 406/837-2447). You can even mail some home.

Burgers and Beer

For the best burger and beer after hiking in Jewel Basin, stop at **Garden Bar and Grill** (451 Electric Ave., 406/837-9914, 10 A.M.–2 A.M., $6–8). You can eat in the bar or out back in the funky garden where live music cranks out tunes on summer evenings. You'll have trouble choosing from the 20 microbrews on tap. In Montana, kids can enter bars usually until 8 P.M. The bar also serves as headquarters for the annual whitewater festival and features music most weekends.

Eclectic Cuisine

Known for exceptional food at modest prices, **Ⓒ Showthyme!** (548 Electric Ave., 406/837-0707, www.showthyme.com, Tues.–Sat., at 5 P.M., $14–28) dishes up a repertoire of fresh fish and pasta to wild game and steaks. One friend swears by the before-dinner wicked gin and tonic. Start dinner with the warm brie cheese salad or just dive straight into an entree with the angel's chicken-stuffed green chiles—a chicken and cheese-stuffed chile covered with red sauce. An extensive wine selection features Australian and New Zealand imports as well as West Coast vintners. For dessert, try the house specialty: a huckleberry ice cream crepe floating in huckleberry sauce. The cozy two-story brick old bank building opens up for outside seating, too, in summer. For theatergoers, the restaurant is extremely convenient—right next door.

French

Who knows better how to cook French delicacies than a native? **La Provence** (408 Bridge St., www.bigforklaprovence.com, 406/837-2923, Tues.–Sat. 5:00–10 P.M., $15–22) features gourmet Southern French and Mediterranean cuisine concocted by Marc Guizol, the owner-chef from Provence. Start off your evening with escargot and traditional French onion soup with Gruyère. Entrees sauced with wines come in fish, duck, rack of lamb, and venison or pork tenderloins. Finish with a traditional soufflé. An extensive wine list accompanies the menu, of course, featuring French vintages. Sit inside surrounded by the works of local artists, or in summer outside on the patio. For lunch and takeout, the restaurant operates as the **La Petite Provence Bistro** (Tues.–Sat. 10 A.M.–2 P.M., $4–9), serving gourmet sandwiches, French homemade pastries, and quiche.

COLUMBIA FALLS

Columbia Falls has never been known as a dining mecca, but recently, new restaurants have opened, giving it options beyond the fast-food enterprises along the highway. However, if you do crave fast-food, head for the local one-of-a-kind place—**Fox's Drive In** (Hwy. 93 and 9th St., 406/892-2020, Mon.–Sat.), but expect a brief wait while they slap your burger on the grill—no precooking here! **Truby's,** a popular wood-fired pizza restaurant that used to be in Whitefish, is slated to open in 2009; if so, look them up.

Cafés

Coffee Traders Pines Café (1st Ave. W. and Hwy. 2, 406/892-7633, 7 A.M.–5 P.M. daily) is not just a place to grab an espresso from the local coffee roasters—Montana Coffee Traders, but also a place for breakfast (until 11 A.M.) and lunch (11 A.M.–3 P.M. daily, Sun. until 2 P.M.). The ambience still clings fondly to memories of the old local dive Pine Tree Cafe, with the pine tree still standing in the middle of the room. The menu ($5–8) features huge breakfast omelets, deli sandwiches (to be really decadent, go for the lobster artichoke melt), wraps, and salads. Given its location en route to Glacier, many folks grab an espresso with muffins, scones, or cookies for the drive and a sandwich to go for the trail. Check your email here on the free Internet. Montana Coffee Traders has two other valley cafés (328 W. Center St., Kalispell, 406/756-2326; 110 Central Ave., Whitefish, 406/862-7667).

Ribs

When locals want down-home cooking, they head for the favorite place to get greasy, **Ⓒ The Back Room of the Nite Owl** (Hwy. 2, 406/892-3131, Sun. 2–9 P.M., Mon.–Thurs. 4–9 P.M., Fri. and Sat. 4–10 P.M., $6–14). The restaurant serves strictly old-time Montana feasts: gooey ribs and broasted chicken. You can order the ribs country, spare, or baby-back, or if you can't decide, a gigantic combo plate. Don't look for commercial sauces smothering the ribs; the restaurant makes their own concoction of secret spices. Fry bread with honey, coleslaw, and homemade french fries fill the plate to overflowing. A waitress may still call you "Hon" as she delivers you a roll of paper towels instead of napkins to handle

A GUIDE TO LOCAL BREWS

Montanans relish their local microbreweries. To help you navigate the mystery of the brews, here's a guide to the local beers you'll find.

Bayern Brewing (Missoula): Their Bayern Amber is the backbone of their brew pub. They also just added the Dancing Trout, a filtered German wheat ale.

Big Sky Brewing (Missoula): One of the most popular brown ales in northwest Montana, Moose Drool may have gained its notoriety through merchandising its name, but it tastes darn good, too. Their other two most popular brews are Scape Goat Pale Ale – a lighter English-style ale – and Trout Slayer – a filtered wheat ale.

Blackfoot River Brewing (Helena): Look for Woollybugger Wheat, a German Hefeweisen, and Missouri River Steamboat Lager, a light, hoppy amber. Or for something more roasty and full-bodied, try the Double Black Diamond Extreme Stout.

Flathead Lake Brewing (Bigfork): The young brewery, which opened in 2005, names its headliner light-bodied, hoppy ale after Flathead Lake's waves: Whitecap Pale Ale. Also, try the Wild Mile Wheat, an unfiltered summer wheat beer named after the town's famous whitewater.

Glacier Brewing (Polson): This brewery produces three lighter beers: the light-bodied German Kolsch Golden Grizzly Ale, the sweet and malty North Fork Amber Ale, and the Port Polson Pilsner. For a good creamy roasted chocolate flavor, pick up a Slurry Bomber Stout.

Great Northern Brewing (Whitefish): Their popular lighter beers include a Hefeweisen called Wheatfish and the light-bodied Hell Roaring Amber. If you haven't overdosed on huckleberries here, you can try them in beer with the Wild Huckleberry Wheat Lager. In winter, look for Snow Ghost, named for the snow-laden trees on top of Whitefish Mountain Resort.

Lang Creek Brewery (Marion): On the lighter end, look for the golden Dutch Skydiver Blonde, named for the local skydiving in Marion. For more richness, sip the English-style Tri-Motor Amber. To satisfy a sweet tooth, try the light-bodied seasonal Huckleberry 'N Honey.

Tamarack Brewing (Lakeside): Northwest Montana's newest brewery puts out a light golden Bear Bottom Blonde and robust amber Yard Sale Ale (named for the famous splats that sprawl ski gear across slopes).

the colossal mess. Abandon all thoughts of calories or cholesterol; dig in, and when you're done, lick your fingers. You won't have room for dessert!

KALISPELL

Kalispell has most of the common national chain restaurants along Highway 93, but not in the few blocks of the downtown core. Hit **Reds, Wines, and Blues** (30 Second St. E., 406/755-9463) for the under 40 singles scene, hopping with brews and music.

Cafés

With its bright colorful interior displaying local art, the **◖ Knead Café** (25 2nd Ave. W., 406/755-7510, www.theknead.com, Mon.–Fri.

10:30 A.M.–9:30 P.M., Sat. 9 A.M.–9 P.M., Sun. 9 A.M.–3 P.M.) can please both a vegetarian and a meat lover with its fresh and slightly different Mediterranean flavors. The weekend brunch ($5–8) features an eclectic collection of wraps, omelets, and frittas, while lunches ($6–9) grill up a salmon and brie cheese sandwich or a black bean burger. Dinners ($15–19) steer more away from the café fare with fish, beef, and vegetarian entrees. A full line of beers, wines, and espressos complement any meal here, as do goods from its own bakery.

For burgers and shakes à la 1950s, drop in at **Norm's News** (34 Main St., 406/756-5466, Mon.–Sat. 9 A.M.–5 P.M., Sun. 11 A.M.–4 P.M., $3–6). A tradition since 1938, the soda fountain lets you munch while you browse over

2,500 magazines and newspapers. The kids will also go crazy with the candy collection, featuring over 400 different sugar treats. For nostalgia buffs, the jukebox and ornate back bar are just worth a look, and, of course, the menu features traditional soda fountain fare: hamburgers, hot dogs, sundaes, shakes, and ice-cream sodas.

Pizza

For those with beer and pizza taste buds, head to **Moose's Saloon** (173 N. Main, 406/755-2337, www.moosessaloon.com, daily 11 A.M.–1:30 A.M., $6–16), where peanut shells and sawdust cover the floor in this funky old-time bar that's been a valley staple since 1957. It will be just what you imagine a Montana bar to be—dark and loud, loud, loud. But the pizza is darn good with one of the best crusts around. You'll get the kitchen sink on the combination pizza, and beer prices are cheap. If you want to forgo the atmosphere, you can order to go.

Fine Dining

[**North Bay Grille** (139 First Ave. West, 406/755-4441, www.nbgrille.com, Mon.–Sat., 11:30 A.M.–10 P.M., bar open until 2 A.M., Sundays opens at 4 P.M., $10–33) is one of Kalispell's newest hotspots serving inventive lunches and dinners. You can grab lighter meals of upscale sandwiches, burgers, pizzas, salads, and pasta in the bar or dining room. House dinner specialties include mango-chokecherry duck breast and beef tenderloin with prawns with a veal demi glace sauce. The bar serves up both domestic and imported wines as well as a long list of imaginative martinis and margaritas.

WHITEFISH

As a resort town, Whitefish is overloaded with outstanding restaurants. Because of crowds, you'll need to make reservations to avoid long waits in high summer or winter. In off-seasons (spring and fall), a few restaurants alter their hours or close for a month on a whim to go fishing; call ahead to be sure they are open. For the best burgers in town, head to the **Bulldog**

Saloon (144 Central Ave., 406/862-5601), but keep the kids out of the X-rated decorated bathrooms.

Cafés

For breakfast and lunch, you might have to arm wrestle a local's claim to a daily seat at **The Buffalo Cafe** (516 E. 3rd St., 406/862-2833, weekdays 6:30 A.M.–2 P.M., Sat. 7 A.M.–2 P.M., Sun. 9 A.M.–2 P.M., $6–9) to order the house Buffalo Pie with hash browns, ham, and cheese, and topped with two poached eggs. A few blocks away, **Loula's** (300 2nd Ave., 406/862-5614, daily 7 A.M.–3 P.M., $6–10) is the place for lemon-stuffed French toast with raspberry sauce or portobello mushroom, roasted red pepper, and cream cheese sandwich. Before leaving, pick up one of their trademark fresh-baked fruit whole pies to go ($18–24).

Located a few blocks outside the downtown mayhem, **Rising Sun Bistro** (549 Wisconsin Ave., 406/862-1236, Tues.–Sat. 9 A.M.–2:30 P.M. and 5:30–9 P.M., Sun. 9 A.M.–2 P.M., $6–19) serves up French bistro comfort foods like tomato basil soup and Burgundian meatloaf. Their breakfast and lunches include both typical café fare like biscuits and gravy or burgers, but also specialties such as smoked salmon benedict and salad nicoise. Daily dinner specialties are worth trying—pasta, crepes, and braised lamb shanks. Brunch is served all day on Sundays. You can dine next to the cozy fire, or in summer out in the garden. They also serve beer and wine.

Italian

Mambo Italiano (234 E. 2nd St., 406/863-9600, 5–10 P.M., $9–20) transports you beyond the Flathead to Italy with its cramped noisy dining room lilting to tunes of Frank Sinatra and Andrea Bocelli. You can also enjoy a view of Big Mountain from their upstairs deck. Start with the Tootsie Roll appetizer, a ricotta cheese–stuffed phyllo on marinara. You can feast on the huge Dotter Gordon salad topped with eggplant or meatballs, or a house pasta like fettuccine alla Lulubella, a carbonara well worth knocking your cholesterol through the roof. Order a jug of house red wine for the table—you'll be charged by how many glasses you drink (a guess on the waitstaff's part) rather than the bottle. And it's decent wine, too.

For pizza, Montana's homegrown chain **MacKenzie River Pizza** (9 Central Ave., 406/862-6601, 11 A.M.–9 P.M., until 10 P.M. on weekends, $8–20) makes a great family restaurant. It serves up traditional and eclectic (chicken fajita, Thai) pizzas with sourdough or natural grain crusts. You'll also find giant salads, sandwiches, and pasta on the menu and local microbrews on tap.

Asian

Although most people don't see sushi and Montana going together, the sushi at **❮ Wasabi Sushi Bar and Ginger Grill** (419 2nd St., 406/863-9283, Tues.–Sun., opens at 5 P.M., $8–25) is downright unbeatable. Here sushi rolls, sake, and grilled Asian specialties are served in a relaxed, bright atmosphere surrounded by wasabi-green walls. Large mirrors reflect the deft fingers of the sushi chefs in action as they make your rolls. While the menu also carries full teriyaki dinners, many make a feast of ordering several sushi rolls. Try the Black Widow, a peppered albacore topped with hot Sri Racha. You can get rolls to go, too.

Cajun and Creole

At **❮ Tupelo Grille** (17 Central Ave., 406/862-6136, www.tupelogrille.com, nightly at 5 P.M., $15–22), the flavors come from New Orleans. Start with a duck, chicken, and andouille gumbo followed by their tasty version of shrimp and grits, where grilled shrimp doused in a spicy tasso cream sauce smothers grilled grits. If you can't decide between the Louisiana flavors, order the Cajun Creole combo plate, which piles up a platter of crawfish étouffée, shrimp Creole, and chicken and sausage jambalaya. Don't leave without your dessert: the bread pudding is scrumptious without being overly sweet.

Mexican

❮ Pescado Blanco (235 E. First St., 406/862-3290, www.pescadoblanco.com, daily

farmers market flowers

© BECKY LOMAX

© BECKY LOMAX

downtown Whitefish Farmers Market on Tuesday evenings

5 P.M.–9 P.M., $16–23) has more than a cute variation on the name of Whitefish; their chefs excel at mountain Mexican cuisine. Try their popular bison enchilada. They also fly in fish twice week for dishes such as halibut tacos with orange sauce and seared scallops with sauces appearing in the Mexican flag. Their signature margaritas are made with fresh lime and a 14 percent distilled agave wine, and they serve a full range of south-of-the-border beers and local microbrews.

Fine Dining

Whitefish also has more than its share of fine restaurants. For prime rib, Montana game, and high-end steaks accompanied by an extensive wine list, make reservations at **Whitefish Lake Restaurant** (1200 Hwy. 93 N., 406/862-5285, www.golfwhitefish .com). At Whitefish Lake Golf Course, the 1937 log building was renovated in 1999, upgrading the facility but retaining its original historic ambience. During the golf season, the restaurant is open daily for lunch (11 A.M.–3 P.M.) and dinner (5:30–10 P.M., $16–44), but in winter, it only opens in the evening for dinner (until 9:30 P.M.). For an appetizer, try the New Zealand mussels followed by one of the restaurant's fish favorites, a halibut baked in phyllo with feta, roasted garlic, and spinach. The house specialty is roasted rack of lamb topped with a three-onion demi-glace.

GROCERIES

The Flathead Valley has no shortage of supermarket chains and local grocers. But for seasonal, locally grown produce, try one of the summer **farmers markets,** which usually congregate May–September in Whitefish (Tues., north end of Central Ave.; Thurs., Mountain Mall parking lot), Bigfork (Wed., Bigfork School), Columbia Falls (Thurs., across from the firehall), and Kalispell (Tues. and Sat., Center St. and Fifth Ave.). You can also get organic foods at several local shops, including **Third Street Market** (3rd and Spokane Ave., Whitefish, 406/862-5054).

FLATHEAD VALLEY

Information and Services

SHOPPING

While Flathead Valley, thank goodness, has no Mall of America clone or factory outlet mall, it does have its share of strip malls and chain stores. However, if you can, head to the few strikingly different shops worth browsing: art galleries, jewelry, and eclectic gift shops. Most of the one-of-a-kind locally owned stores cluster in the few blocks of downtown Whitefish, Bigfork, and Kalispell.

For classy, high quality toys—inventive, classic, and educational—stop in **Imagination Station** (221 Central Ave., Whitefish, 406/862-5668, and 132 Main St., Kalispell, 406/755-5668). They'll even ship your toys home for you, so you don't have to haul everything on the airplane. In Kalispell, visit **Sassafras** (120 Main St., 406/752-2433), an artist co-op, featuring the works of 30–40 local northwest Montana artists. Pieces range from watercolors and cards to pottery, jewelry, clothing, furniture, and sculptures. You'll find works with Glacier Park themes here, too. In Whitefish, be sure to pick up exquisite handmade chocolates at **Copperleaf Chocolate Company** (242 Central Ave., 406/862-9659).

Outdoor Gear

For outdoor gear—camping, backpacking, skiing, snowboarding, and fishing clothing and equipment—several shops carry good brandname selections and know how to fit equipment to individual people. **Rocky Mountain Outfitter** (135 Main St., Kalispell, 406/752-2446) specializes in hiking, backpacking, climbing, and skiing. Don Scharfe, the owner, is well known for first ascents on several of Glacier's peaks.

The folks at **The White Room** (130 Lupfer Ave., Whitefish, 406/862-7666) are the local telemark and backcountry ski experts, but in summer, the shop outfits hikers, backpackers, and climbers with gear and clothing. With two stores, **Sportsman Ski Haus** (145 Hutton

MADE IN MONTANA

Looking for souvenirs to take home? Keep a lookout for the blue Made in Montana logo. Only arts, crafts, food, and other products made by Montana residents and grown or produced within the state may bear the label. More than 2,600 businesses – some producing only one item – use the distinctive label.

What products bear the Made in Montana logo? Look for foods like coffee, jams and jellies, preserves, teas, pasta, salad dressings, barbecue sauces, herbs, cheese, jerky, and cookies. Personal health care products range from soaps and shampoos to lotions and oils. Toys, games, pet goodies, furniture, and clothing also may sport the Made in Montana logo, as can arts and crafts, like photography, music, lithographs, paintings, candles, and more.

One Made in Montana company, **Montana Coffee Traders** has been roasting beans in Flathead Valley since 1981. Their coffees celebrate Montana with the light- and medium-roasted Montana Blend and the light-roasted with a bit of vanilla and almond Glacier Blend. The Grizzly Blend promotes the protection of crucial grizzly bear habitat, and the Wild Rockies Blend promotes protection and restoration of wildlands habitat. Look for these products in local grocery stores, at four Montana Coffee Traders cafés and outlets (5810 Hwy. 93 South and 110 Central Ave., Whitefish; junction First Ave. W. and Hwy. 2, Columbia Falls; 328 W. Center St., Kalispell) or order by phone (800/345-5282; 406/862-7633) or online: www .coffeetraders.com.

If you need a Made in Montana product fix after you get home, check www.made inmontanausa.com for companies that sell Made in Montana products online.

Ranch Road, Kalispell, 406/755-6484, and 6475 Hwy. 93, Whitefish, 406/862-3111) carries gear and clothing for skiers, snowboarders, hikers, backpackers, anglers, hunters, campers, tennis players, bicyclists, and ice skaters. In three locations, **Stumptown Snowboards** (128 Central Ave., Whitefish, 406/862-0955; Depot Park Square, Kalispell, 406/756-5721; and Whitefish Mountain Resort, Whitefish, 406/862-5828) are the local experts in snowboarding and skateboarding with full equipment and clothing lines.

Maps and Books

To stock up on good topographical maps of Glacier and Flathead National Forest, you'll find the widest selection at Rocky Mountain Outfitter or Sportsman Ski Haus. Likewise, both shops carry guidebooks for hiking, fishing, and cross-country skiing in the area—a few field guides, too. You can also find guidebooks, natural history, Lewis and Clark, Montana history, and field guides for flowers, birds, and animals at **Books West** (101 Main St., Kalispell, 406/752-6900) and **Bookworks** (244 Spokane Ave., Whitefish, 406/862-4980).

SERVICES
Spas

Whitefish is home to two unique day spas. **Remedies Day Spa** (105 Wisconsin Ave., 406/863-9493, www.remediesdayspa.com, 10 A.M.–6 P.M., Tues.–Sat., Sun.–Mon. by appt.) makes all their products for massages, soaks, and wraps from natural food ingredients found in the kitchen. Located in one of the town's cozy older homes, the spa offers its signature kitchen fassage (massage for the face), whipped cream wrap, honey and cream hot rock foot rub, scrubs, soaks, and traditional massages ($10–135 per treatment). In an upscale quiet lakeside setting, **The Spa at Whitefish Lake** (1380 Wisconsin Ave., 406/863-4050, www.lodgeatwhitefish lake.com, 9 A.M.–7 P.M., daily, $95–175 per treatment) offers traditional spa facials, waxing, massage, scrubs, wraps, manicures, and

pedicures ($45–175). Their 90-minute Stone Silence uses hot Flathead Valley river stones and aromatherapy oils, like coconilla, in a deep muscle massage ($175).

Gyms, Pools, & Waterparks

Flathead Valley houses two large physical fitness complexes that include weights, cardio machines, indoor swimming pools, and hot tubs. To drop in for a day (adults $12, kids $5–10), call for current hours. **The Summit** (205 Sunnyview Ln., Kalispell, 406/751-4100) also has a climbing wall. **The Wave** (1250 Baker Ave., Whitefish, 406/862-2444) has a fun kids pool with a slide and water fountain.

Two seasonal outdoor pools attract kids in summer. Drop in for $2–5 per person. The recently renovated **Pinewood Family Aquatic Center** (925 4th Ave. W., Columbia Falls, 406/892-3500, June–Aug., Mon.–Sat.) has a bromine 25-meter pool and kids play pool. Kalispell opened their new **Woodland Park** outdoor pool in 2004 (406/758-7812, June–Aug, daily) with slides, a current stream, and diving pools. Call for current schedules.

Big Sky Waterslides (7211 Hwy. 2 E., Columbia Falls, 406/892-5025, June–Labor Day, daily 10 A.M.–8 P.M., $16–26) is a great place to take the kids to unwind after a hot day and a long drive. The park has 10 slides—both big and little—mini-golf, and bumper cars. After 4 P.M., rates drop a couple dollars per person.

Post Offices

Each major town in Flathead Valley has one post office; Kalispell has two. Hours are generally Monday–Friday 8:30 A.M.–5:30 P.M. and Saturday 10 A.M.–2 P.M. Exceptions are noted with locations as follows: Bigfork (265 Holt Dr., 406/837-4479), Columbia Falls (65 1st Ave. E., 406/892-7621, closes at 4:30 P.M. on weekdays), Kalispell (350 N. Meridian Rd., 406/755-6450; 248 First Ave. W., 406/755-0187, closes at 1 P.M. on Sat.), and Whitefish (424 Baker Ave., 406/862-2151). Somers (150 Somers Rd., 406/857-3330, Mon.–Fri.

8 A.M.–4:45 P.M., closed Sat.) and Lakeside (7196 Hwy. 93 S., 406/844-3224, Mon.–Fri. 7:30–11 A.M. and noon–4 P.M., closed Sat.) each have a post office, too.

Banks

Banks and ATMs are common in Flathead Valley, but several have branches in more than one town. Glacier Bank (www.glacier bank.com) has offices and ATMs in Kalispell (202 Main St., 406/756-4200), Bigfork (Old Town Center, 406/837-5980), Columbia Falls (822 Nucleus Ave., 406/892-7100), and Whitefish (319 E. 2nd St., 406/863-6300). First Interstate Bank (www.firstinterstate.com) is located in Kalispell (2 Main St., 406/756-5200) and Whitefish (3rd St. and Spokane Ave., 406/863-8888). First Citizens Bank is located in Columbia Falls (540 Nucleus Ave., 406/892-6800) and Kalispell (490 W. Reserve Dr., 406/758-8200).

Cell Phones and Internet

Contrary to Glacier's sketchy cell and Internet service, Flathead Valley sees nearly ubiquitous coverage. You may still encounter a few old-fashioned dial-up Internet in some motels, but most have added wireless and DSL Internet services. You can also get online in the local public county libraries on their computers for a limited amount of time in Kalispell (247 1st Ave. E., 406/758-5820), Columbia Falls (130 6th St. W., 406/892-5919), Bigfork (525 Electric Ave., 406/837-6976), and Whitefish (9 Spokane Ave., 406/862-6657). Each library has its own policies and hours (mostly Mon.–Sat., but hours vary by the day and library); call for details.

You won't find large Internet cafés with oodles of terminals, but a few cafés have one computer with Internet access available for patrons. **Montana Coffee Traders Cafes** (110 Central Ave., Whitefish, 406/862-7667; 1st Ave. W. and Hwy. 2, Columbia Falls, 406/892-7633) have a free Internet computer for browsing while you drink a latte. In Bigfork, you can get on the Internet at **Wild Mile Deli** (435 Bridge St., 406/837-3354, www.wildmiledeli .com, Mon.–Sat. 8 A.M.–9 P.M. and in summer on Sun. until 8 P.M.).

INFORMATION
Newspapers and Magazines

The local valley daily news comes in the *Daily Interlake* and the weekly news in the free *Flathead Beacon* with their daily updated online version at www.flatheadbeacon.com. You'll also find other northwestern Montana newspapers around, such as *Great Falls Tribune* and *The Missoulian*. Community weeklies, which cover everything from local events to politics, include Columbia Falls' *Hungry Horse News,* the *Whitefish Pilot,* and the *Bigfork Eagle.* For a peek into the local lifestyle, pick up a copy of the free quarterly *Flathead Living* magazine, found in the airport, hotels, stores, and resorts. For a look at northwestern Montana from a more down-to-earth approach, pick up a free copy of Missoula's *Independent.*

Emergencies

For medical, fire, or police emergencies in Flathead Valley, call 911. For medical emergencies in Whitefish and Columbia Falls, the new **North Valley Hospital** (1600 Hospital Way, Whitefish, 406/863-3631) is closest. For emergencies in Kalispell, Bigfork, and Lakeside, the newly upgraded **Kalispell Regional Medical Center** (310 Sunny View Ln., Kalispell, 406/752-5111) is closest.

City police stations have jurisdictions inside city limits only; much of Flathead Valley is covered by the county sheriff's department. In an emergency, when you dial 911, you don't have to think about whether you are inside city boundaries or not; your emergency will be relayed to the appropriate jurisdiction. But just in case, here are the police and sheriff contacts you may need: Flathead County Sheriff (920 S. Main St., Kalispell, 406/758-5585), Columbia Falls Police (130 6th St. W., 406/892-3234), Kalispell Police (312 1st Ave. E., 406/758-7780), and Whitefish Police (2nd St. and Hwy. 93, 406/863-2420).

Ranger Stations

With Flathead National Forest surrounding the Flathead Valley you can pick up maps, current trail and camping information, forest and ski conditions, and regulations in several national forest offices and ranger stations: Flathead National Forest and Talley Lake Ranger Station (650 Wolfpack Way, Kalispell, 406/758-5200) and Swan Lake Ranger Station (200 Ranger Station Rd., Bigfork, 406/837-7500).

BACKGROUND

The Land

GEOLOGY

Glacier's mountains tell a long story—approximately 1.6 billion years of geologic history. During that eon, sediment deposition, uplifts, erosion, intrusions, and glaciation all left their footprints. Sculpting Glacier and Waterton's scenery into its characteristic jagged parapets with swooping valleys, three geologic events occurred. First, sediments layered on top of each other. Then, mountains moved, and last, an ice age gouged formations.

Ever since, erosion relentlessly continues to shape the landscape. Wind and water chip away at peaks. Freeze-melt cycles wreak havoc on cliffs, prying off slabs of rock. Over time, weather leaves its thumbprint on the land.

Ancient Belt Sea

Approximately 1.6 billion to 800 million years ago, a shallow lake formed—the ancient Belt Sea. Covering parts of Washington, Idaho, Montana, and Canada, the Belt Sea accumulated sands washing down from adjacent highlands. Through pressure

© BECKY LOMAX

© BECKY LOMAX

Blackfoot Glacier is one of the park's larger glaciers.

and heat, dolomites, limestone, argillites, siltites, and quartzites layered like a colorful cake, one on top of the other. In a geologic feat found in very few places in North America, Glacier retained its sedimentary rock instead of watching it metamorphose over time. You can easily pick out its layers. Check at Logan Pass, where multihued sediments stripe Mount Clements.

Uplift of Mountains

Between 150 and 60 million years ago, massive tectonic movement along monstrous faults created mountains. During this uplift, a several-mile-thick Belt Sea chunk slid 50 miles east and atop much younger rock. Precambrian rocks—showing only pre-oxygen life forms from 1,500 million years older—shifted on top of younger Cretaceous volcanic and shale dinosaur-age rocks in a formation known as the **Lewis Overthrust Fault.** Look for its evidence where geologists originally discovered the fault in 1890: north of Marias Pass on U.S. Highway 2. In the whole Rocky Mountain

range, Glacier has the oldest exposed sedimentary rock because of the uplift.

During the uplift, rock heated and became pliable like bread dough. Sometimes it simply folded. Look for evidence of folding on Waterton Lake's east shore, above the Ptarmigan Tunnel trail, and between Josephine and Bullhead Lakes on the Swiftcurrent Trail.

Glaciation

More recently, glaciation carved the landscape. Two million years ago, the Pleistocene ice age engraved the park's topography through advancing and retreating glaciers. Only the tops of Glacier's highest peaks poked out as nunataks, a mountaintop completely surrounded by glacial ice. Ice—thousands of feet deep—gouged out valleys.

These ancient ice rivers bit into the landscape. When three or more glaciers gnawed away on a peak, a horn resulted, such as Mount Reynolds or Triple Divide. Sometimes two glaciers chewed ridges paper thin into arêtes; the Iceberg Wall even looks like a ragged

ANCIENT ROCKS

ARGILLITES

Of Glacier's colorful rock formations, the most striking is the argillite, an iron-rich mudstone formed in layers on the floor of the shallow ancient Belt Sea 800 million–1.6 billion years ago. Its blue-green and purple-red hues leap off mountainsides and intensify under water. This clay and silt contains iron, which changes to red hematite when exposed to oxygen, thus giving Grinnell argillite its burgundy color. The Appekunney argillite did not oxidize, remaining green. Driving down the east side of Going-to-the-Sun Road, notice the colors on Red Eagle Mountain. Also, look for both argillites on the Grinnell Glacier Trail, the Iceberg Trail, at Red Rocks Falls, and while rafting on the Middle Fork of the Flathead.

RIPPLE ROCK AND MUD CRACKS

Raindrop impressions, water ripples, and mud cracks remain etched in stone – all evidence of ancient sea origins. Ripple rocks, found most often in red, blue, or beige layers, look like sands on a beach where waves left their marks. As the sea dried up, sediments compacted and cracked, similar to a mud puddle drying up in a driveway. Large blocks show webs of cracks filled in with other sediments – an effect looking like dull maroon or turquoise tiles. Look for slabs with both ripple marks and mud cracks along the Many Glacier Valley trails.

MAGMA INTRUSIONS

Don't be fooled. Yes, Granite Park and its namesake chalet are dubbed for the igneous rock; however, no granite is in Glacier. When early prospectors found Purcell lava or pillow lava – rounded blue-gray formations – they mistakenly called it granite. This lava intruded up through sediment layers, billowing out in ropey coils and bubbles. See this lava on the Highline Trail between Granite Park Chalet and Ahern Pass.

One of the most visible magma intrusions is the diorite or Purcell sill. It appears from a distance like a 100-foot-thick horizontal black line sandwiched between thinner whitish layers.

When magma boiled up between limestone layers 800 million years ago, it superheated the limestone, turning it white. You can see the diorite sill from Many Glacier Road, visible as a thick dark line on Mount Gould and Mount Wilbur. Hikers see it as black jagged teeth above Iceberg Lake or the solid line above Grinnell Glacier. The Highline Trail passes through the sill approximately one mile beyond Haystack Saddle. Look for a crystallized green sheen covering deep black. You'll notice your footing changes abruptly when you step onto the sill; instead of broken shard slabs, you'll find something more solid – something volcanic.

STROMATOLITES

The Belt Sea became habitat for blue-green algae. Six species of this petite primitive life formed there, doing what algae does best: As sunlight hit the algae, its cells removed carbon dioxide from the water and gave off oxygen. During this process, calcium carbonate formed into stromatolites, a round rock formation looking like Van Gogh's *Starry Night* swirls. You'll find stromatolites along Going-to-the-Sun Road and on the Highline Trail before climbing up to Haystack Saddle. The presence of these algae forms in the Belt Sea produced an oxygen-rich atmosphere that allowed other life forms to develop – yes, humans.

© BECKY LOMAX

stromatolites

"fish bone"—its meaning in French. Large lakes filled in U-shaped valleys, the mark of glacial carving: Compare the rounded valley floor of the McDonald Valley with river-carving, such as Grand Canyon's V shape. As glaciers retreated, they left large piles of debris—rocks, sand, and gravel—in the form of moraines, like a big pile of dirty laundry. Large moraines like Howe Ridge remain from Pleistocene ice, whereas smaller rubble piles in Grinnell or Sperry Glacier basins resulted this past century.

In holes where the ice carved deeper, melting water made tarns or small glacial lakes. The upper ends of glaciers often carved out cirques, steep-walled round basins such as Avalanche Lake basin. Lower ends of glaciers plummeted off cliffs, forming hanging valleys: Bird Woman Falls dives from a hanging valley suspended between Mount Oberlin and Mount Cannon. As you hike, look for glacial striations or large scratches on rocks where ice abraded the surface. Check for striations on erratics—large boulders strewn about from receding glaciers—on the Avalanche Lake trail.

While ancient Pleistocene ice melted in Glacier about 12,000 years ago, several miniature ice ages have shaped the land. The glaciers currently in the park are products of the last 8,000 years. During the **Little Ice Age**, 1500–1850, most glaciers grew. Park tree ring studies show evidence of more than 150 glaciers in the early 1900s. Less than 25 percent of those remain in Glacier today, the largest of which is Blackfoot Glacier at 0.7 square miles. Climatologists expect the 25 remaining glaciers to melt by 2030. Sadly, Waterton no longer has active glaciers, only snowfields, but at Cameron Lake, you can look across the border to Herbst Glacier.

Glaciers and Snowfields

In Glacier Park, it's often hard to tell the difference between a glacier and a snowfield. In early summer, they look the same, covered with fresh snow from winter. But they are distinctly different.

It's simple math. When more snow adds than melts annually, glaciers form. The snow transforms into icy grains through freeze-thaw cycles. Snows build up on the upper end of glaciers and push down, compressing ice crystals. Over years, the ice compacts in layers, mounting into a huge mass with a rigid surface and supple base.

Glaciers are moving ice—moving so slow that you can't detect movement by watching them. Aided by gravity, ice presses down, forming a thin elastic barrier that carries the ice mass toward the glacier's toe where it may calve off in chunks. Sperry Glacier moves about 12–20 feet per year, while Grinnell moves much more—30–50 feet per year. When the ice travels over convex ground features, its surface cracks, forming crevasses sometimes hundreds of feet thick. When hidden, crevasses make glaciers deadly for travel.

To move, a certain amount of ice is needed—usually a surface of 25 acres and depth of 100 feet. Less than that, and the ice becomes static—just a permanent snowfield. Moving glaciers behave similarly to a bulldozer, gouging out broad valleys. You'll often be able to recognize them by their tell-tale debris bands—lines of rocks on the surface. When the ice recedes, or melts, rocks and debris are left in large moraines or as erratics. Contrary to the ice fields that Glacier once had, today's glaciers are considerably smaller and fast on their way to becoming snowfields.

CLIMATE

Glacier and Waterton live on a collision course for both Arctic Continental and Pacific Maritime weather. Wet weather races in from the Pacific, with accompanying moderate temperatures. Precipitation results in an annual average 29 inches of rainfall and 157 inches of snow near West Glacier. Waterton also sees more precipitation than the rest of Alberta.

Although the east side of the Continental Divide sees just as much precipitation as the west, one factor produces more extremes—wind. While winter winds often blow snow

PRECIPITATION AND TEMPERATURES

Taken from West Glacier.

Month	Average number rainy/snowy days	Average snowfall (inches)	Average temperature (low-high)
Jan.	17	40	12-28°F
Feb.	13	23	18-34°F
Mar.	13	15	22-41°F
Apr.	11	4	29-52°F
May	13	0.4	37-64°F
June	13	0.2	44-71°F
July	9	0	47-79°F
Aug.	9	0	46-78°F
Sept.	9	0.1	39-67°F
Oct.	11	2	32-53°F
Nov.	15	17	25-37°F
Dec.	17	38	18-30°F

from slopes, providing forage for ungulates, they also have been known to blow trains off their tracks near East Glacier. Several east-side high passes are notorious for raging unpredictable winds causing hikers to crawl on all fours. **Chinook** winds—warm winds with speeds reaching over 90 miles per hour—happen any time of the year, but they are most obvious in winter. Native Americans called them "snow eaters" for the snow they rapidly melted. When a chinook descends the Continental Divide's east side, it becomes warm and dry, fooling trees into thinking it's spring and catapulting their cells into spring water absorption. When temperatures plummet again, the cold freezes the water in their cells and kills the trees. This "winter kill" accounts for the number of dead

silver trunks dotting east-side forests, especially visible in Two Medicine and Waterton.

Glacier is a country of weather extremes. Its maximum high hit 99°F while its low kneeled to -36°F. Elevation makes a huge difference, too: While Lake McDonald beckons swimmers to sunny beaches, frigid winds can rage across Logan Pass. Sometimes, you can experience four seasons in one day, so always dress in layers and carry extra clothing, no matter what the weather looks like in the morning! Rains move in fast, and snows may fall any month of the year.

Spring

While March, April, and May are appealing off-months to travel, in Glacier they are wet and cold, still clinging to winter. Snow buries the high country and much of the lowlands until late spring. May is rather moody: It can be extremely wet with frequent late snowstorms and avalanches in the high country.

Summer

During summer months, June habitually monsoons, but July and August usher in warmer, drier skies. Often higher elevations are substantially cooler—up to 15 degrees chillier than valley floors. While cool breezes are welcome on baking summer days, they can also bring snows in August.

Fall

Autumn begets lovely bug-free warm days and cool nights. While golds paint aspen and larch trees, temperatures bounce through extremes—from highs of 75–80°F during the day to below freezing at night. Seemingly schizophrenic, rains and snows descend for a few days followed by clearing and warming trends.

Winter

Winter temperatures in Glacier vary depending on elevation but mostly hang in the 10–25°F

© BECKY LOMAX

blanketflower

range, producing voluminous snows. Logan Pass is buried under 350–650 inches of snow per year. Temperatures can spike above freezing, with its companion rain, or below zero with an Arctic front. Because chinooks visit Waterton more than the rest of Alberta, it is one of the warmest places in the province in winter. While the Canadian prairies suffer below freezing temperatures, Waterton may be reveling in 30–50°F.

Daylight

Given Glacier's latitude and placement on the mountain time zone's western edge, hours of daylight fluctuate wildly during the year. In June, over 16 hours of sun leaves lots of time to play outdoors. First light fades in around 5 A.M., and dark doesn't descend until almost 11 P.M. By late August, however, it's dark at 9 P.M. with daylight shortening throughout autumn. At the winter solstice, the sun rises around 8 A.M. and sets at 4:30 P.M.

FLORA

Glacier and Waterton parks sprout rich floral diversity. Forests, prairies, and tundra all burgeon with different vegetation specific to elevation, habitat, and weather. Glacier is home to 46 rare Montana plants, four of which are found only in the park. In addition, the park houses 1,150 vascular plants, 400 mosses, and 275 lichens. It harbors species at the edges of their distribution: Great Plains flowers to arctic bulbs. The Lake McDonald Valley shelters nearly 100 Pacific Coast species.

For a small park, Waterton has a corner on the rare plant market: 30 grow only within its borders, including the rarest plant, the Waterton moonwort. Waterton can also brag a total of 970 vascular plants, 190 mosses, and 220 lichens, ironically chalking up more diversity than its larger park sisters to the north— Banff and Jasper.

Grasslands

More than 100 grass species proliferate across the Glacier-Waterton bunchgrass prairies, which poke into valley drainages on the Continental

Divide's east side and have been preserved by natural fires in the North Fork Valley. Waterton houses one of two prairie lands in the Canadian national park system and one of North America's last places where grizzly bears range into historic grassland habitat.

Aspen Parklands

Aspens dominate east-side slopes, populating the valleys of Many Glacier, Belly River, Two Medicine, St. Mary, and Waterton. Harboring elk herds in winter and broken by wildflower meadows of arrowleaf balsamroot and sticky geranium, groves of quaking aspen shake their leaves in the slightest breeze—hence their name. They mark the transition between grasslands and coniferous forests.

Montane Forests

In low- to mid-elevations, dense montane forests mix poplars and firs, which vary substantially depending on moisture and winds. Cedar-hemlock forests with birch dominate wetter western valleys, while drier slopes yield limber pine, Douglas fir, white spruce, and lodgepole pines. The western larch, a conifer that loses its needles each winter, also inhabits lower elevation forests. Below the canopy, twinflower, foamflower, and orchids find their niche along with juniper, Pacific yew, thimbleberry, and serviceberry.

Subalpine Zone

Between 5,000 and 7,000 feet in elevation, stately forests surrender to subalpine firs, dwarfed and gnarled in their struggle to survive in a short growing season, brutal winds, frigid temperatures, and heavy snows. For survival, trees develop a bent, stunted krummholz, forming a protective mat rather than growing upright. Whitebark pine and Englemann spruce also sneak into the subalpine. Between tree islands, lush mountain meadows bloom with a colorful array of columbine, bog gentians, valerian, fleabane, and beargrass.

Alpine Tundra

Nearly 25 percent of Glacier and Waterton is alpine tundra. Above the tree line, the land appears to be barren rock. But a host of miniature plants adapt to the harsh conditions of high winds, short summers, cold temperatures, and little soil. Low-growing perennials and hairy leaves provide protection from winds and the sun's high elevation intensity. Mats of pink moss campion, delicate spotted saxifrage, purple butterworts, and Jones columbine fling their energies into showy flowers, however tiny they may be.

Huckleberries

Of all Glacier's flora, the huckleberry draws the most attention. While several varieties grow throughout the park, from lowlands to subalpine, they all have one thing in common: a sweet berry. Look for a low-growing shrub with small green to reddish leaves. About the size of a small blueberry, huckleberries ripen into a rich dark purple-blue. You can find lowland berries in late July, but mid-August to early September is known as "huck" season. Grizzly bears carbo-load on hucks to survive winter.

Wildflowers

Glacier's wildflowers peak in late June–early August, depending on snowmelt and elevation. Early summer brings on fields of yellow glacier lilies and white spring beauties poking their buds up through the snowpack. In lower elevations, large white heads of cow parsnip bloom alongside roads and continue into higher elevations as summer progresses. Some years, beargrass—a tall white lily—blooms so thickly in July on subalpine slopes that the hillsides look snow-covered. Paintbrush spews fields in yellow, red, fuchsia, white, salmon, and orange. Just a reminder: Picking flowers in national parks is prohibited. Use your camera instead.

Poisonous Plants

Very few plants in Glacier are poisonous to the touch. Several can be toxic if eaten, so it's best to avoid eating plants or mushrooms unless you know what you're doing. Most of Glacier is inhospitable for poison ivy, oak, and sumac. But keep your eyes open for stinging nettles, which line many of the trails: Although not poisonous, they leave an obnoxious itchy residue on contact. A few people have allergic reactions to cow parsnip: If you have sensitive skin, wear long sleeves and long pants to avoid contact with the plant.

FAUNA

Glacier and Waterton teem with wildlife: 24 fish species, 63 mammals, and 272 birds. The Crown of the Continent remains a North American bastion of an intact ecosystem, with many animals present that were here before the human impact of the past 150 years. In the late 1980s, wolves migrated from Canada, completing more of the original members of Glacier's wildlife family. Only mountain bison and woodland caribou remain extirpated.

Bears

Two bears roam Glacier's mountains: the black bear and grizzly bear. Omnivores and opportunistic feeders, bears will eat anything that is easy pickings. Spending most of their waking time eating to gain 100–150 pounds before winter, Glacier's bears feed on a diet heavy in plant matter: bulbs, roots, berries, shoots, and flowers. Ants, insects, carrion, and ground squirrels fill in proteins. Contrary to popular opinion, humans are not on their menu of favorite foods.

Because bears learn fast, they adapt quickly to new food sources, be it a pack dropped by the side of the trail or dog food left out in a campground. For this reason, Glacier imposes strict rules for handling food and garbage in picnic sites, campgrounds, and backcountry areas. All garbage cans and dumpsters are bear resistant. Bears that eat human foods and garbage find themselves moved to a new habitat, or worse, destroyed.

Because grizzly and black bears are integral to Glacier's ecosystem, the National Park Service employs several bear rangers whose jobs entail monitoring and deterring bears from trouble. For bruins who hang near roadways and front country campgrounds, the

bear team uses hazing methods—loud noises, gunshots, pellet beanbags, and sometimes Karelian bear dogs—in an attempt to teach bears to stay away. Nuisance bears are transplanted to remote park drainages or destroyed if their offenses warrant. "A fed bear is a dead bear," the truism goes. For a bear that dabbles in human food often becomes aggressive to seek more.

Bears are one of the least productive mammals, giving birth once every two or three years. While black bears have a gestation of 220 days, for grizzlies spring mating season is followed by delayed implantation, where the fertilized eggs simply "hang" until winter. Pending the sow's health, the egg or eggs implant, resulting in one, two, or three cubs born during winter's deep sleep. If her health is severely threatened, she may abort the egg instead.

Bears don't actually hibernate, for their respiration and pulse remain close to normal. Instead, they enter a deep sleep in which the body temperature drops slightly. Before crawling into their dens, they scarf down mountain ash berries, rough grasses, and twigs to form an anal plug—which inhibits eating, urinating, or defecating during winter. Bears emerge in the spring ravenously hungry, bee-lining for avalanche chutes to rummage for snow-buried carcasses.

Megafauna

Megafauna are the big animals everyone wants to see, like bears. Glacier and Waterton harbor three elusive members of the cat family: mountain lions, bobcats, and Canadian lynx. Quiet hunters and mostly nocturnal, cats may see you while you have no idea that they linger nearby. For mountain lion, deer are tops on the menu, while lynx favor snowshoe hares. Both cat populations rise and fall with their prey populations. With keen eyesight and hearing, these three cats stalk their prey, the lynx with the help of large "snowshoe" feet.

Gray wolf packs inhabit fairly large ranges, 100–300 square miles, so chances of seeing a wolf are fairly rare in spite of the fact that they have a relatively high reproductive potential

Mule deer are much larger than their white-tailed cousins.

of 4–7 pups per year. Coyotes, foxes, wolverines, and badgers round out the large carnivore list. Although wolverines are the most obscure of creatures, Glacier provides prime habitat with remote terrain, snowfields, and plentiful ground squirrels. Many hikers spot them along the Highline Trail.

Ungulates crowd Glacier's high and low country. Moose frequently browse in streambeds and along lakes. Keep your eyes open in the Swiftcurrent Valley, especially around bogs and willow thickets. Elk, mule deer, and white-tailed deer live park-wide at tree line and below, while mountain goats and bighorn sheep cling to rocky alpine slopes. During late spring, goats congregate at the Goat Lick on U.S. Highway 2 looking for minerals for their depleted systems. They also are a regal staple at Logan Pass.

In Waterton, a small bison herd grazes in a paddock—a tiny remnant of what once roamed the prairies here by the thousands. Visitors may drive the viewing road and hike a short overlook trail to see the bison.

Small Mammals

Members of the weasel family—fishers, pine martens, minks, and weasels—inhabit forests and waterways. The short-tailed weasel changes color in winter: Its fur becomes white, except for the small black tip of its tail. Snowshoe hares also change to white in winter, their large namesake feet providing extra flotation on snow. In subalpine country, a chorus of eeks, screams, and squeaks bounce through rockfalls. The noisemakers are pikas, which look like big-eared tail-less mice, and the ubiquitous Columbian ground squirrel, easily recognized by its reddish tint. Looking like fat housecat-size fur balls, hoary marmots splay on rocks sunning themselves. Scampering between high alpine rocks, golden-mantled ground squirrels look like oversized chipmunks with their tell-tale gold stripes.

Fish

With 750 lakes and 1,500 miles of streams, Glacier provides abundant habitat for fish, both native and nonnative species. Bull trout, westslope cutthroat, and whitefish are among the 17 species of native fish. To promote recreational fishing, lakes were stocked with nonnative fish such as rainbow trout, arctic grayling, and kokanee salmon. Introduced species flourished, threatening native fish whose populations are now waning. Since the 1970s, fish are no longer stocked in Glacier or Waterton.

Fish in Waterton Lakes feed on a tiny crustacean, the opossum shrimp—a relic species that inhabited the area prior to the Pleistocene Ice Age. As glaciers melted, the tiny shrimp returned through the Missouri-Mississippi watersheds. Spending its entire life in darkness, it lingers on the lake bottom during the day, surfacing only at night.

Birds

With more than 200 species of birds here, every park visitor can see wildlife. Bird checklists are available at visitors centers in both parks to assist with identification. In summer, trees teem with songbirds—cedar waxwings, thrushes, chickadees, vireos, sparrows, dark-eyed juncos, and finches, to name a few. Brilliant-colored western tanagers and striking mountain bluebirds flit between treetops. Woodpeckers, including the large, red-capped pileated woodpecker, pound at bark in search of bugs. Ground birds such as the chicken-sized grouse surprise hikers on trails, while smaller ptarmigans—whose plumage turns white in winter—blend with summer coloration into rocks. Steller's jays and Clark's nutcrackers add to the cacophony, as do common sightings of rufous and calliope hummingbirds.

Because of Glacier's profuse rivers, streams, and lakes, waterfowl finds plentiful habitat. Loons, grebes, mergansers, and goldeneyes fill almost every lake, while harlequin ducks migrate to rapidly flowing streams in spring for nesting. Tundra swans use Glacier's lakes as a stopping ground during their annual migration to and from their arctic breeding grounds. American dippers, or water ouzels, nest near waterfalls: The dark bird's obvious bobbing action is a dead giveaway as to species.

Raptors

Nothing is more dramatic than sighting a golden eagle soaring along the Continental Divide. Common nesters in remote spots, goldens often return yearly to the same location. Glacier also boasts about 10 nesting pairs of bald eagles, who can be seen along waterways year-round. Above lakes, ospreys dive for fish from impressive heights while red-tailed hawks and American kestrels hover over field mice. Listen carefully, for nights are haunted by the small pygmy owl's "whew" and the great horned owl's six deep hoots.

Snakes and Insects

For the most part, Glacier and Waterton are devoid of poisonous snakes and spiders. The climate is too harsh for rattlesnakes. However, you will find garter and bull snakes on some trails. Due to colder conditions, spiders here are small, although a bite may produce swelling or an allergic reaction.

ENVIRONMENTAL ISSUES
Global Warming

Although earth's temperatures have spiked tropically and dropped icily several times, the current increase in global temperatures affects Glacier Park. While glaciers have shrunk since 1850, climatologists predict that the park's namesakes will melt by 2030—producing not just a loss of ice, but a shift in flora and fauna. As temperatures warm, the tree line advances up in elevation, encroaching on alpine zones. Glacier's tree line was once 3,200 feet lower than today; how far it will climb is unknown.

A rising tree line will cause basins scoured clean by ice and blooming with wildflower meadows to succumb to heavy forests of spruce, fir, pines, shrubs, and bushes. Plants at the fringes of their distribution may disappear. Shifts in habitat may force wildlife to change elevation or latitude in search of food sources. Species such as the heat-intolerant pika may suffer extinction. Because of Glacier's easily accessed alpine areas, scientists are monitoring melt rates of Grinnell and Sperry Glaciers to help predict future impacts on the park's biodiversity.

Endangered and Threatened Species

In the 1800s, more than 100,000 **grizzly bears** roamed grasslands and foothills in the Lower 48. Today, in less than 1 percent of their historic range, fewer than 1,000 grizzlies forage for food. In 1975, grizzly bears were listed as threatened on the Endangered Species List. Since then, a bear management plan assisted recovery in Glacier, Flathead National Forest, and the Bob Marshall Wilderness Complex.

In an effort to count the grizzly population, the U.S. Geological Survey conducted two studies 1998–2004 in Glacier and surrounding lands. Collecting scat and bear hairs via barb-wire stapled to rub trees and surrounding scent lures, scientists used tweezers to bag the hairs for DNA genotyping of species, sex, and individual. The study found a healthy grizzly population with 765 bears spread across 7.8 million acres in northwest Montana. Glacier houses the

densest populations. While Yellowstone's grizzlies have been delisted from the Endangered Species List, Glacier's population as of 2009 has not.

Grizzlies require a large range; many travel outside the park and across international boundaries. Human pressures from road and house building, agriculture and livestock, timber harvesting, and mineral, oil, and gas mining impact their habitat. Just outside Waterton, legal Canadian hunting and predator-control programs subject bears to high mortality rates. In northwest Montana, poaching, management actions, and private landowners account for the deaths of 20–30 grizzlies per year. While bad berry crops and encroaching rural developments may contribute to bears getting into trouble, inappropriate attractants—garbage, livestock grain, and bird feeders—lead to many of the deaths.

Gray wolves once ranged throughout most of North America. By 1920, predator-control programs extirpated them from Glacier and Waterton; in 1973 they were placed on the

Bighorn sheep ewes sport shorter horns than their male counterparts.

© BECKY LOMAX

Endangered Species List. In 1986, following the natural migration of the Magic Pack from Canada, Glacier saw its first litter of pups born in over 50 years. By 2007, statewide numbers climbed to over 400, pushing the animal toward a stable enough status that the federal government pursued delisting in 2008.

Of all the ungulates, **bighorn sheep** face the greatest risk. Once widely scattered across most western mountain ranges, the sheep today live in fragmented pockets. Hunting, disease, agriculture, mining, competition for food, fire-suppression policies, and habitat destruction forced this grassland forager into the more rugged fringes of its historic range. Today, 400–600 bighorn sheep graze in Glacier, with an additional population in Waterton. Recent studies used GPS radio collars to track the sheep, and DNA samples revealed two genetically different populations in northern and southern Glacier.

Recorded sightings of the **Canada lynx** have declined substantially in the past 40 years, prompting it to be listed in 2000 as threatened. In coniferous forests, the lynx follows its chief prey, the snowshoe hare, with the cat's cyclical rising and falling populations in sync with hare numbers. Ongoing park studies follow tracks in snow to ascertain the lynx's status.

Two indigenous trout descended from ice-age lakes that formed as glaciers retreated: **westslope cutthroat trout** and **bull trout.** Glacier provides a stronghold for these fish; while bull trout populations have declined 90 percent (it's been listed since 1998 as an endangered species), pure cutthroat have yet to be placed on the list. While habitat degradation and overfishing contributed to the demise, one menace came from nonnative species stocked for recreational fishing, turning them into fast cuisine for lake trout. But the species sees the most danger through hybridization with other trout, like rainbows. Removing nonnative species is impractical; the park uses fishing regulations to protect pure populations.

Fire

Like snow, wind, or rain, lightning-caused fire is a natural process. It is healthy for the ecosystem, for it removes bug infestations, reduces deadfall and nonnative plants, releases nutrients into the soil like a good fertilizer, and maintains a natural mix of vegetation. Following years of heavy fire suppression policy, forest fuels built up to high levels in the park. Each summer, Glacier averages 13 fires with 5,000 acres burned; some summers, like 2003 when 150,000 acres blazed, see more. Most fires burn unevenly, creating a mosaic of charred timber amid greenery. That patchwork ultimately leads to more vegetation and wildlife diversity. In the natural process of regrowth, the burns flourish rapidly with wildflowers, birds, and wildlife.

Historical Protection

Glacier has substantial cultural and historical resources, but to date, the park has no full-time archaeologist to oversee protection of archaeological and historic assets. At 50 years old, artifacts—even garbage dumps—are considered historic, according to federal law. To date, Glacier has identified 429 archaeological sites and Waterton 358. But many have not been cataloged. While the park does all it can to protect its cultural and historical resources, more funding is needed for adequate protection.

Non-Native Plants

Sometimes the prettiest flowers can be the most noxious. Such is the case with exotic weeds such as spotted knapweed, St. John's wort, and the oxeye daisy, introduced through horses, cars, livestock, and railroads. With their broad roots, high seed production, and chemicals that inhibit growth of native plants, these exotics infest grasslands, lessening diversity and reducing wildlife habitat. Both Parks Canada and Glacier's National Park Service curb the spread of nonnative plants through roadside mowing, herbicides, or natural means.

History

Human use of the Crown of the Continent dates back 10,000 years. Evidence of fishing in Upper Waterton Lake and driving bison across the Blakiston Valley prairies most likely belonged to the ancestors of native peoples living near Glacier and Waterton today.

Native Americans

Spanning what became the U.S.-Canadian border, the **Blackfeet** or Nitsitapii (meaning "real people") included three nomadic groups who based much of their livelihood on hunting bison in the vast prairies on the Continental Divide's east side. The most northerly group, the Sitsika or Blackfoot, were the first to meet European traders. (To refer to the collective, Canada prefers Blackfoot, but Blackfeet is used the U.S.) The other two—the Blood or Kainai and Piegan or Piikani—made up the southern groups. For thousands of years, according to the Blackfeet, their lands ran between the Saskatchewan and Yellowstone Rivers.

During summers, Blackfeet groups convened for the Sun Dance, a ceremony held on the plains. But during the rest of the spring and summer, efforts focused individually on stocking food: hunting, digging roots, and collecting berries. As bison moved northwest to their wintering ranges, groups met again for hunts—sometimes buffalo jumps, where hunters funneled bison over a cliff. Afterward, they returned to their winter camps sheltered in deep mountain forests.

For the Blackfeet, the Glacier Park area was known as the "Backbone of the World." Used for spiritual sanctuary, the mountains provided places for prayer and sacred ceremonies. A place to gather guidance, the mountains also yielded holy plants and roots used for their healing properties. Some of Glacier's peaks, lakes, and rivers still use Blackfeet names today: Going-to-the-Sun Mountain, Two Medicine Lake, Pitamakin Pass, and Running Eagle Falls.

On the Continental Divide's west side, the **Salish** and **Kootenai** hunted, trapped, and fished, ranging east over the mountains on annual bison hunts. Known as the Ktunaxa, the Kootenai (variously spelled Kootenay, Cootenay, or Kutenai) comprised seven bands spanning the western Rockies from southern Alberta to Missoula, Montana. The Kootenai typically used mountain passes like Marias, Cut Bank, Red Eagle, and Brown to cross through Glacier and Waterton to hunt, and the Blackfeet used the same passes for raiding parties. For the Kootenai, the Lake McDonald area was a place for sacred dances, hence its original name of Sacred Dancing Waters.

Two other native people lived in the Glacier-Waterton vicinity: the Assiniboines or Stoney Indians and the Gros Ventres. Both of these tribes find namesakes in the park, with a lake, a pass, and three peaks named for the Stoney. In the park's northeast corner, the Gros Ventres, which means Big Belly, left their names on the Belly River and Mokowanis (which means "Big Belly") drainages with Gros Ventre Falls. Little evidence remains in the park of the presence of the Flathead and Kalispel tribes.

As westward expansion brought more people, Native Americans moved within government reservation boundaries: The Sitsikas settled near Calgary. The Blood moved onto a reserve adjacent to Waterton, while the Piegans, the largest of the three Blackfeet groups, split into two, with the North Piikani settling near Pincher Creek and the South Piikani on the Continental Divide's west side in Montana. The Salish and Kootenai moved to the Flathead Reservation southwest of Glacier. Smallpox and whiskey took their toll on the tribes.

Development

In 1803, when Lewis and Clark came west, they bypassed Glacier. At Camp Disappointment located today on the Blackfeet Reservation, they came within 25 air miles, but never found Marias Pass—one of the lowest passes through the treacherous Rocky Mountains.

Soon, French, Spanish, and English fur

trappers entered the Glacier-Waterton area. Westward expansion also brought miners looking for copper and gold. But lands between the Continental Divide and the plains belonged to the Blackfeet. In 1895, the federal government negotiated a settlement with the Blackfeet to purchase the land. During the turn of the 20th century, mining boomed in Many Glacier and Rising Sun. Western Canada's first oil well spewed at Waterton, and Montana's first at Kintla Lake. Neither oil nor mining paid off, both easily supplanted by burgeoning tourism.

Building a Park

Pressure to find rail passages through the northern Rockies began in the mid-1800s. When Great Northern Railway finally succeeded in 1891 to lay track over the Continental Divide, the face of Glacier changed. The railroad company needed a destination for its wealthy train riders. Their economic needs and pressure from preservationists spawned the idea of Glacier National Park, which finally became

reality on May 11, 1910. The park celebrates its centennial in 2010. (Check www.glaciercentennial.org for events.)

William Logan—for whom Logan Pass is named—took the reins as the first superintendent of the nation's 10th park. Charged with building a headquarters, hiring rangers, constructing trails, and surveying for a road through the park's interior, Logan did little his first year but put out fires. Literally. Over 100,000 acres went up in flames. His second summer finally saw steps toward readying Glacier for visitors.

Great Northern Railway created many of the park's attractions: hotels, tent camps, chalets, roads, trails, and boats. Competing for travel time and dollars from wealthy Americans taking steamships to Europe, the railroad pitched the slogan, "See America First" to lure vacationers to Glacier, which became known as "America's Switzerland."

Horse concessionaires operating from every hotel and chalet in the park merged

© BECKY LOMAX

Granite Park Chalet was built in 1914 opposite Heavens Peak.

into the Park Saddle Horse Company. By the mid-1920s, horseback provided the way to see the park. At its peak, the Park Saddle Horse Company operated more than 1,000 horses and led more than 10,000 visitors through the park each summer.

The demand for a road bisecting Glacier's interior increased. Although the western portion began in 1919, the 52-mile project was not completed until 1932. The opening of Going-to-the-Sun Road ushered in a new era of park visitation. A fleet of 32 red buses hit Glacier's roads for touring. With increased motorized travel, camping gaining popularity, and budget motor inns added to Great Northern's property collections, saddle trips and the chalets met their demise.

During World War II and the Depression, travel curtailment and fuel conservation dropped visitation significantly, forcing hotels and chalets to close. Several fell into massive disrepair and had to be razed. Bus tour business began to usurp rail travel, the Park Saddle Horse Company folded, private car travel increased, and the railroad's lodges lost $500,000 annually, which it offset with ridership profits. Finally, in 1954, Great Northern unloaded the remaining chalets on the National Park Service for $1. In 1957, the company sold the rest of the hotel chain to a Minneapolis hotel corporation, which subsequently sold three years later to Glacier Park, Inc., which would sell again 21 years later to Dial Corporation.

International Peace Park

In 1932, Glacier and Waterton took to front headlines as the world's first peace park. Due to the brainchild and work of Alberta and Montana chapters of Rotary International, lobbying efforts paid off, as the Canadian Parliament and U.S. Congress officially recognized the continuity between the parks. With credit to the longest undefended border in the world, they dedicated the parks together as **Waterton-Glacier International Peace Park.**

Biosphere Reserve and World Heritage Site

In 1976, UNESCO (United Nations Educational, Scientific, and Cultural Organization) designated Glacier Park as a Biosphere Reserve. Three years later, Waterton Lakes received the same recognition. As a Biosphere Reserve, the parks are recognized for their huge diversity of wildlife, plants, and habitats. In 1995, UNESCO followed the biosphere designation with declaring the parks a World Heritage Site for natural beauty and unique geological features, such as Triple Divide Peak and the continent's oldest exposed sedimentary rock.

Recreation

WALKING TRAILS

Glacier is known as a "hiker's park," and no wonder! With 732 miles of trails, everything from a short, leisurely amble to a multiday top-of-the-world Continental Divide backpack trip crams in its borders. Ranger stations and visitors centers have brochures describing hikes in their locales; the same information is also available online (www.nps.gov/glac).

No permits are needed for day hikes—only for backpacking. However, if you plan on day hiking across the Blackfeet Reservation, you will need a $10 conservation permit, available in East Glacier, Browning, and at St. Mary Visitor Center.

Both free and pay shuttles (see *Essentials*) hit trailheads. Shuttles particularly ease hiking point-to-point routes on day trips or backpacking.

Trail Status

Conditions on Glacier's trails vary significantly depending on the season, elevation, recent severe weather, and bear closures. Swinging and

EDUCATION

One of the best ways to become intimate with Glacier's wildlife, geology, birds, and cultural history is to join the regionally and nationally recognized experts from **Glacier Institute** (406/756-1211, www.glacierinstitute.org, $50-1,750). Offered year-round, the courses blend in-the-field experiences with hands-on learning at Big Creek Camp in the North Fork or Glacier Field Camp near the west park entrance. You can join a sea-kayaking trip to Wild Horse Island in Flathead Lake, track animals on snowshoes, hike to Ptarmigan Tunnel to look at Glacier's ancient geology, or take a nighttime walk to look for owls. College credit is available for some of the workshops and classes. Adult seminars cover wilderness first-aid to art, photography, science, and ecology. Youth camps for ages 7-16 emphasize outdoor science. Single-day courses average $60-90; most multi-day courses range $105-400, including lodging and meals.

For those looking for an intimate experience in Glacier, **Glacier National Park Associates** (406/387-4299, www.nps.gov /glac) looks for volunteers each summer for backcountry projects. Some tasks restore historic log structures, reconstruct damaged trails and backcountry campsites, and transplant seedlings from the park's native-plant nursery. Past projects have included work at Sperry Chalet and backcountry patrol cabins. Led by a backcountry ranger intern, participants usually work on one project during a three- to five-day stay in the backcountry. No special skills are required – just a desire to help.

---

plank bridges across rivers and creeks are not installed until late May–June. Some years, bridges have been installed, only to be removed a few weeks later to wait for rivers swollen with runoff to subside. Most years, higher passes are snowbound until early July, and steep snowfields often inhibit hiking on the Highline Trail until then. Large drifts across trails must be blasted to open the paths even late in July. Ptarmigan Tunnel's doors usually open early July–early October. To find out about trail conditions before hiking, you can stop at ranger stations and visitors centers for updates or consult Trail Status Reports (usually updated June–Sept. only) on the park's website.

Signage

All park trailheads and junctions have excellent signage. Be prepared, however, to convert kilometers to miles in your head to understand distances. Some signs show both kilometers and miles, others simply kilometers. This is, after all, the International Peace Park, and kilometers are definitely more international. If you hike in Waterton, all trail sign distances use kilometers. Just pull out your math skills: To convert kilometers to miles, multiply the kilometers listed by 0.6. (Example: Multiply 3 kilometers by 0.6 to get 1.8 miles.) To convert miles to kilometers, multiply the miles by 1.6. (Example: Multiply 2 miles by 1.6 to get 3.2 kilometers.) These calculations are simple, easy approximations you can remember for the trail. Some hikers enjoy kilometers—the number is always higher, so the accomplishment is greater! (For more accurate conversions, multiply by 0.62 to convert kilometers to miles; to convert miles to kilometers, multiply by 1.61.)

Trailheads may also display yellow **bear warnings** or orange **bear closure** signs to alert hikers to frequent bear activity. Heavily trampled areas may have a **footprint with a red slash**—universally recognized as "Don't walk here." Obey these signs: They are protecting fragile alpine meadows from abuse or protecting an area replanted with native plants.

Solo Travelers

Even though solo hiking in bear country is not recommended, some hikers do venture into the backcountry alone. If you're one of them, make tons of noise while hiking and brush up on your bear country hiking skills. Solo travelers looking for trail companionship should hook up with park naturalist hikes (check *The Glacier Explorer* for times and dates) or sign on with a commercially-guided hike through Glacier Guides (406/387-5555 or 800/521-7238, www.glacierguides.com).

Hitchhiking to Trailheads

You may see hitchhikers sticking a thumb out. In Montana, hitchhiking is legal. If hitchhiking, be cautious of where you stand on the road. Choose a spot where a car can get completely off the road to pick you up. Don't bother hitchhiking where no pullout is available; no one will stop.

BACKPACKING

Glacier National Park's backpacking is unrivaled. Sixty-six designated backcountry campgrounds spread campers out, so you never feel crowded. You can hit the popular trails—The Highline, The Belly, and Gunsight Pass—or head for something really remote, like the Nyack-Coal Loop or Waterton to Kintla. Backpacking information, permit applications, trail status reports, and backcountry campsite availability are online: www.nps.gov/glac. Call the park (406/888-7800) to speak with someone in person regarding conditions and routes. Use hiker shuttles to create easy point-to-point routes. While you can get permits and information at ranger stations (Two Medicine, Many Glacier, Polebridge) and visitors centers (Logan Pass, St. Mary), the main place to pick up permits is Apgar Backcountry Office (406/888-7859, May–Oct.).

Guides

Glacier Park allows only one backpacking concessionaire, and that's **Glacier Guides** (406/387-5555 or 800/521-7238, www.glacierguides.com), a company that has been guiding in Glacier for over 25 years. Guide services, shuttles, food, group equipment, and permits are included for roughly $135 per person per

Backpackers on the Gunsight Pass trail take in Glacier's colorful layered rock.

© BECKY LOMAX

GETTING INTO THE BACKCOUNTRY

Miles of well-marked scenic trails makes Glacier rate high with backpackers.

Backcountry camping is by permit only. Each campground has 2-7 sites with four people allowed per site. All backcountry campgrounds have pit toilets (some with great views), community cook sites, and separate tent sites. No food, garbage, toiletries, or cookware should ever be kept in the tent sites. Near the cook sites, a bear pole or bar makes hanging food easy. Some campsites have bear-proof food storage boxes.

Many backcountry campsites do not allow fires, so carry a lightweight stove for cooking. Take low-odor foods to avoid attracting bears, and practice Leave No Trace principles religiously.

In addition to regular backpacking gear (tent, sleeping bag, pad, clothing, rain gear, topographical maps, compass or GPS device, first-aid kit, bug juice, sunscreen, fuel, cook gear, and stove), bring a 25-foot rope for hanging food, a small screen or strainer for sifting food particles out of gray water, a one-micron or smaller filter for purifying water (tablets and boiling can do the job, too), and a small trowel for emergency human waste disposal when a pit toilet is unavailable.

Permits may be acquired two ways: by mail, permits may be reserved for $20 (a limited number of sites are assigned this way, and you still have to pay your per-person fee when you pick up the actual permit); or stop by a permit office no more than 24 hours in advance (8 A.M.-4:30 P.M., May-Nov.; some permit offices stay open later in the evening). Permits ($4 per person per night) are available at Apgar Permit Office (406/888-7859), St. Mary Visitor Center (406/732-7751), Many Glacier Ranger Station (406/732-7740), Two Medicine Ranger Station (406/226-4484), and Polebridge Ranger Station (406/888-7742). In winter, call 406/888-7800.

SUGGESTED ROUTES: 3-4 DAYS

- **Gunsight Pass Trail:** This 20-mile trail between Jackson Overlook and Lake McDonald Lodge crosses two passes and connects with Sperry Chalet. Stay at Gunsight Lake, Lake Ellen Wilson, and Sperry, but leave time for the spur trail to Sperry Glacier.

- **Highline Trail:** For an international hike, begin at Logan Pass and finish 30 miles later at Goat Haunt to catch the boat across Waterton Lake into Canada. Camp at Granite Park, Fifty Mountain, and Kootenai Lakes.

- **St. Mary to Two Medicine:** A 35-mile trail links prime fishing lakes along several high passes in bighorn sheep country. Camp at Old Man Lake, Morningstar Lake, and Red Eagle Lake.

SUGGESTED ROUTES: 5-10 DAYS

- **Continental Divide National Scenic Trail:** The trail runs 110 miles from Marias Pass to Waterton in a stunning conclusion to the 3,100-mile trail. For this route, connect front country and backcountry campgrounds.

- **Northern Traverse:** Between Chief Mountain Customs and Kintla Lake, the 58-mile trail crosses three passes as it wanders just south of the Canadian border. Camp at Cosley Lake, Glenn's Lake, Stoney Indian Lake, Lake Francis, Boulder Pass, Upper Kintla, and Kintla Lake.

- **North Circle Tour:** Following in the footsteps of the historic horseback tours through Glacier, this 54-mile loop connects Many Glacier via Ptarmigan Tunnel with The Belly and the northern Highline. Camp at Elizabeth, Cosley, Glenn's, and Stoney Indian Lakes, Fifty Mountain, and Granite Park.

day. Trips depart weekly for three, four, and six days. Custom trips ($160 per person per day with four-person minimum) and two 10-day Continental Divide trips are also available. If you want the backpacking experience but don't want to carry more than a day pack, you can hire a sherpa to haul up to 40 pounds of your gear ($165 per day). The company also rents packs, tents, sleeping bags, and pads. Reservations are required.

CLIMBING

Glacier's peaks and off-trail scrambles are irresistible; however, the park's crumbly sedimentary rock makes climbing risky. Loose handholds, wobbly footholds, rockfall, and unstable scree and talus slopes are hazardous. Safety while climbing is imperative. Each year, accidents and fatalities occur from falling while climbing. Only venture off the trail for climbing if you know the terrain and inherent risks. Do not attempt climbing in Glacier alone or without experience. Most ascents are actually scrambles, but still not for the inexperienced. For routes, J. Gordon Edwards's *A Climber's Guide to Glacier National Park* is the undisputed bible.

Begin all off-trail adventures by registering at a ranger station or visitors center and go prepared. Be aware of closures for bears and fragile vegetation, especially around Logan Pass. (Check with visitors centers or ranger stations for status or call 406/888-7800.) Always practice Leave No Trace principles. For emergencies, carry a cell phone along, but don't depend on its ability to work everywhere in the park. Instead, be ready to self-rescue.

No commercial guiding outfitters operate climbing trips in Glacier. For those looking to hook up with climbers, **Glacier Mountaineering Society** offers volunteer-led climbs for members usually on weekends, and each summer they pack one week in July full of climbs for their Mountaineering Week. Only $25 buys an annual membership! Their website is loaded with climbing info, too: www.glacier mountaineers.com.

FISHING
Licenses

Glacier National Park does not require fishing licenses, but fishing outside the park does. Outside Glacier, anglers must possess a Montana State Fishing License. Residents pay $13–18 for two days to full season; conservation licenses are free for resident seniors. Nonresidents can purchase 2-day ($25), 10-day ($43.50), or seasonal licenses ($60), which can be purchased in sporting-goods stores and fly shops across Montana. You can also order one online from Montana Fish, Wildlife, and Parks at www.fwp.mt.gov.

On the Blackfeet Reservation, you'll need a Blackfeet tribal fishing permit (Blackfeet Fish and Game Department, 406/338-7207, www .blackfeetfishandwildlife.com, $20 per day, $30 for three days, or $65 per season). Permits for boats and float tubes are included in those rates.

Regulations

Fishing regulations vary substantially by area; anglers are required to know the rules and know their fish. You can pick up regulations when and where you buy your license. In general, the fishing season begins the third Saturday in May and ends November 30, but lake fishing is permitted year-round. While strict daily fishing limits regulate catches in Glacier (5) and the Bob Marshall Wilderness Complex (3), many species have higher limits or no limit at all. Bull trout are a protected species and must be thrown back into the water immediately. Look for the lack of black on the dorsal fin: No black, throw it back.

Inside the park, lead is prohibited in weights, lures, and jigs; outside the park, it's recommended to use weights made of non-lead materials. To dispose of entrails in the front country, use a bear-resistant garbage container. In the backcountry, puncture the air bladder and throw entrails 200 feet out into the water away from trails and campsites.

For Glacier's regulations, stop by a ranger station or visitors center or check the park website (www.nps.gov/glac) for a complete list. For a complete list of the State of Montana (www .fwp.mt.gov) and Blackfeet Reservation (www .blackfeetfishandwildlife.com) regulations, check the websites. For Waterton's fishing licenses and regulations, see the *Waterton* chapter.

BOATING

Out-of-state boats over 12 feet in length must have a home state registration and can be used in Montana up to 90 consecutive days. In-state boats must have Montana registration and decals on the boat. For a complete list of Montana boating regulations, see www.fwp .mt.gov. For boating on Blackfeet Reservation lakes, you'll need a $20 conservation permit (406/338-7207, www.blackfeetfishandwildlife

.com), available in St. Mary, Browning, and East Glacier.

HUNTING

Although hunting is illegal in Glacier National Park, much of the surrounding tribal and national forest lands are prime big game and bird hunting areas. For hunting in the Bob Marshall Wilderness or in national forests, get hunting regulations, seasons, and license info from Montana Fish, Wildlife, and Parks (406/444-2535, www.fwp.mt.gov). For hunting on tribal lands, check with the Blackfeet Reservation (406/338-7207, www.blackfeet fishandwildlife.com) for regulations and licenses.

Tips for Travelers

FOREIGN TRAVELERS
Entering the United States

International travelers entering the United States must be aware that border requirements are rapidly changing. In addition to passports, many travelers will need a visa to visit. Those visiting the United States from selected countries in the Visa Waiver Program don't need visas but must have machine-readable passports and limit their stay to 90 days. These countries are Andorra, Australia, Austria, Belgium, Brunei, Denmark, Finland, France, Germany, Iceland, Ireland, Italy, Japan, Liechtenstein, Luxembourg, Monaco, Netherlands, New Zealand, Norway, Portugal, San Marino, Singapore, Slovenia, Spain, Sweden, Switzerland, and United Kingdom. If you are from a country not recognized in the Visa Waiver Program, give yourself plenty of time to apply for your visa. For additional information, check www.state.travel.gov.

Travel requirements are also changing for international visitors from Canada, Mexico, the Caribbean, and Bermuda no longer permitting simply a government-issued photo ID and proof of citizenship, such as birth certificates, for admittance. All air travelers are

required to have passports or passport cards, and as of June 1, 2009, all land and sea travelers, too. Upon entry to the U.S., you must fill out an I94 form. (Check www.cbp.gov for more info.) Note: Only Canadian and U.S. citizens are permitted to enter and exit through Goat Haunt.

Entering Canada

For international travelers entering Canada, visas are not required from the same countries recognized by the United States for visa waivers, plus Antigua and Barbuda, Bahamas, Barbados, Botswana, Cyprus, Greece, Hungary, Israel (National Passport holders only), Lithuania, Malta, Mexico, Namibia, Papua New Guinea, Poland, Republic of Korea, Slovakia, St. Kitts and Nevis, St. Lucia, St. Vincent, Solomon Islands, Swaziland, United States, and Western Samoa. Check for visa updates to be sure: www.cic.gc.ca.

DRIVING ACROSS THE U.S.-CANADIAN BORDER
Identification

Through May 2009, drivers from the U.S. and Canada may cross the international border either way between Montana and Alberta without a passport. But you will need to bring two items: a photo ID (such as a driver's license) issued by federal, provincial, or state governments; and proof of citizenship, such as a birth certificate or passport. Single parents must have proof of child custody. After June 1, 2009, passports or passport cards are required. Resident aliens must possess a permanent resident card.

Road Ports of Entry

Chief Mountain Customs (9 A.M.–6 P.M. May and after Labor Day, 7 A.M.–10 P.M. June–Labor Day) is a seasonal east-side port of entry on Chief Mountain International Highway. A year-round port of entry on Waterton-Glacier's east side, **Piegan/Carway** (7 A.M.–11 P.M.) sits on U.S. Highway 89/Canada Highway 2. Because Trail Creek Customs closed several years ago during flooding up the North Fork Valley, the only west-side port of entry now is **Roosville** on U.S. Highway 93, north of Eureka. It's open 24 hours 365 days per year, but is also 90 miles from West Glacier.

Goat Haunt

Even though Goat Haunt, U.S.A., is out in the middle of nowhere, the tightening of border policies has affected the small seasonal port of entry. Because of its relationship in the International Peace Park, special regulations are in effect here. For visitors in Canada traveling down Waterton Lake in private boats or touring on the MV *International,* clearing customs is not required, even though you cross the border partway down the lake. At Goat Haunt, you can get off the boat and wander around freely along the beach and walkway between the International Peace Park Pavilion and the boat dock. That is not considered seeking admission into the United States, even though you have stepped on to U.S. soil from Canada. However, should you choose to hike beyond Goat Haunt, you must show proof of citizenship. Only Canadian and U.S. citizens (legal resident aliens of the United States included) are permitted to hike beyond Goat Haunt,

after passing inspection. For further information on crossing from Canada into the United States, call 406/889-3865.

For day hikers to return to Canadian soil, a customs inspection is not required; however, backpackers hiking into Canada must call into Canadian customs upon reaching the Waterton Townsite. Those catching the Waterton boat will be given immigration forms to fill out. For information in advance of your trip, call the Canada Customs and Revenue Agency at 403/653-3535.

Foreign visitors (non-Canadian and non-U.S.) may not use the Goat Haunt port of entry, but rather must enter the U.S. through Chief Mountain, Piegan/Carway, or Roosville. They may, however, visit Goat Haunt briefly and return on the next boat to Waterton. Foreign visitors already in the United States may hike across the border into Canada or take the boat, but they must report to customs by phone upon reaching the Waterton Townsite.

Border No-Nos

In general, Canada and the United States have similar border laws: no fresh fruits, vegetables, plants, drugs, firearms, firewood, fresh meat, or poultry products. Pets are permitted across the border only with a certificate of rabies vaccination within 30 days prior to your crossing. Bear sprays are considered firearms in Canada; they must have a USEPA-approved label to go across the border. For clarification, call 250/887-3413. If you purchase Cuban cigars in Waterton, they are not permitted back across the U.S. border.

Money and Currency Exchange

Those popping into Waterton for a day or two may not even want to exchange money. Waterton has no bank, but the Tamarack Village (214 Mount View Rd., 403/859-2378, www.watertonvisitorservices.com, late May–early Oct.) does offer money-exchange services. Most stores and businesses in Waterton accept U.S. currency, but expect Canadian currency as change. Although it's convenient to use U.S. currency, stores will vary slightly on the exchange rates honored. To receive the best exchange rates, use credit cards; banks always give a better rate than the stores.

There will also be some Canadian coins floating in your change in Montana. These are sometimes treated at par; loonies, toonies, and dollars are not. For Canadians visiting the Glacier and Flathead Valley area, some businesses accept Canadian currency. They are used to converting it. If you're traveling farther south in the state where cashiers may be unfamiliar with loonies, convert into U.S. currency. Credit cards will receive the most accurate exchange rate. On Glacier's east side, you'll find no banks to exchange currency—only on the park's west side in Flathead Valley.

For both Canada and the United States, travelers checks in smaller amounts ($50 and under) work best for short trips on either side of the border; then you're not left dragging around scads of foreign currency. International travelers should exchange currency at their major port of entry (Seattle, Vancouver, Calgary).

TRAVELING WITH CHILDREN
Junior Ranger Program

Kids can earn a Junior Ranger Badge by completing self-guided activities in the *Junior Ranger Newspaper,* available at all visitors centers. Most activities target ages 6–12 and coincide with a trip over Going-to-the-Sun Road. When kids return the completed newspaper to any visitors center, they are sworn in as Junior Rangers and receive Glacier Park badges.

Discovery Cabin

The Discovery Cabin in Apgar serves up educational kid-fun during summer. Hands-on activities guided by interpretive rangers teach children about wildlife, geology, and habitats. Check with Apgar Visitor Center for directions and hours.

Hikes

For kids, short hikes work best. On Going-to-the-Sun Road, go for Avalanche Lake, Hidden Lake Overlook, and St. Mary and Virginia Falls. In Many Glacier, hike to Red Rocks

© BECKY LOMAX

backcountry camping with kids at Kintla Lake

Lake or hop the boat across Swiftcurrent and Josephine Lakes to hike to Grinnell Lake. In Two Medicine, take the boat uplake to hike to Twin Falls or Upper Two Medicine Lake. When hiking with children, always take snacks and water along. If toting a wee one who still needs to be carried, Glacier Outdoor Center (11957 Hwy. 2 E., West Glacier, 406/888-5454 or 800/235-6781, www.glacierraftco.com) rents kiddie packs at $20 per day.

TRAVELING WITH PETS

Pets are allowed in Glacier Park, but only in limited areas: campgrounds, parking lots, and roadsides. They are not allowed on trails, beaches, off-trail in the backcountry, nor at any park lodges or motor inns. When outside a vehicle, pets must be on a six-foot or shorter leash or be caged. In a campground, pets must be leashed or caged. Be kind enough to not leave them unattended in a car anywhere. Be considerate of wildlife and other visitors by keeping your pet under control and disposing of waste in garbage cans.

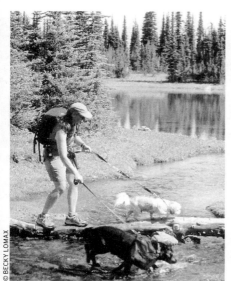

Pets are permitted on national forest trails, but not on Glacier National Park trails.

If you prefer to kennel your pet while you are in Glacier, Flathead Valley has the only options. Two of the closest are in Columbia Falls—**Stage Stop Farm and Kennels** (1892 Columbia Falls Stage, 406/892-5719) and **Triple R Kennels** (636 Kelley Rd., 406/892-3695)—but you can check the phone book for Kalispell, Whitefish, and Bigfork choices.

Trail Restrictions

No pets are allowed on Glacier Park trails, except the paved 2.6-mile Apgar Bike Trail where they are allowed on a leash. (The trail is okay for hikers, too.) Protection of fragile vegetation and preventing conflicts with wildlife are two main reasons; bears stand alone in their own class of reasons to leave poochie home. If you must hike with Fido, head to Flathead National Forest where pets are permitted. Contrary to Glacier, Waterton does permit dogs on its trails, but bring a leash along and use it.

SENIORS
Park Entrance

National parks (as well as lands run by the U.S. Fish and Wildlife Service, U.S. Forest Service, and Bureau of Land Management) have a great deal for seniors age 62 and older who are U.S. citizens or permanent residents: $10 buys the National Parks and Federal Recreational Lands Pass, good for life. To purchase, bring proof of age (state driver's license, birth certificate, or passport) in person to any national park entrance station. In a private vehicle, the card admits four adults within a vehicle plus all kids under 16 are free.

Senior Discounts

The lifetime park pass also grants 50 percent discounts on fees for federally run tours, campgrounds, parking, and boat launching; however, discounts do not apply to park concessionaire services—like hotels, boat tours, and bus tours. Also, Glacier's historic hotels do not give discounts to seniors, but some private lodging establishments surrounding the park do. Ask to be sure.

© BECKY LOMAX

ACCESSIBILITY

Visitors with special needs should pick up an *Accessible Facilities and Services* brochure. You can get these at Logan Pass, St. Mary, or Apgar visitors centers, all of which are accessible by wheelchair. Entrance stations also have them. Park information is available also by TDD: 406/888-7806.

Park Entrance

A National Parks and Federal Recreational Lands Access Pass is available free for any blind or permanently disabled U.S. citizen or permanent resident. The lifetime pass permits free access to all national parks and sites run by the U.S. Fish and Wildlife Service, U.S. Forest Service, and Bureau of Land Management. The pass admits the person who signs for the pass plus three other adults in the same vehicle; kids under 16 are free. This pass also grants a 50 percent discount on fees for federally run tours, campgrounds, parking, and boat launching, but discounts do not apply to concessionaire services. Passes may only be acquired in person at entrance stations with proof of medical disability or eligibility for receiving federal benefits.

Park Facilities

Five campgrounds in Glacier reserve 1–2 sites each for wheelchair needs: Apgar, Fish Creek, Rising Sun, Sprague Creek, and Two Medicine. Picnic Areas at Apgar, Rising Sun, and Sun Point also have wheelchair access. So do all lodges within the park boundaries, although they have a limited number of ADAAG rooms. Other wheelchair-accessible sites include boat docks at Lake McDonald, Many Glacier, and Two Medicine as well as evening naturalist programs in Apgar Amphitheater, Lake McDonald Lodge Auditorium, Many Glacier Hotel Auditorium, Rising Sun Campground, and Two Medicine Campground. Most parking lots offer designated parking.

Trails

Glacier and Waterton both offer wheelchair-accessible trails. In Glacier, the Apgar Bike Trail, Trail of the Cedars at Avalanche, Running Eagle Falls Nature Trail in Two Medicine, Goat Lick Overlook, Oberlin Bend Trail, and the International Peace Park Pavilion at Goat Haunt are all wheelchair-accessible. Admittedly, some of the pavement can be a little rough in places; just be prepared for it. In Waterton, wheelchairs may access Linnet Lake Trail, Waterton Townsite Trail, and Cameron Lake Day Use Area.

While pet dogs are not permitted on backcountry trails, aid dogs are allowed—although, due to bears, they are discouraged. If you choose to hike with an aid dog, be safe by sticking to well-traveled trails during midday.

Interpretive Services

Special programs and sign-language interpretation may be available with a two-week notice. Call 406/888-7930 to schedule.

HEALTH AND SAFETY

Bears

Safety in bear country starts from knowledge and behaving appropriately. With the exception of Alaska and Canada, Glacier beats out any other North American location for the highest density of grizzly bears, and black bears find likable habitat here, too. Regardless of bruin species, one caveat affects the safety of humans and bears: food. Proper use, storage, and handling of food and garbage keeps bears from being conditioned or habituated to situations in which they may become aggressive. With strict food and garbage rules, Glacier has minimized aggressive bear encounters, attacks, and deaths—both of humans and bears.

Camp safely. Use low-odor foods, keep food and cooking gear out of sleeping sites in the backcountry, and store it inside your vehicle in front-country campgrounds. In front-country campgrounds, you'll find detailed explanations of how to safely camp in bear country stapled to your picnic table. For information on camping in bear country, pick up a copy of *Waterton-Glacier Guide* and Glacier's *Backcountry Guide* at entrance stations, visitors

BEAR TIPS

HIKING IN BEAR COUNTRY

Many of Glacier's most heavily tromped trails march smack through prime bear habitat, where a surprise encounter on the trail with a grizzly can turn one's insides to Jell-O. With a few precautions, you can eliminate scares from surprise meetings.

- **Make noise.** Glacier is one park where peace and quiet on the trail could be dangerous. To avoid surprising a bear, use your voice – sing loudly, hoot, or holler – and clap your hands. Bears tend to recognize human sounds as ones to avoid; they'll usually wander off if they hear people approaching. Consciously make loud noise in thick brushy areas, around blind corners, near babbling streams, and against the wind. You'll often hear hikers just hooting out nonsense; it's okay. They're not crazed. It's just their signature bear noise.

- **Hike with other people.** Avoid hiking alone. Keep children near. Very few bear attacks happen to groups of four or more.

- **Avoid bear feeding areas.** Since bears must gain weight before winter, feeding is their prime directive. Often, they'll pack in 20,000 calories in a day. In early season, glacier lily bulbs attract grizzlies for their high nutritional value. By midseason, cow parsnip patches provide sustenance, in between high-protein carrion. If you stumble across an animal carcass, leave the area immediately and notify a ranger. Toward summer's end, huckleberry patches provide high sugars. Detour widely around feeding bears.

- **Hike in broad daylight.** Avoid early mornings, late evenings, and night.

- **Never approach a bear.** Watch the body language: A bear who stands on hind legs may just be trying to get a good smell or better viewpoint. On the other hand, head swaying, teeth clacking, laid-back ears, a lowered head, and huffing or woofing are signs of agitation: Clear out slowly!

- **If you do surprise a bear, back away.** Contrary to all inclinations, do not run! Instead, back away slowly, talking quietly and turning sideways or bending your knees to appear smaller and nonthreatening. Avoid direct eye contact – a challenge in the animal kingdom. Instead, avert your eyes. Leave your pack on; it can protect you if the bear attacks.

- **Use pepper spray or play "dead."** If you surprise a bear that attacks in defense, aim pepper spray at the bear's eyes. Protect yourself and your vulnerable parts by assuming a fetal position on the ground with your hands around the back of your neck. Play "dead." Move again only when you are sure the bear has vacated the area.

- **If a bear stalks you as food, or attacks at night, fight back.** While bears stalking humans as prey is extremely rare, use any means at hand – pepper spray, shouting, sticks, or rocks – to tell the bear you are not an easy food source. Try to escape up something, like a building or tree.

- **Pay attention to trail signage.** Special bear signage is used at trailheads to inform hikers of concerns. Yellow **bear warning** signs indicate bears are frequenting the trail; use extra caution and make more noise than usual on these trails. Orange **bear closure** signs indicate a trail is closed, usually because one has been aggressive or is defending a carcass. Even when trailheads have no signs, hikers still need to be cautious, for Glacier is a bear's park.

- Two books are plump with accurate information on bears: Bill Schneider's *Bear Aware* and Stephen Herrero's *Bear Attacks: Their Causes and Avoidances*.

BLACK BEARS VS. GRIZZLY BEARS

While neither black nor grizzly bears are safer, it's good to know what the bear is when you see one. Even though colors are used to name the bears ("grizzly" means "silver-haired"), bears appear with a variety of fur hues regardless of species. A reddish-black bear can give birth to three cubs of different colors: blond, black, and brown. And grizzly bears appear in all colors of the spectrum. Don't be fooled by color; look instead for body size and shape.

Although hard to assess through binoculars, the bears are two different sizes. Grizzlies are bigger than black bears, standing on all fours at three-four feet tall. They weigh in at 300-600 pounds. Black bears average 12-18 inches shorter on all fours. Adult females weigh around 140 pounds, while males bulk up to 220 pounds.

In profile, the grizzly has one notable feature: a hump on its shoulders. The solid muscle mass provides the grizzly's arms with power for digging and running. Black bears lack this hump. Face profiles are also different. On the grizzly, look for a scooped or dished forehead-to-nose silhouette; the black bear's nose will appear straighter in line with its forehead. Note the ears, for the grizzly's will look a little too small for its head while a black bear's ears seem big, standing straight up. While you don't want to get close enough to check the real thing, paw prints in mud reveal a difference in claws and foot structure. Grizzly claws are four inches long with pads in a relatively straight line, while black bear claws are 1.5 inches with pads arced across the top of the foot.

Although both bears have mediocre vision, they are fast runners. In three seconds, a grizzly bear can cover 180 feet. And contrary to popular lore, humans are not a food source. In fact, both bears are omnivores, feeding primarily on vegetation and carrion.

centers, ranger stations, permit offices, or on-line: www.nps.gov/glac.

Hike safely. When taking your first hike, you'll hear jingle bells. When entering your first gift shop, you'll see them—**bear bells.** They're everywhere. And so are the jokes, calling them "dinner bells." While making noise while hiking is the best safety assurance in bear country, bells are not the best way to do it. And many hikers hate them. To check their effectiveness, see how close you come to hikers before you hear their ringing. Sometimes, it's too close! Bear bells are best as a souvenir, not as a substitute for human noise on the trail. Human noise is best; so talk, sing, hoot, and holler. You'll feel silly at first, but after a while, you'll realize it's something everyone does here.

While firearms are not permitted in national parks, **pepper sprays** are. Many hikers carry pepper sprays for deterring aggressive, attacking bears; however, they are not repellents like bug sprays to be sprayed on the human body, tents, or gear. Instead, you spray the capsicum derivative directly into a bear's face, aiming for the eyes and nose. While pepper sprays have repelled some attacking bears, wind and rain may reduce effectiveness, as will the product's age. Small purse-sized pepper sprays are not adequate for bears—only an eight-ounce can will do. Practice how to use it. Pepper spray is not protection: Carrying it does not lessen the need for making noise. Be aware that pepper sprays are not allowed by airlines unless checked in luggage, and only brands with USEPA labels may cross through Canadian customs.

Bears are dangerous around food, be it a carcass in the woods, a pack left on a trail, or a cooler left in a campsite. Protecting bears and protecting yourself starts with being conscious of food—including wrappers and crumbs. Gorp tidbits dropped along the trail attract wildlife, as do "biodegradable" apple cores chucked into the forest. Pick up what you drop and pack out all garbage; don't leave a Hansel and Gretel trail for bears. Bear attacks can be avoided.

Mountain Lion Encounters

These large cats rarely prey on humans, but they can—especially smaller two-legged munchkins. Making bear noise will help you avoid surprising a lion. Hiking with others and keeping kids close is also a good idea. If you do stumble upon a lion, above all, do not run. Be calm. Group together to appear big. Look at the cat with peripheral vision rather than staring straight on as you back slowly away. If the lion attacks, fight back with everything: rocks, sticks, or kicking.

Water Hazards

Contrary to popular opinion, bears are not the number one cause of death and accidents in Glacier, but rather drowning. Be extremely cautious around lakes, fast-moving streams, and waterfalls where moss and clear algae cover the rocks, making them slippery. Waters here are swift, frigid, plumb-full of submerged obstacles, unforgiving, and sometimes lethal.

Giardia

Lakes and streams can carry parasites like *Giardia lamblia*. If ingested, it causes cramping, nausea, and severe diarrhea for a long period of time. It's easy to avoid giardia by boiling water (for one minute plus one minute for each 1,000 feet of elevation above sea level) or using a one-micron filter. Bleach also works (add two drops per quart and then let it sit for 30 minutes). Tap water in the park campgrounds and picnic areas has been treated, and you'll definitely taste the strong chlorine in the hotel water systems.

Dehydration

Many first-time hikers to Glacier are surprised to find they drink substantially more water here than at home. Glacier's winds, altitude, and lower humidity can add up to a fast case of dehydration—which often manifests first as a headache. If you are hiking, drink lots of water—more than you normally would. If you hike with children, monitor their fluid intake.

Altitude

Some visitors from sea level feel the effects of altitude—a lightheadedness, headache, or shortness of breath—in high zones like Logan Pass. Slowing down a hiking pace helps, as does drinking lots of fluids and giving the body time to acclimatize. If symptoms are more dramatic, descend in elevation as soon as possible. Altitude also increases the effects of UV radiation: You might feel cool, but your skin will still burn. To prevent sunburn, use a strong sunscreen and wear sunglasses and a hat.

Crevasses and Snow Bridges

While ice often looks solid to step on, it harbors unseen caverns beneath. Crevasses (large vertical cracks) are difficult to see, and snow bridges can collapse as a person crosses. You're safer just staying off the ice; even Glacier's tiny ice fields have caused fatalities. Also, steep slopes can run into rocks or trees; if sliding for fun, slide only where you have a safe run out.

Hypothermia

Hypothermia is insidious and subtle; it targets exhausted and physically unprepared hikers. The body's inner core loses heat, reducing mental and physical functions. Watch for uncontrolled shivering, incoherence, poor judgment, fumbling, mumbling, and slurred speech. Avoid becoming hypothermic by staying dry, donning rain gear and warm moisture-wicking layers. Leave the cotton clothing back in the car! If someone in your party is hypothermic, get him or her sheltered and into dry clothing. Give warm liquids, but be sure they're nonalcoholic and decaffeinated. If the victim cannot regain body heat, get into a sleeping bag, with you and the victim stripped for skin-to-skin contact.

Blisters

Ill-fitting shoes and incorrect socks cause most blisters. Although cotton socks feel good, they are not the best choice for hiking because they absorb water from the feet

Slick rocks require caution around water.

and hold it, providing a surface for friction. Synthetic or wool-blend socks wick water away from the skin. To prevent blisters, recognize "hot spots" or rubs, applying Moleskin or New Skin to the sensitive area. In a pinch, duct tape can be slapped on trouble spots. Once a blister occurs, apply special blister Band-Aid bandages or Second Skin, a product developed for burns that cools the blister off and cushions it. Cover Second Skin with Moleskin to absorb future rubbing and hold the Second Skin in place.

Hantavirus

The Hantavirus infection, which causes flu-like symptoms, is contracted by inhaling the dust from deer mice urine and droppings. If you suspect you have the virus, get immediate medical attention. To protect yourself, avoid areas thick with rodents—burrows and woodpiles. Store all food in rodent-proof containers. If you find rodent dust in your gear, disinfect with water and bleach (a cup and a half of bleach to one gallon of water).

Mosquitoes and Ticks

Bugs carry diseases such as West Nile virus and Rocky Mountain spotted fever. Protect yourself by wearing long sleeves and pants as well as using bug repellents in spring and summer when mosquitoes and ticks are common. If you are bitten by a tick, remove it and disinfect the bite; see a doctor if lesions or a rash appears.

Hospitals and Emergencies

For emergencies inside the park, call 406/888-7800. For emergencies outside the park, call 911. On Glacier's west side, the nearest hospitals are in Flathead Valley. Kalispell Regional Medical Center (310 Sunny View Ln., 406/752-5111) and the new North Valley Hospital (1600 Hospital Way, Whitefish, 406/863-3631) are 35 minutes from West Glacier and can be up to 90 minutes from Logan Pass depending on traffic. On Glacier's east side, Northern Rockies Medical Center (802 2nd St. E., Cut Bank, 406/873-2251) is approximately an hour from East Glacier and just under two hours from St. Mary.

ESSENTIALS

Getting There

ORIENTATION

Getting your bearings in Glacier is not difficult; the park splits along the Continental Divide into an east and west side, each with several entrances following valley drainages. Two Medicine, St. Mary, and Many Glacier dominate the east, while Lake McDonald and the North Fork cover the west. Although Highway 2 passes briefly through the park's southern tip en route between East and West Glacier, southern entrances into the park's core are all via foot or horseback trails. On the north side, Waterton Lakes National Park provides access via boat, foot, or horseback across the Canadian-U.S. border into Glacier's interior.

Only one route bisects the entire park: Going-to-the-Sun Road. If there is a rush hour in Glacier, it's on this road 11 A.M.–4 P.M. But rush hour is not restricted to weekdays; it's seven days per week mid-July–mid-August.

Most summer visitors love the park's expansive east-side views. Here, tiny seasonal towns fall away into miles and miles of broad prairie. On a clear day, not much obstructs a view to Ohio. By autumn, not many services remain open to take the Rocky Mountain Front's brutal winds.

The park's heavily forested west side balances remote corners of the North Fork with the busy hub of West Glacier. Mountain snows feed large rivers that drain through the Flathead Valley into Flathead Lake. Mixed with farmland, rural pockets, and resort towns, the fast-growing valley—anchored in winter by recreational skiing—is a year-round enclave for 87,000 people.

SUGGESTED ROUTES
From Western Montana

From I-90 just west of Missoula, U.S. Highway 93 North (Exit 96) leads 103 miles to Flathead Valley. This scenic route passes below the craggy Mission Mountains and along Flathead Lake, the largest freshwater lake west of the Mississippi. Drivers coming from Spokane can cut off miles by exiting I-90 at St. Regis and following the signs to Glacier Park (north on Hwy. 135, northwest on Hwy. 200, east on Hwy. 28). You'll pass the funky little towns of Paradise and Hot Springs, shooting back several decades, before joining Highway 93 heading north at Flathead Lake.

In Kalispell, you'll begin a confusing maze through Flathead Valley as the highway jogs and turns onto different streets. To help, follow signs to the park or West Glacier. In downtown, turn right onto U.S. Highway 2 East, which is also East Idaho Street. Travel for two miles past easily recognizable box stores and car dealerships. Highway 2 will turn left at LaSalle (LaSalle and Highway 2 are the same road), running north 12 miles toward Columbia Falls. At the intersection with Montana Highway 40, the highway turns right; follow it through Columbia Falls, continuing another 16 miles on Highway 2 to West Glacier. Total mileage from I-90 to West Glacier is 145 miles; driving time on the mostly two-lane highway is usually less than 3.5 hours, but can be four hours or more with heavy traffic, snow, or road-

construction delays. Spokane to West Glacier (271 miles) is a four-hour drive.

From Eastern Montana

This long but extremely scenic approach follows the Rocky Mountain Front, a highway for golden eagle migrations, and the buttress for the Bob Marshall Wilderness Complex. This is also the route for those stitching together a visit to both Yellowstone National Park and Glacier. Leave I-90 in **Butte,** turning north toward Helena onto I-15 (Exit 129/227). Drive 101 miles, about 1.5 hours, from I-90 to Exit 228 two miles north of Wolf Creek. Turn north here onto U.S. Highway 287.

Northward from here, high sideways winds

PARK ENTRANCE FEES

National parks survive in part on entrance fees. Glacier is no different. Entrance fees are collected at Two Medicine, St. Mary, Many Glacier, West Glacier, Polebridge, and Camas. When stations are unstaffed, self-pay kiosks allow for purchasing passes.

No single-day passes are sold, only seven-day passes:

	May–Oct	Nov–Apr
Single vehicle	$25	$15
(admits all persons in vehicle)		
Single person	$12	$10
(on foot, bicycle, or motorcycle)		

Two annual passes are also available, but can only be purchased when entrance stations are staffed. Use of these non-transferable passes also requires showing photo ID, but they admit all people in a single vehicle.

- Glacier National Park Pass $35

  (This pass can ONLY be purchased at entrance stations.)

- National Park and Federal Recreation Lands Pass $80

  (You can also buy these online (www.nps.gov) or call 888-ASK USGS, Ext. 1. This pass admits a maximum of four adults in the vehicle; children under 16 are free.)

- In addition, lifetime passes to all national parks are available for U.S. senior citizens ($10) and U.S. citizens with permanent disabilities (free). These must be purchased in person with appropriate documentation at a park entrance station. This pass admits a maximum of four adults in the vehicle; children under 16 are free.

- Glacier and U.S. park passes are NOT valid for entrance to Waterton Lakes National Park in Canada.

can slow travel—gusts strong enough to rock RVs and trailers. Follow the narrow two-lane Highway 287 north 66 miles through Augusta to Choteau (pronounced "SHOW-toe"), the epitome of a Rocky Mountain Front town with 1,700 residents, grain elevators, and a hunting mecca. Here, the road turns left for a bit onto U.S. Highway 89, also Main Street. From Choteau, head north 72 miles to Browning. Again, narrow curves slow driving time, but you will soon see Glacier's peaks jutting up from the plains. Just before Browning, you'll join U.S. Highway 2. At Browning's west end, turn left as Highway 2 leaves town. It leads 13 miles to East Glacier. Total driving time from I-90 to East Glacier is about five hours to cover 253 miles. High winds and traffic may slow travel, but the scenery is worth the drive.

From **Great Falls,** two routes lead to East Glacier, both with spectacular views of the Rocky Mountain Front as it pops up off the plains. For easy interstate and highway driving,

hop on I-15 heading north to Shelby and then U.S. Highway 2 westward to East Glacier (143 miles). Folks who want to get to Glacier quickly take this 2.5-hour route.

A much more interesting approach with a few less miles, however, strikes off through small rural Rocky Mountain Front towns. From Great Falls, head 10 miles north on I-15 to catch Highway 89 north toward Browning. The route travels past Freezeout Lake, known for its snow goose migration. Connect with the Butte route in Choteau. While this 139-mile route is a few miles shorter, the narrow road makes for slower driving, taking two hours and forty-five minutes to get to East Glacier—longer if you stop for explorations.

From the Canadian Rockies

Many travelers link Glacier with a trip in the Canadian Rockies national parks—Jasper, Banff, Yoho, and Kootenay. The Flathead Valley connects directly to the Canadian

Rockies via Highway 93, which runs north–south from Banff. To get to Glacier, travel south on Highway 93 through British Columbia toward Cranbrook. Four miles (six kilometers) before Cranbrook, merge with Canada 3 heading 36 miles (58 km) east toward Elko. From here, you can head to Waterton and Glacier's east side or go south toward West Glacier.

To head to Waterton, stay on Canada 3 for 60 miles (96 km) over Crow's Nest Pass and turn south onto Highway 6 at Pincher. Drive 20 miles (32 km) to Waterton Lakes National Park. From here, the seasonal Chief Mountain Highway connects with Glacier Park's east side.

To head to West Glacier, take Highway 93 south at Elko, driving 24 miles (39 km) toward Roosville on the Canadian-U.S. border. After crossing through customs, continue south 63 miles on Highway 93 through Eureka to Whitefish. Drive with caution: Deer frequent the road between Eureka and Whitefish, earning it the nickname "Deer Alley." In downtown Whitefish (with 25 miles left to go), Highway 93 turns south again at the third stoplight. Drive two miles to a junction with Montana Highway 40; you'll see signs to Glacier Park. Turn left, toward Columbia Falls. En route Highway 40 becomes U.S. Highway 2. Follow the signs to Glacier Park. Expect total driving time from Banff to West Glacier to be nearly six hours.

From Calgary
From Calgary, Alberta, head south for 113 miles (181 km) on Canada Highway 2 toward Fort Macleod. Just before town, the highway merges with Canada 3 for a few miles heading east.

If you are starting your Glacier adventure in Waterton Lakes National Park, turn west onto Canada 3 toward Pincher Creek (17 miles, 27 km). At Pincher, turn south onto Canada Highway 6 for 20 miles (32 km) to the park entrance. From Calgary to Waterton is 149 miles (240 km) via Pincher Creek. With speed limits in Canada being slightly slower than in the United States, the distance can be covered in

two hours and forty-five minutes. (Posted in kilometers; 80 kph is 50 mph.)

To head straight to Glacier, continue from Fort Macleod south through Cardston to the Carway-Piegan border crossing. The 165 miles (266 km) from Calgary to the border at Carway should take about three hours. As a general rule, Canadian highway speed limits tend to be a little lower than U.S. speed limits, especially compared to Montana's rural narrow two-laners, which can hit 70 mph. From Carway, drop over the Canadian-U.S. border onto U.S. Highway 89. Drive 19 miles to St. Mary for Going-to-the-Sun Road's east entrance, 25 minutes from the border. To enter the park instead at Many Glacier, turn right at Babb 10 miles south of the border and drive 12 miles to Many Glacier Hotel and Swiftcurrent (40 minutes total).

FLATHEAD VALLEY
The closest and easiest access to Glacier National Park is Flathead Valley. If flights arrive before evening, you can catch a shuttle and be at Lake McDonald inside Glacier Park in time to catch the sunset. Because the airport has no lodging in the immediate vicinity, those coming in on late flights (or wishing to explore Flathead Valley a bit) will need to stay in Kalispell, Whitefish, or Columbia Falls. While many choose Columbia Falls for its proximity between the airport and the park, Whitefish lures others for its shopping, nightlife, nearby Whitefish Lake, and Whitefish Mountain Resort.

Airports
The closest airport to Glacier National Park—**Glacier Park International Airport**—services only a few airlines coming from a handful of locations: Skywest/Delta from Salt Lake City, Northwest from Minneapolis, United from Denver and Chicago, and Horizon Air from Seattle. But don't ask travel agents for a flight to Glacier airport; they won't know what you're talking about. Known with the airlines as Kalispell Airport or **Flathead County Airport (FCA),** the airport's "international" reputation

comes from a few charter flights from Canada. With only three gates, this tiny airport is easy for meeting up with groups, walking to the baggage claim just a few hundred feet from your gate, or finding the car rental desk. In the terminal, the **Kindred Spirit Gift Shop** (10 A.M.–4:30 P.M. daily in winter and till 5:30 P.M. in summer) carries local arts, crafts, and, of course, huckleberry products, and **The Glacier Grille** (5 A.M.–6 P.M. daily) serves cafeteria food, espresso, beer, and wine. Inside the airport, you'll find desks for Avis, Hertz, National/Alamo, and Budget rental cars. Hotel and prearranged shuttles are right outside.

Although the airport sits within Kalispell city limits, many visitors are surprised to find the Kalispell hotels 10–15 minutes away in the opposite direction of the park. In fact, the airport sits almost equidistant between downtown Kalispell, Whitefish, and Columbia Falls. But because the airport is only 25 miles from West Glacier, you can sit on the beach at Lake McDonald the day you arrive if you want to maximize your park time.

Although Spokane, Washington, can be an alternative airport, it requires a longer drive to get to the park—about 4.5 hours; however, it may fit better in a travel itinerary.

Train

For those arriving by train, station stops in West and East Glacier make for a no-brainer arrival adjacent to the park. **Amtrak's** Empire Builder service (800/USA-RAIL or 800/872-7245, www.amtrak.com) between Chicago and Seattle or Portland runs once daily each direction. Both the east- and westbound trains stop in Whitefish, West Glacier, and Essex year round and summers only in East Glacier. Between Seattle and Shelby, Montana, National Park Service guides offer educational services aboard. From Seattle ($92 one-way), the eastbound train lands riders conveniently in West Glacier in early morning. Eastbound trains hit Whitefish at 7:26 A.M., West Glacier at 8:16 A.M., Essex at 8:55 A.M., and East Glacier at 9:54 A.M. Westbound arrivals run between 6:45 P.M. (East Glacier) and 8:56 P.M.

Amtrak from Seattle or Chicago connects with Whitehead, Essex, and East Glacier.

© BECKY LOMAX

red jammer tour bus

(Whitefish). Departures are 5–10 minutes later. The train has a reputation for running late; be prepared to arrive in the middle of the night. In winter, avalanches disrupt the schedule.

Special Amtrak deals are available. Kids ages 2–15 are half-price. Seniors, veterans, AAA and NARP members, military personnel, and students can also get 10–15 percent discounts: check Amtrak's website for details. High summer travel makes reservations highly recommended. Amtrak's federal funding frequently goes in and out of limbo, with the Glacier route high on the chopping block. Check with Amtrak for changes to schedules and service.

Bus

Bus service to Glacier is nil; no buses connect directly with East or West Glacier. Trailways' **Rimrock Stages** (800/255-7655, www.rim rocktrailways.com) runs one bus daily between Missoula and Whitefish ($39 one-way). It leaves Missoula at 8 A.M., arriving at 11:25 A.M. in Whitefish, where you need to grab a place

to overnight until the train ($6 one-way) to West Glacier departs at 7:46 A.M. the next morning. Likewise with your return connection: The westbound train arrives in Whitefish at 8:56 P.M., but you won't be able to catch your bus to Missoula until 11:35 A.M. the next day. On the upside, if you have to hang out, Whitefish is the place to be.

Taxis and Shuttles

Headquartered one mile north of the airport, **Flathead-Glacier Transportation** (406/892-3390 or 800/829-7039, www.fgtrans.com) provides shuttles and transportation to all east- and west-side hubs in Glacier, all towns in Flathead Valley, and Whitefish Mountain Resort. Drivers will meet any airport flights, as well as pick you up at any of the park lodges, at trailheads, or surrounding towns to transport you back to the airport. They even accommodate the early morning and late night flights. Sample one-way rates from the airport are $36 to West Glacier, $50 to Lake McDonald Lodge,

$130 to East Glacier, $12 to Whitefish, $10 to downtown Kalispell, and $38 to Bigfork. Call ahead for reservations.

Taxi companies come and go here, but usually Whitefish and Kalispell have taxi service. Check the phone book for current operators.

Tours

Most tours in Glacier Park originate in or adjacent to the park, rather than in Flathead Valley. However, the **Glacier Park, Inc.** (406/892-2525, www.glacierparkinc.com) six-day Great Lodges of Glacier tour includes a pickup at Glacier Park International Airport in Flathead Valley.

Car Rental

Glacier Park International Airport terminal has four rental-car agencies with desks in the airport: Hertz (U.S. 406/758-2220 or 800/654-3131, www.hertz.com), National/Alamo (406/257-7144 or 800/CAR-RENT, www.nationalcar .com), Avis (406/257-2727 or 800/230-4898, www.avis.com), and Budget (406/755-7500 or 800/527-0700, www.budget.com). Kalispell and Whitefish also have rental-car agencies (find list at www.iflyglacier.com), which will deliver a car to the airport or pick you up.

RV Rental

The closest RV rentals are located near the airport, a 20-minute drive from Glacier. **J & L RV Rentals** (1805 Hwy. 2 West, Columbia Falls, 406/892-7666, www.jandlrvrentals .com) has motor homes and trailers. Although somewhat expensive (starting around $210 per day), RVing is an easy way to tour national parks with the good parts of camping but without the hassle of tents. Be aware, however, of Going-to-the-Sun Road's vehicle length restrictions (21 feet). Only the smallest RVs will be able to cross the highway. With larger RVs, you must use shuttles or bus tours to see the historic road, or rent a car.

Equipment Rental

Glacier Outdoor Center (11957 Hwy. 2 East, West Glacier, 406/888-5454 or 800/235-6781, www.glacierraftco.com) has the most comprehensive collection of rental gear. The center rents outdoor gear for rafting, bicycling, camping, backpacking, fishing, snowshoeing, and cross-country skiing—everything from sleeping bags to stoves, life jackets, rods and waders, headlamps, rain gear, tents, and coolers. Complete camping setups for rafting ($150 plus) and car camping packages ($125 plus) are available as well as all items singly. Fishing gear ranges $5–50 plus. Reservations are recommended, and you'll need a valid ID to rent.

Other recreational rental gear—skis, kayaks, boats, bicycles—is available through specialty outdoor shops and marinas in Flathead Valley. (See *Recreation* in the *Flathead Valley* chapter.)

Food and Accommodations

Because Glacier is so close to the airport, many travelers go directly into the park on the same day. Likewise with flying out. However, for those adding Flathead Valley explorations to their itineraries, lodging varies from dirt cheap to high end, and many offer complimentary airport shuttles. No lodging exists in the immediate airport vicinity, but rather in Columbia Falls, downtown Kalispell, and Whitefish (check the *Flathead Valley* chapter for accommodations and rates). To be closest to Glacier at 20 minutes away, head to Columbia Falls nine miles from the airport. Lodging in "C Falls" runs the gamut from a budget motel to a golf resort. Downtown Kalispell with its chain hotels also is nine miles from the airport, but in the opposite direction from the park. The resort town of Whitefish sits 11 miles away, with independent motels, B and Bs, and ski and golf resorts. Both Kalispell and Whitefish are approximately a 40-minute drive from West Glacier.

Other than the cafeteria inside the airport, no restaurants are close. En route to Glacier, Columbia Falls has fast food, sandwiches, gooey ribs, and Mexican fare. Those looking for fine dining experiences should gravitate to Whitefish or Kalispell. Check the *Flathead Valley* chapter for restaurant options.

GREAT FALLS

Straddling the mighty Missouri River, Great Falls, Montana, is an east-side gateway to Glacier. But the lack of easy connections with Amtrak and buses make renting a car preferable to drive the 143 miles to the park. With a flight arriving by late afternoon, you can be in East Glacier to watch the sunset that same day.

If you have time to spend in Great Falls, there are two things worth exploring. Squeeze in the **Lewis and Clark National Historic Trail Interpretive Center** (4201 Giant Springs Rd., 406/727-8733, 9 A.M.–6 P.M. daily late May–Sept., 9 A.M.–5 P.M. Tues.–Sat. and Sun. noon–5 P.M. Oct.–May, adults $5, kids 15 and under free). Lewis and Clark followed the Missouri through Great Falls missing Marias Pass at Glacier's southern end, one of the easiest passes over the Continental Divide. The Forest Service–operated center is well worth a walk through historical displays, live demonstrations, and multimedia shows.

Take in the **C.M. Russell Museum** (400 13th St. N., 406/727-8787, www.cmrussell.org, 9 A.M.–6 P.M. daily May–Sept., 10 A.M.–5 P.M. Tues.–Sat. Oct.–Apr., adults $8, students $3). The museum collection celebrates the work of the famous western painter Charlie Russell (1864–1926), who summered in his cabin on Glacier's Lake McDonald, and is known for his early west scenes—depictions of cowboys, mountains, hunters, and horses.

For travelers coming fairly prepared, Great Falls can work as a travel hub. But for those requiring camping equipment or RV rentals, none are available in the city itself nor on Glacier's east side. The nearest equipment and RV rentals are on the park's west side in West Glacier and Flathead Valley, both a convoluted detour out of the way from Great Falls.

Airport

Great Falls International Airport (GTF) (406/727-3404, www.gtfairport.com) receives air service from Delta/Sky West from Salt Lake City, Northwest from Minneapolis, United from Denver, and Horizon Air from Seattle. Like the Kalispell airport, its international label comes from a couple charter flights from Canada. Located outside town, the airport is convenient for picking up on-site rental cars but requires hotel-provided shuttles or a taxi ride to access hotels and restaurants in town 10 minutes away.

Train

From Great Falls, the closest westbound train depot is Shelby, 87 miles north, where **Amtrak's** Empire Builder (800/USA-RAIL or 800/872-7245, www.amtrak.com) runs from Chicago westbound once daily past Glacier. (Chicago to East Glacier starts at $204.) Catch a bus to Shelby, and you can nab a really cheap ticket to East Glacier ($11 one-way). National Park Service interpretive guides join the train between Shelby and Seattle. From Shelby, the train leaves daily at 5:22 P.M., arriving in East Glacier at 6:45 P.M., Essex at 7:41 P.M., West Glacier at 8:23 P.M., and Whitefish at 8:56 P.M. On this route, Amtrak tends to run late. Not just five minutes late, but up to several hours behind schedule, especially in winter with avalanches. Be prepared to contend with arriving in the middle of the night.

Special Amtrak deals are available. Kids ages 2–15 are half-price. Seniors, veterans, AAA and NARP members, military personnel, and students can also get 10–15 percent discounts: check Amtrak's website for details. Amtrak is frequently threatened to have its federal funding yanked. If funding is cut, the Empire Builder usually faces the axe. Check with Amtrak for any changes to schedules and service.

Bus

Trailways' **Rimrock Stages** (800/255-7655, www.rimrocktrailways.com) connect Montana locales via Butte to Great Falls, but not with Glacier Park nor Shelby for connecting with Amtrak. However, in 2008, **Northern Transit Interlocal** (406/470-0727; www.toolecounty mt.gov) started running a 15-passenger van between Shelby and Great Falls, once each direction on Mondays and Thursdays. With prior arrangement, the service will pick you up at the Great Falls Airport, or you can catch the bus at the Great Falls Transit Transfer Center (326 1st Ave. S.). It stops at the Amtrak depot in Shelby. It's a free service, but they do accept donations. This same bus service also operates a Great Falls-Kalispell route twice a week. The bus passes through Browning, East Glacier, Essex, and West Glacier. Call for schedules for both services.

Taxis

Some hotels provide airport shuttle service. Otherwise, **Diamond Cab** (406/453-3241) is the only option to hop into town from the airport.

Car Rental

Great Falls has most national rental car chains. Alamo (406/727-0273 or 800/462-5266; www.alamo.com), Hertz (406/761-6641 or 800/654-3131; www.hertz.com), Dollar (406/453-3535 or 800/800-4000; www.dollar.com), National (406/453-4386 or 800/227-7368; www.nationalcar.com), and Avis (406/761-7610 or 800/230-4898; www.avis.com) are located right in the airport terminal. The airport's website (www.gtfairport.com) lists other rental-car agencies with offices elsewhere than the airport terminal. They will either pick you up by shuttle or deliver your car to you.

Food and Accommodations

Great Falls has hotels and motels ranging from low end to moderately priced accommodations, but nothing too upscale. Most national hotel chains are downtown. For hotels offering airport shuttles, check the Great Falls Airport website (www.gtfairport.com) or the Great Falls Convention and Visitors Bureau (800/735-8535, www.greatfallscvb.visitmt.com).

For a filling meal at a reasonable price, head for **MacKenzie River Pizza Company** (500 River Dr. S., 406/761-0085, open 11 A.M.–9 P.M. daily, until 10 P.M. Fri. and Sat. nights, closing time one hour later in summer, $7–20), Montana's creative answer to pizza chains. The restaurant serves cowboy nachos, giant salads and sandwiches, and of course eclectic pizzas. If you're out on the town, try one of Montana's microbrews—a Moose Drool Brown Ale if you like dark beers, or a Scape Goat Pale Ale, both from Big Sky Brewing in Missoula.

CALGARY

Calgary, Alberta, may provide the perfect hub for some travelers depending on the city of origin, and if you schedule your trip in mid-July, you can take in one of the biggest rodeos in the region—the Calgary Stampede (403/269-9822 or 800/661-1767; wwwcalgarystampede.com). However, travel from Calgary to Glacier or Waterton can be a challenge. No train connection is available. No bus route goes all the way to Waterton, nor Glacier. For ease, most visitors traveling from Calgary rent a vehicle. With an early afternoon flight arrival, you can be walking the beach at Waterton Lake in the evening.

Airport

Calgary International Airport (403/735-1200, www.calgaryairport.com, code YYC) bustles with flights from Tokyo, London, and Frankfurt. It has restaurants, shopping, and over 25 airlines servicing the area. Airport shuttles connect with downtown, hotels, rental-car agencies, and the Greyhound Bus Terminal. Because Calgary is still 149 miles (240 km) from Waterton, most visitors heading to the park rent a car. Others chop off part of the distance by flying via Air Canada (888/247-2262, www.aircanada.com) on to Lethbridge (www.lethbridgecountyairport.com, code YQL), where they rent a car to drive 87 miles (140 km) to Waterton.

Train

If you're traveling by **VIA Rail Canada** (800/VIA-RAIL or 800/842-7245, www.viarail.ca), you'll see lots of Canada, but have a difficult time getting to Waterton and Glacier. Canadian trains hit Winnipeg and Vancouver, which are roughly the same latitude as Waterton, but in between the route jogs north bypassing southern Alberta and southeastern

British Columbia. The closest you can get to Waterton is Edmonton, 332 miles (534 km) away. Most train travelers switch to air or bus travel to Calgary and then rent a car.

Bus
Greyhound Canada (403/265-9111 or 800/661-8747, www.greyhound.ca, no reservations accepted) services cities in southern Alberta, but not Waterton. Bus service connects with Calgary International Airport, and daily buses run from Calgary to Pincher Creek, but no farther: in Pincher Creek, you're stuck 31 miles from Waterton with no car rentals available. You can, however, hire a cab (Crystal Taxi (403/627-4262), but it's pricey—around CDN $70 one way.

Car Rental
Most major car-rental chains have desks inside the Calgary Airport terminal or within a shuttle hop down the road. Vehicles can be booked from home through American sister companies: Alamo (800/462-5266; www.alamo.com), Hertz (800/654-3131; www.hertz.com), Dollar (800/800-4000; www.dollar.com), National (800/227-7368; www.nationalcar.com), Budget (800/472-3325; www.budget.com), and Avis (800/230-4898; www.avis.com). Rates range CDN$79–250 per day, depending on the vehicle's size.

RV Rental
Two RV rental companies are within three kilometers (less than two miles) from the Calgary Airport and offer transfers from the airport and airport hotels: **Canada RV Rentals** (250/814-0251 or 866/814-0253, www.canada-rv-rentals.com) and **CanaDream** (403/291-1000 or 800/461-7368, www.canadream.com). Calgary also has other large RV rental chains. Check in the phone book for listings.

RVing is a fun but somewhat pricey way (small rigs start at CDN$165 per day) to tour national parks without having to put tents up and down each day; however, be aware of Going-to-the-Sun Road's vehicle-length restrictions (21 feet). You may have to supplement your RV tour with shuttles or red bus tours to see the historic road. Only the smallest RVs will be able to cross the highway.

Equipment Rental
For those needing outdoor gear, **Calgary Outdoor Centre** (2500 University Dr. NW, 403/220-5038, www.calgaryoutdoorcentre.ca) rents equipment for reasonable rates. It has gear for camping, backpacking, boating, fishing, snowshoeing, climbing, and skiing. Tents start at CDN$10, backpacks CDN$8, GPS units CDN$7, stoves CDN$4, and sleeping bags CDN$6 daily. Rafts, kayaks, skis, canoes, mountain bikes, climbing gear, and car racks are also available as well as clothing, rain gear, and hiking boots. Call to reserve equipment ahead of time, a must during midsummer; a nonrefundable deposit by credit card is required (rate based on half-day). When you pick up your gear, try it on to be sure it fits and have the staff demonstrate how to use unfamiliar equipment. You'll also need a driver's license or photo ID to rent gear.

Food and Accommodations
The airport terminal itself houses the extremely convenient **Delta Calgary Airport Hotel** (403/250-8722 or 877/814-7706, www.deltahotels.com, CDN$229–414). Within a few miles of the airport, major chain hotels start at $110 per night. Some offer airport shuttles. For additional hotel information and reservations, check http://calgary.airporthotelguide.com or contact Tourism Calgary (403/263-8510, www.tourismcalgary.com).

Budget-minded travelers may want to head for a hostel. The **Calgary City Centre Hostel** (403/670-7580, www.hihostels.ca) has dorm beds costing CDN$30 per night. If you are planning on staying in hostels across Canada as part of your Glacier-Waterton trip, consider purchasing a Hostelling International $35 membership, which gives 10–15 percent discounts on nightly rates. Waterton Lakes National Park also offers lodging in a Hostelling International lodge, as does East Glacier.

Canadian cuisine is somewhat bland, but a

few Alberta specialties merit a taste. Calgary is in the heart of cattle country; grass-fed Alberta beef graces menus in all forms. Buffalo, too. At the high end, it's amazingly tender and sweet; at the lower end, it's still decent. Expect to find the fries accompanying your burger in Canada to be different: they may have gravy on top.

And contrary to many towns east of the Rocky Mountains where steak and potato fare reigns, Calgary is much more internationally cosmopolitan with a good share of ethnic restaurants. Don't forget: Canada's 7 percent GST (Goods and Services Tax) will be added on lodging and food bills.

Getting Around

DRIVING

Driving in Glacier National Park is not particularly easy. Narrow roads built for cars in the 1930s barely fit today's SUVs, much less RVs and trailers. With no shoulders and sharp curves, roads require reduced speeds and shifting into second gear on extended descents to avoid the fumes of burning brakes. Two roads cross the Continental Divide: Going-to-the-Sun Road bisects the park, while U.S. Highway 2 hugs Glacier's southern border. Both are two-laners; however, Going-to-the-Sun Road is the more difficult drive, climbing 1,500 feet higher on a skinnier, snakier road than Highway 2. It's also currently undergoing reconstruction. Going-to-the-Sun Road completely opens in summer for about three months, while Highway 2 is open year-round. Going-to-the-Sun Road does not permit RVs and trailer-rig combos over 21 feet long.

Paved two-lane roads also lead to Two Medicine, St. Mary, Many Glacier, and Waterton. But don't have fantasies here: Just because roads are paved doesn't mean that they are smooth. Frost heaves and sinkholes pockmark them, bouncing passengers and slowing travel. Montana is also the land of dusty, potholed dirt roads: on the west side, two notorious bumpy roads lead up the North Fork Valley; on the east side, a dirt road leads into the Cut Bank Valley. In some places they are decent; in others they are as bad as they can be without requiring a four-wheel drive. Larger RVs and those with trailers will not be comfortable on some dirt roads.

Service Stations

Gas up before you go! You won't find service stations on every corner here. Gas is available in West Glacier, East Glacier, St. Mary, Babb, and Waterton, but few of the stations can mend severely broken-down vehicles. For big vehicle work, you'll need to hit Browning or Flathead Valley.

MAPS AND PLANNERS

Park maps that include both Glacier and Waterton are handed out at every entrance station and available at visitors centers, ranger stations, and online (www.nps.gov/glac). These maps are perfect for driving tours and perhaps a short walk or two. However, for those heading into the backcountry on day hikes and backpacking trips, a topographical map is more useful. Glacier's *Trails Illustrated* (includes Waterton) and the *USGS Glacier Park* (not including Waterton) topographical maps are each $10 through **Glacier Natural History Association** (406/888-5756, www.glacier association.org). For more detailed maps, USGS maps are available in the 7.5 Minute Series at Flathead Valley sporting goods store or through USGS (888/ASK-USGS or 888/275-8747, http://store.usgs.gov). For hiking Waterton, you'll find the best topographical map at the Waterton Visitor Information Center (403/859-5133). You can also order it online (www.gemtrek.com). The Gem Trek Publishing map (CDN$9) not only includes roads, trails, and bike routes, but trail descriptions for easy, moderate, and strenuous hikes. It also includes the eastern end of

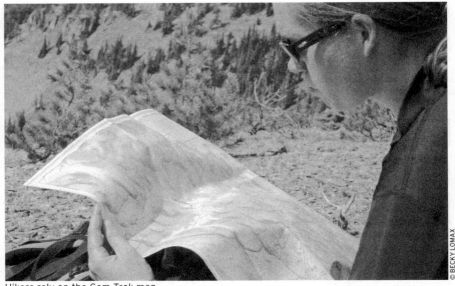

© BECKY LOMAX

Hikers rely on the Gem Trek map.

Akamina-Kishinena Provincial Park and the Goat Haunt area of Glacier.

For hiking trails, area brochure maps (Many Glacier, Lake McDonald, Two Medicine, Logan Pass, and St. Mary) are available at ranger stations, visitors centers, hotel activity desks, and online. These do not have as much detail as topographical maps but can work in a pinch for day hikes on well-signed trails.

Yearly, the park service updates its *Glacier Vacation Planner,* a newspaper listing current campground, road, park, visitors center, border, trail, and safety concerns. Call the park for a mailed copy (406/888-7800) or the current edition is also online (www.nps.gov/glac).

For maps and information about national forests and the Bob Marshall Wilderness adjacent to the park, contact the **Hungry Horse Ranger Station** (10 Hungry Horse Dr., Hungry Horse, 406/387-3800; www.fs.fed .us/r1/flathead). For Lewis and Clark National Forest, call the Rocky Mountain Ranger Station (1102 Main Ave. NW, Choteau, 406/466-5341, www.fs.fed.us/r1/lewisclark).

SHUTTLES
Bus Shuttles

Inside Glacier, the National Park Service runs several **free shuttle** routes July 1–Labor Day. These are shuttles, not guided tours. Between Apgar and St. Mary, they stop at 16 points denoted by interpretive signs on Going-to-the-Sun Road. Get on or off at any of the stops. No tickets are needed; no reservations are taken. These extremely popular shuttles enable point-to-point hiking on some of Glacier's most spectacular trails. West-side Sun Road shuttles depart every 15–30 minutes with stops at the Apgar Transit Center, Sprague Creek Campground, Lake McDonald Lodge, Avalanche Creek, The Loop, and Logan Pass. The 30-mile ride from the transit center to Logan Pass takes 90 minutes or more. East-side shuttles depart every 30 minutes from St. Mary Visitor Center. The one-hour shuttle reaches Logan Pass in 18 miles after stopping at Rising Sun, Sun Point, Sunrift Gorge, St. Mary Falls Trailhead, Gunsight Pass Trailhead, and Siyeh Bend. Both routes begin uphill service at 7:00 A.M. with the last

CELL PHONES

Probably one of the best inventions for emergencies, cell phones allow immediate access to help. However, in an area as mountainous as northwest Montana, they do not always work.

Flathead Valley has comprehensive cell phone coverage. But when driving around Glacier, your phone may not get service. Dealing with a flat tire may require more than a cell phone call to AAA. Throughout much of Going-to-the-Sun Road and Glacier Park, cell-phone reception is sporadic to nonexistent. You can get service in parts of St. Mary, East Glacier, West Glacier, and Waterton.

Hikers and backpackers should carry a cell phone for emergencies, but do not rely on it as the sole means of rescue. High mountains and deep valleys often prevent reception. Be prepared to deal with emergencies and self-rescue.

When phones do work in Glacier, use of cell phones in the backcountry requires etiquette:

- Turn off ringers because phone noise catapults hikers and campers from a natural experience back into the hubbub of modern life.

- If you must make a call (and the phone does work), move away from campsites and other hikers to avoid disrupting their experience.

- In backcountry chalets, go outside and away from people.

- On trails, refrain from using phones in the presence of other hikers.

- Be considerate of other people in the backcountry and their desire to "get away from it all."

departures from Logan Pass at 7 P.M. On the west side, several routes service the road; confirm your destination when you board to be sure you have the right shuttle.

Glacier Park, Inc. (406/892-2525, www .glacierparkinc.com, $8–40 one-way) runs a daily van service north-south on the park's east side early June–late September. It links East Glacier, Two Medicine, Cut Bank Creek, St. Mary, Many Glacier, Chief Mountain Customs, and Waterton. No reservations are taken, and you pay in cash when you board. Between July–Labor Day, additional shuttles run from Many Glacier to St. Mary—usually two in early morning and two in late afternoon to accommodate hikers on the Highline-Swiftcurrent and Piegan Trail. Call or check online for current schedules.

By reservation, **Sun Tours** (406/226-9220 or 800/786-9220, www.glaciersuntours.com, June–Sept.) also shuttles hikers from St. Mary or East Glacier to east-side trailheads. Costs vary with numbers of passengers, gear, time, and location.

Running shuttles year round by reservation, **Flathead-Glacier Transportation** (406/892-3390 or 800/829-7039, www.fgtrans.com, $36–260 one-way) picks up travelers and backpackers at Glacier International Airport and transports them to Chief Mountain Customs, Many Glacier, St. Mary, Two Medicine, East Glacier, West Glacier, Polebridge, and Highway 2 trailheads. The cost of the drop-off or pickup can be split between all the people in your group. They also run shuttles to Flathead Valley locations.

In Waterton, **Waterton Visitor Services** (Tamarack Village Square, 214 Mount View Rd., 403/859-2378, www.watertonvisitorservices.com, late May–early Oct., CDN$12–22) shuttles hikers to the popular Carthew-Alderson trailhead or to Chief Mountain Customs to catch GPI's east side Glacier shuttle.

Boat Shuttles

Hikers and backpackers also use tour boats as hiking shuttles to lop off foot miles. In Glacier, **Glacier Park Boat Company** (406/257-2426, www.glacierparkboats.com, June–Sept., $5.50–9 one-way, kids half-price) carts hikers across Two Medicine Lake and in Many Glacier across Swiftcurrent and Josephine Lakes. Both add early morning Hiker Express shuttles July–August. Pay with cash at the docks; you do not need reservations for catching a return boat. If the last boat back is full, the boat company continues to run shuttles until all hikers are accommodated.

In Waterton, **Waterton Shoreline Cruises** (403/859-2362, www.watertoncruise.com, adults CDN$16–32, kids CDN$8–16) runs boat shuttles to the Crypt Lake Trailhead (May–early Oct.) and the tour boat to Goat Haunt, USA, functions as a hiker shuttle, too, but only June–late September.

TOURS
Bus Tours
Two bus-tour companies operate in Glacier Park, both traveling the scenic Going-to-the-Sun Road. You'll get the "inside story" on the park from both of their guides.

Departing from East Glacier, Browning, St. Mary, and West Glacier, **Sun Tours** (406/226-9220 or 800/786-9220, www.glaciersuntours.com, June–Sept., adults $40–70, kids $15–20, park entrance fees not included) leads four- and seven-hour daily tours over Going-to-the-Sun Road in 25-passenger air-conditioned buses with huge windows. Interpretation is steeped in Blackfeet cultural history and park lore.

The historic **red buses** with roll-back canvas tops are operated by Glacier Park, Inc. (406/892-2525, www.glacierparkinc.com, late May–late Sept.). Daily tours (adults $35–90, kids half-price, park entrance fees and meals not included) depart from all the park lodges for Going-to-the-Sun Road, Waterton, and other park environs. The company also guides the popular **Great Lodges of Glacier** tour (single $2,290; double $1,689 per person, kids 11 and under $619), a six-day romp through four of the park's historic lodges offered late June–mid-September. The tour begins and ends in East Glacier, but the package includes pickup at Glacier Park International Airport

in Flathead Valley. Traveling by historic red jammer buses, the tour stays at Glacier Park Lodge, Prince of Wales Hotel, Many Glacier Hotel, and Lake McDonald Lodge. Rates include lodging, some meals, and transportation around Glacier. All 18 of their tours sell out, so reserve early for this.

Hiking Tours
For hikers, **Glacier Guides** (406/387-5555 or 800/321-7238, www.glacierguides.com) runs several tours July–August. Their six-day inn trip ($1,949) stays in the park lodges. Their five-day camping safari tents in front-country campgrounds with the guides cooking homestyle meals ($910). Their most popular trip is the six-day Ultimate, which hikes to both historic backcountry chalets (Granite and Sperry) and includes a stay at Belton Chalet ($1,700). On each of these tours, the guides lead daily hikes from 6–12 miles in length. The company also departs weekly with three-, four-, and six-day backpacking trips and offers two popular Continental Divide 10-day backpacking trips. You can also hire a sherpa ($165/day) to carry your gear. Equipment, guide service, transportation in Glacier, and most meals are included.

Boat Tours
Five lakes in Waterton-Glacier International Peace Park have scenic boat tours. In Glacier, **Glacier Park Boat Company** (406/257-2426, www.glacierparkboats.com, June–Sept., $11–20, kids half-price) operates daily boat tours on Lake McDonald, Two Medicine Lake, St. Mary Lake, and in Many Glacier on Swiftcurrent and Josephine Lakes. Departure times vary. Buy tickets (cash only) early in the day at the docks in high season, for tour boats fill up fast. In Waterton, scenic boat tours travel down Waterton Lake across the international border. **Waterton Shoreline Cruises** (403/859-2362, www.watertoncruise.com, late May–early Oct., adults CDN$32, teens CDN$16, kids 4–12 CDN$10, under 4 free) departs several times daily with a stop at Goat Haunt, U.S.A. (except in late Sept.). Purchase tickets at the dock.

© BECKY LOMAX

Two Medicine Lake and the *Sinopah* boat tour

BY RV
Road Restrictions

Going-to-the-Sun Road restricts RVs and trailers. From bumper to bumper, vehicles must be 21 feet or shorter to drive the road between Avalanche Campground on the west and Sun Point on the east. A truck- or car-trailer combination must also be under 21 feet. The maximum width allowed, including mirrors, is 8 feet; maximum height is 10 feet. Despite meeting width and height requirements, camper drivers still feel pinched as they navigate the skinny lanes hemmed in by a vertical 1,000-foot wall and a three-foot-tall guardrail in construction zones.

Don't lose heart just because you travel by RV! You can still see the famed Going-to-the-Sun Road via GPI's red bus tours, Sun Tours, and free park shuttles or rent a car in West Glacier, East Glacier, or St. Mary.

Camping

Several campgrounds inside the park accommodate larger RVs and fifth wheels. Apgar can handle the largest RVs, up to 40 feet. Fish Creek, Many Glacier, and St. Mary have sites that can fit RVs up to 35 feet. Two Medicine can accommodate RVs up to 32 feet. Only the shorter RVs can fit into sites at Rising Sun (up to 25 feet), Avalanche (up to 26 feet), and Sprague Creek (up to 21 feet, but no towed units). Large units are not recommended at Bowman Lake, Cut Bank, Kintla Lake, Logging Creek, and Quartz Creek.

Campgrounds inside the park do not have hookups, nor do campgrounds in adjacent national forests or the North Fork. Waterton Lakes National Park, however, is an exception, for the Townsite Campground has hookups. If hookups are essential, head outside Glacier Park to commercial campgrounds in West Glacier, East Glacier, St. Mary, Flathead Valley, outside Waterton Park, and along Highway 2.

Disposal Stations

Seven locations inside Glacier Park have disposal stations: Apgar, Fish Creek, Many Glacier, Rising Sun, St. Mary, Two Medicine, and Waterton. Many private campgrounds at West Glacier, St. Mary, and East Glacier have disposal stations. The North Fork has none. In Waterton National Park, you'll find dump stations at the Townsite and Crandell campgrounds and commercial campgrounds outside the park.

Repairs

Should you need repair services, drive into the Flathead Valley, where your best bet is to consult RV repairs in the phone book and start calling to find who can fit you in to their repair schedule the soonest. If you cannot drive to the Flathead, **Rocky Mountain Repair** (181 Kelly Rd., Kalispell, 406/253-9694) offers mobile services and can repair many things where you are, but you'll definitely pay more for them to come to Glacier. In Waterton, **Pat's Gas Station** (224 Mount View Rd., 403/859-2266, www.watertoninfo.ab.ca) can do minor repairs.

BY BICYCLE

Glacier is a tough place to bicycle. No shoulders, narrow roads, curves, and drivers gawking at scenery instead of the road all shove the biker into a precarious position. With that caveat said, for a cyclist nothing competes with bicycling Going-to-the-Sun Road! It's one of the country's premier bicycling routes. Other roads surrounding Glacier also make good rides, particularly the 142-mile loop linking Going-to-the-Sun Road and Highways 89, 49, and 2. Roadie racers do it in one day; tourers ride the loop in two or three days.

Bike Trails

Designated bike trails are few and far between in Waterton-Glacier. In fact, Glacier has only two trails, both in the Apgar area—one paved, one dirt. No bicycles are allowed on any other backcountry trails in Glacier. In Waterton, however, four trails permit bicycles.

Campsites

Several of Glacier's campgrounds maintain campsites specifically for bikers and hikers:

Apgar, Fish Creek, Sprague Creek, Avalanche, Rising Sun, St. Mary, Many Glacier, and Two Medicine. Held until 9 P.M., the sites are shared, holding up to eight people who pay $5 per person. If these sites are full, you must find a regular designated unoccupied tent site (impossible during high season late at night). Hiker-biker sites have special bear-resistant food storage.

Safety

Because of narrow, shoulderless roads, bikers should have some riding ability before hitting Glacier's roads. Drainage grates, ice, and debris can throw bikes off balance quickly, adding to the challenge. Although bicyclists on Going-to-the-Sun Road are fairly commonplace, many drivers are so agog at the view that they may not be fully conscious of your presence—which is a good reason to wear a helmet and bright colors. Skinny, shoulderless roads demand riding in single file. For added protection, be sure

biking Going-to-the-Sun Road

© BECKY LOMAX

your bike has reflectors on both ends, and use lights in fog and at dawn, dusk, or night.

Restrictions

Because of high traffic and narrow lanes, Glacier enforces bicycling restrictions on Going-to-the-Sun Road's west side. Between June 15 and Labor Day, two sections of the road are closed 11 A.M.–4 P.M.: between Apgar turnoff and Sprague Creek Campground; eastbound (going uphill only) from Logan Creek to Logan Pass. The ride from Sprague to Logan Creek takes about 45 minutes; the climb from Logan Creek to Logan Pass usually takes about three hours.

Repairs

Bring spare tubes and brake pads, a pump, and equipment to effect minor repairs yourself. The park doesn't have bike shops to bail you out. For big repairs, head to the bike shops in Flathead Valley. (See the *Flathead Valley* chapter for suggestions.)

BY MOTORCYCLE

Motorcyclists relish riding Going-to-the-Sun Road. On sunny days, the ride is unparalleled; on inclement days, it's bone-chilling. Many motorcyclists gravitate to Montana because the state requires helmets only for those 17 years old and younger. However, since most drivers on Going-to-the-Sun Road find their attention severely divided between the scenery and the road, you may want to consider wind-in-the-hair versus protection if hit. In Waterton, helmets are required.

Motorcyclists are also allowed to use the shared biker-hiker campsites ($5 per person) at the park's major campgrounds. These are first-come, first-serve and held until 9 P.M.

If you need repairs, the Flathead Valley has several motorcycle shops. Some specialize in one brand over another, including Harley-Davidsons. Your best bet is to check under motorcycle repair in the phone book to pick the appropriate service for your machine.

RESOURCES

Suggested Reading

DRIVING GUIDES

Guthrie, C.W., Martha Cheney, and Diane Krage. *Glacier National Park Legends And Lore: Along Going To The Sun Road.* Helena, MT: Farcountry Press, 2002. An 88-page, mile-by-mile tour of the historic road in Native American tales from Hugh Monroe, known as Rising Wolf of the Blackfeet.

Peterson, Chris, ed. *Glacier National Park Auto Tours.* Columbia Falls, MT: Hungry Horse News, 2000. This large 16-page guide describes four auto tours in the park: Going-to-the-Sun Road and Many Glacier Road, Two Medicine and East Glacier, Waterton, and the North Fork. Each road details specific stops and what to see there.

Schmidt, Thomas. *Glacier-Waterton Lakes National Park Road Guide.* Washington, DC: National Geographic, 2004. A handy 93-page guide to driving the park's roads. Each section is complete with a map, nature notes, landscape features, and stops.

GEOLOGY

Alt, David, and Donald W. Hyndman. *Roadside Geology of Montana.* Missoula, MT: Mountain Press, 1986. Although Glacier's roads are treated minimally here, the diagrams and descriptions are useful even to non-geologists. It is the best resource for geology on roads outside the park.

Raup, Omar B., Robert L. Earhart, James W. Whipple, Paul E. Carrara. *Geology Along Going-to-the-Sun Road.* West Glacier, MT: Glacier Natural History Association, 1983. An easy-to-read 63-page geology guide for folks with no science background. Maps, 21 stops, and diagrams describe the geologic phenomenon on the historic highway along with great photos showing rock formations.

GRIZZLY BEARS

Chadwick, Doug. *True Griz.* San Francisco, CA: Sierra Club Books, 2003. True stories of four grizzly bears—their survival and deaths. Chadwick is a very reputable bear biologist.

Herrero, Stephen. *Bear Attacks: Their Causes and Avoidance.* Guilford, CT: The Lyons Press, 2002. Somewhat sensationalized with attention to gory detail, Herrero's book paints a picture of the myriad reasons for bear attacks while also covering safety and how to avoid attacks. Not for light sleepers who plan to go into the backcountry, Herrero is one of the leading authorities on bear research.

McMillion, Scott. *Mark of the Grizzly.* Helena, MT: Falcon Press Publishing Company, 1998. McMillion tells the stories behind 18 different grizzly bear attacks. He doesn't shy away from the gore, nor does he become preachy or judgmental, but he does examine each attack in detail to determine what we learn about bears.

Schneider, Bill. *Bear Aware.* Helena, MT: Falcon Press Publishing Co., 2004. This handy little 96-page book is packed with advice on how to hike safely in bear country. One section tackles bear myths, debunking them with facts.

HISTORY

Buchholtz, C.W. *Men in Glacier.* West Glacier, MT: Glacier Natural History Association, 1976. It's a hard book to read because of its large size with small print (it would be much better as a regular-sized paperback), but it's thick with information on Glacier's human history, from early Native Americans to park rangers.

Djuff, Ray, and Chris Morrison. *Glacier's Historic Hotels and Chalets: View with a Room.* Helena, MT: Farcountry Press, 2001. Loaded with historical photos, this quasi-coffee-table book tells the story behind each of Glacier Park's lodges and chalets, including chalets no longer existing. A great background read for anyone who falls in love with Glacier's historic lodges.

Guthrie, Carol. *All Aboard for Glacier: The Great Northern Railway and Glacier National Park.* Helena, MT: Farcountry Press, 2004. For train buffs, the history of the Great Northern Railway building up Glacier as a destination for their riders.

Hanna, Warren L. *Montana's Many-Splendored Glacierland.* Grand Forks, ND: University of North Dakota Foundation, 1987. The fact that Hanna's book is somewhat outdated doesn't matter here; he covers historical detail that no one else does—from Marias Pass to Native Americans, dude-wranglers, and celebrity visitors. Historical photos are also included.

Holterman, Jack. *Place Names of Glacier National Park.* Helena, MT: Riverbend Publishing, 2006. A list of 663 park names—how peaks, passes, lakes, rivers, and valleys in Glacier acquired their monikers.

Lawrence, Tom. *Pictures, a Park, and a Pulitzer: Mel Ruder and the Hungry Horse News.* Helena, MT: Farcountry Press, 2000. Photos and stories from Lawrence, a Pulitzer Prize-winning journalist and editor for 32 years at the *Hungry Horse News.* Much of the history covers Glacier.

Schultz, James Willard. *Blackfeet Tales of Glacier National Park.* Helena, MT: Riverbend Publishing, 1916. Original Blackfeet stories collected by Schultz in the late 1800s, including the history of Two Medicine, Cut Bank, St. Mary, Swiftcurrent, and Chief Mountain.

NATURAL HISTORY

DeSanto, Jerry. *Logan Pass.* Guilford, CT: Globe Pequot Press, 1995. Gorgeous photos and short, easy-to-read desciptions of the Logan Pass environment, from grizzly bears to bikes, red buses, hiking, climbing, winter, wildflowers, and geology.

Fisher, Chris. *Birds of the Rocky Mountains.* Edmonton, AB: Lone Pine Publishing, 1997. A Lone Pine Field Guide for birds found in the Rocky Mountains—every species from raptors to waterfowl, songbirds to woodpeckers. Large drawings help with identification, and descriptions include details on size, range, habitat, nesting, and feeding. Details point out differences between similar species.

Fisher, Chris, Don Pattie, and Tamara Hartson. *Mammals of the Rocky Mountains.* Edmonton, AB: Lone Pine Publishing, 2000. A Lone Pine Field Guide for 91 species of animals found in the Rocky Mountains—a breeze to use. Each animal has details on physical description, behavior, habitat, food, denning, range, and young. Similar species are described to point out differences for identification.

Kershaw, Linda, Andy MacKinnon, and Jim Pojar. *Plants of the Rocky Mountains.* Edmonton, AB: Lone Pine Publishing, 1998. A Lone Pine Field Guide for eight types of flora found in the Rocky Mountains: trees, shrubs, wildflowers, aquatics, grasses, ferns, mosses, and lichens. Although the pictures are small, the detailed descriptions of appearance, season, and habitat help in identification. Notes on each of the 1,300 species given include fun tidbits on the origin of names and Native American uses.

Kimball, Shannon Fitzpatrick, and Peter Lesica. *Wildflowers of Glacier National Park and Surrounding Areas.* Kalispell, MT: Trillium Press, 2005. One of the best regional flower guides. Flowers are categorized by color with big sharp photos allowing easy identification. Trees, ferns, and grasses are included, too.

Rockwell, David. *Glacier National Park: A Natural History Guide.* New York: Houghton Mifflin Company, 1995. A rather dense with detail but accurate description of Glacier Park's natural history not only on the big scale, but with personal narrative included, too. Rockwell covers geology, glaciers, flora, fauna, fires, and human impact on the ecosystem in the best in-depth natural history book available on the park.

Strickler, Dr. Dee. *Alpine Wildflowers, Forest Wildflowers,* and *Prairie Wildflowers.* Helena, MT: Falcon Press Publishing Co., 1990. Three books cover the flowers of different northern Rocky Mountain habitats. Descriptions and excellent photos make for easy identification.

Ulrich, Tom J. *Mammals of the Northern Rockies.* Missoula, MT: Mountain Publishing Company, 1990. Wildlife photographer Ulrich uses photos and descriptions to detail the life and habits of area mammals, from the little brown bat to the mountain goat. All the big megafauna are here—moose, bison, sheep, bear, wolf—as well as tiny pikas and mice.

Wilkinson, Todd, and Michael H. Francis, *Watching Glacier's Wildlife.* Helena, MT: Riverbend Publishing, 2002. A 96-page guide to when, where, and how to see Glacier's wildlife.

OUTDOOR RECREATION

Arthur, Jean. *Montana Winter Trails: The Best Cross-Country Ski and Snowshoe Trails.* Guilford, CT: Globe Pequot Press, 2001. Trail descriptions include five detailed trips for Glacier and several more for Flathead Valley.

Duckworth, Carolyn, ed. *Hiker's Guide to Glacier National Park* and *Short Hikes and Strolls in Glacier National Park.* West Glacier, MT: Glacier Natural History Association, 1996. Two books covering Glacier only, not Waterton. The hiker's guide contains 110 pages describing popular trails. The short hikes is a 46-page book covering 16 favorite one- to four-mile walks.

Edwards, J. Gordon. *A Climber's Guide to Glacier Park.* Helena, MT: Falcon Press Publishing Co., 1995. The definitive guide to mountaineering in Glacier National Park. Edwards pioneered many of the routes up Glacier's peaks and is considered the park's patron saint of climbing. Routes cover technical climbs and off-trail scrambles.

Good, Stormy R. *Day Hikes Around the Flathead* and *Nordic Dreams: Flathead Valley Nordic and Snowshoe Guide.* Whitefish, MT: Flathead Guidebooks LLC, 2005. Two self-published books cover 85 day hikes and 33 cross-country ski and snowshoe trails. Both have maps, route descriptions, distances, and difficulty, with special emphasis on labeling trails as dog friendly or not. Available only through local bookstores and outdoor shops.

Meador, Mike, and Lee Stanley. *Mountain Bike Rides of the Flathead Valley.* Whitefish, MT: self-published, 2005. A 60-page roundup of the Flathead's best fat tire rides with maps, directions, and elevation profiles. Available only at Glacier Cyclery in Whitefish.

Molvar, Erik. *Best Easy Day Hikes in Glacier and Waterton Lakes.* Helena, MT: Falcon Press Publishing Co., 2001. A roundup of day hikes in both Glacier and Waterton. At half the size of his hiking guidebook, this focuses only on day hikes with emphasis on well-signed, less strenuous trails.

Molvar, Erik. *Hiking Glacier and Waterton Lakes National Parks.* Helena, MT: Falcon Press Publishing Co., 1996. The most definitive trail guide for Glacier and Waterton Parks. Molvar gives detailed trail descriptions, including maps and elevation charts, for all the popular trails inside the parks as well as less-traveled trails. Routes cover day hikes, overnights, and extended backpacking trips. Hiker safety, campsite details, and fishing information are also included.

Molvar, Erik. *Hiking Montana's Bob Marshall Wilderness.* Helena, MT: Falcon Press Publishing Co., 2001. A detailed trail guide covering the Great Bear, Bob Marshall, and Scapegoat wilderness areas. Trail descriptions include maps, elevation charts, and accurate information on how to find even the more difficult to locate trailheads.

Sande, Nathan. *Instant Gratification: Selected One-Day Ski Trips in the Flathead Backcountry.* Kalispell, MT: self-published. A 66-page guide with maps and route descriptions for backcountry telemark and randonee ski trips in the Swan Mountains, Flathead Range, and Glacier Park. Available only at Rocky Mountain Outfitter in Kalispell.

Schneider, Russ. *Fishing Glacier Park.* Helena, MT: Falcon Press Publishing Co., 2002. The most definitive fishing guide to Glacier. Schneider explains what flies to use to catch certain fish, where you'll catch arctic grayling or westslope cutthroat trout, and where you'll get skunked.

Internet Resources

GLACIER PARK

Glacier National Park
www.nps.gov/glac
The official website for Glacier National Park. It provides information on park conditions, roads, campsites, trails, history, and more. Six webcams update every few minutes. In addition to trip planning information, the site includes downloadable maps, publications, and backcountry permit applications as well as a Going-to-the-Sun Road status report updated daily.

Glacier Natural History Association
www.glacierassociation.org
The best resource for books, maps, posters, and cards on Glacier Park. A portion of the proceeds from book sales are donated back to the park.

Northern Rocky Mountain Research Center
www.nrmrc.usgs.gov
The research center works under the United States Geological Survey. The website contains current research in Glacier on grizzly bears, glaciers, climate change, bighorn sheep, and amphibians.

The Glacier Fund
www.glacierfund.org
As an official nonprofit park partner, The Glacier Fund works with the National Park Foundation to raise money to assist with wildlife research, historic preservation, trails, and education to preserve Glacier's natural and cultural history. It supports what government funds cannot cover.

Glacier Centennial
www.glaciercentennial.org

In 2010, Glacer celebrates its centennial. This is the best resource for special events marking its anniversary.

The Glacier Institute
www.glacierinstitute.org

An educational nonprofit park partner, The Glacier Institute presents programs for kids and adults in field settings taught by expert instructors. Field classes take place in Glacier as well as surrounding ecosystems.

Glacier National Park Associates
www.nps.gov/gla/partners/gnpa.htm

This volunteer nonprofit assists with historic preservation and trail work and is always looking for volunteers to help for a few days on projects.

National Park Service Reservation Center
http://reservations.nps.gov

Two campgrounds in Glacier—Fish Creek and St. Mary—take reservations using this service.

Glacier Adventure
www.glacieradventure.com

On-demand Internet radio shows highlight Glacier hikes, things to see, and places to go with slideshows. Flathead Valley is included, too.

WATERTON PARK

Waterton Lakes National Park
www.pc.gc.ca/waterton

The official website for Waterton. It contains most of the basic park information on camping, hiking, and Parks Canada–operated services, but not the commercial services in Waterton Townsite.

Waterton Lakes National Park Information Guide
www.watertoninfo.ab.ca

Useful park information on boat tours, hiking, bicycling, dining, and lodging. Includes links for many of the commercial services in Waterton Townsite.

National Park Service Reservation Center
www.pccamping.ca

Log on to make reservations at Waterton's Townsite campground and other Canadian national parks.

Waterton Chamber of Commerce
www.watertonchamber.com

This website covers dining, lodging, recreation, visitor services, and camping for Waterton. Some services adjacent to the park are also included.

Waterton Park Information Services
www.watertonpark.com

This website details lodging, dining, services, and recreation, but also includes maps and a great history section.

FLATHEAD VALLEY

Flathead Valley Convention and Visitors Bureau
www.fcvb.org

The Flathead Valley's tourism board covers info on Kalispell, Columbia Falls, Whitefish, Bigfork, Lakeside, Flathead Lake, and ski resorts. You'll find recreation, lodging, dining, and special events.

MONTANA TRAVEL

Glacier Country
www.glaciermt.com

The official state travel website for northwest Montana. You can find lodging, dining, and activity information here, and it's easy to navigate by activity or location.

Montana Travel
www.visitmt.com
The official travel website for Montana. You'll find access to the state's activities, lodging, dining, and recreation by location or activity.

Montana Department of Transportation
www.mdt.mt.gov
Travel advisories and road conditions for Montana. Glacier's interior roads are not yet included on the website; information on Going-to-the-Sun Road is sporadic. Check the park's website for its most accurate information.

Lewis and Clark National Forest
www.fs.fed.us/r1/lewisclark/
Information on campgrounds, trails, fishing, cabin rentals, and other recreation particularly for the Bob Marshall Wilderness.

Flathead National Forest
www.fs.fed.us/r1/flathead
At the official website for Flathead National Forest, you'll find info on campgrounds, fishing, rafting, wilderness areas, cabin rentals, ski areas, trails, and other recreation. However, the recreation section is limited on specifics for trails.

Montana Fish, Wildlife, and Parks
www.fwp.state.mt.us
Up-to-date fishing and hunting information, licenses, state park, and wildlife refuge details for Montana.

CANADIAN TRAVEL

Alberta Travel Guides
www.albertatravel.ca
Heavily funded by Alberta real estate agencies, the site does have some useful travel information if you can wade through the advertising.

Travel Alberta Canada
www.travelalberta.com
The province's official portal to Alberta resorts, parks, ski areas, festivals, events, cities, outdoor recreation, and touring. It's easy to navigate by location or activity to find what you want.

Alberta Travel and Tourism Guide
www.discoveralberta.com
You can access Alberta travel information here, but it all comes in the preformatted package of the WorldWeb network, which is not as easy to navigate or understand as the Travel Alberta website.

Alberta Transportation
www.tu.gov.ab.ca
Check here for postings of Alberta's road construction, advisories, and closures.

British Columbia Transportation
www.gov.bc.ca/tran
Road reports update travel information, closures, construction, and weather for British Columbia. Webcams will give you a firsthand look.

Akamina-Kishinena Provincial Park
www.gov.bc.ca/bcparks
Information on recreation, camping, and hiking in Akamina-Kishinena Provincial Park. Maps and a photo gallery, too.

Fishing Alberta
www.fishalberta.com
Although this is a television-sponsored website rather than an official government site, it is easier to navigate to find current license info, stocked waters, and regulations.

Index

Map Index

www.moon.com

DESTINATIONS | ACTIVITIES | BLOGS | MAPS | BOOKS

MOON.COM is all new, and ready to help plan your next trip! Filled with fresh trip ideas and strategies, author interviews, informative blogs, a detailed map library, and descriptions of all the Moon guidebooks, Moon.com is all you need to get out and explore the world—or even places in your own backyard. As always, when you travel with Moon, expect an experience that is uncommon and truly unique.